投资坦桑尼亚法律必读

（中英文对照）

Required Readings of Laws on Investment in Tanzania (In Chinese & English)

李 智　何烈辉　朱骁琛　等 编译

上海大学出版社
·上海·

图书在版编目(CIP)数据

投资坦桑尼亚法律必读：汉英对照 / 李智,何烈辉,朱骁琛编译. -- 上海：上海大学出版社,2024.10.
ISBN 978-7-5671-5078-2
Ⅰ.D942.5
中国国家版本馆 CIP 数据核字第 2024KQ0967 号

责任编辑　严　妙
封面设计　缪炎栩
技术编辑　金　鑫　钱宇坤

投资坦桑尼亚法律必读(中英文对照)

李　智　何烈辉　朱骁琛　编译
上海大学出版社出版发行
(上海市上大路 99 号　邮政编码 200444)
(https://www.shupress.cn) 发行热线 021-66135112
出版人　余　洋

*

南京展望文化发展有限公司排版
上海普顺印刷包装有限公司印刷　各地新华书店经销
开本 787mm×1092mm 1/16　印张 30.25　字数 735 千
2024 年 10 月第 1 版　2024 年 10 月第 1 次印刷
ISBN 978-7-5671-5078-2/D·264　定价 88.00 元

版权所有　侵权必究
如发现本书有印装质量问题请与印刷厂质量科联系
联系电话：021-36522998

本书是上大法学文库"非洲法律系列"之三,受江苏秉龙慈善基金会和浙江宁邦律师事务所资助,特此表示感谢!

目　　录

第一编　投　资　法　规

第一部　投资条例［2023 年］

第一部分　总则 ·· 2
  1. 引用 ··· 2
  2. 释义 ··· 2

第二部分　董事会的职责 ··· 3
  3. 董事会的职责 ··· 3
  4. 终止成员资格 ··· 3
  5. 填补空缺职位 ··· 3
  6. 法定人数 ··· 3
  7. 董事会的决定 ··· 3
  8. 循环决议 ··· 3
  9. 成员任命上的缺陷 ·· 3
  10. 利益冲突 ·· 3
  11. 实益权益 ·· 4
  12. 董事会秘书 ··· 4

第三部分　国家投资指导委员会和技术委员会职能的履行 ············ 4
  13. 国家投资指导委员会职能的履行 ······························ 4
  14. 技术委员会 ··· 5
  15. 技术委员会会议 ··· 5
  16. 技术委员会的职能 ·· 5

第四部分　向国家投资指导委员会提交各种事项的程序 ················ 5
  17. 战略投资申请及相关事项 ·· 5
  18. 其他提交文件 ·· 6
  19. 决策程序 ·· 6

第五部　奖励、修复和扩展证书 ··· 6
  20. 奖励证书申请 ·· 6
  21. 证书为决定性证据 ·· 6

22. 名称、股权或控制权的变更 ………………………………………… 6
23. 变更不影响利益 ……………………………………………………… 6
24. 延长额外优惠期限的程序 …………………………………………… 7
25. 奖励证书的延期 ……………………………………………………… 7
26. 奖励证书的撤销程序 ………………………………………………… 7

第六部分　促进、推动和协调投资事项 …………………………………… 7
27. 投资促进计划 ………………………………………………………… 7
28. 计划的实施 …………………………………………………………… 7
29. 项目的监督和评估 …………………………………………………… 8
30. 投资者年度报告 ……………………………………………………… 8
31. 派驻土地官员和向投资者颁发派生产权证 ………………………… 8
32. 居住和工作许可证等 ………………………………………………… 8
33. 派驻官员 ……………………………………………………………… 8
34. 获得保证和利润转让 ………………………………………………… 8

第七部分　其他规定 …………………………………………………………… 8
35. 上诉 …………………………………………………………………… 8
36. 复审 …………………………………………………………………… 9
37. 投资争议的协调 ……………………………………………………… 9
38. 违法行为和处罚 ……………………………………………………… 9
39. 撤销 …………………………………………………………………… 9
40. 保留条款 ……………………………………………………………… 9
附表 ……………………………………………………………………… 9

第二部　移民法(第54章)[1998年][2016年修订版](节选)

第四部分　违禁移民 ………………………………………………………… 19
27. 驱逐出境 ……………………………………………………………… 19

第五部分　入境和居留条件 ………………………………………………… 20
28. 禁止无护照、居留许可证或通行证的人入境 ……………………… 20
29. 签证费 ………………………………………………………………… 21
30. 禁止无证就业、学习等 ……………………………………………… 21
31. 外籍移民委员会的设立、组成和职能 ……………………………… 21
32. 居留许可证类别 ……………………………………………………… 22
33. A类居留许可证 ……………………………………………………… 22
34. B类居留许可证 ……………………………………………………… 23
35. C类居留许可证 ……………………………………………………… 23
36. 居留许可证的颁发条件 ……………………………………………… 23
37. 向部长上诉 …………………………………………………………… 24
38. 变更居留许可证的条件 ……………………………………………… 24
39. 获得居留许可证的受抚养人 ………………………………………… 24

| 40. 欺诈的后果 | 24 |
| 41. 居留许可证的撤销和交还 | 24 |

第三部 土地法(第113章)[2001年][2019年修订版](节选)

第五部分 土地占用的权利和附带条件 ... 27
  19. 土地占用权 ... 27
  20. 非公民占用土地的限制 ... 28

第四部 乡村土地法(第114章)[2001年][2019年修订版](节选)

第四部分 乡村土地 ... 30
  A：管理和行政 ... 30
  17. 非乡村组织使用乡村土地 ... 30

第五部 营业执照法(第208章)[1972年][2002年修订版](节选)

  3. 禁止无证经营 ... 32
  10. 非居民临时许可证 ... 33
  19. 罪行 ... 33

第六部 商业法(杂项修正案)[1930年][2012年修订版](节选)

第二部分 对《商业名称(注册)法》(第213章)的修订 ... 36
  3. 解释 ... 36
  4. 长标题的修订 ... 36
  5. 第1条的修订 ... 36
  6. 第2条的修订 ... 36
  7. 第3条的修订 ... 36
  8. 第6条的修订 ... 37
  9. 第8条的修订 ... 37
  10. 第9条的修订 ... 37
  11. 第11条的修订 ... 37
  12. 第12条的修订 ... 37
  13. 第13条的修订 ... 37
  14. 第18条的修订 ... 37
  15. 第20条的修订 ... 37
  16. 新增第25条 ... 38

第七部 公私合营法(第103章)[2011年][2019年修订版]

第一部分 总则 ... 40
  1. 简称 ... 40
  2. 适用范围 ... 40

3. 释义 40
第二部分 公私合营中心的建立和管理 41
4. PPP 中心 41
5. PPP 中心的职能 42
6. 执行董事 43
7. PPP 指导委员会 43
7A. PPP 指导委员会的职能 44
7B. 公共资金和其他 PPP 项目的支持 44
7C. 部长的一般权力 44
第三部分 公共和私营部门的参与 45
8. 公共和私营部门的作用 45
9. 缔约机构的责任 45
10. 可行性研究 45
10A. 促进基金 46
10B. 资金来源 46
10C. 账簿、记录和年度报告 47
11. 协议 47
12. 土地征用 48
13. 协议的期限和延长 48
14. 协议审查 48
15. 采购流程 48
16. 非邀约投标 49
17. 项目官员 49
18. 协议的签署 49
19. 会计官的职责 49
20. 协议的修订 50
21. 享受优惠 50
22. 纠纷解决机制 50
第四部分 其他规定 50
23. 监督和评估 50
23A. 定期业绩报告 50
24. 利益冲突 50
25. 赋予公民权力 51
25A. 与自然财富和资源有关的项目 51
26. 注意的义务和恪尽职守 51
27. 一般处罚 51
28. 条例 51
29. 保留条款 52

第八部 公私合营法(修正案)[2023年]

第一部分 总则 ······ 54
  1. 简称 ······ 54

第二部分 各项条款的修订 ······ 54
  2. 第2条的修订 ······ 54
  3. 第3条的修订 ······ 54
  4. 第4条的修订 ······ 55
  5. 第5条的修订 ······ 55
  6. 第7条的修订 ······ 55
  7. 第7B条的修订 ······ 55
  8. 第9条的修订 ······ 55
  9. 第13条的修订 ······ 55
  10. 第15条的修订 ······ 55
  11. 增加第18A条 ······ 56
  12. 第21条的修订 ······ 56
  13. 废除和取代第22条 ······ 56
  14. 第23条的修订 ······ 56
  15. 第23A条的修订 ······ 57
  16. 第28条的修订 ······ 57
  17. 第28A条的修订 ······ 57

第二编 劳动法规

第九部 就业与劳动关系法(第366章)[2006年][2019年修订版]

第一部分 总则 ······ 60
  1. 简称 ······ 60
  2. 适用 ······ 60
  3. 本法目的 ······ 60
  4. 释义 ······ 61

第二部分 基本权利和保护 ······ 62
  A子部分:童工 ······ 62
  5. 禁止使用童工 ······ 62
  B子部分:强迫劳动 ······ 63
  6. 禁止强迫劳动 ······ 63
  C子部分:歧视 ······ 64
  7. 禁止工作场所中的歧视 ······ 64
  8. 禁止工会和雇主协会中的歧视行为 ······ 65

D 子部分：结社自由
9. 雇员的结社自由权 65
10. 雇主的结社自由权 65
11. 工会和雇主协会的权利 66

第三部分　就业标准 66
A 子部分：总则 66
12. 本部分适用范围 66
13. 雇佣标准 66
14. 与雇员的合同 66
15. 详细情况书面说明 67
16. 告知员工其权利 67

B 子部分：工作时间 67
17. 本部分的适用范围 67
18. 释义 67
19. 工作时间 68
20. 夜间工作 68
21. 压缩工作周 68
22. 平均工时 69
23. 工作日休息时间 69
24. 每日和每周休息时间 69
25. 公共节假日 69

C 子部分：薪酬 69
26. 工资率的计算 69
27. 支付薪酬 70
28. 有关薪资的扣除和其他行为 70

D 子部分：休假 71
29. 本子部分的适用范围 71
30. 本子部分的释义 71
31. 年假 71
32. 病假 72
33. 产假 72
34. 陪产假和其他形式的假期 73

E 子部分：不公平终止雇佣 73
35. 本子部分适用范围 73
36. 释义 73
37. 不公平解雇 74
38. 基于经营需要的终止 74
39. 不公平解雇诉讼中的举证 75
40. 不公平解雇的补救措施 75

> **F 子部分：其他终止事件** ·· 75
>> 41. 解雇通知 ··· 75
>> 42. 遣散费 ··· 76
>> 43. 运送至招聘地点 ··· 76
>> 44. 支付解雇费和工作证明 ··· 76

> **第四部分　工会、雇主协会和联合会** ································· 77
>> 45. 注册义务 ··· 77
>> 46. 注册要求 ··· 77
>> 47. 宪法要求 ··· 77
>> 48. 注册程序 ··· 78
>> 49. 登记的效力 ·· 79
>> 50. 更改名称或章程 ··· 79
>> 51. 账目和审计 ·· 80
>> 52. 注册组织和联合会的职责 ······································ 80
>> 53. 不遵守章程 ·· 80
>> 54. 注册组织和联合会的合并 ······································ 80
>> 55. 取消注册 ··· 81
>> 56. 解散工会或雇主协会 ··· 81
>> 57. 对注册官裁决的上诉 ··· 81
>> 58. 在《公报》上发表 ·· 82

> **第五部分　组织权利** ··· 82
>> 59. 释义 ··· 82
>> 60. 进入雇主的办公场所 ··· 82
>> 61. 扣除工会会费 ·· 82
>> 62. 工会代表 ··· 83
>> 63. 工会活动假期 ·· 83
>> 64. 行使组织权的程序 ·· 83
>> 65. 组织权利的终止 ··· 84

> **第六部分　集体谈判** ··· 84
>> 66. 释义 ··· 84
>> 67. 获认可为雇员的独家谈判代理 ································ 84
>> 68. 诚信谈判的义务 ··· 85
>> 69. 认可的撤销 ·· 85
>> 70. 披露相关信息的义务 ··· 86
>> 71. 集体协议的约束性 ·· 86
>> 72. 受雇人和工会之间的集体协议 ································ 87
>> 73. 工人参与协议 ·· 87
>> 74. 有关集体协议的争议 ··· 87

第七部分　罢工和停工 ······ 88
　　75. 罢工和停工的权利 ······ 88
　　76. 对罢工或停工权利的限制 ······ 88
　　77. 基本服务 ······ 88
　　78. 基本服务权益争议 ······ 89
　　79. 罢工或停工期间的最低限度服务 ······ 89
　　80. 参与合法罢工的程序 ······ 89
　　81. 参与二次罢工的程序 ······ 90
　　82. 合法停工的程序 ······ 90
　　83. 合法罢工或停工的保护性质 ······ 91
　　84. 罢工和停工不遵守本部分的规定 ······ 91
　　85. 抗议行动 ······ 92

第八部分　争议解决 ······ 93
　　A 子部分：调解 ······ 93
　　86. 根据本法规定将争议提交调解 ······ 93
　　87. 不出席调解听证会的后果 ······ 93
　　B 子部分：仲裁 ······ 94
　　88. 通过强制仲裁解决争议 ······ 94
　　89. 仲裁裁决的效力 ······ 95
　　90. 仲裁裁决的更正 ······ 95
　　91. 仲裁裁决的修订 ······ 95
　　92. 仲裁的适用 ······ 95
　　93. 自愿仲裁法 ······ 95
　　C 子部分：裁决 ······ 96
　　94. 劳工法庭的管辖权 ······ 96
　　D 子部分：集体协议中的争议程序 ······ 96
　　95. 集体协议中的争议解决程序 ······ 96

第九部分　一般规定 ······ 97
　　96. 雇主和雇员应保存的记录 ······ 97
　　97. 文件送达 ······ 97
　　98. 条例 ······ 97
　　99. 准则和良好行为守则 ······ 98
　　100. 豁免 ······ 98
　　101. 保密 ······ 99
　　102. 处罚 ······ 99
　　102A. 与成文法不一致 ······ 99
　　103. 法律的废除和修订以及保留条款 ······ 99
　　附件 1　可比工资率计算表 ······ 99
　　附件 2　法律的废止 ······ 100

附件3　保留和过渡条款 ………………………………………………………… 100

第十部　最低工资令[2022年]

1. 名称和生效 ……………………………………………………………………… 106
2. 使用方法 ………………………………………………………………………… 106
3. 释义 ……………………………………………………………………………… 106
4. 部门和领域 ……………………………………………………………………… 107
5. 就业标准 ………………………………………………………………………… 107
6. 能获得更好利益的员工 ………………………………………………………… 107
7. 废除 ……………………………………………………………………………… 107

第三编　经济特区法规

第十一部　出口加工区法(第373章)[2002年][2012年修订版]

第一部分　总则 …………………………………………………………………………… 114
　　1. 简称和应用 ……………………………………………………………………… 114
　　2. 释义 ……………………………………………………………………………… 115
第二部分　出口加工区的设立或申报 …………………………………………………… 115
　　3. 出口加工区的设立或申报 ……………………………………………………… 115
　　4. 设立出口加工区的目的和宗旨 ………………………………………………… 116
第三部分　许可 …………………………………………………………………………… 116
　　5. 出口加工区进入、居住等的限制 ……………………………………………… 116
　　6. 管理局颁发许可证 ……………………………………………………………… 117
　　7. 取消和暂停执照 ………………………………………………………………… 117
　　8. 许可证不得更改 ………………………………………………………………… 117
　　9. 对管理局决定的上诉 …………………………………………………………… 118
　　10. 禁止其他活动 …………………………………………………………………… 118
　　11. 管理局决定在出口加工区的货物或物品 ……………………………………… 118
第四部分　出口加工区管理局 …………………………………………………………… 118
　　12. 管理局的建立 …………………………………………………………………… 118
　　13. 管理局的目标和职能 …………………………………………………………… 118
　　14. 设立出口加工区管理局理事会 ………………………………………………… 119
　　15. 理事会的职能和权力 …………………………………………………………… 119
　　17. 局长及其他雇员 ………………………………………………………………… 120
　　18. 资金来源 ………………………………………………………………………… 120
　　19. 管理局资金的使用 ……………………………………………………………… 120
　　20. 管理局资金的管理和审计 ……………………………………………………… 120

第五部分　投资激励 ··· 121
　21. 给予出口加工区投资者的激励 ··· 121
　22. 出口加工区投资出口货物进入关税区的限制 ··· 122
　23. 技术员工的工作许可证 ··· 122
　24. 管理局可签订协议 ··· 122

第六部分　其他法律的适用和不适用 ··· 123
　25. 不适用 ··· 123
　26. 印花税法的豁免 ··· 123
　27. 城市规划法的适用 ··· 123
　28. 劳动法的适用 ··· 123

第七部分　收购、补偿和争议解决 ··· 123
　29. 收购和补偿法案 ··· 123
　30. 争议解决 ··· 124
　31. 争议解决不受限制 ··· 124
　32. 部长可以制定规章 ··· 124

第八部分　罪行 ··· 124
　33. 许可证和外国货币有关的罪行 ··· 124
　34. 转运产品等罪行 ··· 125
　35. 与违禁货物或物品制造、加工等有关的罪行 ··· 125

第四编　采矿与环境保护法规

第十二部　采矿法（第 123 章）[2010 年][2019 年修订版]（节选）

第二部分　一般原则 ··· 128
　6. 勘探或者采矿所需的许可 ··· 128
　7. 矿业权和专属权 ··· 128
　8. 矿业权授予的限制 ··· 129

第四部分　采矿权 ··· 130
　B 分部：特别采矿许可证和采矿许可证 ··· 130
　39. 申请人 ··· 130
　41. 特别采矿许可证的申请 ··· 131
　51. 采矿许可证持有人的权利 ··· 131
　C 分部：初级采矿许可证 ··· 132
　54. 初级采矿许可证的申请 ··· 132
　D 分部：矿物加工、冶炼和精炼 ··· 132
　59. 矿业权人将矿物留作加工、冶炼或者精炼之用 ··· 132
　60. 矿产加工许可证的申请和授予 ··· 132

第十三部 环境管理法 [2004 年] (节选)

第十部分　环境质量标准 ········· 135
 141. 遵守标准等 ········· 135
 143. 水质量标准 ········· 135
 145. 空气质量标准 ········· 135
 150. 土壤质量标准 ········· 136

第五编　税 收 法 规

第十四部　增值税法 (第 148 章) [2015 年] [2019 年修订版]

第一部分　总则 ········· 138
 1. 简称 ········· 138
 2. 释义 ········· 138

第二部分　增值税的征收 ········· 145
 (a) 征收和豁免 ········· 145
 3. 征收增值税 ········· 145
 4. 增值税纳税义务人 ········· 145
 5. 增值税税率和应纳税额 ········· 145
 6. 法律规定的豁免和税率 ········· 145
 7. 条约 ········· 146
 (b) 进口增值税 ········· 146
 8. 进口增值税的缴纳与征收 ········· 146
 9. 进口价值 ········· 147
 10. 退货价值 ········· 147
 11. 对进口资本货物延期征收增值税 ········· 147
 (c) 供应品增值税 ········· 148
 12. 供应标的和子类别 ········· 148
 13. 供应的对价 ········· 148
 14. 单一和多重供应 ········· 149
 15. 增值税缴纳时间 ········· 149
 16. 渐进式、临时出售和自动售货机的例外情况 ········· 149
 17. 应税供应的价值 ········· 150
 18. 向相关个体提供供应的例外情况 ········· 150
 19. 渐进式或周期性供应 ········· 150
 20. 经济活动的出售 ········· 150
 21. 权利、凭证和期权的税务处理 ········· 151
 22. 权利、凭证和期权的偿付 ········· 151
 23. 权利、凭证和期权的进项税抵免 ········· 151

24. 电信服务预付款 ··· 151
25. 雇员实物福利 ·· 152
26. 已取消的交易 ·· 152
27. 债务人财产的出售 ··· 152

第三部分 注册 ·· 152
28. 注册要求 ··· 152
29. 需要注册的其他人员 ·· 153
30. 申请注册的时间 ··· 153
31. 申请方式 ··· 153
32. 申请的处理 ··· 153
33. 强制注册 ··· 154
34. 未能处理申请的影响 ·· 154
35. 纳税人识别号和增值税注册号 ··· 154
36. 注册涵盖分支机构或部门 ·· 154
37. 变更通知 ··· 154
38. 定价透明度 ··· 154
39. 申请撤销注册 ·· 155
40. 撤销注册申请的决定 ·· 155
41. 撤销注册的权力 ··· 155
42. 被撤销注册的人员 ··· 155
43. 注册人员名单 ·· 155

第四部分 纳税地点 ·· 155
(a) 在坦桑尼亚大陆制造的货物和服务的供应 ································ 155
44. 货物供应 ··· 155
45. 货物的出入境 ·· 156
46. 与不动产有关的供应 ·· 156
47. 提供与土地直接相关的服务 ·· 156
48. 基本服务的供应 ··· 156
49. 向注册人提供的服务 ·· 156
50. 电信服务 ··· 156
51. 向坦桑尼亚大陆未注册人员提供的服务 ····································· 157
52. 向坦桑尼亚大陆未注册人员提供的其他服务 ································ 157
53. 累进或定期供应 ··· 157
(b) 供联合共和国境外使用的供应 ·· 157
54. 不动产零税率 ·· 157
55. 货物供应零税率 ··· 158
55A. 向坦桑尼亚桑给巴尔供应货物的零税率 ··································· 158
56. 在联合共和国境外使用的租赁物品 ··· 158
57. 用于修理临时进口的货物 ·· 158
58. 向非居民担保人提供的货物和服务 ··· 158

59. 用于国际运输服务的货物 ……………………………………………………… 159
60. 为在联合共和国境外使用而提供的服务 ………………………………………… 159
61. 临时进口相关的服务 …………………………………………………………… 159
61A. 服务供应的零税率 ……………………………………………………………… 159
61B. 零税率的供电服务 ……………………………………………………………… 160
62. 在联合共和国境外使用的知识产权 …………………………………………… 160
63. 运营商之间的电信服务 ………………………………………………………… 160
（c）特别规则 …………………………………………………………………… 160
64. 非居民的增值税代表 …………………………………………………………… 160
65. 国外分支机构提供的服务 ……………………………………………………… 160

第五部分　退货、付款和退款 …………………………………………………… 161
（a）退货和付款 ………………………………………………………………… 161
66. 增值税申报表 …………………………………………………………………… 161
（b）应缴增值税净额 …………………………………………………………… 162
67. 净额的计算和支付 ……………………………………………………………… 162
（c）进项税抵免 ………………………………………………………………… 162
68. 进项税抵免 ……………………………………………………………………… 162
69. 进项税抵免的时间 ……………………………………………………………… 163
70. 部分进项税抵免 ………………………………………………………………… 163
（d）其他调整 …………………………………………………………………… 164
71. 调整事件的后供应调整 ………………………………………………………… 164
72. 对调整的限制 …………………………………………………………………… 164
73. 调整期限 ………………………………………………………………………… 165
74. 供应后坏账调整 ………………………………………………………………… 165
75. 私人使用申请 …………………………………………………………………… 166
76. 支付保险金时的调整 …………………………………………………………… 166
77. 收到保险付款时的调整 ………………………………………………………… 166
78. 纠正小错误的调整 ……………………………………………………………… 167
79. 注册时的调整 …………………………………………………………………… 167
80. 撤销注册时的调整 ……………………………………………………………… 167
（e）退款 ………………………………………………………………………… 168
81. 负净额结转 ……………………………………………………………………… 168
82. 不结转的退款 …………………………………………………………………… 168
83. 超额退款 ………………………………………………………………………… 168
84. 退款申请 ………………………………………………………………………… 169
85. 向外交官、国际机构退款 ……………………………………………………… 169

第六部分　文件和记录 …………………………………………………………… 170
86. 税务发票 ………………………………………………………………………… 170
87. 调整通知 ………………………………………………………………………… 170
88. 由代理人签发或向代理人签发的文件 ………………………………………… 171

89. 记录和账目 ·········· 171

第七部分　行政管理 ·········· 171

90. 税务决定 ·········· 171
91. 合伙企业或非法人社团的连续性 ·········· 172
92. 纳税人、占有抵押权人死亡或破产 ·········· 172
93. 与所得税的相互影响 ·········· 172

第八部分　总则 ·········· 173

94. 制定条例的权力 ·········· 173
95. 废除和保留 ·········· 173
96. 过渡条款 ·········· 173

　　附表　[第6条第(1)款] ·········· 174

第十五部　海关(管理和关税)法(第403章)
[1952年] [2019年修订版] (节选)

第三部分　进口 ·········· 184

入境、检查和交付 ·········· 184

28. 货物入境 ·········· 184
29. 转运货物的入境 ·········· 185

第四部分　货物仓储 ·········· 185

总则 ·········· 185

38. 应税货物可以入库 ·········· 185
39. 入库程序 ·········· 185
40. 未入库货物的移送 ·········· 185
41. 入库货物的进口报关 ·········· 186

第十七部分　海关关税 ·········· 186

194A. 进口时缴纳关税 ·········· 186
194B. 一周年后免征关税 ·········· 186
194C. 在出售或转让任何物品时支付的关税 ·········· 186

第十六部　货物和服务付款的预扣税业务指南[2019年]

1.0　税法 ·········· 188
2.0　目的 ·········· 188
3.0　释义 ·········· 188
4.0　本业务指南的应用 ·········· 188
5.0　适用概念 ·········· 188
6.0　预扣税类型 ·········· 189
7.0　预扣税义务 ·········· 189
8.0　适用于特定类型人 ·········· 190

9.0　预扣款项的计算依据 …………………………………………………… 190

　　10.0　包括福利和设施的情况 ………………………………………………… 190

　　11.0　混合供应品(货物和服务)的预扣税基 ……………………………… 191

　　12.0　建筑工程预扣税基 ……………………………………………………… 191

　　13.0　预扣税适用程序 ………………………………………………………… 192

　　14.0　预扣凭证的签发——《所得税法》第85条 ………………………… 192

　　15.0　扣缴义务人的税收抵免 ………………………………………………… 193

　　16.0　未预扣的后果——《所得税法》第84条 …………………………… 193

　　17.0　未按期申报的后果——《税收管理法》第438章第78条 ………… 193

　　18.0　向税务局提交合同文件 ………………………………………………… 193

第六编　反商业贿赂法规

第十七部　预防和反腐败法(第329章)[2007年][2019年修订版](节选)

第三部分　腐败及相关犯罪 ……………………………………………………… 196

　　15. 腐败交易 ………………………………………………………………… 196

　　16. 合同中的腐败交易 ……………………………………………………… 197

　　17. 采购中的腐败交易 ……………………………………………………… 197

　　18. 拍卖中的腐败交易 ……………………………………………………… 198

　　21. 贿赂外国公职人员 ……………………………………………………… 198

　　22. 使用旨在误导委托人的文件 …………………………………………… 198

　　23. 获取利益的人 …………………………………………………………… 198

　　24. 代表被告获得的利益 …………………………………………………… 199

　　25. 性或任何其他方面的利益 ……………………………………………… 199

　　26. 政府官员提供财产账目 ………………………………………………… 199

　　27. 拥有来历不明的财产 …………………………………………………… 199

　　30. 协助和教唆 ……………………………………………………………… 200

　　31. 滥用职权 ………………………………………………………………… 200

　　32. 串谋 ……………………………………………………………………… 200

　　33. 利用影响力交易 ………………………………………………………… 200

　　34. 腐败所得的转移 ………………………………………………………… 201

　　35. 腐败推定 ………………………………………………………………… 201

　　36. 冒充官员 ………………………………………………………………… 201

　　37. 泄露身份罪 ……………………………………………………………… 202

　　38. 资产冻结 ………………………………………………………………… 202

　　39. 提供信息的义务 ………………………………………………………… 203

Contents

GROUP ONE   INVESTMENT LAWS AND REGULATIONS

TITLE ONE   INVESTMENT REGULATIONS [2023]

PART I   PRELIMINARY PROVISIONS ········· 206
   1. Citation ········· 206
   2. Interpretation ········· 206

PART II   RESPONSIBILITIES OF THE BOARD ········· 207
   3. Responsibilities of Board ········· 207
   4. Cessation of membership ········· 207
   5. Filling of vacant position ········· 207
   6. Quorum ········· 207
   7. Decisions of Board ········· 207
   8. Circular resolutions ········· 208
   9. Defect in appointment of member ········· 208
   10. Conflict of interest ········· 208
   11. Beneficial interest ········· 208
   12. Secretary to Board ········· 208

PART III   IMPLEMENTATION OF FUNCTIONS OF THE NATIONAL INVESTMENT STEERING COMMITTEE AND TECHNICAL COMMITTEE ········· 209
   13. Implementation of Functions of National Investment Steering Committee ········· 209
   14. Technical Committee ········· 209
   15. Meetings of Technical Committee ········· 210
   16. Functions of Technical Committee ········· 210

PART IV   PROCEDURES FOR SUBMITTING VARIOUS MATTERS BEFORE THE NATIONAL INVESTMENT STEERING COMMITTEE ········· 210
   17. Application for strategic investment and related matters ········· 210

18. Other submissions 211

19. Procedure for decision making 211

PART V   CERTIFICATE OF INCENTIVES, REHABILITATION AND EXPANSION
.... 211

20. Application for certificate of incentives 211

21. Certificate to be conclusive evidence 211

22. Change of name, shareholding or control 211

23. Change not to affect benefits 212

24. Procedure for extension of time for additional benefits 212

25. Extension of time for certificate of incentives 212

26. Procedure for revocation of certificate of incentives 212

PART VI   PROMOTION, FACILITATION AND COORDINATION OF INVESTMENT MATTERS 213

27. Investment promotion program 213

28. Implementation of program 213

29. Monitoring and evaluation of projects 213

30. Investor's annual report 213

31. Stationing of land officers and issuance of derivative titles to investors 214

32. Residence and work permits, etc. 214

33. Stationed officers 214

34. Access to guarantees and transfer of profits 214

PART VII   MISCELLANEOUS PROVISIONS 214

35. Appeals 214

36. Review 215

37. Coordination of investment disputes 215

38. Offences and penalty 215

39. Revocation 215

40. Saving provisions 215

TITLE TWO   IMMIGRATION ACT (CHAPTER 54)
[1998] [Revised Edition 2016] (Excerpts)

PART IV   PROHIBITED IMMIGRANT 225

27. Deportation 225

PART V   CONDITIONS OF ENTRY AND RESIDENCE 226

28. Prohibition on entry without passport, permit or pass 226

29. Rates payable for visa 227

30. Prohibition on employment, study, etc., without permit 227

31. Establishment, composition and functions of the Alien Immigrants Board 228
32. Classes of residence permits Act Nos. 228
33. Class "A" residence permit 229
34. Class "B" residence permit 230
35. Class "C" residence permit 231
36. Permits to be issued subject to conditions 231
37. Appeals to the Minister 231
38. Variation of conditions of permits 231
39. Dependants of person granted permits 231
40. Effect of fraud 232
41. Revocation and surrender of permits 232

TITLE THREE LAND ACT (CHAPTER 113) [2001] [Revised Edition 2019] (Excerpts)

PART V RIGHTS AND INCIDENTS OF LAND OCCUPATION 235
  19. Rights to occupy land 235
  20. Occupation of land by non-citizen restricted 236

TITLE FOUR VILLAGE LAND ACT (CHAPTER 114) [2001] [Revised Edition 2019] (Excerpts)

PART IV VILLAGE LANDS 238
  A: **Management and Administration** 238
  17. Occupation of village land by non-village organization 238

TITLE FIVE BUSINESS LICENSING ACT (CHAPTER 208) [1972] [Revised Edition 2002] (Excerpts)

  3. Prohibition on carrying on business without licence 241
  10. Temporary licences for non-residents 242
  19. Offences 242

TITLE SIX BUSINESS LAWS (MISCELLANEOUS AMENDMENTS) ACT [1930] [Revised Edition 2012] (Excerpts)

PART II AMENDMENT OF THE BUSINESS NAMES (REGISTRATION) ACT, (CAP.213) 245
  3. Construction 245
  4. Amendment of the long title 245
  5. Amendmant of section 1 245

6. Amendmant of section 2 245
7. Amendment of section 3 246
8. Amendment of section 6 246
9. Amendment of section 8 246
10. Amendment of section 9 246
11. Amendment of section 11 246
12. Amendment of section 12 246
13. Amendment of section 13 247
14. Amendment of section 18 247
15. Amendment of section 20 247
16. Addition of section 25 247

TITLE SEVEN PUBLIC PRIVATE PARTNERSHIP ACT (CHAPTER 103) [2011] [Revised Edition 2019]

PART I PRELIMINARY PROVISIONS 249
1. Short title 249
2. Application 249
3. Interpretation 249

PART II ESTABLISHMENT AND ADMINISTRATION OF THE PPP CENTRE 251
4. PPP Centre 251
5. Functions of PPP Centre 252
6. Executive Director 253
7. Public Private Partnership Steering Committee 253
7A. Functions of Public Private Partnership Steering Committee 254
7B. Public funding and other support of PPP project 254
7C. Powers of Minister generally 255

PART III PARTICIPATION OF THE PUBLIC AND PRIVATE PARTY 255
8. Roles of Public and Private sector 255
9. Responsibilities of contracting authority 256
10. Feasibility Study 256
10A. Facilitation Fund 257
10B. Sources of funds 257
10C. Books of accounts, records and annual reports 258
11. Agreement 258
12. Land acquisition 259
13. Duration and extension of agreement 259
14. Vetting of agreements 260

15. Procurement process ··· 260
16. Unsolicited bids ··· 261
17. Project officers ··· 261
18. Signing of Agreements ·· 261
19. Responsibilities of accounting officers ·························· 261
20. Amendment of Agreements ·· 262
21. Enjoyment of benefits ·· 262
22. Dispute resolutions ·· 262

PART IV MISCELLANEOUS PROVISIONS ··································· 262
23. Monitoring and evaluation ·· 262
23A. Periodic performance reports ···································· 262
24. Conflict of Interest ··· 263
25. Empowerment of citizens ·· 263
25A. Projects relating to natural wealth and resources ··············· 263
26. Duty to take care and exercise due diligence ····················· 263
27. General penalty ·· 263
28. Regulations ·· 264
29. Saving provisions ·· 264

TITLE EIGHT PUBLIC PRIVATE PARTNERSHIP (AMENDMENT) ACT [2023]

PART I PRELIMINARY PROVISIONS ····································· 266
1. Short title ··· 266

PART II AMENDMENT OF VARIOUS PROVISIONS ··························· 266
2. Amendment of section 2 ·· 266
3. Amendment of section 3 ·· 266
4. Amendment of section 4 ·· 267
5. Amendment of section 5 ·· 267
6. Amendment of section 7 ·· 268
7. Amendment of section 7B ··· 268
8. Amendment of section 9 ·· 268
9. Amendment of section 13 ··· 268
10. Amendment of section 15 ·· 268
11. Addition of section 18A ·· 269
12. Amendment of section 21 ·· 269
13. Repeal and replacement of section 22 ····························· 269
14. Amendment of section 23 ·· 269

15. Amendment of section 23A ··· 269
16. Amendment of section 28 ··· 270
17. Addition of section 28A ·· 270

GROUP TWO   LABOUR LAWS AND REGULATIONS

TITLE NINE   EMPLOYMENT AND LABOUR RELATIONS ACT (CHAPTER 366) [2006] [Revised Edition 2019]

PART I   PRELIMINARY PROVISIONS ································· 272
   1. Short title ··· 272
   2. Application ··· 272
   3. Objects ··· 273
   4. Interpretation ··· 273

PART II   FUNDAMENTAL RIGHTS AND PROTECTIONS ············ 275
   Sub-Part A: Child Labour ·· 275
   5. Prohibition of child labour ······································· 275
   Sub-Part B: Forced Labour ······································· 276
   6. Prohibition of forced labour ······································ 276
   Sub-Part C: Discrimination ······································· 276
   7. Prohibition of discrimination in the work-place ··················· 276
   8. Prohibition of discrimination in trade unions and employer associations ······ 278
   Sub-Part D: Freedom of Association ······························ 278
   9. Employee's right to freedom of association ······················· 278
   10. Employer's right to freedom of association ······················ 279
   11. Rights of trade unions and employers' associations ··············· 279

PART III   EMPLOYMENT STANDARDS ······························ 279
   Sub-Part A: Preliminary ·· 279
   12. Application of this Part ·· 279
   13. Employment standards ··· 280
   14. Contracts with employees ······································· 280
   15. Written statement of particulars ································· 280
   16. Informing employees of their rights ······························ 281
   Sub-Part B: Hours of work ······································· 281
   17. Application of this Sub-Part ···································· 281
   18. Interpretation ·· 281
   19. Hours of work ··· 281

20. Night work ………………………………………………………… 282
21. Compressed working week ……………………………………… 282
22. Averaging hours of work ………………………………………… 282
23. Break in working day …………………………………………… 283
24. Daily and weekly rest periods …………………………………… 283
25. Public holidays …………………………………………………… 283

Sub-Part C: Remuneration …………………………………………… 283
26. Calculation of wage rates ………………………………………… 283
27. Payment of remuneration ………………………………………… 284
28. Deductions and other acts concerning remuneration …………… 284

Sub-Part D: Leave ……………………………………………………… 285
29. Application of this Sub-Part ……………………………………… 285
30. Interpretation in this Sub-Part …………………………………… 285
31. Annual leave ……………………………………………………… 286
32. Sick leave ………………………………………………………… 287
33. Maternity leave …………………………………………………… 287
34. Paternity and other forms of leave ……………………………… 288

Sub-Part E: Unfair termination of employment …………………… 288
35. Application of this Sub-Part ……………………………………… 288
36. Interpretation …………………………………………………… 288
37. Unfair termination ………………………………………………… 289
38. Termination based on operational requirements ………………… 289
39. Proof in unfair termination proceedings ………………………… 290
40. Remedies for unfair termination ………………………………… 290

Sub-Part F: Other incidents of Termination ………………………… 290
41. Notice of termination …………………………………………… 290
42. Severance pay …………………………………………………… 291
43. Transport to place of recruitment ………………………………… 291
44. Payment of termination and certificates of employment ………… 292

PART IV TRADE UNIONS, EMPLOYERS ASSOCIATIONS AND FEDERATIONS
………………………………………………………………………… 292
45. Obligation to register …………………………………………… 292
46. Requirements for registration …………………………………… 292
47. Constitutional requirements ……………………………………… 293
48. Process of registration …………………………………………… 294
49. Effect of registration ……………………………………………… 295
50. Change of name or constitution ………………………………… 295

51.	Accounts and audits	296
52.	Duties of registered organizations and federations	296
53.	Non-compliance with constitution	296
54.	Amalgamation of registered organizations and federations	297
55.	Cancellation of registration	297
56.	Dissolution of trade union or employers association	298
57.	Appeals from decisions of Registrar	298
58.	Publication in *Gazette*	298

PART V ORGANISATIONAL RIGHTS — 298

59.	Interpretation	298
60.	Access to employer's premises	299
61.	Deduction of trade union dues	299
62.	Trade union representation	299
63.	Leave for trade union activities	300
64.	Procedure for exercising organizational right	300
65.	Termination of organizational rights	301

PART VI COLLECTIVE BARGAINING — 301

66.	Interpretation	301
67.	Recognition as exclusive bargaining agent of employees	301
68.	Duty to bargain in good faith	302
69.	Withdrawal of recognition	303
70.	Obligation to disclose relevant information	303
71.	Binding nature of collective agreements	304
72.	Agency Shop agreements	304
73.	Workers participation agreement	305
74.	Disputes concerning collective agreements	306

PART VII STRIKES AND LOCKOUTS — 306

75.	Right to strike and to lockout	306
76.	Restrictions on right to strike or lockout	306
77.	Essential services	307
78.	Disputes of interest in essential services	308
79.	Minimum services during strike or lockout	308
80.	Procedure for engaging in lawful strike	308
81.	Procedure for engaging in secondary strike	309
82.	Procedure for engaging in lawful lockout	309
83.	Nature of protection of lawful strike or lockout	310
84.	Strikes and lockouts not in compliance with this Part	310

85. Protest action ··· 311

PART VIII DISPUTE RESOLUTION ··· 312

Sub-Part A: Mediation ··· 312

86. Referral of disputes for mediation under this Act ··· 312

87. Consequences of not attending mediation hearing ·· 313

Sub-Part B: Arbitration ·· 314

88. Resolving disputes by compulsory arbitration ··· 314

89. Effect of arbitration award ··· 315

90. Correction of arbitration award ·· 315

91. Revision of arbitration award ·· 315

92. Application of Arbitration ··· 315

93. Voluntary arbitration ··· 316

Sub-Part C: Adjudication ·· 316

94. Jurisdiction of Labour Court ··· 316

Sub-Part D: Dispute Procedure in Collective Agreements ································· 317

95. Dispute resolution procedures in collective agreements ···································· 317

PART IX GENERAL PROVISIONS ·· 317

96. Records to be kept by employers and employees ··· 317

97. Service of documents ··· 318

98. Regulations ··· 318

99. Guidelines and codes of good practice ··· 319

100. Exemptions ·· 319

101. Confidentiality ·· 320

102. Penalties ··· 320

102A. Inconsistency with written laws ··· 320

103. Repeal and amendment of laws and savings provisions ··································· 320

FIRST SCHEDULE ·· 321

SECOND SCHEDULE ·· 321

THIRD SCHEDULE ··· 322

TITLE TEN MINIMUM WAGE ORDINANCE [2022]

1. Name and take effect ··· 328

2. Usage ·· 328

3. Translation ··· 328

4. Sectors and areas ·· 329

5. Employment standards ··· 329

6. Employees who get better interests ··· 329

7. Canceled ·· 329

GROUP THREE SPECIAL ECONOMIC LAWS AND REGULATIONS

TITLE ELEVEN EXPORT PROCESSING ZONES ACT (CHAPTER 373) [2002] [Revised Edition 2012]

PART I PRELIMINARY PROVISIONS ·· 336
  1. Short title and application ··· 336
  2. Interpretation ·· 337
PART II ESTABLISHMENT OR DECLARATION OF EXPORT PROCESSING ZONES ··· 337
  3. Establishment or declaration of EPZ ··· 337
  4. Objects and purposes of establishment of Export Processing Zone ················· 338
PART III LICENSING ·· 338
  5. Restriction on entering into, residing in, etc., the Export Processing Zones ······ 338
  6. Authority to issue licence ··· 339
  7. Cancellation and suspension of a licence ·· 339
  8. No variation of a licence ·· 340
  9. Appeal against a decision of the Authority ·· 340
  10. Prohibition of other activities ··· 340
  11. Authority to determine certain goods or articles to be processed in Export Processing Zones ·· 341
PART IV EXPORT PROCESSING ZONES AUTHORITY ··························· 341
  12. Establishment of the Authority ··· 341
  13. Objectives and functions of the Authority ·· 341
  14. Establishment of the Export Processing Zones Authority's Board ················· 342
  15. Functions and powers of the Board ·· 343
  17. Director General and other employees ··· 343
  18. Sources of funds ··· 343
  19. Use of the authority funds ·· 344
  20. Management and auditing of the funds of the Authority ································ 344
PART V INVESTMENT INCENTIVES ·· 344
  21. Incentives granted for investments in the Export Processing Zones ··············· 344
  22. Restriction on exportation of goods into cusloms territory by Export Processing

  Zones Investment ············ 346
 23. Work Permits for technical staff ············ 346
 24. Authority may enter into contractual agreement ············ 346
PART VI APPLICATION AND DISAPPLICATION OF OTHER LAWS ············ 347
 25. Disapplication ············ 347
 26. Exemption of the Stamp Duty Act ············ 347
 27. Application of Urhan Plauning ············ 347
 28. Application of labour laws ············ 348
PART VII ACQUISITION.COMPENSATION AND DISPUTES SETTLEMENT ············ 348
 29. Acquisition and compensation Acts ············ 348
 30. Setlement of drputes ············ 348
 31. Non-limitation for scttlement of disputes ············ 349
 32. Minister may make Regulations ············ 349
PART VIII OFFENCES ············ 349
 33. Offences relating to licences and foreign currency ············ 349
 34. Offence for transhipment of products etc. ············ 349
 35. Offences for manufacture, processing, ctc. of prohibited goods or articles ············ 350

GROUP FOUR MINING AND ENVIRONMENT PROTECTION LAWS AND REGULATIONS

TITLE TWELVE MINING ACT (CHAPTER 123) [2010]
[Revised Edition 2019] (Excerpts)

Part II GENERAL PRINCIPLES ············ 352
 6. Authority required for prospecting or mining ············ 352
 7. Mineral rights and exclusivity ············ 352
 8. Restriction on grant of mineral rights ············ 353
Part IV MINERAL RIGHTS ············ 355
 Division B: Special mining licence and mining licence ············ 355
 39. Applicants ············ 355
 41. Application for special mining licence ············ 355
 51. Rights of holder of mining licences ············ 356
 Division C: Primary mining licences ············ 357
 54. Application for primary mining licence ············ 357
 Division D: Mineral processing, smelting and refining ············ 357
 59. Mineral right holder to set aside minerals for processing, smelting or refining ············ 357

60. Application and grant of licence for processing minerals ········· 357

TITLE THIRTEEN   ENVIRONMENTAL MANAGEMENT ACT [2004] (Excerpts)

PART X   ENVIRONMENTAL QUALITY STANDARDS ········· 360

141. Compliance with standards, etc ········· 360
143. Water quality standards ········· 360
145. Air quality standards ········· 360
150. Soil quality standards ········· 361

GROUP FIVE   TAX LAWS AND REGULATIONS

TITLE FOURTEEN   VALUE ADDED TAX ACT (CHAPTER 148) [2015] [Revised Edition 2019]

Part I   PRELIMINARY PROVISIONS ········· 364
1. Short title ········· 364
2. Interpretation ········· 364

Part II   IMPOSITION OF VALUE ADDED TAX ········· 373
(a) Imposition and exemptions ········· 373
3. Imposition of value added tax ········· 373
4. Person liable to pay value added tax ········· 373
5. Value added tax rate and amount payable ········· 373
6. Exemptions and rates to be specified by law ········· 373
7. Treaties ········· 374
(b) Value added tax on imports ········· 375
8. Payment and collection of value added tax on imports ········· 375
9. Value of import ········· 375
10. Value of returning goods ········· 375
11. Deferral of value added tax on imported capital goods ········· 376
(c) Value added tax on supplies ········· 377
12. Subject matters and sub-categories of supply ········· 377
13. Consideration of supply ········· 377
14. Single and multiple supplies ········· 378
15. When value added tax becomes payable ········· 378
16. Exception for progressive, lay-by sale, and vending machine ········· 378
17. Value of taxable supply ········· 379
18. Exception for supplies to connected person ········· 379

19. Progressive or periodic supply ········· 379
20. Sale of economic activity ········· 379
21. Tax treatment on rights, vouchers and options ········· 380
22. Reimbursements of rights, voucher and option ········· 380
23. Input tax credits of right, voucher and options ········· 381
24. Pre-payments for telecommunication services ········· 381
25. In kind employee benefits ········· 381
26. Cancelled transactions ········· 381
27. Sale of property of debtor ········· 382

Part III REGISTRATION ········· 382

28. Registration requirement ········· 382
29. Other persons required to be registered ········· 383
30. Time of application for registration ········· 383
31. Mode of application ········· 384
32. Processing of application ········· 384
33. Compulsory registration ········· 384
34. Effect of failure to process application ········· 384
35. Taxpayer Identification Number and Value Added Tax Registration Number ······ 384
36. Registration to cover branches or divisions ········· 384
37. Notification of changes ········· 384
38. Transparency in pricing ········· 385
39. Application for cancellation of registration ········· 385
40. Decision on application for cancelation of registration ········· 385
41. Power to cancel registration ········· 385
42. Persons whose registration is cancelled ········· 386
43. List of registered persons ········· 386

Part IV PLACE OF TAXATION ········· 386

(a) **Supplies of goods and services made in Mainland Tanzania** ········· 386
44. Supplies of goods ········· 386
45. Inbound and outbound goods ········· 386
46. Supplies relating to immovable property ········· 387
47. Supply of services directly related to land ········· 387
48. Supply of essential services ········· 387
49. Services supplied to registered person ········· 387
50. Telecommunication services ········· 387
51. Services supplied to unregistered person in Mainland Tanzania ········· 388
52. Other services supplied to unregistered person within Mainland Tanzania ········· 388

53. Progressive or periodic supplies ······ 389

(b) Supplies for use outside the United Republic ······ 389

54. Zero-rating of immovable property ······ 389

55. Zero-rating of supply of goods ······ 389

55A. Zero-rating of supply of goods to Tanzania Zanzibar ······ 389

56. Leased goods used outside United Republic ······ 389

57. Goods used to repair temporary imports ······ 389

58. Supply of goods and services to non-resident warrantor ······ 390

59. Goods for use in international transport services ······ 390

60. Services supplied for use outside United Republic ······ 391

61. Services connected with temporary imports ······ 391

61A. Zero-rating of supply of services ······ 391

61B. Zero rating supply of electricity services ······ 392

62. Intellectual property rights for use outside United Republic ······ 392

63. Inter-carrier telecommunication services ······ 392

(c) Special rules ······ 392

64. Value added tax representatives of non-residents ······ 392

65. Services from foreign branch ······ 392

Part V RETURNS, PAYMENTS AND REFUNDS ······ 393

(a) Returns and payment ······ 393

66. Value added tax returns ······ 393

(b) Net amount of value added tax payable ······ 394

67. Calculation and payment of net amount ······ 394

(c) Input tax credits ······ 394

68. Credit for input tax ······ 394

69. Timing of input tax credits ······ 395

70. Partial input tax credit ······ 396

(d) Other adjustments ······ 397

71. Post supply adjustments for adjustment events ······ 397

72. Limitations on adjustments ······ 398

73. Period of making adjustments ······ 398

74. Post supply adjustments for bad debts ······ 398

75. Application for private use ······ 399

76. Adjustment on making insurance payment ······ 400

77. Adjustment on receiving insurance payments ······ 400

78. Adjustment to correct minor errors ······ 401

79. Adjustment on becoming registered ······ 401

80. Adjustment on cancellation of registration ·················· 401

 (e) Refunds ·················· 402

81. Carry forward of negative net amount ·················· 402

82. Refund without carry forward ·················· 402

83. Refund for overpayment ·················· 403

84. Application for refunds ·················· 403

85. Refund to diplomats, international bodies ·················· 404

Part VI DOCUMENTS AND RECORDS ·················· 405

86. Tax invoice ·················· 405

87. Adjustment notes ·················· 405

88. Documentation issued by or to agents ·················· 406

89. Records and accounts ·················· 406

Part VII ADMINISTRATION ·················· 407

90. Tax decisions ·················· 407

91. Continuity of partnerships or unincorporated associations ·················· 407

92. Death or insolvency of taxable person, mortgagee in possession ·················· 408

93. Interaction with income tax ·················· 408

Part VIII GENERAL PROVISIONS ·················· 408

94. Power to make regulations ·················· 408

95. Repeal and savings ·················· 409

96. Transitional provisions ·················· 409

Schedule (Section 6(1)) ·················· 410

TITLE FIFTEEN CUSTOMS (MANAGEMENT AND TARIFF) ACT (CHAPTER 403) [1952] [Revised Edition 2019] (Excerpts)

Part III IMPORTATION ·················· 421

Entry, examination, and delivery ·················· 421

28. Entry of cargo ·················· 421

29. Entry of transfer goods ·················· 422

Part IV WAREHOUSING OF GOODS ·················· 422

General provisions ·················· 422

38. Dutiable goods maybe warehoused ·················· 422

39. Procedure on warehousing ·················· 422

40. Removal to warehouse of goods entered therefor ·················· 423

41. Entry of warehoused goods ·················· 423

Part XVII CUSTOMS TARIFF ·················· 423

194A. Payment of customs duty when importing ·················· 423

194B. Exemption from customs duty after the first anniversary ... 424
194C. Payment of customs duty on sale or transfer of any item ... 424

TITLE SIXTEEN WITHHOLDING TAX ON PAYMENT FOR GOODS AND SERVICES PRACTICE NOTE TAX ACT [2019]

1.0 Tax Law ... 426
2.0 Purpose ... 426
3.0 Interpretation ... 426
4.0 The Application of this Practice Note ... 426
5.0 Applicable Concepts ... 426
6.0 Types of withholding tax ... 427
7.0 Withholding tax obligations ... 427
8.0 Application to particular types of persons ... 428
9.0 Basis for calculation of the withholding payments ... 428
10.0 Inclusion of value of benefits and facilities ... 429
11.0 Withholding Tax Base for Mixed Supplies (Goods & Services) ... 429
12.0 Withholding Tax Base for Construction Works ... 430
13.0 Procedure Applicable to Withholding ... 431
14.0 Issuance of Withholding Certificate — Section 85 of the ITA ... 431
15.0 Tax Credit to Withholdee ... 431
16.0 Consequences for failure to withhold — Sec. 84 of the ITA ... 431
17.0 Consequences for failure to file returns — Sec. 78 of TAA, Cap 438 ... 431
18.0 Submission of Contract Documents to TRA ... 432

GROUP SIX ANTI-CORRUPTION AND ECONOMIC CRIMES LAWS AND REGULATIONS

TITLE SEVEVTEEN PREVENTION AND COMBATING OF CORRUPTION ACT (CHAPTER 329) [2007] [Revised Edition 2019] (Excerpts)

Part III **Corruption and related offences** ... 434

15. Corrupt transactions ... 434
16. Corrupt transactions in contracts ... 435
17. Corrupt transactions in procurement ... 436
18. Corrupt transactions in auctions ... 436

21. Bribery of foreign public official ······ 437
22. Use of documents intended to mislead principal ······ 437
23. Persons obtaining advantage ······ 437
24. Advantage received on behalf of accused person ······ 438
25. Sexual or any other favours ······ 438
26. Public official to give accounts of properties ······ 438
27. Possession of unexplained property ······ 439
30. Aiding and abetting ······ 440
31. Abuse of position ······ 440
32. Conspiracy ······ 440
33. Trading in influence ······ 440
34. Transfer of proceeds of corruption ······ 440
35. Presumption of corruption ······ 441
36. False pretence to be an officer ······ 441
37. Offence of disclosure of identity ······ 442
38. Freezing of assets ······ 442
39. Duty to give information ······ 443

前　言

　　世界进入新的动荡变革期,百年大变局加速演进,面对错综复杂的外部环境,中国企业出海已成为必然趋势。非洲作为"一带一路"倡议的重要合作区域,将成为中国企业出海的重要目的地。译者自登上"非洲之巅"——出版《投资埃塞俄比亚法律必读(中英文对照)》,其后推开"非洲东大门"——出版《投资肯尼亚法律必读(中英文对照)》,现又于2024年中坦建交60周年之际,踏进"非洲伊甸园"——出版《投资坦桑尼亚法律必读(中英文对照)》,希望推动中国企业家出征坦桑尼亚这片蓝海。

　　坦桑尼亚位于非洲东部、赤道以南。北与肯尼亚和乌干达交界,南与赞比亚、马拉维、莫桑比克接壤,西与卢旺达、布隆迪和刚果(金)为邻,东濒印度洋。坦桑尼亚具有大量待开采的矿产和油气资源,旅游资源同样丰富,三分之一国土为国家公园、动物和森林保护区,非洲第一高峰乞力马扎罗山也主要在其境内。

　　1964年4月26日,中国和坦桑尼亚正式建立外交关系,中坦传统友谊由两国老一辈领导人亲手缔结。1965年2月,中国与坦桑尼亚签订《中华人民共和国政府和坦桑尼亚联合共和国政府贸易协定》。2014年起,中国已给予坦桑尼亚97%输华产品进口免税待遇。自2022年12月1日起,中国给予坦桑尼亚98%输华产品进口免关税待遇。据中国海关统计,2022年,中坦双边货物进出口贸易总额为83.1亿美元,同比增长23.7%。其中,中方出口额77.75亿美元,同比增长27.1%;中方进口额5.36亿美元,同比减少11.3%[①]。农业、旅游业和矿业是坦桑尼亚国民经济的三大支柱。

　　根据世界银行发布的《2020年营商环境报告》,坦桑尼亚在全球190个经济体中排名第141位[②]。截至2024年,中国连续8年成为坦桑尼亚最大贸易伙伴。2023年,中坦双边贸易额达87.8亿美元,同比增长5.7%[③]。中方高质量建成交付达累斯萨拉姆港升级项目、桑给巴尔国际机场航站楼、尼雷尔大桥等重大基础设施项目,可以说,中国企业为坦建设"陆海空网"综合基础设施网络作出了突出贡献,共建"一带一路"有效促进了坦桑尼亚国内及

---

① 商务部对外投资和经济合作司.对外投资合作国别(地区)指南　坦桑尼亚(2023年版)[EB/OL]. [2024－06－04]. http://www.mofcom.gov.cn/dl/gbdqzn/upload/tansangniya.pdf.
② 商务部对外投资和经济合作司.对外投资合作国别(地区)指南　坦桑尼亚(2023年版)[EB/OL]. [2024－06－04]. http://www.mofcom.gov.cn/dl/gbdqzn/upload/tansangniya.pdf.
③ 外交部.驻坦桑尼亚大使陈明健在中非智库论坛第十三届会议开幕式上的致辞[EB/OL].(2024－03－10)[2024－10－12]. https://www.fmprc.gov.cn/web/zwbd_673032/wjzs/202403/t20240311_11257291.shtml.

东非地区的互联互通水平①。

值得一提的是,坦桑尼亚相关法律规定商业贿赂构成犯罪。根据透明国际组织发布的2021年"清廉指数",坦桑尼亚排名全球第87位,在东非地区排名第二名,仅次于卢旺达②。

以往央企、国企和民企进入非洲,却各自为战,缺乏协调,由于政局与外汇等原因,出海企业屡遭困境。在此形势下,中非共建"一带一路"合作模式应运而生,作为"新出海之路"解决中国企业出海非洲的痛点,中企出海已经过了单打独斗的阶段,现在是"抱团出海"的黄金时机。

在2024年9月中非合作论坛北京峰会上,习近平总书记提议将中非关系整体定位提升至新时代全天候中非命运共同体,未来3年推动中国企业对非投资不少于700亿元人民币,并且决定给予包括33个非洲国家在内的所有同中国建交的最不发达国家100%税目产品零关税待遇③。2024年中非合作论坛北京峰会期间,中国、坦桑尼亚、赞比亚三国领导人共同见证签署《坦赞铁路激活项目谅解备忘录》。三方将以本次峰会为契机,推动坦赞铁路激活取得新进展。中方将同坦方继续深化经贸合作,积极培育数字经济、绿色发展、蓝色经济等新增长点④。

不仅企业亟需出海,相匹配的法律服务也需要与企业一同征战海外。这无疑是一条看似艰难,但正确的选择。中国企业特别是民营企业如何顺势出海,从遥远的"非洲蓝海"蛋糕上攫取并捕捉难得的机会?正如同塞伦盖蒂大草原上的动物大迁徙一样,为了食物而抱团冒险一搏!本书或可从法律层面予以助力。

本书第一编介绍投资法规。《投资条例》旨在协调、促进与深化投资事项。《移民法》(节选)规定入境、居留以及驱逐出境的条件。《土地法》(节选)明确土地占用的权利和附带条件。《乡村土地法》(节选)规定村庄土地的管理和行政事宜。《营业执照法》(节选)规定企业营业执照的授权范围、非居民临时许可证以及许可证的撤销等。《商业法(杂项修正案)》(节选)规定以商业名称开展业务的商号、个人和公司的注册事宜。《公私合营法》及《公私合营法(修正案)》规定公共部门与私营部门实体之间执行公私合营关系协议的体制框架;制定管理公私合营关系采购、发展和执行公私合营关系的规则、准则和程序等。

第二编呈现劳动法规。《就业与劳动关系法》规定核心劳动权利,制定基本就业标准,提供集体谈判框架,规定纠纷的预防和解决等。《最低工资令》适用于所有私营部门的雇主和雇员,并规定了各行业最低工资的实施标准。

第三编涉猎经济特区法规。《出口加工区法》对出口加工区的建立、发展和管理作出规定。吸引和促进以出口为导向的工业化投资,以实现坦桑尼亚出口的多样化和便利化,提高国际竞争力;创造和扩大外汇收入;创造和增加就业,以及培养熟练劳动力。

---

① 国际在线.直通使领馆|中国驻坦桑尼亚大使陈明健:建交60年 中坦关系一直走在中非合作前列[EB/OL].(2024-04-26)[2024-06-04]. https://baijiahao.baidu.com/s?id=1797369908414201311&wfr=spider&for=pc.

② 商务部对外投资和经济合作司.对外投资合作国别(地区)指南 坦桑尼亚(2023年版)[EB/OL]. [2024-06-04]. http://www.mofcom.gov.cn/dl/gbdqzn/upload/tansangniya.pdf.

③ 中国政府网.习近平在中非合作论坛北京峰会开幕式上的主旨讲话(全文)[EB/OL].(2024-09-05)[2024-09-28].https://www.gov.cn/yaowen/liebiao/202409/content_6972495.htm.

④ 环球网.中国驻坦桑尼亚大使:中坦将在现代化道路上继续做好同行伙伴[EB/OL].(2024-09-13)[2024-09-28]. https://world.huanqiu.com/article/4JQF8W7D5Qw.

第四编简介采矿与环境保护法规。《采矿法》(节选)规定了一般原则以及对于采矿权进行分类的许可。《环境管理法》(节选)规定了环境可持续管理的法律和制度框架;概述了管理、影响和风险评估、污染预防和控制、废物管理、环境质量标准、公众参与、遵守和执行的原则;规定了执行国家环境政策。

第五编阐释税收法规。《增值税法》对于建立征收、管理和监督增值税的法律框架等作出规定。《海关(管理和关税)法》(节选)规定海关、转让税及相关事务的管理和行政事项。《货物和服务付款的预扣税业务指南》为公众和坦桑尼亚税务局(TRA)官员提供指导,以便根据《所得税法》的相关规定,实现商品和服务预扣税(WHT)管理的一致性。

第六编描述反商业贿赂法规。《预防和反腐败法》(节选)对预防、调查和打击腐败及相关犯罪作出全面规定,确保相关部门开展业务活动独立有效地履行其职能。并向公众宣传贪污和腐败的弊端和影响、与当地和国际组织或个人开展合作与协作、推动和促进公众对反腐败的支持、调查和起诉与腐败有关的罪行。

在达之路控股集团董事长何烈辉博士的引荐下,译者得到中交一公局集团坦桑尼亚办事处商务经理位光辉先生、坦桑尼亚鼎言律师事务所负责人丁长江先生的鼎力支持。本书的资料收集还得益于坦桑尼亚中华总商会会长朱金峰先生的大力支持。

作为上大法学文库"非洲法律系列"之三,本书与系列之一的《投资埃塞俄比亚法律必读(中英文对照)》、系列之二的《投资肯尼亚法律必读(中英文对照)》具有类似的功效:一为已在坦桑尼亚发展的企业与个人更好地投资提供法律参考;二为打算去坦桑尼亚投资的企业与个人提供法律指南;三为政府的决策者提供法律索引;四为相关研究的学者提供法律铺陈。

本书的翻译过程历经坎坷,译者们凭借对坦桑尼亚法律的热情,怀揣着对非洲的赤诚之心,经过数次翻译与校对,才使本书终于得以与读者见面。虽然错误与不当仍在所难免,然译者们从事非洲法律翻译的热情依然可见,恳请各位专家与读者不吝赐教。投资坦桑尼亚本没有路,走的人多了,也便成了路。愿本书成为一盏明灯,为各位出海坦桑尼亚保驾护航。

走,到坦桑尼亚投资去!

本书的翻译分工如下:

1.《投资条例》——李智、万欣怡
2.《移民法》(节选)——朱骁琛、周智皓、文怡筱
3.《土地法》(节选)——张一鸣
4.《乡村土地法》(节选)——张漩
5.《营业执照法》(节选)——阿卜杜海拜尔·阿卜杜热西提
6.《商业法(杂项修正案)》(节选)——巫锦锋
7.《公私合营法》——万欣怡、文怡筱
8.《公私合营法(修正案)》——李智、万欣怡
9.《就业与劳动关系法》——李智、李威威、张漩、王苗苗
10.《最低工资令》——李威威、王苗苗
11.《出口加工区法》——何烈辉、朱骁琛、陈盈盈
12.《采矿法》(节选)——张一鸣

13.《环境管理法》(节选)——张津瑶
14.《增值税法》——张津瑶、巫锦锋、张一鸣、周智皓
15.《海关(管理和关税)法》(节选)——张津瑶、王苗苗
16.《货物和服务付款的预扣税业务指南》——张漩
17.《预防和反腐败法》(节选)——文怡筱、陈盈盈

全书译校统稿：李　智
译校统稿助理：张　漩、张一鸣

翻译团队介绍：
李　智：女,民商法博士,上海大学法学院教授、博士生导师。
何烈辉：男,历史学博士,达之路控股集团董事长。
朱晓琛：女,上海师范大学非洲研究中心博士研究生。
万欣怡：女,上海大学法学院2022级民商法硕士研究生。
张津瑶：女,上海大学法学院2022级民商法硕士研究生。
巫锦锋：男,上海大学法学院2022级法律硕士研究生。
李威威：女,上海大学法学院2022级法律硕士研究生。
王苗苗：女,上海大学法学院2023级民商法硕士研究生。
周智皓：男,上海大学法学院2023级民商法硕士研究生。
张　漩：男,上海大学法学院2023级法律硕士研究生。
张一鸣：男,上海大学法学院2023级法律硕士研究生。
阿卜杜海拜尔·阿卜杜热西提：男,上海大学法学院2023级法律硕士研究生。
文怡筱：女,上海大学法学院2023级诉讼法硕士研究生。
陈盈盈：女,上海大学法学院2020级本科生、2024级民商法研究生。

本书正文最终定稿于2024年6月6日
前言最终定稿于2024年10月10日
于上海大学东区法学院609室

第一编
投 资 法 规

第一部
投资条例 [2023 年]

坦桑尼亚联合共和国

补充第 27 号　　　　　　　2023 年 7 月 21 日

附属法例

《坦桑尼亚联合共和国公报》第 104 卷第 27 号, 2023 年 7 月 21 日

根据政府命令由多多马政府印务局印制

| 第 477 号政府公告,发布日期: 2023 年 7 月 21 日 |

坦桑尼亚投资法
（第 38 章）

条例
［根据第 5 条第（4）款和第 35 条作出］

——

坦桑尼亚投资条例，2023 年

第一部分
总　则

1. 引用

本条例可称为《坦桑尼亚投资条例》(2023)。

2. 释义

在本条例中，除非上下文另有规定，否则——

"董事会" 是指根据本法第 9 条设立的坦桑尼亚投资中心董事会；

"国家投资指导委员会" 是指根据本法第 5 条第(1)款设立的国家投资指导委员会；

"技术委员会" 是指根据本法第 5 条第(3)款设立的技术委员会；

"中心" 是指根据本法第 4 条设立的坦桑尼亚投资中心；

"人" 包括——

(a) 自然人及其继承人、遗嘱执行人、遗产管理人或其他代表，以及根据任何国家或地区的法律被授予法人资格或被承认具有法人资格的任何公司或其他实体；

(b) 任何国家或地区的政府、坦桑尼亚或其他地方的公共当局以及任何国际组织或机构，无论其成员是否包括坦桑尼亚，也无论其是否具有法人资格；

"有关联的人" 是指与某个人有关联的人——

(a) 该个人的父母、配偶、兄弟、姐妹或子女；

(b) 以任何信托的受托人、该信托的主要受益人、其配偶或其任何子女或其控制的法人团体的身份行事的人；

(c) 该个人的合伙人；或者

(d) 直接或间接控制该个人或受该个人控制；

"秘书处" 是指国家投资指导委员会秘书处；

"法令" 是指《坦桑尼亚投资法》；［第 38 章］和

"部长" 是指负责投资的部长。

第二部分
董事会的职责

3. 董事会的职责

根据本法的规定,董事会应——

(a) 持续审查中心的职能,以确保实现其目标;

(b) 持续监测国家投资状况和世界投资环境,并提出拟采取的措施,使坦桑尼亚的投资环境更具竞争力;

(c) 向部长提交关于中心活动的季度进展报告;和

(d) 制定中心工作人员的道德操守与行为准则。

4. 终止成员资格

依照本法规定任命的董事会成员,在以下情况下其成员资格应终止——

(a) 该成员因精神障碍、疾病或受伤而丧失行为能力的;

(b) 该成员书面通知任命机构辞职的,自任命机构收到通知之日起生效;

(c) 该成员被判犯有涉及不诚信的刑事罪行的;

(d) 该成员破产或与债权人达成任何协议或和解的;

(e) 该成员在收到每次会议的适当通知后,未经主席事先书面许可,或主席未经部长事先书面许可的情况下,连续三次缺席董事会会议;或者

(f) 任命机构认为该成员没有能力履行其职责,或者终止其成员资格是有效履行董事会职能所必需的。

5. 填补空缺职位

如果董事会成员因本条例所规定的理由不再担任董事会成员,任命机构可任命一人担任董事会成员,以填补董事会剩余任期内的空缺。

6. 法定人数

董事会会议的法定人数不得少于5名成员。

7. 董事会的决定

董事会的决定应以协商一致的方式作出,但在无法达成共识的情况下,应以表决方式作出,每名成员有一票表决权,在表决票数相等的情况下,主席除拥有其审议票外,还拥有决定票。

8. 循环决议

在符合本法规定的情况下,由董事会法定人数签署的书面决议,与正式召开的董事会会议通过的决议一样有效。

9. 成员任命上的缺陷

尽管事后发现任何成员的任命存在缺陷,或其中任何成员已丧失任职资格或在决定中丧失投票的资格,在董事会会议或董事会委员会会议上作出的任何行为均应有效。

10. 利益冲突

如某个人是董事会成员、董事会委员会成员、执行董事、中心工作人员、董事会聘用的顾问或其他人员,在董事会或董事会委员会必须审议的任何事项中拥有金钱利益或其他实益权益,

或与该任何事项有重大利害关系,该任何事项包括在任何个人、企业、财产、合同、已作出或拟作出的投资或者任何其他事项中的直接或间接利益,则该个人应——

  (a) 在审议该事项之前,在董事会会议上向董事会申报该利益的性质;

  (b) 要求将其发言记录在有关会议的记录中;

  (c) 不得出席董事会就该事项进行的任何审议;和

  (d) 不得就该事项采取行动。

11. 实益权益

  (1) 就本条例第 10 条而言,任何人在以下情况下应被视为具有受益权益——

    (a) 本人或其关联人员,或者其雇员或其任命的人员是在本条例第 10 条所述事项中拥有实益权益或与该事项具有重大利害关系的公司或任何其他机构的成员或合伙人;

    (b) 本人或其关联人员在本条例第 10 条所述事项中拥有实益权益或与该事项有重大利害关系的人员有合伙关系,或受雇于该人员;或者

    (c) 本人或其关联人员是任何合约或协议的当事方,无论依据本条例第 10 条该事项是否可被强制执行。

  (2) 如对任何人实施某种行为是否会导致该人不遵从本条例第 10 条的规定存在质疑,则该质疑应由董事会裁定,裁定的详情应记录在有关会议的记录中。

  (3) 本条例所述人员如未按照本条例第 10 条的规定作出披露,任命机构应决定采取适当行动,包括免除或终止其职务。

12. 董事会秘书

  (1) 董事会秘书应准确记录董事会的所有正式程序和决定。

  (2) 尽管有第(1)款的一般性规定,秘书应——

    (a) 保存准确的董事会文件、记录和决议;

    (b) 将报告存档并注明提交日期;

    (c) 发出书面会议通知;

    (d) 编制董事会会议议程;

    (e) 保存董事会成员名册;

    (f) 编制会议记录;

    (g) 确保在合理的时间内向成员提供董事会会议文件;

    (h) 保存董事会设立的所有委员会的准确名单;和

    (i) 通知被选为委员会成员的人员。

第三部分
国家投资指导委员会和技术委员会职能的履行

13. 国家投资指导委员会职能的履行

  在履行本法规定的职能时,国家投资指导委员会可以——

    (a) 在政府内部达成共识,以促进投资事项的实施;

    (b) 发布指令,消除在该国投资的各种障碍;

(c) 受理并处理妨碍为投资事宜提供优质服务的投诉或部门中的障碍,并迅速化解行政纠纷;

(d) 根据项目使用的资金量、创造的就业机会和使用的技术,接收、发布指令和批准对国民经济有重大影响的投资项目。

14. 技术委员会

在符合本法第 5 条第(3)款规定的情况下,技术委员会应由以下人员组成:

(a) 投资、工业和贸易部负责投资事务的常务秘书,担任主席;

(b) 投资、工业和贸易部负责财政(政策)的副常务秘书,担任副主席;

(c) 投资、工业和贸易部负责财政的分析专员;

(d) 土地专员;

(e) 总检察长办公室合同与条约处主任;

(f) 坦桑尼亚税务局大额纳税人事务专员;

(g) 投资、工业和贸易部负责投资事务的投资发展主任;

(h) 投资、工业和贸易部负责工业事务的工业发展主任;和

(i) 主席可能邀请的与讨论事项相关的部门的任何人员。

15. 技术委员会会议

(1) 技术委员会应至少每 3 个月举行一次会议。

(2) 技术委员会应自行规定举行会议的程序。

(3) 技术委员会会议的法定人数应至少为其成员的一半。

16. 技术委员会的职能

(1) 技术委员会应履行以下职能:

(a) 受理并处理秘书处提出的旨在改善投资环境的各项事宜,并向国家投资指导委员会提供建议;

(b) 受理并处理秘书处提出的额外财政和非财政福利申请,并向国家投资指导委员会提供建议;和

(c) 履行国家投资指导委员会可能指示的任何其他职能。

(2) 在处理第(1)条第(b)款规定的申请时,技术委员会可邀请并听取申请人的陈述,并在提出建议时考虑本法第 19 条第(2)款和第(3)款规定的条件。

第四部分
向国家投资指导委员会提交各种事项的程序

17. 战略投资申请及相关事项

(1) 申请战略投资和特别战略投资,以获得额外的财政和非财政福利,应在缴纳本条例附表 2 规定的费用后,以本条例附表 1 所列表格 1 的形式提交国家投资指导委员会秘书。

(2) 根据第(1)款规定提出的申请应附有以下文件:

(a) 奖励证书复印件;

(b) 说明国家和投资者的实际成本、利润,以及国家投资指导委员会为促使投资者

有效实施项目而要求其提供的额外利益的项目分析报告;和

(c) 说明第(b)项规定的投资者申请中的关键问题的简要报告。

(3) 根据第(1)款提出的申请,如果不符合本法规定的条件,则不予批准。

(4) 在不影响第(2)款规定的情况下,申请在有挑战的领域进行战略投资,应表明项目面临的挑战以及提出如何克服这些挑战的建议。

(5) 就本条例而言,国家周边地区面临的挑战包括基础设施和训练有素的人力的短缺。

18. 其他提交文件

除投资争议外,其他与投资有关的事项应通过本条例附表1所列的表格1交由国家投资指导委员会决定或指示。

19. 决策程序

(1) 国家投资指导委员会秘书在收到根据第17条和第18条提出的申请后,应将其提交给技术委员会,技术委员会应在最后一次处理该申请的会议后14天内进行处理并向国家投资指导委员会提出建议。

(2) 国家投资指导委员会在收到技术委员会的建议后,应决定接受或拒绝技术委员会的建议,并在接受建议的情况下,指示秘书处将此决定通知相关部委、部门和机构或相关人员。

第五部
奖励、修复和扩展证书

20. 奖励证书申请

(1) 工商企业法人在缴纳本条例附表2规定的费用并符合本法要求后,可使用本条例附表1所列的表格3向中心提交奖励证书申请。

(2) 中心收到第(1)款规定的申请后,应进行处理,并可——

(a) 受理申请并对企业进行认证;或者

(b) 驳回申请。

(3) 如果中心已受理申请并根据第(2)款对企业进行认证,则应向认证合格的企业颁发奖励证书。

(4) 如果中心根据第(2)款驳回申请,应告知申请人驳回申请的理由。

21. 证书为决定性证据

中心为工商企业颁发的奖励证书应为企业符合本法和本条例所有要求的决定性证据。

22. 名称、股权或控制权的变更

如果经过认证的工商企业需要变更名称、所有权或与股东有关的股权控制权,中心在收到根据《公司法》或《商业名称(登记)法》或任何其他相关法律的法定要求作出的变更确认后,应出具经修订的奖励证书,以符合具体情况。

[第212章;第213章]

23. 变更不影响利益

在符合本法规定的最低资本要求的前提下,第22条所述的任何变更不得影响企业的任何权利或义务。

24. 延长额外优惠期限的程序

（1）获得额外优惠的战略投资者或特殊战略投资者，可在首次申报期届满之前向国家投资指导委员会秘书提交信函，说明申请的合理理由，申请延长优惠期限。

（2）国家投资指导委员会秘书应将根据第（1）款提出的申请提交国家投资指导委员会，由其作出决定，国家投资指导委员会秘书应以书面形式将该决定通知申请人。

（3）在对根据第（1）款提出的申请作出决定时，国家投资指导委员会，除其他事项外，还应考虑在批准投资用地、审批投资资金及其他相关投资许可证和执照方面是否存在延误。

25. 奖励证书的延期

（1）获得奖励证书的工商企业可在先前授予的时间届满之前，通过向中心提交信函说明延期理由，申请延长奖励证书的有效期。

（2）中心在考虑根据本条例延长证书的有效期时，除其他事项外，还应考虑在获取项目土地、资金或者许可证或各种执照方面是否存在延误。

（3）中心应在收到第（1）款规定的申请之日起 7 个工作日内予以处理，并将处理结果以书面形式通知申请人。

26. 奖励证书的撤销程序

（1）中心在确认投资者违反了本法的规定后，可根据本法第 20 条第（3）款规定的理由撤销其奖励证书。

（2）中心在根据第（2）款的规定查明撤销奖励证书的原因后，应在撤销证书前向证书持有者发出通知，要求其在通知规定的时间内纠正已查明的异常情况。

（3）如果证书持有者未能在根据第（2）款规定的通知指明时间内纠正异常情况，中心应提前 7 天发出撤销其证书的意向通知，并要求其在通知期满后说明不应撤销其证书的理由。

（4）如果证书持有者未能提交答辩，或其答辩未被中心接受，中心应撤销其证书，并将决定理由通知证书持有者。

第六部分
促进、推动和协调投资事项

27. 投资促进计划

（1）中心应根据本法履行投资促进职能。

（2）在履行第（1）款规定的职能时，中心应编制并向董事会提交一份投资促进计划供董事会批准。

（3）计划一经批准，董事会应采取一切必要措施，确保投资促进计划的实施。

28. 计划的实施

（1）为实施投资促进计划，中心应——

  （a）通过传播信息、组织公共关系活动和宣传投资机会，向潜在的当地和外国投资者将坦桑尼亚作为投资目的国宣传，以树立和提升坦桑尼亚作为投资目的地的良好形象；

  （b）持续审查在实现本法目标和宗旨方面取得的进展，并发布报告和提供信息，以提高投资者和公众对这些进展以及坦桑尼亚投资环境方面存在的挑战和补救

措施的认识;和

(c) 开发专业知识、技能和其他技术能力,以就促进投资和相关事宜向政府提供建议。

29. 项目的监督和评估

(1) 中心负责对已登记的项目进行监测和评估。

(2) 在履行第(1)款规定的职责时,中心应制定监测和评估框架,每 3 个月编制一次报告。

(3) 在进行监测和评估时,中心应考虑本法第 19 条第(2)款和(3)款规定的条件。

(4) 中心应向国家投资指导委员会报告战略投资和特殊战略投资项目的实施进展情况。

30. 投资者年度报告

(1) 根据本法获得奖励证书的工商企业,应负责向中心提交关于项目进展情况的年度报告。

(2) 新获认证的工商企业应在奖励证书颁发之日起 12 个月内提交年度报告。

(3) 现有注册工商企业应在上一年度最后提交之日起 12 个月内提交年度报告。

(4) 本条规定的报告应按本条例附表 1 表格 4 规定的方式编制。

31. 派驻土地官员和向投资者颁发派生产权证

(1) 根据本法第 6 条第(1)款第(e)项和第 18 条第(2)款的规定,派驻中心的土地官员应负责根据本法就投资用地做出快速通道安排。

(2) 派驻中心的土地官员应受理并处理指定用于投资的土地派生产权申请,并建议执行主任根据《土地法》向投资者颁发此类派生产权证。[第 113 章]

(3) 执行主任在收到土地官员建议的 7 个工作日内,认为其符合法律规定的,应向投资者颁发指定土地的派生产权证。

32. 居住和工作许可证等

根据本法第 6 条第(1)款第(f)项和第 18 条第(1)款的规定,中心应在收到投资者的申请后 7 个工作日内协助投资者获得居留和工作许可证、商业登记证和必要的许可证。

33. 派驻官员

根据本法第 18 条第(2)款的规定,各部委、部门和机构派驻中心的官员应根据通过该中心提交的申请,协调和促进各种许可证的办理,以确保在收到此类申请后 7 个工作日内发放许可证。

34. 获得保证和利润转让

中心应主动向持有根据《采矿法》授予的矿业权或根据《石油法》授予的许可证的投资者颁发奖励证书,以保证其能够享有本法第 28 条规定的资本、利润和红利转让;以及确保其依据本法第 29 条和本法第 2 条第(3)款的规定免于征用。

[第 123 章;第 392 章]

第七部分
其 他 规 定

35. 上诉

(1) 对中心下列事项的决定不满意者——

(a) 拒绝奖励证书的申请;

(b) 拒绝有关恢复或扩大工商企业的申请;

(c) 拒绝延长奖励证书有效期的申请;或者

(d) 撤销奖励证书,

可以在决定作出之日起 21 天内致函部长提出上诉。

(2) 收到上诉后,部长可确认、撤销或更改该决定,或就中心作出的决定发布具体指示。

(3) 部长根据第(2)款作出的决定为终局裁定。

36. 复审

(1) 对国家投资指导委员会根据第 18 条提交的关于给予奖励的决定或其他事项不满意的投资者,可在收到该决定之日起 21 天内,向国家投资指导委员会提出复审申请,并说明复审理由。

(2) 向国家投资指导委员会提出的复审申请应提交给国家投资指导委员会秘书。

(3) 收到申请后,委员会将进行审议并作出终局裁定。

37. 投资争议的协调

(1) 根据本法第 33 条的规定,中心应在收到提交给中心的与登记投资有关的争议后 30 天内受理并解决该争议。

(2) 面临争议的投资者应在争议发生之日起 21 日内向中心提交书面争议说明,以及所寻求的救济。

(3) 在收到根据第(2)款提交的材料后,中心应尽力与相关责任方召开会议,以便及时友好地解决争议。

38. 违法行为和处罚

任何人违反本条例规定,即属犯罪,一经定罪,应依照本法规定予以处罚。

39. 撤销

特此废除《坦桑尼亚投资条例》(2002)。

[2002 年第 381A 号政府公告]

40. 保留条款

尽管《坦桑尼亚投资条例》(2005)已被废止,但根据该条例做出的所有行为将继续有效,如同根据本条例做出的一样,直至其根据本条例被宣布无效。

附表 1

表格

表格 1

[根据第 17 条第(1)款制定]

战略投资者和特别战略投资者身份申请表

致:执行主任

坦桑尼亚投资中心,

邮政信箱 938 号,

达累斯萨拉姆

1. 对于申请战略/特别战略投资者身份的企业，请注明董事或股东（公司）的名称 _____

2. 指明公司注册地点及住所 _____

3. 附上以下文件的复印件：
   （a）奖励证书；和
   （b）项目概要，表明符合本法规定的注册要求，包括项目融资结构、实施期限和运营日期

   4. 以坦桑尼亚先令或美元表示公司的拟投资资本金额 _____

   5. 申请费缴纳声明
   我/我们随函附上一张支票/现金，抬头请写"坦桑尼亚投资中心"，不可退还，金额为 _____ 先令/美元。作为战略/特别战略投资者，我，_____ 邮政编码 _____ 谨此郑重声明：本人为 _____ 之董事/正式授权代理人，并已遵守《坦桑尼亚投资法》(2022)中关于注册工商企业的先决事项和附带事项的所有要求，本人在此郑重声明，并确保声明内容属实。

   宣布于 _____
   _____ 年 _____ 月 _____ 日
   在我面前：

   _____
   宣誓专员

仅在适用时附上，否则请注明"不适用"。

申请概要和补充信息

公司名称：_____
奖励证书编号：_____ 和日期：_____
邮箱：_____
城市：_____
部门：_____ 分部门：_____
投资融资计划（百万美元/坦桑尼亚先令）

外国股本	本地股本	外国贷款	本地贷款
_____	_____	_____	_____

项目目标 _____
_____
产能：_____
直接就业：国外：_____ 本地：_____ 总计：_____

间接就业：_____
实施期限：_____
项目地点
场地/地块/区块编号：_____
街道：_____   地区：_____   区域：_____
（附项目位置示意图）

股东	国籍	%
....	....	....
....	....	....
....	....	....

投资明细（美元/坦桑尼亚先令）
土地/建筑_____
工厂_____
车辆_____
家具与配件_____
前期费用_____
其他_____
营运资本_____
总计_____

联系方式
姓名：_____   职务：_____
电话：_____   传真：_____
电子邮件：_____

要求提供的其他具体财政和非财政激励措施

序号	激励措施名称	项目/商品/服务名称	计量单位	估计数量	激励金额估计额（美元）	激励措施实施期间	激励措施的合理性
1.							
2.							
3.							
4.							
5.							
6.							
7.							
8.							

表格 2

(根据第 18 条制定)

提交国家投资指导委员会决定和审议的投资相关事项

致 国家投资指导委员会执行主任兼秘书,
  坦桑尼亚投资中心,
  邮政信箱 938 号
  达累斯萨拉姆

1. 填写提交需要国家投资指导委员会指导的投资事项的企业或政府实体的名称。
   ....

2. 填写需要国家投资指导委员会干预的投资相关事项
   ....

3. 在提交材料时附上以下文件的复印件:
   (a) 阐述该事项的详细书面报告复印件,
   (b) 负责的部委、部门或代理机构,
   (c) 已采取的行动和建议国家投资指导委员会采取的干预措施;

4. 申请人声明
   我,_____邮政编码_____谨此郑重声明:本人为_____之董事/正式授权代理人

   ....
              申请人

5. 联系方式:
   姓名:_____ 职务:_____
   电话:_____ 传真:_____
   电子邮件:_____

提交摘要

序号	事项详情	责任机构	对投资环境或企业的影响	采取的行动	拟议的国家投资指导委员会干预措施

表格 3

[根据第 20 条第（1）款制定]

奖励证书申请表

致 执行主任
坦桑尼亚投资中心，
邮政信箱 938 号
达累斯萨拉姆

1. 写明_____的董事/代理人的姓名

2. 说明公司或工商企业注册办事处的名称和住所

3. 附上以下文件的复印件：
   （a）公司备忘录和章程细则/或合伙协议
   （b）公司注册/登记证书
   （c）项目简介或可行性研究报告复印件，说明实施期限、实施计划和实施日期；
   （d）项目的资金证明和土地所有权证明

4. 写明项目地点名称

5. 公司的主要管理人员为：
   （a）_____
   （b）_____
   （c）_____

6. 以坦桑尼亚先令或美元为单位写明公司法定股本

7. 以坦桑尼亚先令或美元为单位写明项目的拟投资资本金额

8. 附上支票/现金，以证明已缴付不可退还的注册费；

9. 声明
   我，_____邮政编码_____谨此郑重声明：本人为_____之董事/正式授权代理人，并已遵守《坦桑尼亚投资法》（2022）中关于注册工商企业的先决事项和附带事项的所有要求，本人在此郑重声明，并确保声明内容属实。

   宣布于_____ ｝   申请人
   _____ ｝
   ____年____月____日｝

在我面前：

宣誓专员

仅在适用时附上，否则请注明"不适用"。

申请概要和补充信息

企业名称：--

注册类型：--

注册编号：------------------   注册日期：----------------

邮箱：----------

城市：------------------

部门：----------   分部门：----------

投资融资计划（百万美元/坦桑尼亚先令）

外国股本	本地股本	外国贷款	本地贷款
----------	----------	----------	----------

项目目标

项目产能：----------

就业：国外：----------   本地：----------   总计：----------

实施期限：----------

项目地点

场地/地块/区块编号：--------------------

街道：----------   地区：----------   区域：----------

（附项目位置示意图）

股东	国籍	%
----------	----------	----------
----------	----------	----------
----------	----------	----------

投资明细（美元/坦桑尼亚先令）

土地/建筑 ----------

工厂 ----------

车辆 ----------

家具与配件 ----------

前期费用 ----------

其他 ----------

营运资本 ....
总计 ....

联系方式
姓名：........................ 职务：........................
电话：........................ 传真：........................
电子邮件：........................

表格 4

[根据第 30 条第(4)款制定]

投资者年度报告

致 执行董事
　　坦桑尼亚投资中心，
　　邮政信箱 938 号，
　　达累斯萨拉姆

1. 报告应显示
　　（a）这一时期的计划活动
　　（b）迄今在项目实施方面取得的成就：
　　　　（即从项目获批之日起至撰写报告之日止）
　　（c）说明已开展活动的情况,如建筑施工、物资采购、设备安装等。
2. 报告将提供以下方面的最新信息：

序号	信息	说明	项目现状
1.	股东信息	现有股东姓名、国籍和持股比例	
2.	公司通信信息	电子邮件地址	
		手机号码	
		座机电话号码	
		实际地址（地块编号、座号、街道、地区和区域）	
3.	联系人	名称	
		职位	
		通信详情（电子邮件、手机和电话）	
4.	公司注册	公司注册证书编号	
5.	TIN 信息	TIN 证书编号	

续表

序号	信息	说明	项目现状
6.	项目目标	项目核心活动	
7.	产能	项目年产能	
8.	直接就业	外国男性	
		外国女性	
		当地男性	
		当地女性	
9.	间接就业	预估总数	

序号	信息	说明	项目现状
		间接就业类型/领域	

3. 项目财务支出报告(美元)：

	外币(美元)	当地(美元)	总计(美元)
土地和建筑物			
设备和机械			
车辆/飞机			
家具			
办公设备			
保险范围			
运营前费用			
营运资本小计			
总计			

4. 项目融资报告

说明项目的融资方式,如股权、贷款、贷款来源、条件等,参见下表。

	金额(美元)	来源国
本地股本		坦桑尼亚
本地贷款		坦桑尼亚

续 表

	金额(美元)	来源国
外国股本		
外国贷款		
投资总额		

5. 说明问题和解决方案的报告

说明管理层在执行项目过程中遇到的问题,以及为解决这些问题所采取的措施。

6. 说明未来计划的报告

说明未来6个月的计划和计划的融资承诺。

7. 说明建议和任何其他意见的报告

附表 2

[根据第17条第(1)款和第20条第(1)款制定]

收 费 表

	签 发 服 务	适用费用(美元或等值的坦桑尼亚先令)
1.	奖励证书申请	1 200
2.	战略投资者和特别战略投资者身份申请	3 000
3.	投资项目扩建和改造申请	1 200
4.	一站式服务	发证机构所收取费用的10%

多多马,

2023年7月4日

阿沙图·卡丘万巴·基贾济,

投资、工业和贸易部长

第二部
移民法（第54章）［1998年］［2016年修订版］（节选）

坦桑尼亚联合共和国

移民法

第54章

［主要立法］

2016年修订版

本版《移民法》（第54章）纳入了截至2016年11月15日（含该日）的所有修正案，并根据《法律修订法》（第4章）第4条的授权印刷。

达累斯萨拉姆 2016年12月20日	乔治·马萨祖 总检察长

移 民 法
（第54章）

旨在对控制进入联合共和国的移民和有关移民事项作出规定的法案。

[1998年2月1日]

[1998年政府公告第51号]

第四部分
违 禁 移 民

27. 驱逐出境

（1）除坦桑尼亚公民外的任何人，因违反本法任何规定而被定罪，经主任专员建议驱逐出境，可根据部长作出的命令将其驱逐出坦桑尼亚。

（2）部长可作出命令，要求：

（a）任何违禁移民（除持有有效通行证或根据本法向其颁发的其他授权书之外的违禁移民）；

（b）非法进入坦桑尼亚或在坦桑尼亚境内非法逗留的人；或者

（c）除坦桑尼亚公民以外的任何人，如果总统认为其行为或其继续在坦桑尼亚的逗留可能对坦桑尼亚的和平与良好秩序构成威胁，或者其行为或其继续在坦桑尼亚的逗留由于任何其他原因不受欢迎，应无限期或在命令规定的期限内被驱逐出境并禁止入境。

（3）根据第（1）款或第（2）款作出的任何命令应以部长指示的方式生效。

（4）如果部长指示，被驱逐出境的人在等待驱逐出境和被送往离境地期间，可以被拘留，则此期间的拘留应被视为合法拘留。

（5）如果任何人根据本法的规定被带至法院，并且法院被告知已根据本条对其提出了驱逐令申请，则法院有权对其进行不超过28天的拘留。

（6）驱逐令在其中规定的期限内有效，除非部长提前更改或撤销，或者如果没有规定期限，则其在部长更改或撤销之前一直有效。

（7）如果根据本条对正在服刑的人发出驱逐令，尽管刑期尚未满，但如果总统作出指示，驱逐令仍应执行，且总统作出的任何该等指示应足以授权将该人从监狱释放，以便将其驱逐出境。

[2015年第8号法案第3条]

第五部分
入境和居留条件

28. 禁止无护照、居留许可证或通行证的人入境

（1）除第（2）款和第（3）款另有规定外,本条适用的任何人不得从坦桑尼亚境外的任何地方进入坦桑尼亚或在坦桑尼亚逗留,除非——

  （a）其持有附有签证的护照;

  （b）其是根据本法规定颁发的居留许可证的持有人,或其姓名被签注;或者

  （c）其是根据本法规定颁发的通行证的持有人,或其姓名被签注。

（2）尽管有第（1）款的规定,但在任何特定情况下,主任专员可允许任何人在不持护照的情况下进入坦桑尼亚,但须遵守其规定的条件。

（3）部长可免除任何人或任何类别的人持有护照的要求。

（4）如任何许可证或通行证上的签注被取消,且未再签发或签注居留证或通行证,则该许可证或通行证的前持有人或其姓名被签注在该证上的人（视情况而定）出现在坦桑尼亚境内,除非部长另有指示,否则不得仅以第（1）款的规定为理由,在根据第48条对相关类别的许可证、通行证或签注作出有关规定的开始期间、有效期届满或取消日期之前,将所涉许可证、通行证或签注视为非法。

（5）第（1）款第（a）项和第（b）项的规定适用于以下人员以外的任何人——

  （a）外国主权国家派驻坦桑尼亚的特使或其他代表,以及该特使或代表的正式工作人员和国内工作人员;

  （b）被坦桑尼亚政府任命并认可的外国主权国家派驻坦桑尼亚的领事官员或领事雇员;

  （c）外国主权国家派驻坦桑尼亚的特使或其他代表的,或该特使或其他代表的正式工作人员的,或外国主权国家派驻坦桑尼亚并经坦桑尼亚政府承认的领事官员或领事雇员的妻子和受抚养子女;

  （d）为坦桑尼亚政府或桑给巴尔革命政府服务并驻扎在坦桑尼亚、持有有效护照且移民官对其身份和职业满意的人,以及此人的妻子和受抚养子女;但坦桑尼亚政府或桑给巴尔革命政府可要求其以保证金或现金存款的方式提供担保,以支付政府或其雇主将其本人、妻子和受抚养子女遣返回原籍国可能产生的任何费用;

  （e）部长已指示,豁免其受本条第（1）款第（a）项和第（b）项规定约束的任何其他人。

（6）根据第（5）款获得豁免者的妻子或任何受抚养子女,在未事先获得为此目的颁发的或被视为已颁发的居留许可证之前,不得在坦桑尼亚从事任何工作、商业、贸易或职业。

（7）其中:

  （a）第（5）款第（a）项所指的任何人不再担任该职务;

  （b）第（5）款第（d）项所指的任何人不再为坦桑尼亚政府或桑给巴尔革命政府服务,或不再驻扎在坦桑尼亚;或者

(c) 部长发出指示,撤销或撤回根据第(5)款第(e)项给予的任何豁免,则自终止、撤销或撤回豁免之日起 1 个月(视情况而定),或部长允许的更长的期限内,第(5)款第(a)、(b)、(d)或(e)项所指人员及其妻子和受抚养子女在坦桑尼亚的居留,除非本法另有授权,否则被视为非法。

(8) 部长可在与桑给巴尔总统协商并征得其同意后,通过在《公报》上发布的命令,对前往坦桑尼亚的游客进出桑给巴尔作出补充规定。

[2004 年第 15 号法案第 25 条;2015 年第 8 号法案第 3 条]

29. 签证费

(1) 根据本法签发的签证费用应符合本法附表中的规定。

(2) 部长可在《公报》上发布公告,废除或修订该附表。

[2004 年第 15 号法案第 25 条]

30. 禁止无证就业、学习等

(1) 除非根据《非公民(就业管理)法》的规定获得许可,否则任何人不得在坦桑尼亚居民雇主手下从事带薪工作。

(2) 除非符合根据《非公民(就业管理)法》颁发的适当许可证的条款,否则任何人不得为获得利益或报酬而从事任何规定的贸易、商业、行业或其他职业。

(3) 除非持有根据本法颁发的适当的有效许可证,否则任何人不得在坦桑尼亚的教育机构开始任何课程的学习。

[第 436 章;2015 年第 1 号法案第 28 条;2015 年第 8 号法案第 3 条]

31. 外籍移民委员会的设立、组成和职能

(1) 特此设立一个委员会,称为外籍移民委员会。

(2) 委员会由以下人员组成:

(a) 主席 1 名,为由总统任命的负责移民事务的高级官员;

(b) 联邦政府劳工事务专员或其代表,即为委员会秘书;

(c) 桑给巴尔革命政府劳工专员或其代表;

(d) 6 名高级公职人员,分别来自联邦政府和桑给巴尔革命政府,代表下列机构——

(i) 负责贸易和工业的部门;

(ii) 负责规划事务的机构;

(iii) 负责行政事务的机构。

(3) 委员会的职能如下:

(a) 就主任专员或有关当局决定向外籍移民发放营业执照或 B 类居留许可证之前需要考虑的因素,向主任专员和其他有关当局提供建议;

(b) 就根据第(a)项申请并获发营业执照或 B 类居留许可证的任何外籍移民的入境、居留或流动的管制和监测条件及方式,向主任专员和其他有关当局提供建议;

(c) 就外籍移民拟从事的商业或就业空缺是否能由坦桑尼亚公民有偿填补,向主任专员和其他有关当局提供建议;

(d) 就为更有效地执行本节规定而采取的任何措施向主任专员提供一般性建议。

(4) 部长可通过在《公报》上发布条例,规定委员会成员的任期和议事程序,以及与委员会有关的其他事项。

（5）部长可修改、变更或撤销根据本条第（4）款制定的规章。

[2015 年第 8 号法案第 3 条]

32. 居留许可证类别

（1）居留许可证分为三类，分别称为 A 类居留许可证、B 类居留许可证和 C 类居留许可证。

（2）居留许可证的有效期不超过 3 年，可以由主任专员签发续期签注，续期不超过 2 年，但在任何情况下，原居留许可证及其续期的总有效期不得超过 5 年。

（3）颁发任何类别居留许可证的权力均属主任专员。

（4）根据本法，特别是本部分的规定，任何根据《坦桑尼亚投资法》获得奖励证书的人，在投资开始期间都有权获得最多 5 人的初始自动移民配额。[第 38 章]

（5）根据由坦桑尼亚投资中心代表奖励证书持有人提交的申请颁发许可证时，主任专员应在适当考虑第（4）款规定的移民配额的情况下，自收到申请之日起 14 天内颁发许可证或向该中心说明拒绝颁发居留许可证的理由。

（6）尽管有第（4）款和第（5）款的规定，采矿和石油作业的移民配额应由投资者根据作业性质确定。

（7）根据第（4）款和第（5）款的规定，坦桑尼亚投资中心应在移民配额范围内向主任专员提出增加人员的申请，主任专员在考虑到成为坦桑尼亚人的适格性、商业企业所采用技术的复杂性以及与投资者达成的协议后，可授权增加其认为必要的人员。

[1997 年第 27 号法案第 25 条；2015 年第 8 号法案第 3 条]

33. A 类居留许可证

（1）除被禁止的移民外，任何拟进入或留在坦桑尼亚并从事任何贸易、商业、行业、农业、畜牧业、矿产勘探或制造业的人，如果主任专员考虑劳工专员为此颁发的工作居留许可证条件后认为合适，可在下列情况下获得 A 类居留许可证：

- (a) 该人或代表该人的其他人向移民官交存移民官认为足以支付将该人、其妻子和受抚养子女（如有）送回原籍国或移民官酌情决定送回他可能获准进入的其他国家的费用的款项，再加上不超过上述第一笔款项 25% 的其他款项，以此作为担保；或者
- (b) 按照第（a）项计算的金额，该人通过与移民官批准的一名或多名担保人签订协议，提供担保。

（2）获得 A 类居留许可证的人应获准进入坦桑尼亚或在坦桑尼亚逗留，但受以下条件的限制：

- (a) 该人可以居住的区域；
- (b) 该人可从事的职业或业务种类（如有），以及从事这些职业或业务所受的限制；和
- (c) 主任专员在居留许可证中规定的其在坦桑尼亚的居留期限。

（3）凡获得 A 类居留许可证的人——

- (a) 未能从事或停止从事许可证中规定的贸易、商业、行业或其他职业，或者
- (b) 在任何条件下，从事居留许可证规定的贸易、商业、行业以外的任何贸易、商业、

行业或职业,居留许可证应立即失效,除本法另有规定外,该人在坦桑尼亚的逗留被视为非法。

(4) 除违禁移民外,在坦桑尼亚居住 10 年或 10 年以上,并通过投资贸易、商业、行业、农业、畜牧业、矿产勘探或制造业对坦桑尼亚和坦桑尼亚人民的经济或福祉作出巨大贡献或具有重大价值的人,在考虑到劳工专员为此颁发的工作居留证的条件后,主任专员可在符合本条规定的其他条件的情况下,向其颁发 A 类居留许可证,并决定该许可证有效期。

[2015 年第 1 号法案第 28 条;2015 年第 8 号法案第 3 条]

34. B 类居留许可证

(1) 除违禁移民外,凡已在坦桑尼亚获得特定工作机会的人,如果主任专员认为他具备从事该工作所需的资格或技能,且他的工作将对坦桑尼亚有利,则可在考虑到劳工专员为此颁发的工作居留证的条件后认为合适的情况下,向其颁发 B 类居留许可证,但条件是雇主应在该人及其家属(如有)进入坦桑尼亚之前,或在向其颁发居留许可证之前,为居留许可证和主任专员可能确定的任何其他目的提供担保。

(2) 获得 B 类居留许可证的人应获准进入或在坦桑尼亚逗留,但须遵守第 33 条第(2)款第(a)、(b)和(c)项提及的任何事项或主任专员可能就其他任何事项提出的要求。

(3) 凡获得 B 类居留许可证的人,如:
  (a) 未能从事或停止从事居留许可证中规定的工作;或者
  (b) 在任何条件下,从事居留许可证规定的工作以外的任何职业,居留证应立即失效,除本法另有规定外,该人在坦桑尼亚的逗留被视为非法。

(4) 如果某人因第(3)款的规定,在坦桑尼亚的居留即属非法,则该人居留许可证中标明的雇主应在该持有人未能受雇于或停止受雇于该雇主之日起 30 天内,向移民官报告该持有人未能受雇于或停止受雇于该雇主的情况;任何雇主拒绝报告或不遵守本款规定,即属犯罪。

[2015 年第 1 号法案第 28 条;2015 年第 8 号法案第 3 条]

35. C 类居留许可证

(1) 除违禁移民外,未获 A 类或 B 类居留许可证的人,如主任专员认为合适,可获颁 C 类居留许可证,但须符合第 33 条第(1)款第(a)和(b)项所述事项或主任专员就其他事项要求的条件。

(2) 获得 C 类居留许可证的人应获准进入坦桑尼亚或在坦桑尼亚逗留,但须遵守主任专员规定的条件。

[2015 年第 8 号法案第 3 条]

36. 居留许可证的颁发条件

(1) 根据本法颁发的每份居留许可证都应随时遵守针对该类居留许可证规定的条件。

(2) 根据本法颁发的每份居留许可证,无论其类别如何,均须遵守以下条件,即如果主任专员在任何时候通知其持有人该居留许可证已根据第 41 条被吊销,则该持有人应在主任专员规定的时间内离开坦桑尼亚。

(3) 根据本法向任何打算在居留许可证有效期内访问或逗留桑给巴尔的人颁发的居留许可证,还应附加一个条件,即持有人应遵守根据第 28 条第(8)款作出的任何命令的规定。

(4) 如有证据证明任何获得居留许可证的人违反、不遵守或拒绝遵守居留许可证颁发或被视为颁发的任何条件,则该居留证许可将失效,该人在坦桑尼亚的居留将被视为非法;如果提供的担保——
  (a) 是以保证金的方式提供的,该保证金可被没收,或者
  (b) 是以保函的方式提供的,则主任专员可就保函所担保的款项提起诉讼并追讨。
[2015 年第 8 号法案第 3 条]

37. 向部长上诉

任何人如对主任专员拒绝居留许可证申请或更改居留许可证规定的条件或有效期不服,可向部长提出上诉,部长对上诉的决定为终局裁定,任何法院不得进行质询。
[2015 年第 8 号法案第 3 条]

38. 变更居留许可证的条件

根据本法任何关于居留许可证或居留许可证类别的规定,主任专员可自行或根据本法颁发的居留许可证的持有人以规定方式提出的申请,更改居留许可证中规定的条件和有效期。
[2015 年第 8 号法案第 3 条]

39. 获得居留许可证的受抚养人

(1) 在符合上述规定的条件下,在居留许可证持有人或申请人以规定的格式提出申请时,主任专员可在居留许可证上签注持有人或申请人随行前往坦桑尼亚或居住在坦桑尼亚的妻子和受抚养子女的姓名。

(2) 除非部长在特定情况下另有指示,否则根据第(1)款作出的签注,应在居留许可证持有人死亡或其妻子或子女不再是持有人的受抚养人之日起,或自其姓名被签注的人不再是持有人本法意义上的妻子或子女(视情况而定)之日起 1 个月内或主任专员就此向其提出申请后酌情允许的更长期限届满时失效,除非本法另行授权,否则该妻子或子女(视情况而定)在坦桑尼亚的逗留被视为非法。
[2015 年第 8 号法案第 3 条]

40. 欺诈的后果

(1) 如果:
  (a) 主任专员在履行其职能时确信;或者
  (b) 在根据本法提起的任何诉讼中,有证据证明根据本法颁发的任何居留许可证、通行证、证书或其他授权文件是通过任何欺诈或虚假陈述或隐瞒或不披露任何实质性事项获得或颁发的,无论有意或无意。则该居留许可证、通行证、证书或其他授权文件应自颁发之日起无效或被视为无效。

(2) 如果根据本法颁发的居留许可证、通行证、证书或其他授权根据第(1)款的规定无效或被视为无效,则其持有人在坦桑尼亚的逗留自该居留许可证、通行证、证书或授权颁发之日起被视为非法,对其适用本法第 27 条的规定。
[2015 年第 8 号法案第 3 条]

41. 居留许可证的撤销和交还

(1) 主任专员如确信居留许可证的持有人有以下情况,可以书面撤销任何根据本法颁发的居留许可证:
  (a) 违反了本法的任何规定,或未能遵守本法规定的任何要求;

(b) 通过在任何重大事项上虚假陈述或隐瞒重要信息的方式获得任何居留许可证；

(c) 未能遵守居留许可证规定的任何条件；

(d) 因不能供养自己及其在坦桑尼亚的任何受抚养人，已成为或可能成为坦桑尼亚联合共和国的负担。

(2) 撤销根据本法签发的居留许可证的通知应亲自送达持有人，并应具体说明：

(a) 拟撤销的居留许可证；

(b) 撤销生效的日期，其不得少于通知书送达后的3日；和

(c) 撤销所依据的理由，以及该居留许可证应在第(b)项规定的日期失效；

(3) 根据本法颁发给违禁移民的所有居留许可证均无效，且应被视为从未颁发过。

(4) 根据本法颁发给之后成为违禁移民者的任何居留许可证，在持证人成为违禁移民时停止效力。

(5) 凡获得某一类居留许可证的人，其后又获得另一类居留许可证，则应将原居留许可证交还移民官注销。

(6) 凡获得A类、B类或C类居留许可证的人永久离开坦桑尼亚的，应将居留许可证交还移民官注销。

(7) 任何人违反、拒绝或不遵守本条的任何规定，即属犯罪。

[2015年第8号法案第3条]

第三部
土地法(第113章)
[2001年][2019年修订版](节选)

坦桑尼亚
土 地 法
（第 113 章）

2001 年 5 月 1 日生效

［本文件为 2019 年 11 月 30 日版。］

［注：在总检察长办公室的监督下，根据《法律修订法》1994 年第 7 号、《法律修订和年度修订法》第 356 章（R.L.），以及《法律解释和一般条款法》1972 年第 30 号对本法进行了全面修订与合并。本版本为截至 2002 年 7 月 31 日的最新版本。］

［2001 年第 484 号政府公告；1999 年第 4 号法案；2002 年第 2 号法案；2004 年第 2 号法案；2004 年第 12 号法案；2005 年第 11 号法案；2008 年第 12 号法案；2008 年第 17 号法案；2009 年第 3 号法案；2010 年第 2 号法案；2016 年第 7 号法案；2018 年第 1 号法案；2018 年第 4 号法案；2018 年第 17 号法案］

旨在规定与村庄土地以外的土地、土地管理、争议解决和相关问题有关的基本法的法案。

第五部分
土地占用的权利和附带条件

19. 土地占用权

（1）本法所称"权利持有者"的一个公民、两个或两个以上公民共同组成的团体，无论其是否根据本法或任何其他法律组成社团、合伙企业或法人团体，根据本法所享有的土地占有权，特此声明如下：

  （a）授予占用权；

  （b）授予占用权的派生权利，在本法中称为派生权；

（2）个人或团体（不论是否根据《公司法》组成），或是其他非公民，包括其多数股东或所有者为非公民的法人团体，只能享有以下权利：

  ［第 212 章］

  （a）根据《坦桑尼亚投资法》授予的投资占用权；

  ［第 38 章］

  （b）根据《坦桑尼亚投资法》授予的或根据《出口加工区法》颁发的投资派生权；

  ［第 373 章］

  （c）根据《坦桑尼亚投资法》授予的或根据《出口加工区法》颁发的合资企业中为协助符合发展条件需公民部分转让的土地权益。

（3）第（2）款的规定不适用于——

  （a）根据联合共和国政府为一方的协议，为公众的贫困或困境提供救济或为促进宗教或教育提供保健或其他社会服务的非营利性的外国或本地公司或组织,如不存在此类协议,部长确信该公司或组织的成立纯粹是为了救济公众的贫困或困境,或提供健康或其他社会服务,或促进宗教或教育;

（b）外国政府、外国政府全资拥有的机构,以及国际机构或组织。

（4）除第(3)款的规定外,第47、48和49条的规定应比照适用于违反协议的情况。

［2004年第2号法案第3条;2004年第12号法案附录］

20. 非公民占用土地的限制

（1）为避免疑问,除非根据《坦桑尼亚投资法》的规定用于投资目的,否则非公民不得被分配或被授予土地。

（2）根据第(1)款指定用于投资目的的土地应予以确定、刊登在《公报》上,并分配给为投资者创设派生权的坦桑尼亚投资中心。

（3）就根据本法或任何其他成文法作出的补偿而言,非公民在本法颁布前获得的所有土地应被视为没有价值,但根据本法和任何其他法律可支付补偿的未用完的土地除外。

（4）就本法而言,任何法人团体,其多数股东或所有者为非公民的,应被视为非公民或外国公司。

（5）在非公民或外国公司获得的占用权或派生权利到期、终止或消灭时,土地上的利益或权利应归还给坦桑尼亚投资中心或部长在《公报》中规定的任何其他机构。

［第38章;2004年第2号法案第4条］

第四部
乡村土地法(第114章)
[2001年][2019年修订版](节选)

坦桑尼亚
乡村土地法
（第 114 章）

2001 年 5 月 1 日起生效
［本文件为 2019 年 11 月 30 日版。］
［注：在总检察长办公室的监督下，根据《法律修订法》1994 年第 7 号、《法律修订和年度修订法》第 356 章（R.L.），以及《法律解释和一般条款法》1972 年第 30 号对本法进行了全面修订与合并。本版本为截至 2002 年 7 月 31 日的最新版本。］
［2001 年第 486 号政府公告；1999 年第 5 号法案；2010 年第 2 号法案］
旨在规定村庄土地的管理和行政以及相关事宜的法案。

第四部分
乡村土地

A：管理和行政

17. 非乡村组织使用乡村土地
（1）本节适用的非乡村组织是指——
  （a）政府部门或其任何办事处或该办事处中的部门；
  （b）法人或其他半官方机构或任何办公室、部门、分部或其附属机构；
  （c）法人或其他机构，其大多数成员或股东是根据坦桑尼亚当时有效的、并适用于该法人或其他机构的任何法律注册或获准经营的公民，但该法人或其他机构的成员不占村集体成员的大部分；或该法人或其他机构的任何类似组成的附属机构。

（2）如果在本法生效之时，任何非乡村组织根据授予的使用权使用乡村土地，则该授予的使用权，尽管存在于乡村土地中，在其剩余期限内应继续被视为授予的使用权。

（3）根据土地法的规定，关于使用权的处置，专员将继续负责管理适用本条的使用权。
        ［第 113 章］

（4）如果专员认为一个乡村委员会在有效的方式下管理乡村土地，其可以书面授权将适用本条的使用权管理职能委托给该乡村委员会，但须附加任何他认为合适的条件到授权文件中。

（5）在本法生效之后，如果非乡村组织希望获得一部分乡村土地以更好地开展其业务，可以向村委会申请该土地，并且村委会应向专员建议授予或拒绝此类授予。

（6）任何根据习惯法组成的旨在占用、使用和管理土地的团体，或者任何组织起来并被其所属社区认可的旨在在城市或近郊地区占用、使用和管理土地的协会，如果这些组成该协会的人依照《受托人注册法》的规定进行注册，则本法将予以承认，并且本法相关条款也将相应适用于此类协会。
        ［第 318 章］

第五部
营业执照法(第208章)
[1972年][2002年修订版](节选)

坦桑尼亚
营业执照法
(第208章)

发表于坦桑尼亚政府《公报》
1972年9月1日起生效
［本文件为2002年7月31日版。］

［注：在总检察长办公室的监督下，根据《法律修订法》1994年第7号、《法律修订和年度修订法》第356章(R.L.)，以及《法律解释和一般条款法》1972年第30号对本法进行了全面修订与合并。本版本为截至2002年7月31日的最新版本。］

［1972年第25号法案；1973年第10号法案；1974年第16号法案；1976年第7号法案；1978年第20号法案；1979年第8号法案；1979年第12号法案；1980年第9号法案；1980年25号法案；1981年第12号法案；1982年第9号法案；1987年第10号法案；1989年第13号法案；1990年第17号法案；1991年第13号法案；1991年第18号法案；1993年第3号法案；1993年第10号法案；1994年第16号法案；1996年第13号法案；1997年第25号法案；1998年第8号法案；1999年第12号法案；2000年第11号法案；2001年第14号法案；2002年第10号法案；2002年第18号法案］

旨在规定营业许可及相关事宜的法案。

3. 禁止无证经营

(1) 任何人不得作为委托人或代理人在坦桑尼亚经营任何业务，除非——

(a) 该人持有与该业务相关的有效营业执照；和

(b) 该业务是在执照中所指明的地点经营。

(2) 任何人不得在两个或两个以上地点经营业务，除非他持有就每个地方的业务所颁发的单独营业执照：

但是，在任何以下情况下，如果其中任何营业地（以下简称"主要营业地"）存在有效的营业执照，则持有人应被视为未违反本款的规定——

(a) 如果该人就该等业务持有另一营业地的附属执照，或如果该人在两个或两个以上其他地点经营该等业务，则在每个其他地点经营都需持有营业执照；或者

(b) 如果该业务相关的附属执照没有规定执照费用。

(3) 在不与任何其他成文法相冲突的情况下，本条不得解释为禁止同一人或不同人在同一地点经营两项或多项业务，只要每项业务都是在有效营业执照的授权下经营的：

但是，根据本法制定的法规可规定，该法规中规定的任何业务不得在同时经营该法规所规定的任何其他业务或任何类别或种类的业务的任何地方进行。

(4) 许可机关有权查封任何被发现无证经营的商户的营业场所，在关闭时，许可机关可要

求警务人员或任何其他授权代理人提供协助。

[第 77 章]

10. 非居民临时许可证

（1）本条适用于属于特定职业的人员和建筑承包商。

（2）本条所适用的非坦桑尼亚联合共和国常住居民不得在坦桑尼亚从事以下业务——

（a）就属于某一特定职业的人而言,提供其因身为该职业成员而有资格提供的任何专业服务;

（b）就建筑承包商而言,从事任何建筑工程或与建筑工程有关的工作;

（c）就商务旅行者而言,从事上述附表中某一栏的业务,除非该人是——

（i）持有特定职业或建筑承包商业务（视属何情况而定）的有效营业许可的人;或者

（ii）根据本法免于申请此类执照的人;或者

（iii）持有针对其从事特定职业或建筑承包商业务（视属何情况而定）的临时执照的人。

（3）本条适用的任何人在支付费用后可获得临时执照——

（a）特定职业的人,费用为 500 先令;

（b）建筑承包商,费用为 750 先令;

（c）商务旅行者,费用为 120 先令。

（4）根据本条授予的每个临时执照的有效期为自签发之日起 30 天,或常任秘书在任何情况下指示的更长期限。

（5）临时执照持有人在该许可有效期内,有权在与相应营业执照持有人相同的范围内,从事该执照指定的业务和任何辅助业务。

[第 77 章第 9 条]

19. 罪行

（1）任何人——

（a）未持有有效执照或在第 10 条适用的情况下未持有授权其经营此类业务的有效临时执照的情况下经营业务;

（b）违反第 3 条的规定,在有效营业执照或附属执照未指明的地方经营此类业务;

（c）没有按照第 16 条的要求出示其获得的营业执照;

（d）未能遵守第 17 条的规定;

（e）在根据第 14 条被要求交出营业执照时,没有交出;

（f）在许可证申请或在与许可证申请有关的情况下在重要细节上作虚假陈述;

（g）持有根据本法附条件的营业执照,却未能遵守此类条件;

（h）未能遵守第 18A 条的规定;

（i）意图逃避缴付全额许可费而故意做出或不做出任何行为或事情,即属犯罪,一经定罪,可处以——

（i）如属第（a）项至第（i）项所述的罪行——

(aa) 对于全国性和国际性企业,应处以 10 万以上,50 万以下先令的罚款;和

(bb) 对于营业执照由地方当局颁发和管理的企业,应处以 5 万以上,30 万以下先令的罚款,或处以两年以下的监禁,或两者并罚。

(ii) 如属第(h)项所述的罪行,除许可费用外,还需交付许可费百分之三百(300%)的罚款。

(2) 在对第(1)款第(a)项所述罪行提起的任何诉讼中,如果被告使法庭确信,他涉嫌犯罪的日期是在其先前持有的营业执照到期之日或他首次开始营业之日起的 21 日内(视情况而定),则他可能被判处的最高刑罚应为:对于全国性和国际性企业,罚款 5 万先令;对于营业执照由地方当局颁发和管理的企业,罚款 1 万先令。

[第 17 条]

第六部
商业法(杂项修正案)
[1930年][2012年修订版](节选)

坦桑尼亚联合共和国

法案补充第3号   2012年7月27日

《坦桑尼亚联合共和国公报》第93卷第30号,2012年7月27日
根据政府命令由达累斯萨拉姆印务局印刷

商 业 法
（杂项修正案）[2012 年]

旨在修订管理商业行为，为在坦桑尼亚经商创造更有利的环境的法案。

由坦桑尼亚联合共和国议会颁布。

第二部分
对《商业名称（注册）法》（第 213 章）的修订

3. 解释

本部分应与《商业名称（注册）法》（以下简称"原法"）一起解读。

[第 213 章]

4. 长标题的修订

对原法进行了修订，废除原标题并代之如下："旨在对以商业名称开展业务的公司、个人和企业的注册事宜以及其他相关事项作出规定的法律"。

5. 第 1 条的修订

对原法进行了修订，废除了第 1 条，并代之如下：

"1. 简称

本法可称为《商业名称法》"。

6. 第 2 条的修订

对原法第 2 条通过以下方式进行了修订——

（a）在"业务"一词的定义中出现的"包括"和"职业"之间插入"每个行业和"；

（b）按适当的英文字母次序加入以下新定义：

"开展业务"包括在坦桑尼亚设立营业场所，并从坦桑尼亚境内任何人处招揽或获取订单；

"注册官"指根据本法履行商业名称注册职能的任何注册官或副注册官。

"部长"指负责贸易的部长；

"法人"指具有法人资格的任何法律实体；

"通信地址"包括电子邮件、传真、网站和电话号码；和

"姓"就通常以不同于其姓的头衔为人所知的平辈或个人而言，指该头衔。

7. 第 3 条的修订

对原法第 3 条通过以下方式进行了修订——

（a）删去第（1）款并代之如下：

"（1）部长可任命一名注册官、副注册官和为实现本法目的随时任命的助理注册官"；以及

（b）在"副"和"注册官"之间加入"和助理"。

8. 第 6 条的修订

对原法第 6 条第(1)款通过以下方式进行了修订——

(a) 删除第(1)款中的"邮寄"。

(b) 在第(a)项末尾加入"其邮政地址和任何其他通信地址";和

(c) 删除但书中出现的"21 岁,其只需陈述其已成年",代之以"18 岁,其只需陈述其已成年,并应避免使用笼统的词语来描述业务性质"。

9. 第 8 条的修订

原法第 8 条经过修订,删除了"28",以"21"代之。

10. 第 9 条的修订

原法第 9 条修订如下:

对第(1)款中的第(a)项,通过以下方式进行了修订——

(i) 删除(b)段并以新的(b)段替代:

"(b) 明示或暗示政府的认可、批准或赞助;";

(ii) 删除(d)项中的"句号",代之以"分号",并紧接着加入"和",

(iii) 在紧接(d)项之后加入新的(e)项,如下:

"(e) 注册官认为不合要求的;"。

(b) 在第(3)款中,删除"28",代之以"5 个工作日";和

(c) 在第(4)款中,删除"其决定为终局裁定"。

11. 第 11 条的修订

对原法第 11 条进行了修订,删除了"28",代之以"14"。

12. 第 12 条的修订

对原法第 12 条进行了修订——

(a) 删除第(1)款而代之以以下新款:

"(1) 如果根据本法申请注册的商业名称违反了第 9 条第(1)款的规定,或因疏忽或其他原因而被注册,注册官可以注册登记簿所示的以该名称开展业务的地点为地址,向该名称的相关注册人发出通知:

(a) 说明注册官在不超过 21 天的期限届满时取消或拒绝该名称注册的建议;和

(b) 说明建议取消或拒绝的理由。";

(b) 删除第(2)款中的"其决定为终局裁定"。

13. 第 13 条的修订

对原法第 13 条进行了修订,删除了"200",代之以"50 000"。

14. 第 18 条的修订

对原法第 18 条进行了修订,删除了"5 000",代之以"50 000"。

15. 第 20 条的修订

对原法第 20 条通过以下方式进行了修订——

(a) 删除第(1)款中的"邮寄",代之以"通信地址";和

(b) 在第(4)款之后加入以下新款:

"(5) 任何商号、个人或公司一旦被除名,应在除名通知期满之日起 21 天内,向注册官交还根据本法签发的任何证书。

(6) 在收到第(4)款规定的证书后,注册官应注销该证书。"

16. 新增第 25 条

对原法进行了修订,在第 24 条之后增加了以下新条款:

"25. 表格

根据本法签发的每份证书应采用本法附表 2 规定的形式。"

第七部
公私合营法(第103章)
[2011年][2019年修订版]

坦桑尼亚联合共和国

公私合营法

第103章

[基本法]

2019年修订版

本版《公私合营法》(第103章)的修订日期截至2019年11月30日(含当日),并根据《法律修订法》(第4章)第4条的授权印刷。

多多马	阿德里安·德·科尔吉
2018年11月30日	总检察长

公 私 合 营 法
（第 103 章）

旨在为公共部门与私营部门实体之间执行公私合营协议提供体制框架；
就公私合营采购、发展和执行制定规则、准则和
程序，并对其他相关事项作出规定的法案。

［2011 年 5 月 26 日］
［2011 年第 156A 号政府公告］

法案编号
2010 年第 18 期
2014 年第 3 期
2018 年第 9 期
政府公告编号
2018 年第 483 号

第一部分
总　　则

1. 简称
　　本法可称为《公私合营法》。

2. 适用范围
　　本法适用于坦桑尼亚大陆公共部门与私营部门合作开展的项目。

3. 释义
　　在本法中，除非上下文另有规定，否则：
　　"**会计官**"是指缔约机构的常任秘书或首席执行官，包括地方政府当局的会计官；
　　"**可负担**"在协议中是指缔约方应履行与该协议有关的财务承诺；
　　"**协议**"是指根据本法签订的公私合营协议；
　　"**资产**"包括相关缔约机构的现有资产或为签订协议而购置的新资产；
　　"**或有负债**"是指根据由项目交易产生的未来不确定事件的结果而付款的法律或合同义务，包括政府可能承担的与公私合营项目有关或相关的所有其他或有负债；
　　"**缔约机构**"是指任何部委、政府部门或代理机构、地方政府当局、公共或法定公司；
　　"**执行董事**"是指根据第 6 条任命的公私合营（PPP）中心执行董事；
　　"**促进基金**"是指根据第 10A 条设立的公私合营促进基金；
　　"**地方政府当局**"应具有《地方政府（地方当局）法》和《地方政府（市政当局）法》赋予它的含义；［第 287 章和 288 章］

"部长"是指负责公私合营的部长;

"部门"是指负责公私合营的部门;

"PPP 协议"是指缔约机构与一个或多个私人当事方之间制定的规定公私合营协议条款的书面合同;

"PPP 中心"是指根据第 4 条设立的公私合营中心;

"私人当事方"是指协议中非缔约机构一方的当事人。

"项目"是指根据本法签订的协议实施的项目或服务;

"私营部门"是指公共部门以外的部门,包括非营利性非政府组织;

"公私合营"或其首字母缩写词"PPP"是指缔约机构与私人当事方之间的合同安排,其中私人当事方需要——

(a) 承诺在规定时期内代表缔约机构履行其职能;

(b) 承担代表缔约机构履行职能或使用政府财产所带来的大量财务、技术和操作风险;或者

(c) 代表缔约机构履行职能或利用公共财产可以通过以下方式获得利益:

(i) 由缔约机构从收入基金中支付的对价,或者如果该缔约机构是中央政府或地方政府当局,则从该机构的收入中支付的对价;

(ii) 私人当事方或其代理人向用户或客户收取的费用;或者

(iii) 上述对价与上述费用的组合。

"PPP 指导委员会"是指根据第 7 条设立的公私合营指导委员会;

"公共部门"是指政府部委、部门或机构、地方政府当局以及代表政府部委、部门或机构或者地方政府当局行事的任何其他人;

"招标书"是指项目要求的具体条款、投标程序、评标标准,包括协议范本;

"行业部委"是指对缔约机构负责的部委;

"小规模公私合营项目"指根据本法批准的金额不超过 2 000 万美元的公私合营项目。

[2014 年第 3 号法案第 2 条;2018 年第 9 号法案第 2 条]

第二部分
公私合营中心的建立和管理

4. PPP 中心

(1) PPP 中心即公私合营中心。

(2) 执行董事经公共服务部门负责编制的当局批准后,可确定其他部门的数量。

(3) 中心为法人团体,拥有永久继承权和公章,并能够以自己的名义——

(a) 取得和持有动产,处置财产,签订合同或进行其他交易;

(b) 起诉和应诉;和

(c) 为适当履行本法规定的职能,做出或允许做出法人团体可合法做出或允许做出的所有其他行为和事项。

(4) PPP 中心应负责促进和协调与公私合营项目有关的所有事项。

(5) 第(4)款所指的项目应在符合第(6)和(7)款规定的前提下,在生产和社会部门进行,包括但不限于以下部门:
  (a) 农业;
  (b) 基础设施;
  (c) 工业和制造业;
  (d) 勘探和采矿;
  (e) 教育;
  (f) 医疗;
  (g) 环境和废物管理;
  (h) 信息和传播技术(ICT);
  (i) 贸易和营销;
  (j) 体育、娱乐和休闲;
  (k) 自然资源和旅游业;和
  (l) 能源。

(6) 各缔约机构应在每个预算周期开始时,向PPP中心提交潜在公私合营项目的概念说明和预可行性研究报告:
 条件是——
  (a) 潜在的公私合营项目符合国家发展优先事项;和
  (b) 潜在的公私合营项目的概念说明和预可行性研究由相关部长批准。

(6A) PPP中心应在21个工作日内分析根据第(6)款收到的潜在公私合营项目,并将其转交给公私合营指导委员会。

(7) 就第(6)款而言,部长应在财政年度开始前至少2个月,要求各缔约机构向PPP中心提交潜在公私合营项目的概念说明和预可行性研究报告。

(8) 在本条中,"预算周期"一词应具有《预算法》所赋予的含义。

[2014年第3号法案第4条;2018年第9条法案第4条;政府公告2018年第483号]

5. PPP中心的职能

(1) PPP中心的职能如下——
  (a) 为项目开发和政府对公私合营项目的支持调动资源;
  (b) 建立机制,确保所有部委、政府部门和机构以及地方政府当局将公私合营纳入其部门战略和计划;
  (c) 为缔约机构制定操作指南;
  (d) 设计并实施公平、透明、有竞争力和高性价比的采购流程;
  (e) 处理所有公私合营项目的财务风险分担以及其他财务事项。
  (f) 就所有事项向缔约机构提供与公私合营项目有关的咨询意见;
  (g) 为各部委、政府部门、机构、地方政府当局和私营部门提供技术援助,以规划、管理和评估公私合营项目;
  (h) 审查招标书,确保其符合经批准的可行性研究报告;
  (i) 监督、审查和评估公私合营促进基金的实施情况;

(j) 确保缔约机构向其提交的投标书的相关性和充分性;

(k) 监督和评估公私合营项目的绩效,并定期编写绩效报告;

(l) 为公共和私营部门设计和实施公私合营能力建设计划;

(m) 制定和实施旨在提高公众对公私合营问题认识的计划;和

(n) 进行有关公私合营的研究。

(2) 在不影响第(1)款一般性的前提下,PPP 中心应在收到缔约机构提交项目之日起 30 个工作日内对其进行分析。

(3) PPP 中心在完成第(2)款规定的分析后,应向公私合营指导委员会提交可行性研究报告、首选投标人的选择和公私合营协议,以供批准。

(4) PPP 中心是一站式中心,该中心应寻求负责投资、财政、规划的部委或任何其他部委或机构的建议,以有效履行其职能。

(5) 本条的任何规定均不妨碍缔约机构对其管辖范围内的项目进行必要的技术分析。

(6) 为确保对 PPP 项目的投资,部长应与负责投资的部长协商,通过公私合营安排,制定开发和维护有利投资环境的方案。

[2014 年第 3 号法案第 5 条;2018 年第 9 号法案第 5 条]

6. 执行董事

(1) PPP 中心应由一名执行董事领导,执行董事应根据《公共服务法》通过竞争方式任命。

(2) 符合以下条件者有资格被任命为执行董事——

(a) 至少拥有项目管理、会计、法律、工程、经济或其他相关领域的学位;和

(b) 具有开发、组建或实施公共或私营性质的项目或事业的知识和经验;

(3) PPP 中心应任命在公共或私营性质的项目或事业的形成、发展或实施方面具有资格、知识和经验的人员。

(4) PPP 中心人员应根据《公共服务法》通过竞争方式任命。

[2014 年第 3 号法案第 6 条;第 298 章]

7. PPP 指导委员会

(1) 应当成立一个 PPP 指导委员会,由以下成员组成——

(a) 部委常务秘书担任主席;

(b) 总理办公室常务秘书;

(c) 负责土地事务的部委常务秘书;

(d) 副总检察长;

(e) 一名国家规划主管机构的代表;

(f) 坦桑尼亚投资中心执行董事;

(g) 坦桑尼亚私营部门基金会执行董事;

(h) 坦桑尼亚税务局局长;

(i) 地方政府部门常务秘书;

(j) 部长根据坦桑尼亚私营部门基金会的推荐提名的两名私营部门人员。

(2) 项目提交审议的行业部委常务秘书应参加 PPP 指导委员会的会议。

(3) PPP 指导委员会可以增选任何在审议事项方面具有知识和经验的其他人员。

(4) 执行董事应担任 PPP 指导委员会秘书。

(5) PPP 指导委员会应至少每 3 个月召开一次会议。

(6) 尽管有第(5)款的规定,PPP 指导委员会可在有效履行其职能所必需的情况下召开会议。

[2014 年第 3 号法案第 7 条;2018 年第 9 号法案第 6 条]

7A. PPP 指导委员会的职能

(1) PPP 指导委员会的职能如下——

(a) 审查有关促进、推动和发展公私合营的政策、立法、计划和战略,并向部长提出相应的建议;

(b) 就与实施国家公私合营计划有关的事项向部长提出建议;

(c) 批准可行性研究、详细项目报告和设计、优先投标人的选择、公私合营协议或协议的任何修订;

(d) 批准从促进基金中拨出项目开发资金;和

(e) 向缔约机构指定使用促进基金的条款和条件。

(2) 根据 PPP 中心的建议,PPP 指导委员会应在 21 个工作日内批准可行性研究、详细项目报告和设计、优先投标人的选择、协议和协议修订。

(3) 根据 PPP 中心的建议,PPP 指导委员会应批准可行性研究、优先投标人协议的选择和协议的修订。

[2014 年第 3 号法案第 8 条;2018 年第 9 号法案第 7 条]

7B. 公共资金和其他 PPP 项目的支持

(1) 尽管有第 7A 条的规定,如果项目需要公共资金、任何其他政府支持或政策确定,PPP 指导委员会应将该事项提交部长进行决定。

(2) 部长应在收到 PPP 指导委员会根据第(1)款提出的事项之日起 21 个工作日内——

(a) 对于需要公共资金的事项,按照《政府贷款担保和赠款法》规定的方式处理;[第 134 章]

(b) 对于需要政府支持或政策确定的事项,应作出决定并向 PPP 指导委员会作出相应指示。

(3) 尽管有第(2)款的规定,如果在 21 个工作日内仍未就某一事项做出决定,部长应通知 PPP 指导委员会并说明理由。

[2018 年第 9 号法案第 8 条]

7C. 部长的一般权力

(1) 部长应通过官方《公报》、广泛发行的报纸或公共媒体,向公众通报根据本法批准的所有项目。

(2) 部长应根据相关协议,监督和管理与实施 PPP 项目相关的财政风险和其他财务事项。

(3) 根据本法的规定,部长应向缔约机构的会计官发布关于小规模 PPP 项目的分析和批准或不批准的指示。

[2018 年第 9 号法案第 9 条]

第三部分
公共和私营部门的参与

8. 公共和私营部门的作用

(1) 公共部门应通过如下方式促进公私合作项目的实施:
 (a) 确定项目;
 (b) 进行可行性研究;
 (c) 监督与评估;
 (d) 分担风险;和
 (e) 建立适当的扶持环境,包括:
  (i) 优惠政策;
  (ii) 实施战略;
  (iii) 法律和体制框架。

(2) 私营部门应通过以下方式发挥确立和施行公私合营项目的作用:
 (a) 进行可行性研究;
 (b) 调动资源;
 (c) 风险分担;
 (d) 监测和评估;和
 (e) 提供技术经验和管理技能。

(3) 公共部门和私营部门有责任制定一项宣传战略,以提高认识和达成共识,使公私合营所有利益相关方接受其成果效益、相关成本与风险。

9. 缔约机构的责任

(1) 就本法而言,缔约机构应:
 (a) 确定、评估、开发、管理和监督根据本法实施的项目;
 (b) 在其认为该项目适合根据协议实施时,进行或安排进行可行性研究;和
 (c) 将拟议项目连同可行性研究报告提交 PPP 中心审议。

(2) 在向 PPP 中心提交拟议项目的可行性研究报告之前,缔约机构应与相关监管机构进行磋商。

(3) 第 7A 条和第 7B 条不得被解释为取消或废除缔约机构或会计官就依据本条分配给它的事项承担全面责任的权力。

[2014 年第 3 号法案第 9 条]

10. 可行性研究

(1) 每个缔约机构在认为项目可以根据公私合营协议实施的情况下,应进行或安排进行可行性研究,以评估拟议项目是否具有可行性。

(2) 可行性研究应当:
 (a) 确定和界定政府打算从私人当事方外包的活动;
 (b) 评估拟将有关活动外包给私人当事方对政府人员、资产、负债和收入的预计

影响；
  （c）评估政府对此类活动的需求，包括：
    （i）政府为满足这些需求可采取的方案；
    （ii）每种方案的优缺点；
  （d）在实施协议的策略和运营方面展示比较优势；
  （e）具体说明：
    （i）缔约机构职能的性质、与项目有关的具体职能，以及预期的投入和可交付成果；
    （ii）私人当事人根据协议可以合法有效地履行这些职能的程度；
  （f）表明协议应当：
    （i）在缔约机构负担能力范围内；
    （ii）提供物有所值的服务；
    （iii）将适当的技术、操作以及财务风险转移给私人当事方；
  （g）评估缔约机构有效执行协议的能力，包括监测和管理项目执行情况以及私人当事方按照协议履约的能力；和
  （h）评估私人当事方实施该项目的能力以及资源。
（3）就第（2）款而言，可行性研究应包括技术和社会经济影响分析。
（4）根据第（2）款第（c）项进行的评估应表明以下方面的比较预测：
  （a）该活动不是通过公私合营协议外包的情况下，政府或有关活动的全部成本；和
  （b）该活动是通过公私合营协议外包的情况下，政府承担的该活动的全部成本。
（5）在不影响第（2）款规定的情况下，部长可通过法规规定公私合营项目可能要求的概念说明和可行性研究的附加或详细内容。
（6）如果所承建的项目的性质或类型需要根据《环境管理法》第6部分进行环境影响评估，则缔约机构应确保私人当事方在承建项目前获得环境影响评估证书。［第191章］

     ［2018年第9号法案第10条］

10A. 促进基金

（1）应设立一个促进基金，称为公私合营促进基金。
（2）PPP中心应开设一个银行账户，存放构成促进基金的所有资金。
（3）执行主任为促进基金的会计官。
（4）使用促进基金的资金须经PPP指导委员会批准。

   ［2014年第3号法案第10条；2018年第9号法案第11条］

10B. 资金来源

（1）促进基金的资金来源应是议会为此目的划拨的款项，以及从以下任何来源筹集的任何其他资金——
  （a）发展伙伴、公共实体、半官方组织和社会保障基金；和
  （b）促进基金先前根据项目支持协议向缔约机构全部或部分追回的资金。
（2）经PPP指导委员会批准后，促进基金将用于以下方面——
  （a）为缔约机构可能要求的全部或部分可行性研究和其他项目筹备提供资金；

(b) 提供资源,以提高那些经济效益虽高但财政可行性有限的项目可行性;和

(c) 本条例规定的任何其他用途。

(3) 第(2)款的规定不得解释为限制或阻止缔约机构使用自有资金为可行性研究和其他项目筹备提供资金。

[2014年第3号法案第10条;2018年第9号法案第2条]

10C. 账簿、记录和年度报告

(1) PPP中心应根据可接受的会计标准,对促进基金的运作进行账目登记和妥善记录。

(2) PPP中心应随时及在每个财政年度结束时请财务主管和审计长审计基金的账目。

(3) PPP中心应向部长提交经审计的报告和年度报告,其中包含截至6月30日的上一年度促进基金活动的详细信息。

(4) 部长应向国民议会提交经审计的账目报表和PPP中心的报告。

(5) 部长应编写并向内阁提交关于公私合营计划执行情况的年度报告。

[2014年第3号法案第10条]

11. 协议

(1) 尽管有任何其他成文法的规定,缔约机构仍可与私人当事方制定协议,以履行该缔约机构的一项或多项职能。

(2) 就第(1)款而言,缔约机构的会计官应组建一个多学科的、对拟议项目的主题事项具有知识、技能和经验的谈判团队,以便向负责缔约机构的部长提供建议。

(3) 在不影响第(2)款的前提下,谈判应确保协议以书面形式制定,并且——

(a) 明确缔约机构和私人当事方的责任;

(b) 明确相关财务条款;

(c) 确保私人当事方的绩效管理;

(d) 规定缔约机构向私人当事方承诺获得实施项目所需的执照和许可证;

(e) 规定在协议终止或期满时向缔约当局归还资产(如有);

(f) 明确双方的作用和承担的风险;

(g) 规定从私人当事方向其提供服务的用户或客户收取的费用形成的收入基金中以补偿的方式向私人当事方支付费用;

(h) 规定私人当事方向缔约机构支付的款项;

(i) 规定任何一方违约时的补救措施;

(j) 对私人当事方施加财务管理职责,包括与内部财务控制、预算、透明度、问责和报告相关的程序;

(k) 规定在任何一方违反条款和条件的情况下终止协议;

(l) 如有必要,规定提供服务的条件;

(m) 规定执行期限;和

(n) 规定其他必要的信息。

(4) 在不影响第(3)款规定的前提下,协议应包含以下条件并明确:

(a) 私人当事方承诺代表缔约机构在规定的期限内履行缔约机构的职能;

(b) 私人当事方应对履行其职能所产生的风险负责;

(c) 项目的环境影响评价证书已经颁发;

(d) 项目所需的政府设施、设备或其他国家资源及时转移或提供给私人当事方;和

(e) 公私资产明确划分。

(5) 根据本法签订的每项协议均应受坦桑尼亚大陆的法律管辖,并根据坦桑尼亚大陆的法律进行解释。

(6) 未经缔约机构事先书面同意,不得将本协议项下任何项目中私人当事方的权利、义务和控制权转让或让与第三方。

(7) 缔约机构应确保涉及公私合营项目的协议按照本法规定的程序并通过本法规定的机构执行。

[2014 年第 3 号法案第 11 条]

12. 土地征用

如果项目的实施需要征用土地,征用土地应根据《土地法》《乡村土地法》《土地使用规划法》《土地征用法》和任何其他相关法律进行征收。

[第 113、114、116 和 118 章]

13. 协议的期限和延长

(1) 协议的期限应在协议中规定,不得延长,除非:

(a) 任何一方无法控制的情况造成完工延迟或业务中断;

(b) 协作单位或缔约机构的要求造成费用增加,而这些要求是协议中没有预见到或没有包括在内的;和

(c) 如果服务必需,但缔约机构没有能力或近期无意接管和运行该项目。

(2) 协议任何一方违反第(1)款的规定,违约方应对另一方遭受的任何经济损失负责。

14. 协议审查

根据本法拟签订的每一项协议都应提交给总检察长办公室获取法律意见。

15. 采购流程

(1) 本法规定的所有公私合营项目均应通过公开竞标程序进行采购。

(2) 尽管有第(1)款的规定,但如果非招标项目的采购符合以下标准,部长可以免除竞标程序:

(a) 项目应是政府在特定时期的优先事项,并与政府的战略目标基本一致;

(b) 私人提议者不需要政府担保或任何形式的政府财政支持;

(c) 项目应具有独特的属性,因而有理由不采用竞争性招标程序;

(d) 项目规模大、范围广,并根据条例规定的条件,需要大量资金;

(e) 项目应证明物有所值、可负担,并应将重大风险转移给私人提议者;

(f) 项目具有广泛的社会经济效益,包括改善服务、就业和税收;和

(g) 提议者承诺承担进行可行性研究的费用。

(3) 非招标提案项目概念获批后,私人提议者应通过缴纳不超过拟开展项目预估费用3%的可退还保证金,承诺承担该项目。

(4) 部长可制定条例,规定基于第(3)款的承诺保证金的存入和退还程序。

(5) 所有招标项目和非招标项目均应按照本法规定的方式进行采购。

(6) 本条规定的条例除其他事项外,应规定以下事项——

（a）将本地公司和专家纳入顾问合同；

（b）在工程和非咨询服务中使用本地商品和专家；

（c）在评估过程中优先考虑本地商品；

（d）提高当地企业的能力；和

（e）与增强当地公司和坦桑尼亚公民能力有关的任何其他事项。

［2014 年第 3 号法案第 12 条；2018 年第 9 号法案第 12 条］

16. 非邀约投标

（1）私人当事方应就非招标的项目提案进行可行性研究,并向相关缔约机构提交可行性研究报告。

（2）根据第（1）款进行的可行性研究应考虑技术、财务、社会环境影响、经济或本法可能要求的任何其他相关事项。

（3）在不影响第（2）款的一般性的前提下,非招标的项目提案的可行性研究应当：

（a）具体说明拟议的项目活动；

（b）规定环境事项；

（c）解释拟议项目对政府的意义和益处；和

（d）说明私人当事方实施和管理拟议项目的财务能力。

（4）部长应制定条例,规定处理根据本法通过非邀约投标发起的公私合作项目提案的程序。

［2014 年第 3 号法案第 13 条］

17. 项目官员

（1）一旦缔约机构启动一个可能属于公私合营的项目,会计官应从缔约机构内部或外部任命一位具有适当技能和经验的人作为该项目的项目官员。

（2）项目官员应负责：

（a）协助会计官监督私人当事方的履约情况,确保协议得到妥善的执行；和

（b）履行会计官根据本法授予他的任何其他职责或权力。

18. 协议的签署

（1）根据本法签订的协议经 PPP 指导委员会的审议和批准,并经过总检察长办公室的审查后,应由相关缔约机构的会计官签署。

（2）会计官应在完全确信协议符合本法和任何其他相关法律的规定后签署协议。

（3）任何人违反本条的任何规定,即属犯罪。

［2014 年第 3 号法案第 14 条；2018 年第 9 号法案第 12 条］

19. 会计官的职责

签订协议的会计官除承担本法规定的任何其他责任外,还应采取一切必要和合理的措施以确保：

（a）外包活动按照协议切实有效地进行；

（b）根据协议,任何由私人当事方控制的公共财产都应得到适当的保护,以防止被没收、盗窃、损失、浪费和滥用；和

(c) 缔约机构具有足够的合同管理和监督能力。

20. 协议的修订

依据第 7B 条的规定,各方可对协议进行审查和修订,但审查或修订须经 PPP 指导委员会同意,并由总检察长审核。

[2018 年第 9 号法案第 13 条]

21. 享受优惠

(1) 不符合本法规定实施的项目,如果有资格享受《坦桑尼亚投资法》规定的类似投资的优惠,则有权享受该法规定的此类优惠。

(2) 第(1)款提及的优惠不适用于税收优惠。

[第 38 章]

22. 纠纷解决机制

在协议执行过程中出现的任何争议应——

(a) 通过协商解决;或者

(b) 在调解或仲裁的情况下,由在坦桑尼亚联合共和国设立的司法机构或其他机关根据坦桑尼亚法律作出裁决。

[2018 年第 9 号法案第 14 条]

第四部分
其 他 规 定

23. 监督和评估

(1) 本法项下的所有公私合营项目均应由实施项目的部委、行业部委、政府部门、机构或地方政府当局进行监督。

(2) 第(1)款规定的监督目的应纳入协调一致的监督和定期审查机制,其中包括:

(a) 可衡量的绩效目标;

(b) 有意义的激励和奖励;和

(c) 有效处罚。

(3) 部委、行业部委、司局、机构或地方政府当局应尽可能让其他利益相关方参与进来,以更好地实施和开展监督与评估工作。

23A. 定期业绩报告

(1) 会计官应按照法规规定的方式向 PPP 中心提交关于公私合营项目实施情况的年中业绩报告。

(2) PPP 中心应汇总缔约机构的年中业绩报告,并向部长提交报告。

[2018 年第 9 号法案第 15 条]

24. 利益冲突

(1) 如果 PPP 指导委员会成员、PPP 中心官员或缔约机构在任何项目、拟议项目或其他事项中直接或间接拥有金钱利益,并参与或参与了该项目、拟议项目或其他事项作为审议对象的程序,则他应在该程序开始后尽快披露这一事实,并不得参与或出席与该项目、拟议项目或其他事项有关的审议或讨论。

(2) 在符合本款规定的情况下,就本条而言,在以下情况下,某人应被视为在某一项目或其他事项中拥有直接或间接的金钱利益:

  (a) 某人或某人的被提名人是某家公司或其他组织的成员,或持有该项目或拟议项目的公司的股份或债券,或在该项目、拟议项目或考虑事项中拥有直接或间接的金钱利益;或者

  (b) 某人是与该项目合作或拟合作者的合伙人或受其雇佣的人,或与该项目、拟议项目或其他正在考虑的事项有直接或间接金钱利益的人。

(3) 在本条中,与 PPP 中心或缔约机构官员的配偶或任何家庭成员的直接或间接利益,如为该官员所知,则应被视为 PPP 中心或缔约当局官员的直接或间接利益。

(4) 任何人违反本条的规定,即属犯罪。

[2014 年第 3 号法案第 16 条;2018 年第 9 号法案第 2 条;第 4 章第 8 条]

25. 赋予公民权力

PPP 协议应根据《国家经济赋权法》的规定,努力为赋予坦桑尼亚公民权力提供机会。

[第 386 章]

25A. 与自然财富和资源有关的项目

涉及自然财富和资源的 PPP 项目应考虑《自然财富和资源(永久主权)法》和《自然财富和资源合同(不合理条款再审查和再谈判)法》条款的规定。

[2017 年第 5 号法案;2017 年第 6 号法案;2018 年第 9 号法案第 16 条]

26. 注意的义务和恪尽职守

根据本法或与公私合营有关的任何其他成文法履行任何职能、履行任何职责或行使任何权力的每一位公职人员都有义务根据本法和任何其他相关法律规定,在履行职能、履行职责和行使权力时采取合理的谨慎措施并尽职尽责。

27. 一般处罚

任何人犯有本法规定的罪行且未规定具体处罚的,应处以 500 万先令以上 5 000 万先令以下的罚款,或处以 3 个月以上 3 年以下的监禁,或两者并罚。

[2018 年第 9 号法案第 16 条]

28. 条例

(1) 部长可制定条例,以更好地执行本法的规定。

(2) 在不影响第(1)款规定的前提下,部长可制定条例,对以下事项作出规定:

  (a) 收费;

  (b) 投资机会和宣传;

  (c) 本法规定的地方政府当局的职能以及执行部门与地方政府有关机构之间的明确联系;

  (d) 根据本法对项目进行评估、运作和管理;

  (e) 促进基金的管理以及使用促进基金的条款和条件;

  (f) 私人当事方的采购程序及其附带事项;

  (g) 坦桑尼亚公民赋权的实施方式,包括坦桑尼亚企业家提供商品和服务、培训和

技术转让、雇佣坦桑尼亚人以及承担企业社会责任；

(h) 审查和分析需要政府支持的项目的过程和程序；

(i) 坦桑尼亚公民赋权的实施方式；和

(j) 促进和推动本法目标的任何其他事项。

(3) 尽管有第(1)款和第(2)款的规定，部长仍可制定规则和指导方针，以更好地实施本法。

[2014年第3号法案第17条；2018年第9号法案第17条]

29. 保留条款

任何缔约机构与私人当事方在本法生效前签订的所有现有协议或谅解备忘录不受本法生效的影响。

第八部
公私合营法(修正案)[2023 年]

坦桑尼亚联合共和国

第 6 号 2023 年 7 月 14 日

法案补充

《坦桑尼亚联合共和国公报》第 104 卷第 28 号,2023 年 7 月 14 日

根据政府命令由多多马政府印务局印刷

坦桑尼亚联合共和国
No.2023 年第 4 号

旨在对《公私合营法》作出修正的法案。
由坦桑尼亚联合共和国议会颁布

第一部分
总　　则

1. 简称

本法可称为《公私合营法(修正案)》(2023)应与《公私合营法》(以下简称"原法")一并解读。

[第 103 章]

第二部分
各项条款的修订

2. 第 2 条的修订

对原法第 2 条进行了修订,删除了第(2)款,替换如下:

"(2)尽管有相反的规定,本法的规定不得妨碍已经得到内阁批准的在联合共和国内制定战略发展特殊安排的协议实施:

但该协议在提交内阁批准前必须经过总检察长的审查。"

3. 第 3 条的修订

对原法第 3 条进行了修订——

（a）按适当的字母顺序插入以下新定义:

"'特殊目的载体'是指在签署协议前由成功签约的私人当事方成立的私人公司,以实施 PPP 项目为目的,该公司可以有包括公共实体在内的其他方作为成员,其责任和财务风险以股份为限;

'标准文件'包括标准资质请求书、标准建议书和标准 PPP(Public Private Partnership)协议;

'战略项目'是指由国家规划主管部门确定的战略项目";

（b）在"公共部门"一词的定义中,删除"和任何其他代表政府部委、部门、机构或地方政府当局行事的人"并将其替换为"区域秘书处或任何其他公共机构和任何其他代表政府部委、部门、机构、地方政府当局或区域秘书处行事的人";和

（c）在"征求建议书"一词的定义中,删除"示范协议"一词,并将其替换为"标准

4. 第 4 条的修订

对原法第 4 条进行了修订。

(a) 在第(3)条第(a)款中,在"动产"和"财产"之间加入"和不动产";

(b) 删去第(6)款并替代如下:

"(6) 每一个缔约机构应在每个预算周期开始时向部长提交潜在的公私合营项目的预可行性研究报告,以供国家发展计划考虑:

前提是——

(a) 潜在的公私合营项目符合国家发展优先事项;和

(b) 潜在的公私合营项目的预可行性研究已由相关部长批准。";

(c) 删去第(6A)款并替代如下:

"(6A) 在收到来自缔约机构的潜在公私合营项目的预可行性研究报告后,部长应在 7 个工作日内将该研究转交 PPP 中心进行分析。";

(d) 在紧接第(6A)款之后加入以下内容:

"(6B) PPP 中心应在 21 个工作日内分析根据第(6A)款收到的潜在公私合营项目的预可行性研究报告,并将其提交公私合营指导委员会以便通知。";

(e) 删去第(7)款;和

(f) 将第(8)款重新编号为第(7)款。

5. 第 5 条的修订

对原法第 5 条进行了修订,删除了第(2)款,替代如下:

"(2) 在不影响第(1)款一般性规定的前提下,PPP 中心应在收到缔约机构提交的潜在公私合营项目预可行性研究报告、招标书、优选投标人评估报告和 PPP 协议之日起 30 个工作日内对其进行分析。"

6. 第 7 条的修订

对原法第 7 条第(6)款进行了修订,在"公共"一词之后添加了"私营"一词。

7. 第 7B 条的修订

对原法第 7B 条进行了修订,在第(3)款后增加了以下内容:

"(4) 就本条而言,'公共资金'是指构成与 PPP 项目有关的财政承诺或或有负债的政府财政支持。"

8. 第 9 条的修订

对原法第 9 条第(1)款进行了修订,在紧接第(c)项之后增加以下内容:

"(d) 每三个月向 PPP 中心提交一份由 PPP 中心提出建议的实施报告。"。

9. 第 13 条的修订

对原法第 13 条第(1)款进行了修订,删除了第(b)项中的"协调单位或者"字样。

10. 第 15 条的修订

对原法第 15 条进行了修订——

(a) 删去第(3)及第(4)款,替换如下:

"(3) 根据 PPP 指导委员会的建议,如果招标项目符合第(2)款规定的标准,并满足以下

任何条件,部长可免除招标项目的采购竞标程序:

(a) 项目交付品属于紧急需要,且其他任何采购方法均不可行:
但引起紧急的情况是缔约机构所不能预见的;

(b) 私人当事方对项目所需的关键方法或技术拥有知识产权;或者

(c) 特定的私人当事方对该项目拥有专有权,并且没有合理的替代方案或替代品。

(4) 在未经招标的项目被豁免竞标程序后,政府与私人提议者应就协议的条款和条件展开谈判。";

(b) 在第(6)款中,通过——

(i) 在紧接第(c)项之后加入以下内容:
"(d) 开始就协议条款和条件进行谈判的时限;

(ii) 将第(d)款和第(e)款重新命名为第(e)款和第(f)款。"

11. 增加第 18A 条

在原法紧接第 18 条之后新增:

"18A. 设立特殊目的载体

(1) 在签署 PPP 协议之前,私人当事方应根据《公司法》设立专门从事该项目的特殊目的机构。[第212章]

(2) 根据第(1)款设立的特殊目的机构可包括作为少数股东的公共实体,但该公共实体应——

(a) 持有特殊目的机构的股份不超过出资额的 25%;

(b) 证明在特殊目的机构中股权出资的财务能力;和

(c) 证明承担和减轻与项目实施有关的风险的能力。"

12. 第 21 条的修订

对原法的第 21 条进行了如下修订——

(a) 删除第(2)款;和

(b) 将第(1)款的内容指定为第 21 条。

13. 废除和取代第 22 条

将原法的第 22 条废除,替换为以下内容:

"22. 争议的解决

(1) 在 PPP 协议执行过程中出现争议的,应努力通过友好协商解决争议。

(2) 未能通过谈判解决的争议,经当事方双方同意,协商提交如下仲裁——

(a) 符合《坦桑尼亚仲裁法》的;

(b) 根据国际投资争议解决中心的仲裁程序规则的;或者

(c) 在联合共和国政府与投资者所在国政府签订的任何双边或多边投资保护协议的框架内的。"

14. 第 23 条的修订

对原法第 23 条进行了如下修订——

(a) 在第(1)款的"监督"一词之后加入"并评估";和

(b) 在第(2)款中"监督"一词之后加入"并评估"。

15. 第 23A 条的修订

对原法第 23A 条进行了如下修订——

(a) 在第(1)和(2)款中"年中"一词之后加入"和年度";和

(b) 在第(2)款出现的"报告"和"提交给部长"之间加入"在提交给 PPP 指导委员会之前"。

16. 第 28 条的修订

对原法第 28 条第(2)款第(b)项进行了修订,在"投资"一词之前添加了"PPP"一词。

17. 第 28A 条的修订

对原法进行了修订,在第 28 条之后增加:

"28A. 与其他法律不一致

本法规定与任何其他成文法关于公私合营的开发、采购和实施之间存在任何不一致之处,应以本法的规定为准。"

国民议会于 2023 年 6 月 13 日通过

内内尔瓦-J-姆维汉比
国民议会书记官

第二编
劳 动 法 规

第九部
就业与劳动关系法（第366章）
［2006年］［2019年修订版］

坦桑尼亚联合共和国

就业与劳动关系法

［主要立法］

2019年修订版

本版《就业与劳动关系法》（第366章）的修订时间截至2019年11月30日（含当日），

并根据《法律修订法》第4章第4条的授权印刷。

多多马 2019年11月30日	阿德里安·德·科尔吉 总检察长

就业与劳动关系法
（第366章）

旨在规定核心劳动权利，制定基本就业标准，提供集体谈判框架，对争议的预防和解决及相关事项作出规定的法案。

[2006年12月20日]

[2007年第1号政府公告]

法案编号

2004年第6号法案

2006年第8号法案

2009年第21号法案

2010年第2号法案

2010年第17号法案

2015年第24号法案

2016年第4号法案

第一部分
总　　则

1. 简称

本法可称为《就业与劳动关系法》。

2. 适用

（1）本法适用于坦桑尼亚大陆的所有雇员，包括坦桑尼亚政府公共服务部门的雇员，但不适用于以下机构的临时或永久成员：

（i）坦桑尼亚人民国防军；

（ii）警察部队；

（iii）监狱管理局；或者

（iv）国民服务队。

（2）部长可以在与理事会和负责本条第（1）款规定所排除的一项或多项服务的有关部长协商后，通过在《公报》上发布通知，确定受雇于上述服务的雇员类别，这些雇员可以被排除在本法适用范围之外。

（3）第5、6和7条的规定应适用于第（1）款提及的部队和军队成员。

3. 本法目的

本法的主要目的是——

（a）通过提高经济效率、生产力和社会公平正义，促进经济发展；

（b）为有效和公平的雇佣关系和关于工作条件的最低标准提供法律框架；

（c）为自愿集体谈判提供框架；

（d）规范以劳工行动作为解决争议的手段；

（e）为通过调解、仲裁和裁决解决争议提供框架；

（f）实施1977年《坦桑尼亚联合共和国宪法》中适用于就业和劳动关系以及工作条件的条款；和

（g）全面实施国际劳工组织的核心公约以及其他经过批准的公约。

4. 释义

在本法中，除非上下文另有规定，否则——

"**仲裁员**"是指根据《劳工机构法》第19条任命的仲裁员；

"**基本工资**"是指就雇员在正常工作时间内所完成的工作而支付的部分薪酬，但不包括——

（a）津贴，不论是否按雇员的基本工资计算；

（b）根据第19条第(5)款规定支付的加班费；

（c）在星期日或公共假期工作的额外报酬；或者

（d）第20条第(4)款规定的夜班额外工资；

"**儿童**"是指未满14周岁的人；但在危险部门就业的儿童是指未满18周岁的人；

"**集体协议**"是指注册工会与雇主或注册雇主协会就任何劳工事务制定的书面协议；

"**委员会**"是指根据《劳工机构法》第12条设立的调解和仲裁委员会；[第300章]

"**申诉**"是指因以下各项的适用、解释或实施而引起的任何争议——

（a）与雇员制定的协议或合约；

（b）集体协议；

（c）本法或由部长管理的任何其他成文法；

（d）《商船法》第七部分；[第72章]

"**理事会**"是指根据《劳工机构法》第3条成立的劳工、经济和社会理事会；[第300章]

"**争议**"是指——

（a）任何雇主或注册雇主协会与任何雇员或注册工会之间有关劳资事务的任何争议；和

（b）包括诉称的争议；

"**利益争议**"是指除申诉以外的任何争议；

"**雇员**"是指以下人员——

（a）已签订雇佣合同的；或者

（b）已签订任何其他合同的，根据该合同——

（i）该个人承诺亲自为合同另一方工作；和

（ii）另一方不是该个人从事的任何职业、业务或事业的客户或顾客；或者

（c）根据第98条第(3)款被部长视为雇员的人；

"**雇主**"是指雇用雇员的任何人，包括政府和执行机构；

"**雇主协会**"是指为调节雇主与其雇员或代表这些雇员的工会之间的关系而自行联合起

来或为其他目的而联合起来的任何数量的雇主；

"**雇佣**"是指合同双方当事人在雇主与雇员关系下履行雇佣合同；

"**基本服务委员会**"是指根据《劳工机构法》第29条设立的基本服务委员会；[第300章]

"**联合会**"是指工会联合会或雇主协会联合会；

"**劳工专员**"是指根据《劳工机构法》第43条(1)款任命的劳工专员；[第300章]

"**劳工法庭**"是指根据《劳工机构法》第50条设立的高等法院劳资争议庭；

"**劳资事务**"是指与雇佣或劳动关系有关的任何事务；

"**停工**"是指一个或多个雇主完全或部分拒绝让其雇员工作，以迫使其雇员接受、修改或放弃可能形成利益纠纷标的的任何要求；

"**调解员**"是指根据《劳工机构法》第19条任命的调解员；[第300章]

"**部长**"是指目前负责劳工事务的部长；

"**业务要求**"是指基于雇主的经济、技术、结构或类似需求的要求；

"**组织**"是指工会或雇主协会；

"**抗议行动**"是指雇员为促进或维护工人的社会经济利益而全部或部分停止工作，但不包括以下目的——

（a）罢工定义中提及的罢工；或者

（b）可通过法律途径解决的争议；

"**注册组织**"是指注册工会或注册雇主协会；

"**注册官**"是指根据《劳工机构法》第43条(2)款任命的注册官；[第300章]

"**复职**"是指雇佣合同及其所有附带条件恢复生效，雇员有权享有其在未实际服务期间的所有权利；

"**薪酬**"指因雇佣雇员而支付或应付予该雇员的所有金钱或实物付款的总值；

"**罢工**"是指雇员的全部或部分停工，以迫使其雇主、任何其他雇主或雇主所属的雇主协会接受、修改或放弃可能形成利益纠纷标的的任何要求；

"**特定任务**"是指偶然性或季节性、非连续性的任务；

"**工会**"是指为调节雇员与其雇主或雇主所属的雇主协会之间的关系而自行联合起来或为其他目的而联合起来的任何数量的雇员。

[第300章;2015年第24号法案第4条]

第二部分
基本权利和保护

A 子部分：童工

5. 禁止使用童工

（1）任何人不得雇佣14周岁以下的童工。

（2）14周岁的儿童只能受雇从事轻体力劳动，且该劳动不得对儿童的健康和发育造成损害，也不得妨碍儿童上学、参加主管当局批准的职业指导或培训方案，也不得妨碍儿童从所接受的教育中获益。

(3) 未满18周岁的儿童不得受雇于矿山、工厂、船舶或任何其他工作场所,包括部长可能认为其工作环境有危险的非正规环境和农业。

(3A) 就第(3)款而言,"船舶"包括用于航行的任何类型的船只。[第4章第8条]

(4) 任何人不得雇佣儿童从事以下工作——

 (a) 不适合该年龄段儿童的工作;

 (b) 危及儿童福祉、教育、身心健康,或精神、道德或社会发展的工作。

(5) 尽管有第(3)款的规定,任何规范培训规定的成文法均可允许未满18周岁的儿童从事以下工作——

 (a) 在训练船上工作,作为该儿童训练的一部分;

 (b) 在工厂或矿山工作,如果工厂或矿山的工作是儿童培训的一部分;

 (c) 在任何其他工作场所,条件是儿童的健康、安全和道德得到充分保护,而且该儿童已经或正在接受相关工作或活动方面充分的专业指导或职业培训。

(6) 部长应制定规章——

 (a) 禁止雇用或培训未满18周岁的儿童,或为其设定条件;

 (b) 确定本法第(4)款所述的工作形式,并为定期修订和更新危险工作形式清单作出规定。

(7) 任何人有以下行为,均属违法——

 (a) 违反本条规定雇用儿童;

 (b) 违反本条规定招揽儿童受雇。

(8) 在根据本条进行的任何法律程序中,如果对儿童的年龄有争议,则应由雇用或促成该儿童受雇的人承担举证责任,证明经调查后有理由相信,该儿童未达到本条规定的年龄。

(9) 在不影响本条规定的前提下,每个雇主应确保在考虑到年龄和不断发展的能力的情况下,根据本法合法雇用的每个儿童都受到保护,使其免受歧视或可能产生负面影响的行为的侵害。

[2009年第21号法案第172条]

B 子部分:强迫劳动

6. 禁止强迫劳动

(1) 任何人促成、要求或强迫劳动,均属犯罪。

(2) 就本条而言,强迫劳动包括抵债劳动或在惩罚威胁下强迫某人从事的任何未经该人同意的工作,但不包括[第192章]——

 (a) 根据《国防法》要求进行的任何纯军事性质的工作;

 (b) 构成坦桑尼亚联合共和国公民正常公民义务一部分的任何工作;

 (c) 任何人因被法院定罪而被迫从事的任何工作,但是该工作是在公共当局的监督和控制下进行的,并且该人非受雇于私人或安排给私人处置;

 (d) 在紧急情况下或在可能危及全部或部分人口的生存或福祉的情况下所进行的任何工作;

 (e) 社区成员之间或社区成员与其直接代表就服务需求进行协商后,为该社区的直接利益而提供的小型社区服务。

C 子部分：歧视

7. 禁止工作场所中的歧视

(1) 每位雇主应确保促进就业机会均等，并努力消除任何就业政策或实践中的歧视。

(2) 雇主应向劳工专员登记一项促进平等机会和消除工作场所歧视的计划。

(3) 劳工专员可要求雇主——

　　(a) 发展第(2)款规定的计划；和

　　(b) 向专员登记该计划。

(4) 任何雇主不得在任何就业政策或实践中，以以下任何理由直接或间接歧视雇员：

　　(a) 肤色；

　　(b) 国籍；

　　(c) 部落或原籍地；

　　(d) 种族；

　　(e) 民族血统；

　　(f) 社会出身；

　　(g) 政治观点或宗教；

　　(h) 性；

　　(i) 性别；

　　(j) 怀孕；

　　(k) 婚姻状况或家庭责任；

　　(l) 残疾；

　　(m) 艾滋病毒/艾滋病；

　　(n) 年龄；或者

　　(o) 生活状况。

(5) 对雇员的骚扰是一种歧视，应禁止基于第(4)款规定的任何一项或多项理由组合的骚扰雇员行为。

(6) 以下不构成歧视——

　　(a) 采取与促进平等或消除工作场所歧视相一致的平权行动措施；

　　(b) 基于工作的固有要求而区分、排斥或偏袒任何人；或者

　　(c) 按照《国家就业促进服务法》雇用公民。[第243章]

(7) 任何人违反第(4)款和第(5)款的规定，即属犯罪。

(8) 在任何诉讼中——

　　(a) 如雇员根据第(4)款规定的任何理由举出初步证据证明受到了雇主的歧视，则雇主有责任证明——

　　　　(i) 没有发生所指控的歧视行为；或者

　　　　(ii) 该歧视行为或不作为并非基于上述任何理由；

　　(b) 如果歧视确实是基于第(5)款规定的理由而发生的，雇主应根据第(6)款的规定提出抗辩；或者

　　(c) 劳工法庭或仲裁员（视情况而定）应考虑根据本条向劳工专员登记的任何计划。

(9) 就本条而言——
    (a)"雇主"包括职业介绍所；
    (b) 雇员包括求职者；
    (c)"就业政策或惯例"包括与招聘程序、招聘广告和遴选标准、任命和任命程序、职务分类和分级、薪酬、就业福利、就业条款和条件、工作分配、工作环境和设施、培训和发展、绩效评估系统、晋升调动、降职、解聘及纪律处分相关事项。
(10) 为避免产生疑问,每个雇主都应采取积极措施保证男女同工同酬。

8. 禁止工会和雇主协会中的歧视行为
(1) 任何工会或雇主协会都不得在以下方面依据第 7 条第(4)款规定的任何理由直接或间接作出歧视行为——
    (a) 在接纳、代表或终止成员资格方面；
    (b) 在第 7 条第(9)款规定的任何雇佣政策或做法上；或者
    (c) 在任何集体协议中。
(2) 任何人违反第(1)款的规定,即属犯罪。

D 子部分：结社自由

9. 雇员的结社自由权
(1) 每个雇员都应该有如下权利——
    (a) 组织和加入工会；或者
    (b) 参加工会的合法活动。
(2) 尽管有第(1)款的规定——
    (a) 地方法官只能组织或加入仅限司法人员加入的工会；
    (b) 检察官只能组织或加入仅限于检察官或法院工作人员加入的工会；
    (c) 高级管理雇员不得加入代表雇主非高级管理雇员的工会。
(3) 任何人不得以以下理由歧视雇员——
    (a) 行使或已经行使本法或由部长管理的任何其他成文法规定的任何权利；
    (b) 属于或曾经属于工会；或者
    (c) 参加或曾经参加工会的合法活动。
(4) 任何人不得歧视因代表工会或联合会而参与其合法活动的官员或职务人员。
(5) 任何人违反第(3)和第(4)款的规定,即属犯罪。
(6) 就本条而言——
    (a)"雇员"包括求职者；
    (b)"高级管理雇员"是指员具有如下职责——
        (i) 代表雇主制定政策；以及
        (ii) 有权代表雇主签订集体协议。

10. 雇主的结社自由权
(1) 每个雇主都应该有权——
    (a) 组织并加入雇主协会；或者

(b) 参加雇主协会的合法活动。

(2) 任何人不得以以下理由歧视雇主——

(a) 行使或已经行使本法规定的权利；

(b) 属于或曾经属于雇主协会；或者

(c) 参与或曾经参与雇主协会的合法活动。

(3) 任何人不得歧视因代表雇主协会或联合会而参与其合法活动的官员或职务人员。

(4) 任何人违反第(2)和第(3)款的规定，即属犯罪。

11. 工会和雇主协会的权利

每个组织都有权——

(a) 决定自己的章程；

(b) 规划和组织其行政管理和合法活动；

(c) 加入并组织联合会；

(d) 参加联合会的合法活动；

(e) 与任何国际工人组织或国际雇主组织或国际劳工组织有联系，并参与其事务，并向这些组织捐款或接受其财政援助。

第三部分
就 业 标 准

A 子部分：总则

12. 本部分适用范围

(1) 在符合第(2)款规定的情况下，A 至 D 部分和 F 部分的规定不适用于其雇佣条款和条件受《商船法》规管的海员。[第72章]

(2) 尽管有第(1)款的规定，本部分的规定适用于在渔船上工作的海员，如果本法的规定与《商船法》及其规章之间有任何冲突，应以本法的规定为准。

(3) 如果任何与职业培训有关的成文法规定了第 13 条第(1)款规定的就业标准，则应适用该其他法律的规定。[第72章]

13. 雇佣标准

(1) 本法中关于工资确定的条款，凡规定最低就业期限和条件的，均为雇佣标准。

(2) 雇佣标准构成与雇员签订的合同条款，除非——

(a) 合同条款中包含对雇员更有利的条款；

(b) 协议中的某项规定在本部分条款允许的范围内改变了雇佣标准；

(c) 任何集体协议的条款、规范就业的成文法、工资决定或根据第 100 条授予的豁免条款改变了雇佣标准。

14. 与雇员的合同

(1) 与雇员签订的合同应属于以下类型——

(a) 不定期合同；

(b) 专业人员和管理人员的特定期限合同；

（c）特定任务合同。

（2）如果与雇员签订的合同规定该雇员将在坦桑尼亚联合共和国境内或境外工作,则该合同应采用书面形式。

[2015 年第 24 号法案第 5 条]

15. 详细情况书面说明

（1）在符合第 19 条第（2）款的情况下,雇主应在雇员开始工作时以书面形式向雇员提供以下详细情况,即——

  （a）雇员的姓名、年龄、永久地址和性别；

  （b）招聘地点；

  （c）职位说明；

  （d）生效日期；

  （e）合同的形式和期限；

  （f）工作地点；

  （g）工作时间；

  （h）酬金、计算酬金的方式以及任何福利或实物支付的细节；和

  （i）其他规定事项。

（2）如第（1）款所提述的所有情况均载于书面合同,而雇主已向雇员提供该合同,则雇主可以不提供第 14 条所述的书面声明。

（3）如果雇员不理解书面说明,雇主应确保以雇员能理解的方式向其解释。

（4）如第（1）款所规定的任何事项发生更改,雇主须在与雇员协商后,修订书面细节以反映有关变化,并以书面形式通知雇员有关变化。

（5）雇主应将第（1）款所规定的书面详情保存至雇佣终止后的五年。

（6）在任何法律诉讼中,如果雇主未能提供第（1）款规定的书面合同或书面详情,则雇主应当承担证明或反驳第（1）款规定中诉称的雇佣条款的责任。

（7）本节的规定不适用于一个月内为雇主工作少于 6 天的雇员。

16. 告知员工其权利

每个雇主应在显著处以规定的格式展示出雇员依本法享有的权利。

B 子部分：工作时间

17. 本部分的适用范围

（1）本部分的规定不适用于代表雇主管理其他雇员的雇员,以及直接向第 9 条第（6）款第（b）项规定的高级管理雇员汇报的雇员。

（2）第 19 条第（1）款、第 19 条第（3）款、第 23 条第（1）款、第 24 条第（1）款和第 25 条第（1）款的规定不适用于在正常工作时间内无法由员工完成的紧急情况。

18. 释义

就本部分而言——

  （a）"日"是指从雇员正常开始工作的时间起算的 24 小时,"每日"具有相应的含义；

  （b）"加班"是指超出正常工作时间的工作；

(c)"周"是指从雇员正常开始工作周的那一天起算的 7 天时间,"每周"具有相应的含义。

19. 工作时间

(1)在符合本部分规定的情况下,雇主不得要求或允许雇员在任何一天内工作超过 12 小时。

(2)在符合本部分规定的情况下,雇员可获准或被要求工作的普通日数或小时数的上限为——

    (a)每周 6 天;

    (b)每周 45 小时;和

    (c)每天 9 小时。

(3)在符合本部分规定的情况下,雇主不得要求或允许员工超时工作——

    (a)根据协议规定的除外;和

    (b)在任何四周周期内加班超过 50 小时。

(4)根据第(3)款制定的协议不得要求雇员工作时间超过第(1)款规定的 12 小时限制。

(5)雇主向雇员支付的任何加班费均不得少于雇员基本工资的 1.5 倍。

20. 夜间工作

(1)在本条中,"夜间"是指 20 时之后至 6 时之前的时间。

(2)禁止雇主要求或允许——

    (a)有以下情况的怀孕员工在夜间工作——

        (i)预产期前两个月的;或者

        (ii)在该日期之前,如果雇员出示医疗证明,证明其不再适合从事夜班工作的;

    (b)有以下情况的母亲在夜间工作——

        (i)其婴儿 2 个月大的;

        (ii)在该日期之前,如果该母亲要求工作并出示医疗证明,证明其和婴儿的健康状况不会受到威胁的;

        (iii)在该日期之后,如果该母亲出示医疗证明,证明其尚不适合从事夜间工作,或婴儿的健康状况不容许其从事夜间工作的;

    (c)未满 18 周岁的儿童在夜间工作;

    (d)经医学证明不适合从事夜间工作的雇员在夜间工作。

(3)任何从事夜间工作的雇员如经证明不适合从事夜间工作,雇主应将其调离,除非实际上不可行。

(4)雇主应为雇员在夜间工作的每小时支付至少相当于该雇员基本工资 5% 的工资,如果工作时间为加班时间,则这 5% 的工资应按雇员的加班费率计算。

(5)就本条而言,医疗证明是指由注册医生或雇主接受的任何其他医生签发的证明书,雇主不得无理拒绝接受。

21. 压缩工作周

(1)书面协议应要求或允许雇员一天工作不超过 12 小时,包括任何用餐时间,且不领取加班费。

(2)根据第(1)款制定的协议,不得要求或允许雇员工作时间——

    (a)一周超过 5 天;

(b) 每周超过45小时;

(c) 每周加班超过10小时。

22. 平均工时

(1) 尽管有第19条或第24条的规定,集体协议应规定在一个议定期间内平均计算普通工时和加班工时。

(2) 第(1)款中的集体协议不得要求或允许雇员平均工作时间超过——

(a) 在约定期限内的每周正常工作的40小时;

(b) 在约定期限内的每周加班的10小时。

(3) 第(1)款规定的集体协议不得允许超过一年的平均期限。

23. 工作日休息时间

(1) 在符合本部分规定的情况下,雇主应给予连续工作超过5小时的雇员至少60分钟的休息时间。

(2) 雇主只有在工作不能无人看管或不能由其他雇员完成的情况下,才可要求雇员在休息时间工作。

(3) 除非雇员在休息期间被要求工作或可以工作,否则雇主没有义务支付雇员休息期间的工资。

24. 每日和每周休息时间

(1) 雇主应允许雇员——

(a) 在结束工作和重新开始工作之间,每日至少有连续12个小时的休息时间;

(b) 从一周的最后一个正常工作日到下一周的第一个正常工作日之间,每周至少有24个小时的休息时间。

(2) 在以下情况下,每日休息时间可减至8小时——

(a) 有这方面的书面协议;和

(b) 正常工作时间中断至少3小时;或者

(c) 雇员居住在工作场所内。

(3) 每周休息时间可通过书面协议规定——

(a) 每两周至少连续休息60小时;或者

(b) 如果下一周的休息时间相应延长,则每周休息时间减少8小时。

(4) 在雇员同意的情况下,该雇员仅可在第(1)款中提到的每周休息时间内工作,但雇主应为该雇员在该期间内工作的每小时支付双倍的小时基本工资。

25. 公共节假日

如果雇员在《公共节假日法》规定的公共节假日工作,雇主应为该雇员在当日工作的每小时支付双倍的基本工资。

[第93章]

C 子部分: 薪酬

26. 工资率的计算

(1) 本条规定适用于为本法的任何目的而必须确定适用的小时、日、周或月工资率。

(2) 每小时、每日、每周或每月的工资率应根据附表 1 中的表格确定。

(3) 如雇员的工资不是基于工作时间计算的,则就本条而言,该雇员应被视为按周计酬,并且该雇员的每周基本工资应按其所赚取的金额计算,即——

(a) 随后的 13 周内赚取的金额;或者

(b) 如果雇员受雇时间不足 13 周,则指该期间赚取的金额。

27. 支付薪酬

(1) 雇主应向雇员支付雇员有权获得的任何金钱报酬——

(a) 在约定发薪日的工作时间内在工作地点支付;

(b) 以现金支付,除非雇员另行同意,在这种情况下,支付方式可为——

(i) 支付给雇员的支票;或者

(ii) 直接存入雇员书面指定的账户;和

(c) 如果支付方式是以现金或支票支付,则应将其装入密封信封。

(2) 第(1)款规定的每笔付款均应附有一份详细的书面说明,其中应包括以下规定的具体内容——

(a) 如果支付方式是以现金或支票支付,则应随附付款;或者

(b) 如果支付方式是直接存款,则应将其装在密封的信封内交给雇员。

(3) 薪酬应在合同期结束时支付,但雇主可在双方约定的日期到期之前支付预付款,如果没有约定日期,则至少在合同期过半时支付一次;这种预付款不应就其贷款,也不应就其收取利息。

[第 4 章第 8 条]

(4) 尽管有第(1)款的规定,部长仍可通过条例规定以实物津贴的形式支付部分薪酬,但不得以酒精饮料或有毒药品的形式支付薪酬,在将以实物津贴的形式支付薪酬作为惯例或视为可取的行业或职业中,任何此类实物津贴应供雇员及其家人个人使用,且此类津贴的价值应公平合理。

(5) 任何雇主违反本条规定,即属犯罪。

28. 有关薪资的扣除和其他行为

(1) 雇主不得从雇员的报酬中扣除任何款项,除非——

(a) 根据成文法、集体协议、工资决定、法院命令或仲裁裁决要求或允许的扣减;或者

(b) 在符合第(2)款规定的情况下,雇员以书面同意就债务扣除款项。

(2) 根据第(1)款第(b)项作出的扣除,只有在以下情况下,才能用于向雇主赔偿损失或损害——

(a) 损失或损害发生在雇佣过程中,并且是由于雇员的过失造成的;

(b) 雇主已以书面形式向雇员说明债务的原因、金额和计算方法;

(c) 雇主已给予雇员合理的机会对原因、金额或计算方法提出质疑;

(d) 债务总额不超过损失或损害的实际金额;

(e) 根据本款从雇员薪酬中扣除的总额不超过该雇员薪酬的四分之一。

(3) 根据第(1)款第(b)项就雇员购买的货物或服务进行扣除的协议,应具体说明债务的原因、数额和计算方法。

(4) 雇主如果根据第(1)款从雇员薪酬中扣除款项以支付给他人,应按照协议、法律、裁定、法院命令或仲裁裁决中规定的任何要求将款项支付给该人。

(5) 雇主不得要求或允许雇员——

(a) 退还任何报酬,但雇主先前因计算雇员报酬错误而多付的报酬除外;或者

(b) 确认收到的数额大于实际收到的报酬。

(6) 尽管有任何其他法律关于雇主企业破产或清算的规定,雇员或代表雇员对雇员根据本法有权获得的任何薪酬提出的索赔,应为在宣布破产或清算之日前26周内累计的索赔。

(7) 任何人违反本条规定,即属犯罪。

D 子部分:休假

29. 本子部分的适用范围

(1) 在符合第(2)款规定的情况下,服务期不足6个月的雇员无权根据本部分的规定享有带薪休假。

(2) 尽管有第(1)款的规定——

(a) 季节性受雇的雇员有权根据本部分的规定享有带薪休假;

(b) 服务期不足6个月,但在一年内为同一雇主工作超过一次的雇员,如果在该年为该雇主工作的总时间超过6个月,则有权根据本部分的规定享有带薪休假。

30. 本子部分的释义

(1) 就本子部分而言——

(a) "日"包括第24条规定的任何休息时间;

(b) "休假周期"是指——

(i) 就年假而言,在以下情况下连续受雇于雇主满12个月——

(aa) 除第(2)款另有规定外,在雇员开始受雇;或者

(bb) 完成最近12个月的休假周期后;

(ii) 就本款授予的所有其他形式的休假而言,在以下情况下连续受雇于雇主满36个月——

(aa) 除第(2)款另有规定外,在雇员开始受雇;或者

(bb) 完成最近36个月的休假周期;

(c) "带薪休假"是指根据本部分规定并依据雇员基本工资计算的任何休假。

(2) 尽管有第(1)款第(b)项第(i)目(aa)和第(ii)目(aa)的规定,只要不损害雇员根据本部分享有的带薪休假权利,雇主和雇员可商定一个标准休假周期。

31. 年假

(1) 雇主须在每个假期周期内给予雇员至少连续28天的假期,而该假期应包括可能在休假期间内的任何公共假日。

(2) 第(1)款提及的天数,可以按雇主应雇员要求准予该雇员带薪偶尔休假的休假周期内的天数减去。

(3) 雇主可决定休年假的时间,但不得晚于——

(a) 休假周期结束后6个月;或者

（b）如有以下情况,则不得晚于休假周期结束后 12 个月,除非——
    （i）雇员同意;和
    （ii）雇主因业务需求延长休假。

（4）雇主应向雇员支付雇员在休假开始前的休假期间工作所应获得的薪酬。

（5）雇主不得要求或准许雇员以年假代替雇员根据本部分所享有的任何假期。

（6）经雇员同意,雇主可要求或允许该雇员在年假期间为雇主工作,但不得连续工作两年。

（7）除第（6）款和第（8）款另有规定外,雇主应向雇员支付一个月的工资,以代替该雇员有权享有或被要求工作的年假。

（8）雇主应按比例向雇员支付累计年假的工资——
    （a）除第（9）款另有规定外,在终止雇佣时支付;或者
    （b）在每个季节结束时,为季节性雇佣的员工发放。

（9）如雇员未在第（3）款规定的期限和情况下休假,则该雇员无权就累计年假获得按比例支付的薪酬。

（10）第（8）款所提述的年假按比例计算,应按雇员工作或有权工作的每 13 天的一日基本工资来计算。

[2015 年第 24 号法案第 6 条]

32. 病假

（1）在任何休假周期内,雇员均有权享受至少 126 天的病假。

（2）第（1）款所述病假应按以下方式计算——
    （a）前 63 天应支付全额工资;
    （b）后 63 天应支付半薪。

（3）尽管有第（2）款的规定,在以下情况下,雇主无须向雇员支付病假工资——
    （a）该雇员未能出示医疗证明;或者
    （b）根据任何法律、基金或集体协议,该雇员有权享受带薪病假。

（4）就本条而言,"医疗证明"是指由注册医生或雇主认可的任何其他医生签发的证明书,雇主不得无理拒绝接受。

33. 产假

（1）雇员应在预产期前至少 3 个月通知雇主其打算休产假,并应提供医疗证明。

（2）在以下情况下,雇员可开始休产假——
    （a）预产期 4 周前的任何时候;
    （b）如果医生证明这对雇员或其未出生的孩子的健康是必要的,则可在更早的时间开始。

（3）任何雇员不得在其子女出生后 6 周内工作,除非医生证明其适合工作。

（4）在符合第（2）款和第（3）款规定的情况下,雇员可在产假结束后按相同的雇佣条款和条件恢复工作。

（5）任何雇主不得要求或允许怀孕员工或正在哺乳期的员工从事危害其健康或其子女健康的工作。

（6）在符合第（7）款和第（8）款规定的情况下,雇员在任何休假周期内至少有权——

(a) 享有 84 天的带薪产假;或者

(b) 如雇员同时生育一个以上子女,可享有 100 天的带薪产假。

(7) 尽管有第(6)款第(a)项的规定,如果婴儿在出生后一年内死亡,雇员有权在休假周期内额外享受 84 天带薪产假。

(8) 根据本条规定,雇主仅能给予雇员 4 个月的带薪产假。

(9) 如果雇员从事的工作对其本人或其子女的健康有害,其雇主应在可行的情况下,以不低于其工作条件的条款和条件为其提供适当的替代工作。

(10) 如果雇员正在母乳喂养子女,雇主应允许雇员在工作时间喂奶,每天最多不超过两小时。

(11) 就本条而言,"医疗证明"是指由注册医生(包括助产士)或雇主认可的任何其他医生签发的证明书,雇主不得无理拒绝接受。

34. 陪产假和其他形式的假期

(1) 在任何休假周期内,雇员有权——

(a) 享有至少 3 天带薪陪产假,条件是——

(i) 在子女出生后 7 天内休假;和

(ii) 该雇员是该子女的父亲;

(b) 因下列原因之一,享有至少 4 天带薪假——

(i) 雇员的子女患病或死亡;

(ii) 雇员的配偶、父母、祖父母、孙子女或兄弟姐妹死亡。

(2) 雇主在根据本条向雇员支付假期工资之前,可要求雇员提供第(1)款规定的事件的合理证据。

(3) 为了明确起见——

(a) 第(1)款第(a)项所提及的 3 天是雇员有权享有的休假总天数,不论该雇员有多少名子女在假期周期内出生;

(b) 第(1)款第(b)项所提及的 4 天是雇员有权享有的休假总天数,无论在一个休假周期内发生多少起该段所规定的事件,但雇员可在同一休假周期内因该事件及其后发生的其他事件而获得雇主批准的更多休假天数,但这些额外的休假天数将是无薪的。

E 子部分:不公平终止雇佣

35. 本子部分适用范围

本部分的规定不适用于为同一雇主工作少于 6 个月的雇员,无论是根据一份还是多份合同。

36. 释义

就本部分而言——

(a) "终止雇佣"包括——

(i) 根据普通法合法终止雇佣关系;

(ii) 雇员因雇主令其无法忍受继续受雇而终止雇佣关系;

(iii) 如果存在续签的合理预期,未按相同或类似条件续签固定期限合同;

（iv）雇员未得到允许在休完根据本法批准的产假或任何商定的产假后恢复工作；和

（v）如果雇主因相同或类似的原因解雇了多名雇员，并已提出重新雇用其中一名或多名雇员，但未重新雇用该雇员；

(b) "终止雇佣"具有与"雇佣关系终止"相对应的含义。

37. 不公平解雇

（1）雇主不公平地解雇雇员属于非法。

（2）如果雇主未能证明以下情况，则解雇是不公平的——

(a) 终止雇佣关系的理由是正当的；

(b) 该理由是公平的，且——

（i）与雇员的行为、能力或适应性有关；或者

（ii）基于雇主的业务需要，和

(c) 终止雇佣关系符合公平程序。

（3）以下原因不得作为解雇雇员的合理理由[第4章第8条]——

(a) 因雇员的原因——

（i）披露其根据本法或任何其他法律有权或必须向他人披露的信息；

（ii）未做或拒绝做雇主不得合法允许或要求雇员做的任何事情；

（iii）行使通过协议、本法或任何其他法律赋予的任何权利；

（iv）属于或曾经属于任何工会；或者

（v）参与合法的工会活动，包括合法罢工；

(b) 以下原因——

（i）与怀孕有关的；

（ii）与残疾有关的；和

（iii）构成本法规定的歧视的。

（4）在决定雇主终止雇佣是否公平时，雇主、仲裁员或劳工法庭应考虑到根据第99条公布的任何良好行为准则。

（5）在法院作出终局裁决以及提出任何上诉之前，对被指控犯有实质相同的刑事罪行的雇员，不得对其处以罚款、解雇或开除等任何纪律处分。

38. 基于经营需要的终止

（1）在因经营需要而终止合同（裁员）时，雇主应遵守以下原则，即应——

(a) 一旦有任何裁员的意向，应立即发出通知；

(b) 披露有关计划裁员的所有信息，以便进行适当协商；

(c) 在裁员或解雇前就以下问题进行磋商——

（i）打算裁员的原因；

（ii）避免或尽量减少预期裁员的措施；

（iii）选择裁减雇员的方法；

（iv）裁员的时间；和

（v）与裁员有关的遣散费；

(d) 根据本分节的规定,对下列组织或人员发出通知、作出披露以及进行协商——
  (i) 第 67 条承认的工会;
  (ii) 任何注册工会,其成员在工作场所未被注册的工会代表;
  (iii) 未被公认或注册的工会所代表的任何雇员。
(2) 如双方在根据第(1)款进行的协商中未达成协议,则该事项应根据本法第八部分的规定提交调解。
(3) 如果调解失败,应将争议提交仲裁,仲裁应在 30 天内结束,在此期间,任何裁员均不得生效,如果雇员对裁决不服,并希望根据第 91 条第(2)款向劳工法庭提出修订,则雇主可继续裁员。

[2010 年第 17 号法案第 8 条;2015 年第 24 号法案第 7 条]

39. 不公平解雇诉讼中的举证

在涉及雇主不公平解雇雇员的任何诉讼中,雇主应证明解雇是公平的。

40. 不公平解雇的补救措施

(1) 如果仲裁员或劳工法庭认为解雇是不公平的,仲裁员或法庭可以命令雇主——
  (a) 在雇员因不公平解聘而缺勤期间,自其被解雇之日起将其复职,且其薪酬不损失;或者
  (b) 按照仲裁员或法院可能决定的任何条款重新雇用该雇员;或者
  (c) 向雇员支付不少于 12 个月薪酬的补偿。
(2) 根据本条发出的赔偿令是雇员根据任何法律或协议有权获得的任何其他金额的补充,而不是替代。
(3) 如果仲裁员或法院作出复职或再聘令,而雇主决定不将雇员复职或重新聘用该雇员,则雇主应从不公平解雇之日起至最后付款之日止,除支付该雇员应得的工资和其他福利外,再支付 12 个月工资的赔偿金。

[第 4 章第 8 条]

F 子部分:其他终止事件

41. 解雇通知

(1) 如果雇佣合同可以提前通知终止,通知期不得少于——
  (a) 如果通知是在受雇的第一个月内发出的,则为 7 天;和
  (b) 在此之后——
    (i) 如果雇员是按日或按周受雇,则为 4 天;或者
    (ii) 如果雇员按月受雇,则为 28 天。
(2) 协议可规定长于第(1)款规定的通知期,但条件是商定的通知期对雇主和雇员而言期限相同。
(3) 解雇通知应以书面形式发出并说明——
  (i) 解雇的原因;和
  (ii) 发出通知的日期。
(4) 解雇通知不得——
  (a) 在本法规定的任何休假期间发出;或者

（b）与任何此类假期同时进行。

（5）雇主无须向雇员发出解雇通知，而可向其支付雇员在通知期内工作本应得到的报酬。

（6）如雇员在通知期内拒绝工作，雇主可从该雇员被解雇时应得的任何款项中扣除该雇员在通知期内工作本应得的款项。

（7）本条规定不影响以下权利——

（a）雇员对根据本法或任何其他法律规定的终止雇佣的合法性或公正性提出异议；

（b）雇主或雇员可因法律承认的任何原因，在不通知的情况下终止雇佣关系。

[第4章第8条]

42. 遣散费

（1）就本条而言，"遣散费"指为该雇主工作10年内，每连续工作满1年，最少相当于7天的基本工资。

（2）在以下情况下，雇主应在终止雇佣时支付遣散费——

（a）该雇员已为雇主连续工作满12个月；和

（b）在不违反第（3）款规定的情况下，雇主终止雇佣。

（3）第（2）款的规定不适用于以下情况——

（a）以不当行为为理由的公平解雇；

（b）雇员因能力兼容问题或雇主的业务要求而被解雇，但无理拒绝接受该雇主或任何其他雇主提供的替代工作；或者

（c）达到退休年龄的雇员或因时间原因服务合同期满或终止的雇员。

（4）根据本条规定支付的遣散费不影响雇员根据本法或任何其他成文法获得任何其他应得款项的权利。

[2010年第2号法案第13条]

43. 运送至招聘地点

（1）如果雇员的雇佣合同在其受聘地点以外的其他地点终止，雇主应——

（a）将雇员及其个人物品运送到招聘地点；

（b）支付雇员前往招聘地点的交通费；或者

（c）按照第（2）款的规定，向雇员支付前往招聘地点的交通津贴，以及从合同终止之日至将雇员及其家属送往招聘地点之日这段期间（如有）的每日生活费。

（2）根据第（1）款第（c）项规定的津贴至少应等于前往离招聘地点最近的公共汽车站的车费。

（3）就本条而言，"招聘"是指雇主或雇主代理人招揽任何雇员就业。

44. 支付解雇费和工作证明

（1）终止雇佣时，雇主应向雇员支付以下费用——

（a）终止前已完成工作的任何报酬；

（b）根据第31条应支付给雇员的该雇员未休年假的薪酬；

（c）根据第31条第（1）款确定的任何不完整休假周期内累积的年假薪酬；

（d）根据第41条第（5）款到期应付的任何通知期内工作报酬；和

（e）根据第42条应支付的任何遣散费；

（f）根据第 43 条可能应付的任何交通津贴。

（2）终止雇佣时，雇主应向雇员签发规定的服务证明。

第四部分
工会、雇主协会和联合会

45. 注册义务

（1）工会或雇主协会应在成立后 6 个月内根据本部分进行注册。

（2）符合第 46 条第（3）款规定的联合会注册要求的联合会可以注册。

（3）工会或雇主协会在以下情况下作为工会或协会运作，即属犯罪——

（a）在其成立满 6 个月之后，未根据本部分规定申请注册的；或者

（b）已根据本部分规定注册的情况除外。

46. 注册要求

（1）工会注册的条件如下：

（a）是一个真正的工会；

（b）是一个不以营利为目的的协会；

（c）独立于任何雇主或雇主协会；

（d）经 20 人以上职工会议设立；

（e）已通过符合第 47 条规定的章程和规则；

（f）采用的名称与另一工会的名称不相似，以免误导或造成混淆；和

（g）地址在坦桑尼亚联合共和国境内。

（2）雇主协会注册的条件如下：

（a）是一个真正的雇员协会；

（b）是一个不以营利为目的的协会；

（c）经 4 人以上雇主会议设立；

（d）已通过符合第 47 条规定的章程和规则；

（e）采用的名称与另一雇主协会的名称不相似，以免误导或造成混淆；和

（f）地址在坦桑尼亚联合共和国境内。

（3）联合会注册的条件如下：

（a）是一个真正的联合会；

（b）是一个不以营利为目的的联合会；

（c）经 5 个以上已登记的同类组织会议设立；

（d）已通过符合第 47 条规定的章程和规则；

（e）采用的名称与另一组织或联合会的名称不相似，以免误导或造成混淆；

（f）只包括已注册的组织；和

（g）地址在坦桑尼亚联合共和国境内。

47. 宪法要求

（1）工会、雇主协会或联合会的章程和规则应——

（a）声明其是一个不以营利为目的的组织；
（b）规定成员资格，并规定终止成员资格的理由和程序；
（c）规定会费或确定会费的方法；
（d）规定召开和举行会议的规则，包括法定人数要求和该等会议须备存的记录；
（e）确定决策方式；
（f）设立秘书办公室并明确其职能；
（g）确定职务人员和官员，并界定他们各自的职能；
（h）规定职务人员的提名和选举程序；
（i）规定官员的任命、提名或选举程序；
（j）规定在何种情况下和以何种方式免除职务人员、官员和工会代表的职务；
（k）确定进行投票的情况和方式；
（l）就成员进行投票作出规定——
　　（i）成员如属工会，对工会号召罢工进行投票作出规定；
　　（ii）成员如属雇主协会，对雇主协会要求停工进行投票作出规定；
　　（iii）成员如属工会联合会，对联合会呼吁参与抗议行动进行投票作出规定；
（m）规定银行业务和货币投资；
（n）确定其资金的用途；
（o）规定财产的取得和管制；
（p）规定修改章程和规则的程序；
（q）规定以下组织从属或合并的程序——
　　（i）工会与其他注册工会；
　　（ii）雇主协会与其他注册协会；
　　（iii）联合会与其他联合会；
（r）规定加入国际工人协会或国际雇主协会的程序；
（s）规定解散组织或联合会的程序；
（t）规定任何其他事项。

（2）注册组织的章程或规则不得——
（a）与以下情况冲突——
　　（i）1977年《坦桑尼亚联合共和国宪法》第三部分规定的基本权利和义务；
　　（ii）本法或任何其他成文法的规定；或者
（b）逃避任何法律规定的义务。

48. 注册程序

（1）任何组织或联合会可申请注册，向注册官提交以下材料——
（a）由该组织或联合会秘书妥善填写并签字的规定表格；
（b）第46条第（1）款第（d）项、第（2）款第（c）项或第（3）款第（c）项规定的成立大会的出席名册和会议记录的核证副本；和
（c）其章程和规则的核证副本。

（2）尽管有第（1）款的规定，注册官可要求提供进一步的资料以支持申请。

(3) 凡注册官认为有关组织或协会已遵从第46和47条的要求,他应注册该组织或联合会。

(4) 如注册官认为有关组织或联合会不符合第46和47条的要求,则他——

(a) 可给予申请人在规定期限内更正其申请的机会;

(b) 可拒绝申请,并向申请人发出书面通知,说明决定和理由。

(5) 在对组织或联合会进行注册后,注册官应——

(a) 将该组织或联合会的名称记入适当的登记册;

(b) 向该组织或联合会颁发注册证书。

49. 登记的效力

(1) 组织或联合会一经注册,即成为法人团体——

(a) 具有永久继承权和共同印章;

(b) 有能力以自己的名义——

(i) 起诉和被起诉;

(ii) 签订合同;和

(iii) 持有、购买或以其他方式获取和处置动产或不动产。

(2) 注册组织或联合会不得为限制贸易的协会。

(3) 一个人是一个注册组织或联合会的成员,该人并不因这一事实而对该工会或组织承担任何义务或责任。

(4) 已登记组织或联合会的成员、职务人员、官员在为或代表该组织或联合会履行职责时,因善意履行或遗漏行为而造成的任何人的损失,概不承担个人责任。

(5) 正式颁发的注册证书足以证明注册组织或联合会是法人团体。

(6) 就本条而言,与工会有关的"职务人员"包括第62条规定的工会代表。

50. 更改名称或章程

(1) 注册组织或联合会名称的更改或章程与规则的更改,只有在注册官根据本条批准后方可生效。

(2) 已登记的组织或联合会可向注册官提交以下材料,申请批准更改名称或更改其章程和规则——

(a) 由秘书妥当填写和签署的规定表格;

(b) 载有变更措辞的决议副本;和

(c) 一份由秘书签署的证明书,说明该决议是按照章程条例通过的。

(3) 尽管有第(2)款的规定,注册官可要求提供进一步的资料以支持申请。

(4) 注册官应——

(a) 审议申请和申请人提供的任何进一步资料;

(b) 如确信章程及规则的更改符合第46和47条规定的要求,则发出批准该项更改的规定的证明书;和

(c) 如确信更改后的名称与另一工会的名称不相似,不会误导或造成混淆、则通过签发反映新名称的新注册证书来批准这一更改。

(5) 如拒绝批准变更,应书面通知该决定及拒绝的理由。

51. 账目和审计

（1）各注册组织和联合会应按照公认的会计实务标准、原则和程序——

（a）保存收入、支出、资产和负债的账簿和记录；

（b）就截至12月31日的每个财政年度，按规定格式编制财务报表；

（c）安排注册审计师对账簿和账目记录以及财务报表进行年度审计；

（d）在次年的3月31日之前，将财务报表和审计报告提交给——

（i）组织或联合会章程规定的会议成员或其代表；和

（ii）注册官。

（2）各注册组织和联合会应在其办事处向会员提供财务报表和审计报告，以供查阅。

52. 注册组织和联合会的职责

（1）除第51条所要求的记录外，每个注册组织或联合会应保存以下记录5年——

（a）符合规定格式的成员名单；

（b）会议记录；

（c）选票。

（2）各注册组织或联合会应向注册官提供以下资料——

（a）在次年3月31日前，提交一份经秘书认证的年度报表，列明截至前一年12月31日的会员总数；

（b）在注册官提出要求后30天内，提交一份与成员资格说明、审计报告或财务报表有关的任何事项的书面解释：

但是，注册官不得调查任何组织的财务事项，除非有重大理由相信该组织违反了法律或该组织的资金被贪污或以其他方式被滥用；

（c）在任命或选举国家职务人员后30天内，提供其姓名和工作地址；

（d）送达文件的新地址生效前30天，通知该地址的变更。

53. 不遵守章程

（1）如果联合会或注册组织没有遵守其章程，联合会或注册组织的注册官或成员可向劳工法庭申请任何适当的命令，包括——

（a）撤销任何决定、协议或选举；

（b）要求该组织或联合会或其任何官员——

（i）遵守章程；

（ii）采取措施纠正违规行为；

（c）限制任何人作出任何不符合章程的行动。

（2）在劳工法庭审理第（1）款规定的申请之前，法庭应确信——

（a）该组织或联合会的内部程序已经用尽；或者

（b）尽管未用尽任何内部程序，但审理申请符合该组织或联合会的最大利益。

54. 注册组织和联合会的合并

（1）任何已注册的——

（a）工会可决定与一个或多个注册的工会合并；和

（b）雇主协会可决定与一个或多个注册雇主协会合并；

（c）联合会可决定与一个或多个联合会合并组成一个联合会。

（2）合并的组织或联合会可向注册官申请注册合并后的组织或联合会,第48条中有关注册程序的规定可比照适用于该申请。

（3）在注册官对合并后的组织或联合会进行注册后,他应从有关登记册中删除合并的每个组织或联合会的名称,从而取消它们的登记。

（4）合并后的组织或联合会的注册,自注册官将其名称列入有关登记册之日起生效。

（5）如注册官已注册一个合并组织或联合会——

　　（a）合并的组织或联合会的所有资产、权利、义务和责任应移交给合并后的组织或联合会；和

　　（b）合并后的组织或联合会在以下方面接替合并的组织或联合会——

　　　　（i）合并的组织或联合会享有的任何权利；

　　　　（ii）根据本法或任何其他法律设立的任何基金；

　　　　（iii）任何集体协议或其他协议；和

　　　　（iv）成员就定期扣除应付给合并组织的征费或会费所作的书面授权。

55. 取消注册

（1）如已注册组织或联合会未能遵守以下规定,注册官可向劳工法庭申请命令取消该组织或联合会的注册——

　　（a）注册要求；或者

　　（b）本部分的规定。

（2）劳工法庭可作出任何适当的命令,包括——

　　（a）取消一个组织或联合会的注册；

　　（b）给予该组织或联合会任何不遵守规定的补救机会。

（3）如组织或联合会的注册被取消,则——

　　（a）其根据本法享有的所有权利将终止；和

　　（b）该组织或联合会应根据第56条的规定解散。

56. 解散工会或雇主协会

（1）注册官可向劳工法庭申请解散任何违反第45条规定的组织。

（2）组织或联合会可向劳工法庭申请解散。

（3）凡劳工法庭根据第55条第(2)款作出取消某组织或联合会注册的命令,它还可作出解散该组织或联合会的命令。

（4）根据与破产相关的法律,任何利害关系人均可以任何破产理由向劳动争议法庭申请解散注册组织或联合会。

（5）破产法应适用于第(3)款规定的申请,在破产法中任何相关法律的解释权均归劳工法庭。

（6）在根据本条发出解散令时,劳工法庭可——

　　（a）按任何适当条件任命任何合适人选为清算人；

　　（b）在章程和规则未规定的情况下,决定剩余资产的归属。

57. 对注册官裁决的上诉

任何人如对注册官根据本部分作出的决定不服的,可向劳工法庭提出上诉。

58. 在《公报》上发表

（1）注册官应在《公报》发布通知，陈述以下事实，即——

  （a）一个组织或联合会已注册；

  （b）任何组织或联合会的注册被取消；

  （c）影响任何注册组织或联合会的名称变更或合并已经注册；

  （d）注册组织或联合会已解散。

（2）凡第（1）款所提及的通知涉及组织或联合会的注册，该通知应包含一项声明，声明任何人可在注册官办公室查看该组织或联合会的章程。

第五部分
组 织 权 利

59. 释义

就本部分而言——

"授权代表"是指工会的职务人员或官员或任何其他获授权代表工会的人；

"雇主场所"包括在雇主控制下进行工作的任何场所或为员工提供的住所；

"劳工法"包括本法和与劳工事务有关的任何其他法律；

"注册工会"包括两个或两个以上联合行动的工会；

"代表工会"是指最具代表性的注册工会。

60. 进入雇主的办公场所

（1）注册工会的任何授权代表有权进入雇主的场所，以便——

  （a）招募成员；

  （b）与成员沟通；

  （c）在与雇主打交道时会见成员；

  （d）在办公场所举行雇员会议；

  （e）根据工会章程在任何投票中投票。

（2）注册工会可在雇用其10名或10名以上成员的任何工作场所设立外地分会。

（3）雇主应为工会提供符合第67条规定的合理和必要的设施，以便其在工作场所开展活动。

（4）本条规定的权利应受任何合理且必要的时间和地点条件的限制，以保障生命或财产安全或防止工作受到不适当的干扰。

61. 扣除工会会费

（1）如果雇员在规定的表格中授权雇主从其工资中扣除注册工会的会费，则雇主应从该雇员的工资中作出相应扣除。

（2）雇主应在扣款月结束后7天内将扣款汇给工会。

（3）如雇主无合理理由而未在第（2）款规定的时间内交纳工会会费，则应在会费未缴纳的每一天向工会支付相当于应付总额5%的款项。

（4）雇员可提前一个月向雇主和工会发出书面通知，撤销授权。

（5）凡雇员根据第（3）款撤销任何授权，雇主应在通知期满后停止扣款。

(6) 在每月汇款时,雇主应向注册工会提供——
(a) 一份规定格式的成员名单,列明需要扣款的成员姓名;
(b) 根据第(3)款发出的任何撤销通知的副本。

62. 工会代表

(1) 注册工会有权——
(a) 设工会代表 1 人,代表 1 至 9 名成员;
(b) 设工会代表 3 人,代表 10 至 20 名成员;
(c) 设工会代表 10 人,代表 21 至 100 名成员;
(d) 在成员超过 100 人的工作场所设 15 名代表。

[第 4 章第 8 条]

(2) 在会员人数超过 100 人的工作场所,至少有 5 名工会代表应代表受雇并加入工会的女雇员(如果有)。

(3) 注册工会的章程应对工会代表的选举、任期和免职作出规定。

(4) 工会代表应履行以下职能——
(a) 代表会员参加申诉和纪律听证会;
(b) 代表会员就规则作出陈述;
(c) 就工作场所的生产力问题进行咨询;
(d) 在监察员就劳工法进行的查询和调查中代表工会;
(e) 监督雇主遵守劳工法的情况;
(f) 根据工会章程履行工会职能;
(g) 促进友好关系;
(h) 履行雇主同意的任何职能或角色。

(5) 工会代表有权享受合理的带薪休假,以履行第(4)款提及的任何职能。

(6) 雇主应向工会代表披露与其履行职责有关的任何信息。

(7) 第 70 条与披露相关资料有关的条文,须比照适用于第(6)款所规定的任何披露。

(8) 本条规定的权利受任何合理条件的限制,以有序行使这些权利,并确保工作免受不适当的干扰。

63. 工会活动假期

雇主应给予以下人员合理的带薪假——
(a) 第 62 条所指的工会代表,以使其参加与其职能有关的培训课程;
(b) 以下机构的职务人员——
(i) 注册工会,以履行其官员的职能;
(ii) 代表工会所属的注册联合会,以履行其职责。

64. 行使组织权的程序

(1) 任何注册工会均可使用规定的表格通知雇主,以谋求行使本部分所赋予的权利。

(2) 在收到第(1)款规定的通知后 30 天内,雇主应与工会会面,以制定一项集体协议,授予该权利并规定行使该权利的方式。

(3) 如果未达成协议或雇主未能在 30 天内与工会会面,工会可将争议提交委员会调解。

(4) 如果调解未能解决争议,工会可将争议提交劳工法庭,劳工法庭应作出适当的裁决。

(5) 就根据本条发出的命令的解释或适用的任何争议应提交劳工法庭裁决。

65. 组织权利的终止

(1) 如果工会严重违反了行使组织权利的条款和条件,则雇主——

 (a) 可将问题提交委员会调解;

 (b) 如果调解未能解决问题,可向劳工法庭提出申请——

  (i) 终止集体协议赋予工会的组织权利;或者

  (ii) 撤销根据第 64 条发出的命令。

(2) 根据本条作出裁决的劳工法庭可下达任何适当的命令,包括——

 (a) 要求工会采取措施,确保遵守行使权利的条件;

 (b) 在一段时间内暂停行使某项权利;

 (c) 终止根据第 64 条制定的集体协议或命令中包含的组织权利。

第六部分
集 体 谈 判

66. 释义

就本部分而言——

 (a) "谈判单位"——

  (i) 指注册工会获认可或有权获认可为本部分规定的独家谈判代理的任何雇员单位;

  (ii) 包括受雇于一个以上雇主的雇员单位。

 (b) "经认可的工会"是指经集体协议认可或经劳动争议法庭根据第 67 条下达的命令认可的工会;

 (c) "注册工会"包括两个或两个以上联合行动的注册工会。

67. 获认可为雇员的独家谈判代理

(1) 已注册工会如代表有关谈判单位的多数雇员,则有权获认可为该单位雇员的独家谈判代理人。

(2) 雇主或雇主协会不得承认工会为独家谈判代理,除非该工会已注册并代表谈判单位中的大多数雇员。

(3) 注册工会可使用规定的表格通知雇主或雇主协会,其将谋求获认可为适当谈判单位内的独家谈判代理。

(4) 在第(3)款规定的通知发出后的 30 天内,雇主应开会达成认可工会的集体协议。

(5) 如果未达成协议或雇主未能在 30 天内与工会会面,工会可将争议提交委员会调解,经协商可延长 30 天期限。

(6) 如果调解未能解决争议,工会或雇主可将争议提交劳工法庭裁决。

(7) 劳工法庭可安排任何适当人员对受影响的雇员进行投票,就有关工会代表性的任何争议作出裁决。

（8）在确定谈判单位的适当性时,劳工法庭应——

（a）考虑以下因素：

（i）双方的意愿；

（ii）双方的谈判历史；

（iii）雇主之间或雇主的雇员之间的工会组织程度；

（iv）员工的利益相似性；

（v）雇主的组织结构；

（vi）雇主的不同职能和流程及其融合程度；

（vii）雇主的地理位置；

（b）促进有序、有效的集体谈判,尽量减少雇主组织结构的分散。

（9）就根据本条发布的命令的解释或适用产生的任何争议,应提交发布命令的当局或法院,由其作出解释并发布其他必要的命令。

（10）根据本条发出的任何命令,应与劳工法庭发出的任何其他命令同样执行。

（11）本条规定不妨碍注册工会、雇主和注册雇主协会通过集体协议建立自己的集体谈判安排。

[2010年第17号法案第9条]

68. 诚信谈判的义务

（1）雇主或雇主协会应本着诚意与经认可的工会进行谈判。

（2）获认可的工会应与已认可其或根据第67条规定必须认可其的雇主或雇主协会进行诚信的谈判。

69. 认可的撤销

（1）如果经认可的工会不再代表谈判单位中的大多数雇员,雇主应——

（a）在3个月内通知工会获得多数席位；

（b）如果工会在3个月期限届满时未能获得多数席位,则撤销对其的唯一认可。

（2）如果某个经认可的工会不再代表谈判单位中的大多数,任何其他工会均可填写规定的表格,以便获认可为唯一的谈判单位。

（3）凡第67条第（10）款规定的集体协议的一方或受认可令约束的一方严重违反该协议或命令,另一方可向劳工法庭提出申请,要求通过以下方式撤销该认可[第4章第8条]——

（a）终止认可协议；

（b）撤销认可令。

（4）劳工法庭可安排任何适当人员对受影响的雇员进行投票,就有关工会代表性的任何争议作出裁决。

（5）劳工法庭可下达任何适当的命令,包括——

（a）给予工会成为代表的机会；

（b）改变谈判单位；

（c）在一段时间内暂停认可；

（d）撤销认可。

[2010年第17号法案第10条]

70. 披露相关信息的义务

（1）根据本部分规定认可工会的雇主应允许工会有效地参与集体谈判。

（2）雇主没有义务披露以下信息——

（a）享有法律上的特权的信息；

（b）雇主不能披露，否则违反法律或法院命令的信息；

（c）属于机密，一旦泄露可能会对雇员或雇主造成重大伤害的信息；

（d）未经雇员同意可披露的，与该雇员有关的私人信息。

（3）根据本条规定接收机密或私人个人信息的工会——

（a）不得向其成员和顾问以外的任何人披露信息；

（b）应采取合理措施确保所披露信息的保密性。

（4）如对信息披露存在争议，争议的任何一方均可将争议提交委员会调解。[第4章第8条]

（5）如果调解未能解决争议，任何一方均可将争议提交劳工法庭裁决。

（6）在作出任何裁决时，劳工法庭可以——

（a）不公开审理；

（b）考虑工会或其会员以前违反保密规定的情况；

（c）如果在权衡利弊后，不披露的后果可能严重妨碍工会的能力，则命令雇主披露任何机密信息，以——

（i）有效地进行谈判；

（ii）有效地代表雇员；

（d）命令披露信息，以限制披露可能造成的任何损害；

（e）命令工会为任何违反保密规定的行为支付损害赔偿金；

（f）中止或撤销披露权。

71. 集体协议的约束性

（1）集体协议应采用书面形式并由双方签字。

（2）除非协议另有规定，否则集体协议在最后一次签字时即具有约束力。

（3）集体协议对以下各方具有约束力——

（a）协议各方；

（b）协议各方的任何成员；

（c）任何非协议一方工会会员的雇员，如果该工会根据第67条被认可为该等雇员的独家谈判代理。

（4）集体协议应继续对在协议生效时为协议一方的雇主或雇员具有约束力，包括从该工会或雇主协会辞职的会员。

（5）集体协议对在协议生效后成为协议各方成员的雇主和雇员具有约束力。

（6）除非集体协议另有规定，协议的任何一方均可在发出合理通知后终止协议，并应说明终止的理由。

（7）集体协议各方必须向劳工专员提交一份协议副本，可推定以这种方式登记的副本是真实的，并可作为法院的一项法令予以执行。

[2006年第8号法案附录；2010年第17号法案第11条]

72. 受雇人和工会之间的集体协议

（1）强制雇员成为工会成员的协议不具有法律的执行力。

（2）被认可的工会和雇主可签订集体协议,对工会代理制企业做出规定。

（3）具有约束力的受雇人和工会之间集体协议的要求如下——

  （a）该协议仅适用于谈判单位的雇员；

  （b）不属工会成员的雇员不得被强制成为工会成员；

  （c）从非工会成员雇员的薪酬中扣除的任何代理费相当于或少于雇主从工会成员薪酬中扣除的工会会费；

  （d）从工会成员和非工会成员处扣除的金额应存入工会管理的单独账户；

  （e）该账户中的资金只能用于促进或维护该工作场所雇员的社会经济利益,不得用于——

    （i）向政党支付入党费；或者

    （ii）任何对政党的捐赠或竞选政治职务的人的捐赠。

（4）尽管有任何法律或合同的规定,雇主仍可根据符合本条规定的受雇人和工会之间的集体协议,从雇员的工资中扣除代理费,且无须征得该雇员的同意；

但这种扣除必须符合条例规定的条款和条件。

（5）签订受雇人和工会之间集体协议的工会应——

  （a）任命一名注册审计师,负责审计第（3）条第（d）款规定的账户；

  （b）在报告发出之日起30天内向劳工专员及注册官提交审计报告；和

  （c）允许任何利益相关者在办公时间内在工会办公室查阅报告。

（6）工会根据本条任命的审计师所作的报告,应包括对本条规定是否已获遵守的意见。

（7）受雇人和工会之间的集体协议应——

  （a）只要工会不具有代表性,则应暂停；

  （b）一旦根据第69条认可被撤销,则应终止。

（8）凡受雇人和工会之间的集体协议被暂停或终止,本条的条文应继续适用于第（3）条第（d）款所规定的账户内的任何剩余款项。［第4章第8条］

（9）就本条而言,"工会代理制企业"是指一种工会保障安排,根据这种安排,谈判单位中的雇员如不属于获认可的工会成员,则必须向工会支付代理费。

［2015第24号法案第8条］

73. 工人参与协议

（1）经认可的工会和雇主或雇主协会可签订集体协议,以在工作场所设立一个职工参与论坛。

（2）如果注册工会、雇主或雇主协会希望在任何工作场所设立一个职工参与论坛,该工会、雇主或协会可请求劳工专员协助促进工会、雇主或协会之间的讨论。

（3）劳工专员应在考虑理事会公布的关于职工参与的任何良好行为守则的情况下,促进关于在任何工作场所设立职工参与论坛的讨论。

［2015年第24号法案第9条；第4章第8条］

74. 有关集体协议的争议

除非集体协议各方另有约定,否则——

(a) 有关集体协议适用、解释或执行的争议应提交委员会调解;和

(b) 如果调解失败,任何一方均可将争议提交劳工法庭裁决。

第七部分
罢工和停工

75. 罢工和停工的权利

(1) 在符合本部分规定的情况下——

(a) 每个雇员都有权就利益争议参加罢工;和

(b) 每个雇主都有权因利益争议而停工。

76. 对罢工或停工权利的限制

(1) 在以下情况下,任何人不得参加罢工或停工,或以任何方式做出打算或推动罢工或停工的行为——

(a) 在符合第(2)款规定的情况下,该人从事的是第77条所述的基本服务;

(b) 该人从事的是第79条规定的最低限度的服务;

(c) 该人受协议约束,该协议要求将争议问题提交仲裁;

(d) 该人受规范争议问题的集体协议或仲裁裁决的约束;

(e) 在确定工资的第一年内,该人受规范争议问题的工资确定办法的约束;

(f) 该人是治安法官、检察官或其他法院工作人员;

(g) 争议问题属于申诉;

(h) 第80、81和82条规定的程序未得到遵守。

(2) 尽管有第(1)条第(a)款的规定,在以下情况下,从事基本服务的人可罢工或停工——

(a) 有一项集体协议规定了罢工或停工期间的最低服务;和

(b) 该协议已由基本服务委员会根据第77条批准。

(3) 禁止以下与罢工和停工有关的行为:

(a) 纠察——

(i) 支持罢工;或者

(ii) 反对合法停工;

(b) 在停工或合法罢工期间使用替代劳工;

(c) 将雇主禁锢在办公场所内;

(d) 阻止雇主进入办公场所。

(4) 就本条而言,"替代劳工"是指在罢工或停工期间雇用任何人以继续或维持生产,但不包括调派雇员从事罢工或被停工雇员的工作,除非调派雇员征得该雇员的同意。[第4章第8条]

77. 基本服务

(1) 就本条而言,"服务"包括任何种类的服务。

(2) 以下服务是基本服务——

(a) 水和卫生设施;

(b) 电;

(c) 保健服务和相关实验室服务;

(d) 消防服务;

(e) 空中交通管制和民用航空电信;

(f) 提供上述服务所需的任何运输服务。

(3) 除第(2)款指定的服务外,如果某项服务的中断会危及民众或部分民众的人身安全或健康,则基本服务委员会可指定该项服务为基本服务。

(4) 在基本服务委员会根据第(3)款指定一项基本服务之前,它应——

(a) 以规定的方式发出调查通知,邀请有关各方进行陈述;

(b) 以规定的方式进行调查;

(c) 提供任何书面陈述以供查阅;

(d) 举行公开听证会,有关各方可在会上作口头陈述;和

(e) 审议上述陈述。

(5) 当基本服务委员会指定某项服务为基本服务时,它应在《公报》上为此刊登公告。

[第4章第8条]

(6) 基本服务委员会可按照第(4)和第(5)款规定的程序比照更改或取消根据本条作出的指定。

(7) 关于某项服务是否属于基本服务或雇主或雇员是否从事基本服务的争议,争议的任何一方应将争议提交基本服务委员会裁决。

(8) 将争议提交基本服务委员会的一方应使委员会确信,争议副本已送达争议各方。

(9) 基本服务委员会应尽快对争议作出裁决。

78. 基本服务权益争议

(1) 除非集体协议另有规定,否则——

(a) 基本服务权益争议的任何一方,可将争议提交委员会调解。

(b) 如果调解失败,争议的任何一方可将争议提交委员会仲裁。

(2) 第(1)款的规定在以下情况下适用——

(a) 双方受集体协议的约束,该协议规定了罢工或停工期间的最低限度的服务;和

(b) 基本服务委员会已根据第79条第(2)款批准该协议。

79. 罢工或停工期间的最低限度服务

(1) 集体协议各方可商定在罢工或停工期间提供最低限度服务。

(2) 集体协议的任何一方,如规定在罢工或停工期间提供基本服务的最低限度,均可以规定的方式向基本服务委员会申请批准该协议。

(3) 在以下情况下,雇主可按规定的方式向基本服务委员会申请指定某项最低限度服务——

(a) 在罢工或合法停工期间,为防止财产、机器或厂房受到损害,有必要提供最低限度服务;和

(b) 没有规定罢工或停工期间最低限度服务的集体协议。

80. 参与合法罢工的程序

(1) 在遵守本条规定的前提下,雇员可以在以下情况下举行合法罢工——

(a) 争议属于权益争议;

(b) 该争议已按既定格式提交委员会调解；

(c) 根据与第 87 条第(1)和第(2)款一并解读的第 86 条第(4)款规定的调解期结束时，争议仍未解决；

(d) 该罢工是由工会发起的，且工会根据工会章程进行了投票，大多数投票者赞成罢工；和

(e) 在第(c)项所述的适用期限过后，雇员或其工会已提前 48 小时通知雇主其罢工的意图。

(2) 如争议涉及单方面更改雇佣条款和条件，雇员和工会可在根据第(1)款提交争议时要求雇主[第 4 章第 8 条]——

(a) 不实施对条款和条件的任何拟定变更；或者

(b) 如果雇主已实施变更，则需恢复变更前适用的雇佣条款和条件。

(3) 如雇主在收到转介后 48 小时内未遵守第(2)款所述的要求，雇员和工会可在不遵守第(1)款第(c)项至(e)项的情况下举行罢工。[第 4 章第 8 条]

(4) 本条的规定不妨碍工会与雇主或雇主协会在集体协议中商定各自的罢工程序，在这种情况下，该协议的规定应予适用，而第(1)款至第(3)款的规定则不适用。

81. 参与二次罢工的程序

(1) "二次罢工"是指以下罢工——

(a) 支持其他雇员针对其雇主（"主要雇主"）的合法罢工（"主要罢工"）；或者

(b) 反对另一雇主（"主要雇主"）对其雇员实施的停工（"主要停工"）。

(2) 工会只有在以下情况下才可号召二次罢工——

(a) 通知第二雇主 14 天内开启二次罢工；

(b) 第二雇主和第一雇主之间存在允许施加压力的关系；

(c) 二次罢工是成比例的，考虑到以下因素——

(i) 罢工对第二雇主的影响；

(ii) 罢工对解决引起初次罢工或初次停工的争议可能产生的影响。

(3) 从事以下服务的雇员不得参与二次罢工：

(a) 第 77 条所述的基本服务，而该等服务并未在第 79 条第(2)款规定获批的集体协议范围之内；或者

(b) 第 79 条规定的商定或确定的最低限度服务。

(4) 本条规定不妨碍工会与雇主或雇主协会在集体协议中约定各自的要求和程序，在这种情况下，该协议的规定应予适用，而第(1)款和第(2)款的规定则不适用。

82. 合法停工的程序

(1) 在符合第(2)款规定的情况下，雇主可以实施以下合法的停工行为——

(a) 争议属于权益争议；

(b) 该争议已按规定格式提交委员会调解；

(c) 在第 86 和 87 条规定的调解期结束时，争议仍未解决；

(d) 在第(c)款所述的适用期结束后，雇主或雇主协会已在 48 小时内向雇员或其工会发出停工意向通知。

(2) 本条规定不妨碍工会与雇主或雇主协会在集体协议中商定各自的程序,在这种情况下,应适用该协议的规定,而不适用第(1)款的规定。

83. 合法罢工或停工的保护性质

(1) 尽管有任何其他法律(包括普通法)的规定,合法罢工或合法停工不属于——
 (a) 违反合同;
 (b) 侵权行为;
 (c) 刑事犯罪。

(2) 雇主不得因以下原因终止雇佣合同——
 (a) 雇员参加合法罢工;或者
 (b) 雇员在停工期间不同意雇主的要求。

(3) 不得对参加合法罢工或合法停工的任何人提起民事或刑事诉讼。

(4) 尽管有第(1)款的规定,雇主没有义务为雇员在合法罢工或合法停工期间未提供的服务支付酬劳,但是——
 (a) 在罢工或停工期间,雇主应继续向法律或雇佣合同规定雇员应归属的任何基金缴款其和雇员的费用;
 (b) 如果雇主提供食宿或其他基本生活保障,在罢工或停工期间,雇主应继续提供此类保障;
 (c) 罢工或停工结束后,雇主可以——
  (i) 从雇员薪酬中扣除(a)项所述的雇员费用;
  (ii) 在雇员同意的情况下,从雇员的薪酬中扣除食宿或便利设施的约定货币价值。

(5) 如雇员不同意第(4)款第(c)项第(ii)目规定的扣除,雇主可将争议提交调解。

(6) 如果第(5)款提及的争议未得到解决,雇主可将其提交劳工法庭裁决。

(7) 第(4)款中的任何规定均不得妨碍工会或雇主或雇主协会缔结一项集体协议,对该款中涉及的事项作出不同的规定。

84. 罢工和停工不遵守本部分的规定

(1) 如果罢工或停工不符合本法的规定,或者工会或雇主或雇主协会从事被禁止的行为,劳工法庭拥有专属管辖权——
 (a) 发出禁制令,禁止任何人作出以下行为——
  (i) 参加非法罢工或停工;
  (ii) 从事任何被禁止的行为;
 (b) 要求对可归因于以下情况的罢工、停工等行为而造成的任何损失支付公平赔偿金——
  (i) 故障程度;
  (ii) 罢工、停工或被禁止的行为发生的原因;
  (iii) 先前的违规记录;
  (iv) 支付能力;
  (v) 伤害的程度;

（ⅵ）集体谈判的利益；

（ⅶ）罢工、停工或被禁止的行为的持续时间。

（2）劳工法庭签发禁止令应提前48小时通知被告。

（3）尽管有第(2)款的规定，法院仍可根据正当理由批准较短的期限，但必须给予被告合理的陈述机会。

（4）除特殊情况外，劳工法庭不得下达可能导致工会、雇主或雇主协会破产的赔偿令。

85. 抗议行动

（1）在不违反第(2)款规定的情况下，雇员可在下列情况下参加抗议行动——

（a）抗议行动是由注册工会或注册工会联合会发起的；

（b）工会或联合会已向理事会发出通知，说明——

（ⅰ）采取抗议行动的理由；和

（ⅱ）抗议行动的期限和形式；

（c）自本通知发出之日起30天后；和

（d）工会或联合会至少在抗议行动开始前14天发出通知。

（2）从事以下服务的雇员不得参与抗议行动：

（a）第77条中所述的基本服务，而该等服务不在第79条第(2)款规定获批的集体协议范围之内；或者

（b）第79条规定的约定或确定的最低限度服务。

（3）理事会应在通知发出后30天内召开会议，以——

（a）解决引起抗议行动的问题；和

（b）如果无法解决问题，确保与要求采取抗议行动的工会或工会联合会就抗议行动的持续时间和形式达成协议，以尽量减少抗议行动可能造成的伤害。

（4）为实现第(3)款规定的目标，理事会可——

（a）成立三方委员会，履行第(3)款规定的职能；

（b）在与委员会协商后任命一名调解员进行调解；

（c）向劳工法庭申请第(5)款规定的宣告令。

（5）任何可能受到或已经受到抗议行动影响的人可向劳工法庭提出申请，要求——

（a）命令限制任何人参加抗议行动，或参与任何不符合本法第(1)款和第(2)款规定的行动的预谋或推进行为。

（b）考虑到以下因素，就建议采取的任何行动的相关性发出宣告令——

（ⅰ）抗议行动的性质和持续时间；

（ⅱ）抗议行动理由的重要性；和

（ⅲ）工会或联合会为尽量减少抗议行动造成的伤害而采取的措施。

（6）在不违反第(7)款规定的情况下，任何参加符合本条规定的抗议行动的人都享有第83条赋予合法罢工的保护。

（7）第(6)款赋予参与合法抗议行动的人的保护，不适用于不遵守根据第(5)款第(b)项签发的宣告令的人。

第八部分
争议解决

A 子部分：调解

86. 根据本法规定将争议提交调解

（1）提交给委员会的争议应采用规定的格式。

（2）根据第（1）款提交争议的一方应使委员会确信，已将提交争议的副本送达争议的其他各方。

（3）在收到根据规定第（1）款提交的争议时，委员会应——
 （a）任命一名调解员调解争议；
 （b）决定调解听证会的时间、日期和地点；
 （c）告知争议各方第（a）项和第（b）项规定的详细信息。

（4）在不违反第 87 条规定的情况下，调解员应在移交后 30 天内或各方书面同意的任何更长期限内解决争议。

（5）调解员应决定调解方式，必要时可要求在第（4）款所述期限内举行进一步会议。

（6）在任何调解中，争议一方可由以下人员代表——
 （a）该党工会或雇主协会的成员或官员；
 （b）辩护人；或者
 （c）当事人自己选择的个人代表。

（7）如调解员未能在第（4）款规定的限期内解决某项争议，争议的任何一方可以——
 （a）如果争议是权益争议，则应根据第 80 或 82 条的规定，发出其打算开始罢工或停工的通知；
 （b）如果争议是申诉——
  （i）将申诉提交仲裁；或者
  （ii）将申诉提交劳工法庭。

（8）即使未能在第（4）款规定的期限内解决争议，调解员仍应继续处理争议，直至争议得到解决，并可在任何罢工、停工、仲裁或裁决之前或期间召集争议各方开会，以解决争议。

[2006 年第 8 号法案附录]

87. 不出席调解听证会的后果

（1）如果雇员或工会根据第 86 条向委员会提交权益争议，调解员可以——
 （a）如果雇员或工会未能出席委员会安排的听证会，则将第 86 条第（4）款的期限再延长 30 天；
 （b）如果争议一方的雇主或雇主协会未出席听证会，则缩短第 86 条第（4）款规定的期限。

（2）如果雇主或雇主协会根据第 86 条向委员会提交权益争议时，调解员可以——
 （a）如果雇主或雇主协会未出席委员会安排的听证会，则将第 86 条第（4）款的期限再延长 30 天；

(b) 如果争议一方的雇员或工会未出席听证会,则缩短第86条第(4)款规定的期限。
 (3) 对于根据本法移交的投诉,调解员可以——
  (a) 如果投诉人未出席调解听证会,则驳回申诉;
  (b) 如果投诉的另一方未能出席调解听证会,则对投诉作出裁决。
 (4) 根据本条作出的决定可作为有管辖权的法院的判决在劳工法庭予以执行。
 (5) 在以下情况下,委员会可推翻根据本条作出的决定——
  (a) 申请是以规定的方式提出的;和
  (b) 委员会确信不出席听证会的理由正当。

B子部分:仲裁

88. 通过强制仲裁解决争议
 (1) 就本条而言,争议是指——
  (a) 权益争议,如果争议各方从事的是基本服务;
  (b) 对以下方面的投诉——
   (i) 雇员被解雇的公正性或合法性;
   (ii) 任何其他违反本法或任何其他劳动法的行为或违约行为,或属于普通法、侵权责任和替代责任范畴的任何就业或劳动事项;
   (iii) 劳工法庭根据第94条第(3)款第(a)项第(ii)目提交仲裁的任何争议。
 (2) 如各方未能根据第86条提交调解解决争议,则委员会应[第4章第8条]——
  (a) 指定一名仲裁员裁决争议;
  (b) 确定仲裁听证的时间、日期和地点;和
  (c) 将第(a)项或第(b)项规定的细节告知争议各方。
 (3) 第(2)款的规定并不妨碍委员会——
  (a) 在调解争议之前任命仲裁员;
  (b) 确定仲裁听证的时间、日期和地点,该日期可与调解听证的日期一致;
  (c) 将第(a)款和第(b)款规定的细节告知争议各方。
 (4) 仲裁员——
  (a) 可以其认为适当的方式进行仲裁,以便公平、迅速地裁决争议;
  (b) 应以最少的法律手续解决争议的实质问题。
 (5) 根据仲裁员对诉讼程序适当形式的自由裁量权,争议一方可以提供证据、传唤证人、询问证人和提出论点。
 (6) 如争议各方同意,仲裁员可暂停仲裁程序,通过调解解决争议。[第4章第8条]
 (7) 调解员可以根据当事人之间的协议或当事人的申请,就其面前的任何未决争议拟定和解协议,该协议应由当事人和调解员签署,该协议应视为法院的判令。
 (8) 如果一方当事人未能——
  (a) 出席任何仲裁员召集的仲裁程序,可根据《劳动机构(调解)规则》第28条的规定单独审理该事项;[2007年第67号政府公号]或者
  (b) 遵守仲裁员作出的任何指示,仲裁员应着手作出裁决。

（9）在任何仲裁听证中，争议一方可由以下人员代理——

（a）该方工会或雇主协会的成员或官员；

（b）辩护人；或者

（c）当事人自己选择的个人代表。

（10）仲裁员可作出任何适当的裁决，但除非一方当事人或代表一方当事人的人行为轻率或无理取闹，否则仲裁员不得作出缴付诉讼费的命令。

（11）在仲裁程序结束后30天内，仲裁员应签发裁决书并说明理由。

[2006年第8号法案附录；2010年第17号法案第12条]

89. 仲裁裁决的效力

（1）根据本法作出的仲裁裁决对争议各方具有约束力。

（2）根据本法作出的仲裁裁决可作为法庭的判决在劳工法庭送达和执行。

90. 仲裁裁决的更正

根据第88条第(10)款作出裁决的仲裁员，可根据申请或主动更正裁决书中的任何笔误或因意外疏忽或遗漏而造成的错误。

[2010年第17号法案第13条]

91. 仲裁裁决的修订

（1）根据第88条第(10)款作出的仲裁裁决的任何一方，如声称委员会主持的任何仲裁程序存在缺陷，可在以下时间内，向劳工法庭申请撤销该仲裁裁决——

（a）裁决书送达申请人之日起6周内，除非所称缺陷涉及不当采购；

（b）如果所称缺陷涉及不当程序，则在申请人发现该事实之日起6周内。

（2）劳工法庭可撤销根据本法作出的以下裁决，理由是——

（a）仲裁员行为不当；

（b）该裁决是以不正当手段获得的；

（c）裁决不合法、不合逻辑或不合理。

（3）劳工法庭可在作出裁决之前暂缓执行裁决。

（4）如果裁决被撤销，劳工法庭可——

（a）以其认为适当的方式裁定争议；

（b）就裁定争议所应遵循的程序下达其认为适当的命令。

[2010年第17号法案第14条]

92. 仲裁的适用

《仲裁法》不适用于委员会进行的仲裁。

[第15章]

93. 自愿仲裁法

（1）本法的任何规定均不妨碍将争议提交仲裁的协议。

（2）《仲裁法》的规定应适用于任何同意将争议提交仲裁的情况，条件是——

（a）尽管有《仲裁法》第3条的规定，任何争议均可提交仲裁；[第4章第8条]

（b）《仲裁法》中涉及提交高等法院的情形，应解释为提交劳工法庭。

（3）根据《劳动机构法》第14条第(1)款第(b)项第(ii)目提出的自愿仲裁应由委员会处

理,如同根据第 88 条第(2)款至第(9)款提及的强制仲裁。[第 300 章]

[2010 年第 17 号法案第 15 条;第 15 章]

C 子部分:裁决

94. 劳工法庭的管辖权

(1) 在不违反 1977 年《坦桑尼亚联合共和国宪法》的情况下,劳工法庭对本法条款的适用、解释和执行,以及属于普通法、侵权责任、替代责任或违约的任何就业或劳工事项,拥有专属管辖权,并有权决定——

 (a) 对注册官根据第四部分作出的决定提出上诉;

 (b) 审查和修订——

  (i) 仲裁员根据本部分条款作出的裁决;

  (ii) 基本服务委员会根据第七部分作出的决定;

 (c) 审查决定、法规、准则或部长根据本法制定的条例;

 (d) 投诉,但根据本法规定由仲裁决定的投诉除外;

 (e) 任何本法规定的劳工法庭处理的争议;和

 (f) 适用,包括——

  (i) 就本法的任何规定发出的宣告令;或者

  (ii) 禁令。

(2) 在下列情况下,劳工法庭可拒绝审理申诉——

 (a) 申诉未根据第 86 条规定提交委员会调解;或者

 (b) 该条的规定没有得到遵守;和

 (c) 申请并非紧急事项。

(3) 如果一方当事人将争议提交给劳工法庭,法庭可——

 (a) 如果根据本法,该争议需要劳动争议法庭——

  (i) 裁决争议;或者

  (ii) 将争议提交委员会通过仲裁决定;

 (b) 如果该申诉是必须提交仲裁的申诉——

  (i) 将申诉提交委员会,由委员会根据第 88 条进行处理;

  (ii) 对申诉作出裁决,但可以就费用问题下达适当的命令。

[2006 年第 8 号法案附录;2010 年第 17 号法案第 16 条]

D 子部分:集体协议中的争议程序

95. 集体协议中的争议解决程序

(1) 本部分的任何规定均不妨碍以工会为一方与以雇主或雇主协会为另一方缔结集体协议,以解决本部分规定之外的争议。

(2) 集体协议可偏离本部分的规定,但必须以独立、中立、快速和专业的方式对争议进行调解或仲裁。

(3) 受本条规定的集体协议约束的人不得根据本部分的规定将争议提交调解与仲裁委员会:

但任何未解决的争议均应由争议的任何一方或调解员或仲裁员提交劳工法庭裁决、裁定和执行。

（4）在不违反第（3）款规定的情况下，调解员或仲裁员分别作出的任何决议或通过的任何裁决对各方均具有约束力，并应作为劳工法庭的判决执行。

（5）经申请，劳工法庭可撤销集体协议中不符合第（2）款规定的条款。

[2006年第8号法案附录]

第九部分
一 般 规 定

96. 雇主和雇员应保存的记录

（1）所有雇主和雇员都应保存以下信息的记录——
  （a）第15条规定的书面细节及对这些细节的任何更改；
  （b）支付给雇员的任何薪酬。

（2）每名雇主应在雇员被解雇后5年内保留第（1）款规定的该雇员的记录。

（3）雇主应将涉及其雇员的任何罢工、停工或抗议行动的规定细节记录在案。

（4）劳工专员可以规定的方式要求雇主提供基于本部分所述记录的信息。

（5）雇主应向劳工专员提交第（4）款所要求的任何信息。

（6）在不违反第101条规定的情况下，劳工专员可——
  （a）对根据本条提交信息收集的统计数据进行汇编、分析和制表；和
  （b）根据部长的指示公布这些统计数据。

97. 文件送达

（1）在任何民事或刑事诉讼中，要求送达的已登记组织或联合会的文件，在以下情况下应视为已妥为送达——
  （a）送交该组织或联合会的注册办事处；
  （b）用挂号邮递方式送达其邮政地址；或者
  （c）亲自送达该组织或联合会的官员。

（2）就本条而言，"文件"包括根据本法要求送达的任何通知、转交、呈件、申请或其他文件。

98. 条例

（1）部长可与理事会协商，为执行或落实本法的原则和规定而制定条例和表格。

（2）在不影响第（1）款所赋予权力的一般前提下，部长可特别就以下事项制定条例：
  （a）本法规定或要求规定的所有事项；
  （b）禁止或管制雇用18岁以下儿童；
  （c）登记消除工作场所歧视的计划；
  （d）向雇员提供书面雇佣详情的形式和方式；
  （e）规范工资支付，包括向已故雇员的继承人支付的该雇员应得的任何款项或该雇员的遗产；
  （f）信息的形式和内容，以及雇主向雇员提供的文件；

(g) 规定组织和联合会的注册程序、应保存的登记簿和注册证书；
(h) 授权工会官员进入雇主办公场所进行招聘、会面和代表成员；
(i) 扣除工会会费，包括授权和向注册工会汇款；
(j) 认可已注册工会的程序；
(k) 向劳工专员提交集体协议；
(l) 基本服务委员会对基本服务和最低限度服务进行调查的程序；
(m) 根据本法应保存的账簿、记录、账目和其他文件；
(n) 雇主须向劳工专员提供的资料；
(o) 雇主须向劳工专员提交的申报表；
(p) 为注册或本法规定或允许的任何其他服务或事项而收取的费用；
(q) 通过适当的检查制度确保职业安全和健康标准以及工作环境；和
(r) 与本法具体提及的事项或主题相关的所有附带事项。

(3) 部长在与理事会协商后，可通过在《公报》上发布公告，基于本节、本法任何条款或部长负责的任何其他成文法的目的，将任何类别的人员视为雇员。

99. 准则和良好行为守则

(1) 部长在征求理事会意见之后，可——
  (a) 发布良好行为守则；
  (b) 发布指导原则，以便本法的执行；
  (c) 更改或取代任何行为准则或指导方针。

(2) 任何良好行为准则或指导方针，或对行为准则或指导方针的任何修改或替换，均应在《公报》上公布。

(3) 任何人在解释或应用本条款时，应考虑到根据本条公布的任何良好行为准则或指导方针，如果该人偏离该行为准则或指导方针，则应说明偏离的理由。

100. 豁免

(1) 部长可豁免任何雇主或任何类别的雇主遵守第19、20、23至25、27、31至34、41、42和43条所载的任何就业标准。

(2) 在部长根据本条授予豁免之前——
  (a) 雇主或雇主组织应向部长证明，其已与受豁免影响的雇员或其注册工会进行了协商；
  (b) 部长应将任何豁免建议通知受影响的雇主和雇员或其注册组织，并要求他们在合理期限内提交申述；
  (c) 部长应考虑雇员或其注册工会提出的申述；
  (d) 部长应在考虑适用的国际劳工组织公约或建议的情况下，公平兼顾雇主和雇员的利益。

(3) 根据第(1)款授予的豁免应符合以下条件——
  (a) 采用部长规定的格式，该格式应包括受豁免影响的雇主或雇主类别的声明；
  (b) 包括授予豁免的任何条件；
  (c) 说明豁免期限，可追溯至不早于申请豁免之日的日期；和
  (d) 如果豁免的对象是某类雇主，则该豁免应在《公报》上公布。

（4）部长可修改或撤销根据本条授予的豁免。

（5）如果豁免已根据第（3）款第（d）项在《公报》上公布，部长只能通过在《公报》上发布公告，从该公告所述日期起修改或撤销豁免。

（6）任何人如对豁免的批准、修改或撤销或其条款或期限不服，均可向劳工法庭申请对该决定进行复审。

101. 保密

（1）根据第（2）款的规定，任何人披露与他人财务或商业事务有关的任何信息，如果该信息是在履行本法规定的任何职能或行使本法规定的任何权力时获得的，即属犯罪。

（2）下列未按本法披露信息的情形，不适用于第（1）款规定——

（a）使人能依据本法履行职能或行使权力；

（b）根据任何成文法；

（c）为适当执行本法之目的；

（d）为司法行政之目的。

102. 处罚

（1）地方法院和驻地治安法院有权对本法规定的罪行处以刑罚。

（2）任何被判定犯有第5和第6条所述罪行的人，可被判处——

（a）500万先令以下的罚款；

（b）监禁一年；或者

（c）同时处以罚款和监禁。

（3）任何被判定犯有第7、8和9条所述任何罪行的人，可被处以500万先令以下的罚款。

（4）任何被判定犯有第27、28、45条第（3）款和第101条所述任何罪行的人，应被处以100万先令以下的罚款。

（5）任何人如对法院根据本条作出的裁决不服，可向高等法院提出上诉。

102A. 与成文法不一致

如果本法与其他任何有关就业标准的成文法发生冲突，应以本法规定的标准为准。

[2015年第24号法案第10条]

103. 法律的废除和修订以及保留条款

（1）在附表3所列的保留和过渡性条款的限制下，附表2所提及的法律被废除。

（2）附表2所提及的每项法律均在该附表所提及的范围内予以修订。

（3）附表3规定了从第（1）款废止的法律的实施到本法规定事项的实施的过渡。

附件1

（根据第26条第（1）款制定）

可比工资率计算表

就本表而言——

"正常工时"不包括加班工时；

"平日"是指雇员在一个星期内通常工作的天数,不包括在第 24 条规定的每周休息日内的任何一天；

"工资率"以雇员的基本工资为基础。

表——可比工资率的计算

付款基础	计算小时费率	计算日费率	计算周费率	计算月费率
基本工资按小时计算的雇员		小时费率乘以每天正常工作小时数	小时费率乘以每周正常工作小时数	计算周费率,然后将计算出的周费率乘以 4 333
基本工资按日计算的雇员	日费率除以每天正常工作小时数		日费率乘以每周正常工作天数	计算周费率,然后将计算出的周费率乘以 4 333
基本工资按周计算的雇员	周费率（或计算出的周费率）除以每周正常工作小时数	周费率（或计算出的周费率）除以每周正常工作天数		周费率（或计算出的周费率）乘以 4 333
基本工资按月计算的雇员	月费率除以 4 333 乘以每周正常工作小时数	月费率除以 4 333 乘以每周正常工作天数	月费率除以 4 333	

附件 2

（根据第 103 条第（1）款制定）

引 用 法 律	废除范围
《雇佣条例》(第 366 章)	整个
《工资和雇佣条款条例》(第 300 章)	整个
1974 年《工资和薪金（总修订）法》(1974 年第 22 号法案)	整个
1998 年《工会法》(1998 年第 10 号法案)	整个
《就业保障法》(第 574 章)	整个
《离职津贴法》(第 487 章)	整个
1967 年《坦桑尼亚工业法院法》(1967 年第 41 号法案)	整个

附件 3

（根据第 103 条第(2)、(3)款制定）
保留和过渡条款

1. 释义

在本附表中,除非上下文另有规定,否则——

"雇主组织"指根据《工会法》注册的雇主组织;

"联合会"指根据《工会法》注册的联合会;

"被废除的法律"指根据第 103 条第(1)款被废除并列于附表 2 的法律;[第 4 章第 8 条]

"工会"指根据《工会法》注册的工会;

"工会法"指 1998 年《工会法》。[1998 年第 10 号法案]

[1998 年第 10 号法案]

2. 现有工会、雇主组织和联合会

(1) 在本法生效前根据被废除的法律注册的工会、雇主组织或联合会,应被视为根据本法注册。

(2) 在本法生效后,注册官应在可行的情况下尽快——

 (a) 将工会、雇主组织和联合会的名称和详细资料录入根据本法第 48 条第(5)款第(a)项规定的适当登记册;

 (b) 根据本法第 48 条第(5)款第(b)项的规定,向(a)项所述的工会、雇主组织和联合会颁发证书。

(3) 如果工会、雇主组织或联合会章程的任何规定不符合本法第 46 和 47 条的要求,工会、雇主组织或联合会应在本法生效后 6 个月内更正其章程,并将更正内容提交给登记官。

(4) 第 50 条的规定,应比照适用于第(3)款所指的更正。

(5) 如果工会、雇主组织或联合会未能遵守第(3)款的规定,或未能做出必要的改变,注册官应向劳工法庭申请取消工会、雇主组织或联合会的注册,因为其未能遵守本款的规定以及本法第 46 条和第 47 条的规定。

(6) 第 55 条应比照适用于根据第(5)款提出的申请。

3. 待处理的注册申请

(1) 任何根据被废除的法律提出的注册、更改名称或章程的待决申请,应视同根据本法提出的申请处理。

(2) 在处理第(1)款所述的申请时,注册官可——

 (a) 宽恕技术上不遵守本法的行为;

 (b) 要求申请人修改其申请,以符合本法的规定。

4. 组织权利和承认

(1) 就本款而言——

 (a) "组织权利"是指下列任何权利:

  (i) 在工作场所代表工会的权利,包括成立委员会或外地分会的权利;

  (ii) 在工作场所为工会代表提供便利的权利;

  (iii) 信息披露权;

  (iv) 扣除工会会费和税款的权利;

  (v) 为招募会员、会见会员和代表会员而进入雇主办公场所的权利;

 (b) "认可"是指根据已废除的法律,为就雇佣条款和条件进行谈判而认可工会的任何协议或惯例。

(2) 工会应保留以下被授予的组织性权利——

（a）所有过去3年间被废除的法律；

（b）本法生效时有效的任何集体协议，直至协议期满，但如果协议在本法生效后2年内期满，则协议应再延长1年，视同被废除的法律未被废除。

（3）在本法生效之前，根据被废除的法律提交给劳工官员的任何争议，应按被废除的法律未被废除的情况处理。

（4）如果一个工会在本法生效时得到认可，雇主应在3年内继续认可该工会，除非另一个工会根据第67条被认可为独家谈判代理。

（5）根据已废除的法律授予的任何组织权利或承认的任何争议应由劳工法庭裁决，视同被废除的法律未被废除。

5. 协商或自愿协议

（1）在本法生效之前通过谈判达成的或自愿达成的任何协议，无论是否已由劳工法庭根据已废除的法律进行了注册，在协议期满之前都具有约束力，条件是——

（a）如果协议在本法生效1年后到期，则协议在该年年底到期。

（b）在符合第4条第（2）款第（b）项规定的情况下，任何此类协议的续签均应根据本法的规定进行。

（2）因适用、解释或执行第（1）款规定的协议而产生的任何争议，应由劳工法庭裁决，视同被废除的法律未被废除。

6. 就业条例

尽管《就业条例》已被废除，但是该条例第100条和第102条有关"提供药品及医疗"和"已故雇员及受养人的殡葬"的条文继续适用，直至被另一法律废除为止。

7. 工业法庭裁决

（1）在符合第（3）款规定的情况下，在本法生效之前发生的、在被废除的法律中规定的任何贸易争议，应按这些法律未被废除的情况处理。

（2）在符合第（3）款规定的情况下，在本法生效前，根据《坦桑尼亚工业法院法》第4条提交给工业法庭或根据该法第8条作为贸易调查提交给法院的任何贸易争议，应按这些法律未被废除的情况处理。

（3）尽管有第（1）款和第（2）款的规定，在本法生效后开始的罢工或停工应根据本法处理。

（4）对工业法庭所作裁决的任何修订或解释，应视同被废除的法律未被废除的情况处理。

（5）工业法庭根据被废除的法律作出的任何裁决在裁决期满之前仍然有效。

8. 提交调解委员会

在本法生效之前发生的关于即时解雇或纪律处分的情形，应按被废除的法律未被废除的情况处理。[第4章第8条]

9. 提交劳工官员的争议

在本法生效之前出现的被废除的法律中所涉及的任何争议，应按被废除的法律未被废除的情况处理。

10. 涉及部长

凡提及被废除的法律所指定的部长时，应按被废除的法律未被废除的情况处理。

11. 普通法院受理的案件

（1）在本法生效之前根据被废除的法律所犯的任何罪行，应按被废除的法律未被废除的情况处理。

（2）在本法生效之前根据被废除的法律产生的任何索赔，应按被废除的法律未被废除的情况处理。

（3）在本法生效之前开始的任何诉讼或其他民事诉讼，应按被废除的法律未被废除的情况处理。

12. 部长可授权委员会履行调解委员会和工业法庭的职能

（1）部长在与委员会协商后，可通过在《公报》上发布公告，授权委员会根据第7款或第8款的规定按以下条件履行调解委员会或工业法庭的职能——

（a）就坦桑尼亚大陆的全部或任何特定部分而言；

（b）自《公报》指定的日期起生效。

（2）委员会根据第（1）款作出的授权不得影响调解委员会或工业法庭根据第7款或第8款的规定，对在《公报》指定的日期进行部分审理的任何事项作出裁决或最后定案的权限。

13. 源于已废除法律的争议

（1）所有因被废除的法律而产生的争议应由本法生效前适用的实体法来裁定。

（2）在本法生效之前，因部长的决定而在下级法院引起的所有未决争议和提出的所有执行申请均应由下级法院裁定。

（3）所有未决争议——

（a）已解散的坦桑尼亚工业法庭的改判应由劳工法庭的三名法官组成的合议庭裁定；和

（b）坦桑尼亚劳工法庭的审理应由劳工法庭决定。

（4）源自坦桑尼亚工业法庭的所有上诉和司法审查申请在高等法院待决，应由高等法院裁定。

（5）委员会有权调解和仲裁提交给委员会的由被废除的法律引起的所有争议，所有此类争议应被视为已根据本法第86条正式提起诉讼。

（6）所有等待部长决定的案件均应——

（a）对于高等法院退回部长重审的案件，由部长决定并最终确定；和

（b）对于尚待部长作出决定的案件，应将其连同各自的完整记录转交劳工法庭裁决。

（7）部长作出决定的日期应为规定表格中注明的日期。

（8）尽管有任何其他成文法的规定，但在计算时效时，应排除作出裁决日期与收到裁决日期之间的时间。

[2010年第11号法案第42条；2016年第4号法案第24条]

14. 最低工资

（1）尽管《工资和雇佣条款条例》已被废除——

（a）部长可在本法生效后3年内——

（i）根据该条例第4条设立最低工资委员会；和

（ⅱ）在总统批准下,根据第 10 条发出工资规管令,规定最低基本工资;

(b) 该条例的有关条文须适用于根据第(a)款设立的委员会及根据第(a)款作出的命令。

(2) 除第(3)款另有规定外,根据《工资和雇佣条款条例》发布的《工资管理条例》在本法生效后继续有效。

(3) 在根据《劳工机构法》公布工资决定的情况下,第(1)款规定的任何适用的工资管理条例令将不再适用于受该决定约束的雇主和雇员。[第 300 章;第 4 章第 8 条]

[1951 年第 15 号命令]

15. 附属立法

根据被废止的法律制定的任何附属立法应继续有效,直至这些法律——

(a) 被部长废除;或者

(b) 被根据本法制定的附属立法所取代。

16. 家政和保安人员的工作时间

尽管有第 19 条的规定,家政工人和保安工人的工作时间应不超过——

(a) 本法生效后第一年的 54 个普通小时;

(b) 本法生效后第二年的 51 个普通小时;

(c) 本法生效后第三年的 48 个普通小时;和

(d) 此后的 45 小时。

17. 书面资料

各雇主应在本法生效后 1 年内提交本法第 15 条规定的适用于本法生效时在职雇员的书面详情。

第十部
最低工资令［2022 年］

坦桑尼亚联合共和国

补充第 45 号　　**2022 年 11 月 25 日**

附属法例

《坦桑尼亚联合共和国公报》第 103 卷第 45 号，2022 年 11 月 25 日

根据政府命令由多多马政府印务局印刷

第 687 号政府公告 2022 年 11 月 25 日

劳工机构法
（第300章）

命令

（根据第39条第（1）款发布）

2022年最低工资令

1. 名称和生效

本命令称为《2022年最低工资令》，并将于2023年1月1日生效。

2. 使用方法

该法令适用于所有私营部门的雇员和雇主。

3. 释义

在本法令中，除非上下文另有规定，否则——

"**农业**"是指由此类活动的经营者或代表经营者进行的农作物生产、林业活动、昆虫的育种和养殖、农产品和动物的预加工，包括使用和修理机械、设备、工具和农业机械，包括与农业生产有关的合作化的农业活动中的加工、储存、经营或运输；

"**良好协议**"指注册工会与雇主或注册雇主协会就任意工作事项达成的书面协议。

"**商业和工业**"包括为获得收入而开展业务、提供专业服务或任何有类似目的的活动，采矿和农业活动除外；

"**承包商**"包括土木工程师、建筑、机械、电工和特种承包商；

"**家政工人**"是指通过从事家政工作获得收入的人；

"**雇员**"具有《就业与劳动关系法》在工作中所赋予的含义；[第366章]

"**雇主**"具有《就业与劳动关系法》在工作中所赋予的含义；[第366章]

"**能源**"包括所有与生产有关的过程或任何来源的能源供应；

"**国际公司**"是指国际组织或涉及各国业务的国际商业公司；

"**采矿活动**"应具有《采矿法》所赋予的含义，不应包括与盐或石灰石生产有关的任何活动；[第123章]

"**大商人**"是指从事高生产、高利润的经济活动的人。

"**私营部门**"是指除公共部门以外的任何部门；

"**小公司**"指除大型公司或国际公司以外的所有公司；

"**大型酒店或旅游酒店**"指所有高水平经营、高利润的酒店，包括为游客提供住宿和其他服务的营地。

4. 部门和领域

（1）根据本法令的规定，各部门最低工资的范围按本法令第一表1的规定予以确定。

（2）以小时、日、周、两周或月为单位计算的可比工资率，将根据《就业与劳动关系法》第26条第（1）款发布的表格1的规定来确定。[第366章]

（3）表2中规定的最低工资应被视为支付给相关部门或地区雇员的最低工资，雇主可以支付给雇员高于最低工资的工资，只要他支付给雇员的工资不低于相关部门或区域规定的水平。

（4）可通过集体协议或其他方式提高最低工资标准。

5. 就业标准

（1）在符合本命令规定的情况下，适用于每一特定部门或地区所有工人的就业率应按照《就业与劳动关系法》第三部分的规定，或在就业合同和条件更好的合同中实施。[第366章]

（2）除带薪年假外，雇员连续为同一雇主工作每两年有权享受一次休假津贴。

（3）雇员有权享受雇主和雇员协商一致的其他津贴。

（4）尽管有本款的一般性规定，卡车司机仍有权领取司机与雇主谈判商定的因旅行距离、在总部外逾期停留、装卸而产生的津贴。

6. 能获得更好利益的员工

如果在本命令生效时，任何雇员获得比本命令所规定的更高的工资和更好的工作条件，如果该雇员受雇于同一雇主，则该雇员也将继续获得更高的工资和更好的工作条件。

7. 废除

《2013年最低工资条例》废除。

[TA. And. 2013年第196号]

表1

（根据第4条第（1）款作出）

最低工资部门和地区

（a）农业部门；

（b）卫生部门；

（c）电信业；

（d）家政和酒店工作；

（e）人身保护服务；

（f）能源部门；

（g）交通运输业；

（h）建筑业；

（i）采矿业；

（j）私立学校服务；

（k）工商部门；

（l）渔业和海洋服务业；

（m）其他行业。

表 2

(根据第 4 条第(3)款作出)

最低工资

	部门和领域	时间	级别(先令)
1.	农业部门	小时 日 一周 两周 月	718 5 385 32 310 64 620 140 000
2.	健康产业	小时 日 一周 两周 月	1 000 7 501 45 003 90 007 195 000
3.	通信行业		
	(a) 通信服务	小时 日 一周 两周 月	2 564 19 232 115 394 230 787 500 000
	(b) 广告和媒体、邮政和包裹递送服务	小时 日 一周 两周 月	1 154 8 654 51 927 103 854 225 000
4.	家政和酒店工作		
	(a) 受雇于外交官和大商人的家政工人	小时 日 一周 两周 月	1 282 9 616 57 697 115 393 250 000
	(b) 受雇于合格官员的家政工人	小时 日 一周 两周 月	1 026 7 693 46 157 92 315 200 000
	(c) 家政工人 但以下人员除外 受雇于外交官、大商人和符合条件的官员 但不住在雇主家里的人	小时 日 一周 两周 月	615 4 616 27 694 55 389 120 000

续　表

	部门和领域	时　间	级别(先令)
	(d) 上述(a)(b)和(c)款未指明的非住家的家政工人	小时 日 一周 两周 月	308 2 308 13 847 27 694 60 000
	(e) 大型酒店或旅游酒店	小时 日 一周 两周 月	1 539 11 539 69 236 138 472 300 000
	(f) 酒店楼层	小时 日 一周 两周 月	923 6 924 41 542 83 083 180 000
	(g) 餐厅、旅馆和酒吧	小时 日 一周 两周 月	769 5 770 34 618 69 236 150 000
5.	私营安保服务		
	(a) 大型国际公司	小时 日 一周 两周 月	1 139 8 539 51 235 102 469 222 000
	(b) 小型公司	小时 日 一周 两周 月	759 5 693 34 156 68 313 148 000
6.	能源部门		
	(a) 国际公司	小时 日 一周 两周 月	3 036 22 771 136 626 273 252 592 000

续 表

	部门和领域	时间	级别(先令)
	(b) 小型公司	小时 日 一周 两周 月	1 154 8 654 51 927 103 854 225 000
7.	运输业		
	(a) 航空运输服务	小时 日 一周 两周 月	2 000 15 001 90 007 180 014 390 000
	(b) 货物运送和配送服务	小时 日 一周 两周 月	1 846 13 847 83 083 166 167 360 000
	(c) 陆运服务	小时 日 一周 两周 月	1 539 11 539 69 236 138 472 300 000
8.	建筑业		
	(a) 一级承包商	小时 日 一周 两周 月	2 154 16 155 96 931 193 861 420 000
	(b) 二级至四级承包商	小时 日 一周 两周 月	1 846 13 847 83 083 166 167 360 000
	(c) 五级至七级承包商	小时 日 一周 两周 月	1 641 12 309 73 852 147 704 320 000

续 表

	部门和领域	时 间	级别(先令)
9.	采矿业		
	(a) 拥有采矿和勘探许可证	小时 日 一周 两周 月	2 564 19 232 115 394 230 787 500 000
	(b) 小规模采矿许可证持有者	小时 日 一周 两周 月	1 539 11 539 69 236 138 472 300 000
	(c) 营业执照持有人	小时 日 一周 两周 月	2 308 17 309 103 854 207 708 450 000
	(d) 持牌经纪人	小时 日 一周 两周 月	1 282 9 616 57 697 115 393 250 000
10.	私立学校服务(小学、小学和中学)工作时间	小时 日 一周 两周 月	1 062 7 962 47 773 95 546 207 000
11.	工商业部门		
	(a) 商业和工业	小时 日 一周 两周 月	769 5 770 34 618 69 236 150 000
	(b) 金融机构	小时 日 一周 两周 月	3 036 22 771 136 626 273 252 592 000

续表

	部门和领域	时间	级别(先令)
12.	渔业和海洋服务业	小时 日 一周 两周 月	1 221 9 155 54 927 109 855 238 000
13.	本命令未指明的其他行业	小时 日 一周 两周 月	769 5 770 34 618 69 236 150 000

多多马，
2022 年 11 月 16 日

乔伊斯
总理府劳动、青年、就业和残疾人事务部长

第三编
经济特区法规

第十一部
出口加工区法(第373章)
[2002年][2012年修订版]

坦桑尼亚联合共和国

出口加工区法

第373章

[主要立法]

2012年修订版

坦桑尼亚联合共和国
出口加工区法

法律第 373 章

[主要立法]

2012 年修订版

本版《出口加工区法》(第 373 章)取代了 2006 年修订版,纳入了截至 2012 年 12 月 31 日(含该日)的所有修订内容,根据《法律修订法》(第 4 章)第 4 条授权印刷,并由政府在 2013 年第 206 号通知中发布。

达累斯萨拉姆,
2013 年 6 月 21 日

弗雷德里克·M.韦尔马
总检察长

第 373 章
出口加工区法

旨在对出口加工区的建立、发展和管理作出规定;为出口增长创造国际竞争力并对相关事项作出规定的法案。

[2002 年 7 月 1 日]

[2002 年第 316 号政府公告]

法案编号
2002 年第 11 号法案
2006 年第 3 号法案
2011 年第 2 号法案

第一部分
总　　则

1. 简称和应用

(1) 本法可称为《出口加工区法》。

(2) [省略]。

(3) 本法适用于坦桑尼亚大陆。

2. 释义

在本法中，除非上下文另有规定，否则——

"**法**"是指《出口加工区法》；

"**管理局**"是指根据本法第 12 条设立的出口加工区管理局；

"**理事会**"是指根据本法第 14 条第(1)款设立的理事会。

"**主任专员**"是指《坦桑尼亚税务局法》定义的坦桑尼亚税务局主任专员；[第 399 章]

"**关税区**"是指坦桑尼亚联合共和国境内不属于出口加工区范围内的地区；

"**出口加工区**"是指根据本法第 3 条第(1)款设立或申报的地区。

"**外国市场**"是指除关税区以外的任何市场；

"**投资者**"是指在坦桑尼亚联合共和国注册成立的公司，该公司申请并获得管理局的许可，在出口加工区生产工业产品并出口到国外市场，还包括为设立或申报为出口加工区的地区的发展提供必要基础设施的人；

"**合资企业**"是指外国投资者与一个当地合作社或半官方组织、外国投资者与地方私人投资者、国内私人投资者与地方半官方组织和合作组织、外国投资者与另一个外国投资者为在出口加工区共同投资而成立的组织，无论其是法人团体或非法人团体；

"**许可证**"是指管理局根据投资者的申请而授予其在出口加工区内进行商业交易的官方许可证；

"**制造**"是指为提升使用价值而改变原材料形态的任何操作或流程，包括组装、加工、包装和重新包装；

"**部长**"是指负责工业的部长；

"**单一工厂**"是指可获得出口加工区待遇但不位于出口加工区内的工业园区；

"**税收减免期**"是指许可证中规定的投资者无须就其进行的任何商业交易缴纳税款和关税的期限。

[2006 年第 3 号法案第 2 条；2002 年第 11 号法案；1969 年第 90 号政府公告]

第二部分
出口加工区的设立或申报

3. 出口加工区的设立或申报

（1）部长可根据理事会的意见，在与有关当局协商后，根据该局的建议，通过《公报》发布通知——

（a）设立或申报任何区域为出口加工区；和

（b）确定第(a)项所述出口加工区的位置、范围、地理特征或边界。

（2）如果部长已根据第(1)款咨询了相关当局，而后者在 30 天内未作出回应或未给出不应将任何该区域设立或申报为出口加工区的理由，则应推定该当局已同意在该区域设立或申报出口加工区。

（3）设立或申报的出口加工区可由已开发、部分开发或未开发的区域组成，也可由单个工厂单位或一组工厂单位组成。

[2006 年第 3 号法案第 2 条]

4. 设立出口加工区的目的和宗旨

设立或申报出口加工区的目的和宗旨是——

(a) 吸引和促进以出口为导向的工业化投资,以实现坦桑尼亚出口的多样化和便利化,并提高其国际竞争力;

(b) 创造和扩大外汇收入;

(c) 创造和增加就业机会,以及培养熟练劳动力;

(d) 吸引和鼓励新技术转移;

(e) 促进本地经济与国际市场的联系;和

(f) 促进本地原材料加工出口。

第三部分
许　　可

5. 出口加工区进入、居住等的限制

(1) 任何人不得——

(a) 除非他持有管理局颁发的许可证——

(i) 就在出口加工区制造或进口的任何货物开展任何业务或从事零售贸易;或者

(ii) 出于除运往另一出口加工区或出口到外国市场或仅为加工这些货物之外的目的,移走在出口加工区制造的任何货物;或者

(iii) 将在出口加工区制造的任何货物用于在该出口加工区或任何其他出口加工区消费;或者

(b) 除非得到管理局的书面授权,否则——

(i) 在符合第(2)款规定的情况下,进入出口加工区;或者

(ii) 居住在出口加工区。

(2) 第(b)项第(i)目的规定不适用于以下人员——

(i) 警务人员;或者

(ii) 公务员,包括海关官员或地方政府官员;或者

(iii) 受雇于投资者或依法负责或授权提供任何公用事业的机构或公司,在履行其各自的职责和职能过程中行事的任何人员。

(3) 管理局可向投资者或任何在出口加工区内的人发出书面通知

(a) 规定关于管制、限制或禁止货物或货物类别进入出口加工区的条件;

(b) 命令出口加工区内的投资者或个人在通知规定的期限内(该期限不得少于14天)——

(i) 从出口加工区移走任何物品、商品或物件;或者

(ii) 中止管理局在通知中指明的出口加工区内的任何活动或业务。

(4) 按照上款收到通知书的收件人,可在收到该通知书后7日内,就该通知书所要求的任何条件或所包含的任何命令,向管理局作出书面陈述。

(5) 任何人违反第(1)款的规定,或不遵守根据第(4)款发出的通知,即属犯罪,一经定罪,须承担以下法律责任——

(a) 如果是自然人,处以 1 500 万先令以下的罚款或 4 年以下的监禁,或两者并罚;

(b) 如果不是自然人,则处以 5 000 万先令以下的罚款。

[2006 年第 3 号法案第 2 条]

6. 管理局颁发许可证

(1) 管理局应负责向任何希望在出口加工区开展业务或活动的人颁发许可证。

(2) 根据第(1)款颁发的许可证应与主管当局根据已废除的《商业许可法》和《国家工业(许可和登记)法》颁发的许可证一样有效。[1972 年第 25 号法案;第 46 章]

(3) 就本条而言,管理局应咨询负责管理《商业活动登记法》和《国家工业(许可和登记)法》的相关部门,以便对在坦桑尼亚开展业务的个人或公司进行协调记录。[第 208 章;第 46 章]

[2006 年第 3 号法案第 2 条]

7. 取消和暂停执照

(1) 如果管理局确定许可证持有人有以下情况,其在向许可证持有人发出书面通知 30 天后,有权取消或暂停该人的许可证——

(a) 在没有书面说明合理理由的情况下,未能在许可证规定的时间内或管理局可能规定的任何期限内,开展已获许可的业务或活动;或者

(b) 未经管理局事先同意或通知,暂停其在出口加工区的活动超过 6 个月;

(c) 在没有书面说明合理理由的情况下,未能遵守许可证的条款或本部分以及任何法规的规定,或向管理局提出延期请求并经其同意后,仍未能在许可证所确定或管理局向其发出的通知所确定的期限内继续经营业务。

(2) 如果管理局向投资者颁发的在出口加工区开展业务或活动的许可证持有人有以下行为,管理局应取消该许可证——

(a) 未就符合征税条件的交易缴税或逃避缴税;或者

(b) 未能遵守本法或根据本法制定的任何规章的规定或未能符合取得许可证的条件;或者

(c) 未经管理局事先批准而将许可证转让给他人;或者

(d) 以欺诈或故意提交虚假或误导性信息或陈述的方式获得此类许可证。

(3) 许可证持有人可在收到第(1)款规定的通知后 21 天内,向管理局提交书面申述,管理局应在考虑该申述后再审议是否取消或吊销许可证。

[2006 年第 3 号法案第 2 条]

8. 许可证不得更改

(1) 管理局不得变更许可证及其附带条件,除非持有人以书面形式请求管理局变更,且此变更的目的是使持有人更好地开展许可证发放所要求的业务或活动。

(2) 如果许可证的变更涉及税收减免期的延长,则该变更不得延长最初给予投资者的税收减免期。

[2006 年第 3 号法案第 2 条]

9. 对管理局决定的上诉

(1) 任何人如对管理局拒绝许可申请、取消或吊销许可的决定不服,可向部长提出上诉,部长可确认、更改或搁置管理局的决定。

(2) 任何人如果对部长根据第(1)款做出的决定不服,可在部长做出决定之日起30天内向高等法院提出上诉。

[2006年第3号法案第2条]

10. 禁止其他活动

(1) 任何人不得在税收减免期内从事所获许可证许可以外的任何行业或业务。

(2) 在不影响第(1)款的情况下,任何人不得从事出口加工区内生产或组装的物品的零售业务,但经管理局决定和授权的除外。

[2006年第3号法案第2条]

11. 管理局决定在出口加工区的货物或物品

(1) 管理局应确定出口加工区应生产的产品或应提供的服务类型。

(2) 根据第(3)款的规定,不得制造、加工、生产或供应本款规定或提及的任何货物或物品,也不得将此类货物或物品带入出口加工区或允许其留在出口加工区——

 (a) 枪支弹药或《武器和弹药法》规定的其他战争物资;

 (b) 危险爆炸物;

 (c) 毒品和麻醉品。

[2006年第3号法案第2条]

第四部分
出口加工区管理局

12. 管理局的建立

(1) 兹设立一个自主的政府机构,称为出口加工区管理局。

(2) 管理局须为法人团体,且应——

 (a) 永久存续和拥有法人公章;

 (b) 能够以其法人名义起诉和应诉;

 (c) 在遵守本法的前提下,能够购买或以其他方式获得和/或转让动产和不动产。

[2006年第3号法案第4条]

13. 管理局的目标和职能

(1) 管理局应当启动、发展和管理公有出口加工区的运营,并为此目的履行本条规定的职责和职能。

(2) 为启动、发展和管理出口加工区的运营,管理局应——

 (a) 与土地部部长和负责地方政府当局事务的部长协商,以其名义购置土地,并就土地向投资者出租或设立派生(/其他)权利,或在土地上建造工业和商业建筑,并向在出口加工区获得许可从事相关业务的投资者出租这些建筑;

 (b) 为出口加工区的经营提供基础设施;

(c) 在出口加工区内为出口加工区投资者和其他用户的利益提供公用设施和排污、排水以及垃圾和废物清除系统;

(d) 制定适当的促进出口加工区发展的国家和国际计划;

(e) 确保安保和监控,维护财产和设备的安全,保证食物和餐饮服务的正常供应;

(f) 为出口加工区投资者的利益提供商业信息;和

(g) 出于改善目的为出口加工区的经营者和投资者或出口加工区产品或服务的消费者提供任何其他必要的公共服务。

(3) 为履行第(2)款规定的职责和职能,管理局有权将第(2)款规定的职责或职能分包给他人执行,特别是可以许可私人投资者或与私人投资者建立合资公司开发出口加工区的基础设施。

(4) 管理局可就在出口加工区提供的服务或设施收取租金、会费和其他费用。

(5) 管理局在履行本法赋予的权力和职责时,可提供其他服务,履行其他职责和职能,行使为体现本法精神所需的权力。

[2006年第3号法案第4条;2011年第2号法案第5条]

14. 设立出口加工区管理局理事会

(1) 为管理局设立一个理事会,称为出口加工区管理局理事会。

(2) 理事会由以下成员组成——

(a) 负责工业的部长担任主席:

(b) 总检察长;

(c) 财政部常务秘书;

(d) 水资源部常务秘书:

(e) 能源部常务秘书;

(f) 主管地方政府当局事务的常务秘书;

(g) 规划委员会执行秘书;

(h) 坦桑尼亚税务局局长;

(i) 地政总署署长;

(j) 坦桑尼亚私营部门基金会主席;和

(k) 坦桑尼亚商业、工业和农业商会会长。

(3) 理事会可增选任何其他人出席理事会会议。

(4) 理事会可不时设立其认为适宜的委员会,以履行其指示的职责和职能。

[2006年第3号法案第4条;2011年2号法案第6条]

15. 理事会的职能和权力

(1) 理事会应负责履行管理局的职能和管理事务。

(2) 为妥善履行管理局的职能,在遵守部长可能就一般政策事项作出指示的情况下,理事会有责任和权力——

(a) 制定出口加工区政策并就出口加工区的发展和经营提供一般性政策指导;

(b) 批准与出口加工区的建立和发展有关的计划和方案;

(c) 根据本法第3条,向部长提供建议;

(d) 确定在特定出口加工区优先推广的部门；

(e) 批准出口加工区发展的具体融资要求；

(f) 批准管理局的预算；

(g) 批准管理局的结构和人员编制；和

(h) 批准业务政策和工作人员薪酬。

(3) 理事会有权规范自身程序。

[2006年第3号法案第4条;2011第2号法案第7条]

(4) 理事长应主持其出席的所有理事会会议。

(5) 理事长缺席时,理事会出席会议的会员应选举一名会员担任会议主席。

(6) 理事会的事宜应由出席会议并参加表决的成员以多数票决定,表决票数相等时,理事长应有权投决定票。

17. 局长及其他雇员

(1) 理事会应与部长协商后,根据理事会确定的条款和条件任命一名管理局局长。

(2) 局长应是管理局首席执行官,并就管理局的日常管理事务直接向理事会负责。

(3) 局长应为理事会的秘书,可参加理事会的审议,但无权对理事会决议或其他事项进行表决。

(4) 理事会可根据其通过的条款和条件委任或聘用管理局高级官员。

[2006年第3号法案第4条;2011年第2号法案第4条]

18. 资金来源

(1) 管理局的资金来源应包括——

(a) 议会为此目的而可能划拨的款项；

(b) 出口加工区的基础设施和工厂的投资回报；

(c) 借款；

(d) 管理局从在出口加工区内履行本法规定的职责的个人或组织处收到的捐赠、赠予或遗赠；

(e) 出口加工区经营活动中产生的租金和其他服务收入；和

(f) 管理局为履行本法规定的职能而收到或取得的任何其他款项。

[2006年第3号法案第4条]

19. 管理局资金的使用

(1) 管理局的资金应用于——

(a) 根据本法的规定启动、发展和管理出口加工区基础设施；

(b) 在出口加工区提供公共设施；

(c) 修复和维护出口加工区的基础设施；和

(d) 清偿因实施本法而产生的债务。

(2) 尽管有第(1)款的规定,管理局应保留其在持续履行职能过程中所累积的所有款项。

[2006年第3号法案第4条]

20. 管理局资金的管理和审计

(1) 管理局的资金应按照《公共财政法》的规定进行管理。

(2) 管理局的资金应由财务总监和审计长或其指定的代为履行其职责的审计员进行审计。

(3) 管理局应编制一份关于出口加工区业务实施情况的年度报告并提交给部长,部长应将报告提交国民议会。

[2006 年第 3 号法案第 4 条;第 348 章]

第五部分
投 资 激 励

21. 给予出口加工区投资者的激励

(1) 出口加工区的投资者有权获得以下激励——

 (a) 在符合适用的条件和程序的前提下,准许加入出口信贷担保计划;

 (b) 减免与出口加工区的生产有关的原材料和资本货物的关税、增值税和其他税费;

 (c) 初始阶段 10 年内免缴公司税,其后应按《所得税法》中的规定缴纳公司税;

 (d) 前 10 年免缴股息和利息预扣税;

 (e) 出口加工区生产的产品免征 10 年地方政府当局征收的所有税费;

 (f) 免除装运前或目的地检查要求;

 (g) 准许在出口加工区海关现场查验货物;

 (h) 规定在入境时为关键技术、管理和培训人员提供时间最长为两个月的商务签证,此后投资者可根据《移民法》要求申请居留许可证;[第 54 章]

 (i) 进口一辆行政车辆、救护车、消防车以及最多两辆供员工往返出口加工区的巴士,并减免涉及的关税、增值税及其他任何应付税款;

 (j) 将运往出口加工区的货物作为过境货物处理;

 (k) 免征公用事业和码头费的增值税;

 (l) 投资者在启动期有权获得最多 5 人初始移民配额,此后的任何额外移民申请应向管理局提交,管理局应与移民局和劳工专员协商,批准额外的移民,同时需要考虑预备移民者的适格性、投资者所采用技术的复杂性以及与投资者达成的协议;

 (m) 提供出口加工区内有竞争力的、现代化的和可靠的服务;和

 (n) 准许通过任何授权交易商银行以可自由兑换货币无条件转让——

  (i) 归属于投资的净利润或股息;

  (ii) 已获得外国贷款的服务费;

  (iii) 与任何技术转让协议有关的特许权使用费、费用和收费;

  (iv) 企业出售或清算时的收益汇款(包括所有税费和其他义务产生的费用)或归属于投资的任何利息;和

  (v) 向在坦桑尼亚的企业雇用的外国职员支付的薪酬和其他福利;

(2) 第(1)款第(e)项的规定不适用在关税区内制造和销售或以其他方式卸载的货物。

(3) 管理局可在符合授予投资激励的前提下向理事会提出对在出口加工区开展业务的人

员获授予的投资激励类型进行变更、添加、更改或一般性修改的建议。

（4）如果理事会认可对投资激励类型的变更、添加、更改或一般性修改，则应向负责财政的部长提交提案，财政部长应着手进行必要的变更、添加、更改或一般性修改。

[2006年第3号法案第6条；2011年第2号法案第4条；第332章；第4章第8条第(k)款]

22. 出口加工区投资出口货物进入关税区的限制

（1）出口加工区内的免税货物不得从该区运出，除非此类货物——

(a) 是出口到关税区外的货物；

(b) 在符合以下条件的情况下，作为出口货物进入关税区内——

(i) 获得来自海关的必要许可证；

(ii) 支付所有适用的进口税、税费和其他费用；

(iii) 遵守所有海关规定程序；和

(iv) 此类出口的百分比不超过该投资者在该企业内年度总产量的20%。

（2）理事会可根据行业或商品的性质和市场情况，授权投资者在关境内销售超出第(1)款规定的范围的数量。

（3）所有卸入关税区销售的货物均应缴纳所有适用的关税和税款。

[2006年第3号法案第7条；2011年第2号法案第4条]

23. 技术员工的工作许可证

（1）政府应为掌握当地无法提供的技能的管理和技术人员提供工作许可证，其数量应由管理局与负责劳工的部门协商后确定。

（2）在符合第(1)款规定的情况下，主管部门应向政府提出建议，以免除培训当地雇员的投资者的培训税，其数额应为上述培训税的50%。

[2006年第3号法案第5条]

24. 管理局可签订协议

（1）管理局可在不违反本法的情况下签订合同，就授予投资激励和在出口加工区内开展业务与投资者达成协议。

（2）根据第(1)款的规定签订的合同，可包含与特别许可证或在特别许可证下进行的商业交易有关的对坦桑尼亚联合共和国具有约束力的条款，该合同——

(a) 在税费、费用和其他财政收入方面有特别规定；

(b) 包含管理局本法或根据本法制定的规章赋予其的自由裁量权的行使情况或方式；

(c) 包含与环境事项有关的事项，包括项目特定事项和一般性法规未涵盖的事项。条款旨在界定范围，并在特定情况下适当限制特别许可证持有者的义务或责任范围。

（3）当本法或条例赋予部长或管理局做任何事情的自由裁量权时，部长或管理局（视情况而定）应依照根据本节规定签订的合同协议中所载的相关规定行使该自由裁量权。

（4）管理局应将拟议的合同协议提交给部长，以便就投资者拟议进行的商业交易或项目获得批准。

[2006年第3号法案第5条]

第六部分
其他法律的适用和不适用

25. 不适用

[《坦桑尼亚投资法》不适用。]

[2006年第3号法案第5条]

26. 印花税法的豁免

不得在出口加工区内外签署与任何动产或不动产的转让、抵押或租赁有关的任何文书,以及不得在该出口加工区内实施或做任何行为,或不得涉及与任何活动、行动、经营、企业、项目有关的任何文件、证书、文书、报告或记录,包括——

(a) 抵押债券;
(b) 关税和消费税单据;
(c) 分期付款或融资租赁协议;
(d) 合伙协议;
(e) 授权委托书;
(f) 转让契约;
(g) 汇票;或者
(h) 本票。

应缴纳《印花税法》规定的任何税。[第189章]

[第189章;2006年第3号法案第5条]

27. 城市规划法的适用

就《城市规划法》与出口加工区建筑物有关的规则而言,这些法律关于规划许可和建筑许可的任何条款提及的地方政府当局,应解释为指管理局。

[2006年第3号法案第2和5条]

28. 劳动法的适用

适用于坦桑尼亚联合共和国的现行劳动法应比照适用于出口加工区。

[2006年第3号法案第2和第5条]

第七部分
收购、补偿和争议解决

29. 收购和补偿法案

(1) 除非符合《坦桑尼亚联合共和国宪法》和《土地征用法》规定的条件,否则政府不得取得出口加工区内任何财产的权益。

(2) 凡按照第(1)款规定获得任何财产,政府应根据第25条的规定,以可自由兑换的货币支付给该财产的所有人,给予其公正和及时的补偿。[2006年第3号法案第2条和第5条]

[第2章;第118章]

30. 争议解决

（1）根据本法获得出口加工区许可证的人，该许可证可以对其与管理局之间就下列事项发生的争议作出规定——

（a）根据第23条规定的在收购情况下应该支付的补偿总额或者其他有关事项；或者

（b）该许可证的有效性或持续有效性；或者

（c）根据本法产生的任何其他争议应通过仲裁解决——

（i）根据国际投资争议解决中心的仲裁规则和程序进行仲裁；或者

（ii）在坦桑尼亚联合共和国政府和投资者国籍国签署的任何双边或多边投资保护协定框架内；或者

（iii）按照国际商会的仲裁规则和程序进行仲裁；或者

（iv）根据各方解决投资争议的任何其他国际机制进行仲裁。

（2）第（1）款中提及的许可证，凡对仲裁作出规定的，即构成许可证持有人和政府对提交仲裁的同意。

（3）本条所述仲裁的任何裁决均为终局裁决，对政府和许可证持有人具有约束力，如果是外国裁决，则可根据《承认及执行外国仲裁裁决公约》予以执行。

［2006年第3号法案第2条和第5条］

31. 争议解决不受限制

第24条的任何规定不得解释为以下情况——

（a）第24条第（1）款所述的许可证没有就争议解决作出规定，以限制该许可证持有人获得任何其他补救的权利；或者

（b）第24条第（1）款所指的许可证确实就争议解决作出了规定，以防止该许可证的持有者或管理局在签订协议中约定，除非该许可证中另有规定，否则该协议中规定或预期的任何特定争议不得通过协议解决。

［2006年第3号法案第2条和5条］

32. 部长可以制定规章

为了更好地执行本法的宗旨，部长可与管理局协商制定一般性法规。

［2006年第3号法案第2条和5条］

第八部分
罪　　行

33. 许可证和外国货币有关的罪行

任何人——

（a）在许可证申请或与许可证申请有关的情况下；或者

（b）为获得或保留任何外汇作出虚假陈述（明知是虚假的或有理由相信不属实的），或故意提供虚假信息，

构成犯罪的，一经定罪，应被处以1 500万先令以下的罚款或4年以下的监禁，或两者

并罚。

[2006年第3号法案第5条]

34. 转运产品等罪行

（1）任何人不得为获得根据双边、多边或区域协议或议定书在贸易配额中给予坦桑尼亚的优势，将产品转运至其他国家，并声称这些产品是在出口加工区生产或制造的。

（2）违反第（1）款的人即属犯罪，一经定罪，可处以——
  （a）如果该人是自然人，则被处以 2 000 万先令以下的罚款，或 5 年以下的监禁，或两者并罚；
  （b）如果该人不是自然人，则被处以 10 亿先令以下的罚款，并关闭和没收其企业或业务。

[2006年第3号法案第5条]

35. 与违禁货物或物品制造、加工等有关的罪行

（1）任何人如违反第 11 条第（1）款的，应被处以 5 000 万先令以下的罚款或 15 年以下的监禁。

（2）除根据第（1）款的规定作出判决外，初审法院还可以命令政府没收与犯罪有关的货物或物品。

[2006年第3号法案第5条]

第四编
采矿与环境保护法规

第十二部
采矿法(第123章)
[2010年][2019年修订版](节选)

采 矿 法
（第 123 章）

2010 年 11 月 1 日实施

［本文件为 2019 年 11 月 30 日版。］

［注：在总检察长办公室的监督下，根据《法律修订法》1994 年第 7 号、《法律修订和年度修订法》第 356 章（R.L.），以及《法律解释和一般条款法》1972 年第 30 号对本法进行了全面修订与合并。本版本为截至 2002 年 7 月 31 日的最新版本。］

［政府公告 2010 年第 396 号；法案编号 2010 年第 14 号法案；2010 年第 17 号法案；2015 年第 23 号法案；2017 年第 4 号法案；2017 年第 7 号法案；2017 年第 9 号法案；2018 年第 4 号法案；2019 年第 6 号法案；2019 年第 14 号法案］

旨在重新颁布并对条款进行重大修改的法案，规定有关矿产勘探、采矿、加工和经营矿产、授予、续期和终止矿产权、支付特许权使用费、费用和其他收费以及任何其他有关事项。

第二部分
一 般 原 则

6. 勘探或者采矿所需的许可

（1）除非持有或者被视为持有本法规定的矿业权许可证，否则任何人不得在本法管辖的任何土地上或土地内进行矿产资源的勘查、开采或加工。

（2）在地质测绘的过程中，机构所进行的活动不应被视为本条第（1）款中规定的矿产资源的勘查或者开采作业。

（3）任何人违反本条第（1）款的规定，即属犯罪，一经定罪，须承担以下法律责任——

    （a）如果是个人，处以 1 000 万先令以下 500 万先令以上的罚款或 3 年以下的监禁，或两者并罚；

    （b）如果是法人，处以 5 000 先令以下的罚款。

（4）在未经许可的勘查、开采或加工作业过程中获得的任何矿产资源，包括参与这些作业的设备，以及未经适当许可而占有的任何矿产资源，均应由坦桑尼亚矿业委员会收归政府，并通过相关的政府资产拍卖程序进行拍卖。

［2015 年第 23 号法案第 30 条］

7. 矿业权和专属权

（1）以下矿业权可根据本法以下规定授予——

    （a）第四部分 A 分部项下的——

        （i）勘探许可证；

            （ii）宝石勘探许可证；
        （b）第四部分 B 分部项下的——
            （i）特别采矿许可证；
            （ii）采矿许可证；
        （c）第四部分 C 分部项下的——初级采矿许可证；
        （d）第四部分 D 分部项下的——
            （i）加工许可证；
            （ii）冶炼许可证；
            （iii）精炼许可证。
    （2）经矿业权人同意，许可机关在同一采矿区域内可以许可多个矿业权，具体如下——
        （a）在已经授予非建筑材料矿产的矿业权的区域内，可以授予建筑材料采矿许可证或建筑材料初级采矿许可证；
        （b）在已经授予非宝石矿产的勘探许可证的区域内，可以授予宝石探矿许可证。
    （3）尽管本条有上述规定，但本法不得妨碍从事隧道、道路、水坝、机场和类似工程性质的公共工程建设的任何人员，将经矿业部长书面批准所得的任何矿物作为建筑材料。
    （4）就本条第（3）款而言，矿业部长不得批准在采矿区域内的任何矿源。
    （5）矿业部长可随时撤销根据本条第（3）款给予的批准。

[2015 年第 23 号法案第 31 条；第 4 章第 8 条]

8. 矿业权授予的限制

（1）矿业权不得授予——
    （a）符合以下情况的个人——
        （i）未满 18 周岁者；
        （ii）不是坦桑尼亚联合共和国的公民，且在联合共和国没有连续居住满 4 年或者其他规定的期限；
        （iii）是未解除破产状态的破产人，其已被判决破产或根据任何成文法，无论是根据坦桑尼亚联合共和国法律或其他地方的法律，或与债权人达成任何协议或和解计划，或利用任何有利于债务人的法律，被宣告破产；或者
        （iv）在过去 10 年内，因为不诚信的行为构成犯罪，或违反本法、任何相关或者坦桑尼亚联合共和国境外有效的类似法律中的规定而被定罪，并被判处监禁或者 2 000 万先令以上的罚款。
    （b）符合以下情况的公司——
        （i）未在坦桑尼亚联合共和国境内设立实际地址和邮寄地址，用于接收法律通知和其他信函；
        （ii）并非根据《公司法》注册成立，并且打算根据采矿许可证开展采矿业务；
        （iii）处于清算状态，但并非属于持有人重建或合并计划一部分的清算；
        （iv）其董事或者股东中有任何根据第（a）款第（iii）和（iv）项规定不符合资格的人员。
（2）任何矿产的初级采矿许可证不得授予个人、合伙企业或者法人团体，除非——

(a) 对于个人而言,该个人是坦桑尼亚公民;

(b) 对于合伙企业而言,其合伙人均为坦桑尼亚公民;

(c) 对于法人团体而言,该法人团体是一家公司——:

 (i) 其成员均为坦桑尼亚公民;

 (ii) 其董事均为坦桑尼亚公民;

 (iii) 公司的直接或者间接控制权,由坦桑尼亚境内的所有坦桑尼亚公民行使。

(3) 尽管有第(2)款的规定,但矿业委员会在驻地矿务官的建议下,如果确信初级采矿许可证持有人需要技术支持,而这种技术支持在坦桑尼亚无法获得的情况下,可以允许初级采矿许可证持有人与外国人签订技术支持合同。

[第4章第8节]

(4) 第(1)款第(a)项第(iii)条和(iv)条的规定适用于聘用外国技术支持人员的情况。

(5) 开采宝石的采矿许可证只能授予坦桑尼亚的公民申请人。

(6) 尽管有第(5)款的规定,如果部长在与委员会协商后,确定在受矿产权约束的某土地区域内开发宝石资源,很可能需要专门技能、技术或者高水平投资,可以向申请人授予宝石开采许可证,同时部长须确信该许可证由该申请人和非公民共同持有,且非公民的未分割参与份额不超过50%,无论是一人单独持有还是多人共同持有。

(7) 个人、合伙企业、法人团体、合伙企业中的合伙人、法人中的股东或者董事,如果在其他矿产权或已过期或被取消的矿产权中存在违约行为,则不能获授予矿产权。但存在如下情形之一的,可以对其授予矿产权——

(a) 存在违约行为的个人、合伙企业或者法人团体;或者

(b) 存在违约行为的合伙企业中的合伙人、法人团体中的股东或者董事,已经纠正违约行为。

(8) 个人、合伙企业、法人团体,或任何合伙企业的合伙人或者法人团体的股东或董事,如果拥有超过20个其他有效勘探许可证的,不得再次获得勘探许可证,除非这些勘探许可证的累计勘探区域不超过2 000平方公里。

[2017年第7号法案第7条]

第四部分
采 矿 权

B分部:特别采矿许可证和采矿许可证
(i) 特别采矿许可证和采矿许可证的申请

39. 申请人

(1) 在符合第42或51条(视情况而定)规定的条件下,本部分下文中称为"有资格的申请人"的A类勘探许可证的持有人有权——

(a) 依据第41条,向委员会申请特别采矿许可证;

(b) 依据第50条,向委员会申请采矿许可证,用于在勘探区内开采勘探许可证所适用范围内的矿产资源。

(2) 如果非有权申请人,向发证机关以规定的方式申请特别采矿许可证或者采矿许可证,并缴纳规定的费用,该申请应当立即根据本法在为此类申请而设的申请登记簿中登记。

(3) 根据第(2)款登记的申请应获分配一个编号,正式的收据上应注明收到申请的日期和时间,然后交给申请人或其授权代理人,或者以挂号信寄交申请人。

(4) 每个根据本法的规定申请特别采矿许可证或者采矿许可证的申请人,应当将其申请的副本提交给部长在条例中指定的人员进行备案。

[2015 年第 23 号法案第 40 条;第 4 章第 8 条]

(ii) 特别采矿许可证

41. 特别采矿许可证的申请

(1) 特别采矿许可证的申请应当按照规定的格式填写,并缴纳规定的费用。

(2) 除了第(3)款规定的要求外,特别采矿许可证的申请还应当标明相关的勘探许可证,并提供勘探区域内拟申请特许采矿许可证的土地的完整描述,以及按照委员会合理要求绘制拟开采区域的平面图并显示细节。

[2015 年第 23 号法案第 42 条;2017 年第 7 号法案第 17 条;第 4 章第 8 条]

(3) 每份申请特别采矿许可证的文件应当包括或者附有以下内容——

(a) 申请许可期限的说明;

(b) 申请人就其所知的拟开采区域的矿产资源的综合说明,以及所有已探明、估算或者推断的矿种、矿石储量和开采条件的详细情况;

(c) 拟开展的采矿作业计划,包括资本投资预测、矿石和矿产品的估计回收率,以及矿石和矿产品的处理和处置方案;

(d) 根据《土地法》制定的开采区域内人员的搬迁、安置和补偿之建议方案;

[第 113 章]

(e) 申请人根据《环境管理法》获得的环境证书;

[第 191 章]

(f) 预期基础设施需求的详细情况;

(g) 在坦桑尼亚联合共和国可获得的货物和服务的采购计划;

(h) 根据《就业和劳动关系法》可能要求的,关于坦桑尼亚公民的就业和培训的拟议计划以及外籍雇员的继任计划;

[第 366 章]

(i) 按照规定的格式作出的诚信承诺的声明;

(j) 本地内容计划;和

(k) 部长为处理申请可能合理要求的其他信息。

(4) 根据本条提出的申请应当提交给委员会。

(iii) 采矿许可证

51. 采矿许可证持有人的权利

采矿许可证赋予持有人在遵守本法和相关规定的前提下,对规定的矿种在采矿区内进行采矿作业所享有的专属权利。为此目的,持有人及其雇员和代理人可以特别做到以下几点——
  (a) 进入采矿区,在地表或地下采取一切合理措施,以便于促进和开展采矿作业;
  (b) 为采矿、运输、加工和处理采矿作业中回收的矿物,建立必要的设备、工厂和建筑物;
  (c) 按照本法和相关条例规定缴纳使用费后,处置任何回收的矿产品;
  (d) 按照适用的条例,以规定的方式堆放或者倾倒任何矿物或者废物;和
  (e) 按照《就业与劳动关系法》的规定,雇佣和培训坦桑尼亚公民,并对外籍雇员实施继任计划,并且可以在采矿区内勘探除宝石以外的任何矿物。

[第 366 章]

C 分部:初级采矿许可证

54. 初级采矿许可证的申请
(1) 根据第 8 条被取消资格的任何人,可以向委员会申请颁发初级采矿许可证。
(2) 每份申请应当——
  (a) 符合规定的格式,并缴纳规定的费用;
  (b) 说明申请初级采矿许可证的区域,该区域不得超过规定的最大面积,并附有一份载有足够细节的草图,以便委员会识别该区域;
  (c) 附有规定格式的诚信承诺书;和
  (d) 附有本地内容计划。
(3) 初级采矿许可证的申请应当包含以下内容:
  (a) 对于个人而言,其应当提供其全名、国籍、住址和邮寄地址,并附有身份证明,如国民身份证、护照、驾驶证或者选民登记卡;
  (b) 对于法人而言,其应当提供其法人名称、注册地、股东和董事的姓名和国籍,以及其身份证明的复印件;
  (c) 对于多人申请而言,其应当提供前述(a)项和(b)项的详细情况;
  (d) 根据相关法律法规作出的环境调查、社会研究和环境保护计划。
(4) 初级采矿许可证应授予持有人按照本部分本分部规定的方式勘探和开采矿产资源的权利。

[2015 年第 23 号法案第 45 条;2017 年第 7 号法案第 21 条]

D 分部:矿物加工、冶炼和精炼

59. 矿业权人将矿物留作加工、冶炼或者精炼之用
  矿业权人应当按照部长在与矿业权人和委员会协商后确定的百分比,预留出一定数量的矿产,用于在坦桑尼亚联合共和国内进行加工、冶炼或者精炼。

60. 矿产加工许可证的申请和授予
(1) 任何在受矿业权约束的区域内或外无权加工矿产的人,可以向委员会申请矿产加工许可证。
(2) 根据第(1)款的规定提出的申请应当使用规定的格式,并附有以下内容——
  (a) 规定的费用;

(b) 根据相关法规描述的环境管理计划;

(c) 加工厂布局;

(d) 采购、运输和加工投入计划;

(e) 补偿、搬迁和重新安置计划,如有需要;和

(f) 许可机关要求的其他文件和信息。

(3) 委员会如果对根据第(2)款的规定提出的申请内容满意,应当为申请人注册,并根据许可证规定的条款和条件颁发许可证。

(4) 根据本条规定颁发的矿产加工许可证,有效期不超过10年,并应续期。

(5) 本条规定的矿产加工许可证的申请和授予程序,应当在法规中规定。

第十三部
环境管理法［2004 年］（节选）

环境管理法
2004 年第 20 号

旨在规定可持续环境管理的法律和体制框架；概述管理、影响和风险评估、
污染预防和控制、废物管理、环境质量标准、公众参与、遵守和执行的
原则；为执行有关环境的国际文书提供基础；规定实施国家环境政策；
废除 1983 年《国家环境管理法》，规定国家环境管理委员会继续
存在；规定设立国家环境信托基金及其他有关事项的法案。

第十部分
环境质量标准

由坦桑尼亚联合共和国国会发布

141. 遵守标准等

从事任何活动的每个人，都必须遵守环境质量的标准和准则。

143. 水质量标准

国家环境标准委员会应当——

(a) 规定衡量水质的标准和程序；

(b) 制定坦桑尼亚所有水域的最低质量标准；

(c) 制定不同用途用水的最低质量标准，包括：

　　(i) 饮用水；

　　(ii) 农业用水；

　　(iii) 娱乐用水；

　　(iv) 渔业和野生动物用水；

　　(v) 工业用水；

　　(vi) 环境用水；和

　　(vii) 任何其他用途的水。

145. 空气质量标准

国家环境标准委员会应当——

(a) 规定测量空气质量的标准和程序；

(b) 制定环境空气质量标准；

(c) 制定职业空气质量标准；

(d) 制定各种来源的排放标准；

(e) 规定移动和固定污染源的空气污染控制标准和准则；和

(f) 任何其他空气排放质量标准。

150. 土壤质量标准

国家环境标准委员会应当——

(a) 制定标准和程序,以衡量和判断土壤质量;

(b) 制定土壤质量管理的最低标准;

(c) 就土壤中废弃物的处置、土壤的最佳利用、土壤的分类和鉴定以及土壤保护所需的措施和禁止土壤退化活动制定指导方针;和

(d) 做任何其他有利于监控和控制土壤退化的必要事项。

第五编
税 收 法 规

第十四部
增值税法(第148章)
[2015年] [2019年修订版]

增 值 税 法
（第 148 章）

2015 年 7 月 1 日起生效

[本文件为 2019 年 11 月 30 日版。]

[注：在总检察长办公室的监督下，根据《法律修订法》1994 年第 7 号、《法律修订和年度修订法》第 356 章(R.L.)，以及《法律解释和一般条款法》1972 年第 30 号对本法进行了全面修订与合并。本版本为截至 2002 年 7 月 31 日的最新版本。]

[2015 年第 224 号政府公报；2014 年第 5 号法案；2016 年第 2 号法案；2017 年第 4 号法案；2017 年第 7 号法案；2017 年第 9 号法案；2018 年第 4 号法案；2019 年第 6 号法案；2019 年第 8 号法案；2019 年第 13 号法案]

旨在为增值税的征收、管理、经营制定法律框架并就其他相关事项作出规定的法案。

第一部分
总　　则

1. 简称

（1）本法可称为《增值税法》。

（2）[略]

2. 释义

（1）在本法中，除非上下文另有规定，否则——

"**调整事件**"——

（a）就供应而言，除（b）项所述的供应外，是指——

（i）取消供应；

（ii）供应对价的变更；

（iii）将所供应的物品或其部分退还给供应商；或者

（iv）全部或部分供应的变更或改动，其结果是该供应成为或不再是应纳税供应；和

（b）就应纳税凭单供应而言，是指免税供应凭单的全部或部分款项；或为零税率；

[2016 年第 2 号法案第 90 条]

"**代理人**"是指在业务中代表他人行事的人；

"**辅助运输服务**"是指装卸服务、捆绑和固定服务、货物检查服务、海关单证准备服务、集装箱装卸服务以及运输货物或待运输货物的仓储服务；

"**社团**"是指在坦桑尼亚大陆创立、组织、设立或认可的合伙企业、信托机构或团体，不包括公司；

"**主任专员**"是指根据《坦桑尼亚税务局法》任命的坦桑尼亚税务局主任专员；

[第 399 章]

"**商业用房**"是指建筑物内的用房,包括作为酒店、汽车旅馆、公寓楼、招待所、旅舍、小屋、别墅、服务式公寓或类似场所经营的建筑物的一部分或一组建筑物,或在开发作为露营地的场地上,定期或通常以定期收费的方式提供的住宿或其他提供给个人短期居住的住宿,但不作为个人的主要住所；

"**公司**"与《公司法》赋予它的含义相同；

[第 212 章]

"**个体**"是指——

（a）两个人,其之间的关系可以合理地预期一个人会按照另一个人的意图行事,或者可以合理地预期两个人都会按照第三人的意图行事；

（b）就个人而言,该个人和——

（i）其丈夫或妻子；

（ii）其亲属的丈夫或妻子；

（iii）其丈夫或妻子的亲属；

（iv）其丈夫或妻子亲属的丈夫或妻子；和

（v）其亲属；

（c）合伙企业和其合伙人,该合伙人单独或与合伙人相关的其他人共同控制该合伙企业 10%或以上的收入或资本权利；

（d）公司和其股东,该股东直接或间接、单独或和与其有关联的主体共同控制该公司 10%或以上的表决权或者收入或资本分配权；

（e）一家公司和另一家公司,某个主体直接或间接、单独或和与其有关联的主体共同控制这两家公司 10%或以上的股权或者收入或资本分配权；

（f）以信托受托人身份行事的个人和是或可能是该信托受益人的个人,或其亲属是或可能是该信托受益人的个人；和

（g）控制另一人的人,前者在法律上或业务上能够对后者进行约束或指示；

"**文件**"是指书面陈述,包括以纸质或电子形式保存的账目、评估、账簿、证书、索赔、票据、通知、命令、记录、申报表或裁决；

"**经济活动**"是指——

（a）个人连续或定期进行的活动,该活动涉及或意图涉及货物、服务或不动产的供应,包括——

（i）以商业、专业、职业、贸易、制造或任何类型的经营形式进行的活动,无论该活动是否以营利为目的；或者

（ii）以租赁、租用、许可或类似安排的方式供应财产；

（b）具有贸易性质的一次性投资或经营；和

（c）在本定义(a)项或(b)项所界定的经济活动开始或终止期间或者就其开始或终止所采取的任何行动,但"经济活动"不包括——

（i）雇员为雇主提供服务的活动；或者

　　　　（ⅱ）以公司董事身份从事的活动，但该董事进行某项经济活动而接受了该项职务的情况除外，在这种情况下，该等服务应被视为是在进行该项经济活动的过程中或促进该项经济活动过程中提供的；

"**娱乐活动**"是指提供食物、饮料、娱乐、消遣或任何形式的招待；

"**豁免**"，就供应或进口而言，是指根据本法规定被指定为豁免的供应或进口，或指获得豁免供应的权利或选择权；

"**出口**"，就货物供应而言，是指货物从坦桑尼亚大陆某地运往联合共和国境外的某地，在没有相反证据的情况下，以下证据足以证明货物已如此出口——

　　（a）货物托运或交付至联合共和国境外地址的证据；或者

　　（b）将货物交付给从事国际运输的船舶、飞机或其他运输工具的所有人、承租人或经营人，以便将货物运出联合共和国的证据；

"**供应的公允市场价值**"是指——

　　（a）在无关联关系的个体之间自由进行的公开市场交易中，该供应可获得的对价；或者

　　（b）在无法根据（a）款确定数额的情况下，在没有关联的个体之间自由进行的公开市场交易中，类似的供应将获得的公允市场价值，且该公允市场价值需根据此类供应与实际供应之间的差异进行调整；

"**融资租赁**"是指根据《融资租赁法》被视为融资租赁的租赁，但不包括分期付款购买协议的租赁；

[第 417 章]

"**金融服务**"是指以下服务——

　　（a）贷款、信贷、信用担保和资金担保的发放、谈判和处理，包括发放者对贷款、信贷或信用担保的管理；

　　（b）与存款、往来账户、付款、转账、债务、支票或流通票据有关的交易，但商账追收或债务保理除外；

　　（c）与金融衍生品、远期合同、购买金融工具期权和类似安排有关的交易；

　　（d）与股份、股票、债券和其他证券有关的交易，但不包括托管服务；

　　（e）在福利基金、公积金、养老基金、退休年金基金、保本基金或类似基金支付或发放福利的计划中，涉及授予或转让权益所有权的交易；

　　（f）涉及提供或转让健康或人寿保险合同的所有权，或者就该合同提供再保险的交易；

　　（g）支付或收取任何股份、债务证券、股权证券、参与式证券、信贷合同、人寿保险合同或期货合同的利息、本金、股息或其他款项；和

　　（h）外汇交易，包括提供外国汇票和国际汇票，

但不包括提供服务、安排或促进第（a）款至（h）款规定的任何服务；

"**固定地点**"，就进行某项经济活动而言，是指进行该项经济活动的地点，即——

　　（a）管理场所；

　　（b）分公司、办事处、工厂或车间；

　　（c）矿井、油井、气井、采石场或任何其他开采自然资源的场所；或者

(d) 建筑工地、建筑或安装工程；

"**货物**"是指各种有形动产,不包括股份、股票、有价证券和货币；

"**政府实体**"是指——

  (a) 坦桑尼亚联合共和国政府或其部委、部门或机构；

  (b) 由联合国政府拥有或经营的法定机构、部门或企业；或者

  (c) 地方政府机关；

"**进口**"是指将货物从联合共和国境外带入或导致货物从联合共和国境外带入坦桑尼亚大陆；

"**进口服务**"是指向纳税人提供的服务,该服务的提供不是根据本法确定在联合共和国境内提供的；

"**不动产**"包括——

  (a) 对土地的权益或权利；

  (b) 要求获得或被授予土地权益或权利的个人权利；

  (c) 占用土地的权利或可在土地上行使或与土地有关的任何其他合同权利；

  (d) 提供住宿；或者

  (e) 获得第(a)款至(d)款所述任何物品的权利或选择权；

"**所得税**"具有《所得税法》赋予的含义；

[第332章]

"**进项税**",就纳税人而言,是指——

  (a) 就向该个人提供的应税供应所征收的增值税,包括该个人就进口服务的应税供应所应缴纳的增值税；

  (b) 对该个人应税进口货物征收的增值税；和

  (c) 根据坦桑尼亚桑给巴尔适用的增值税管理法律征收的进项税；

"**进项税抵免**",就纳税人而言,是指对该个人产生的进项税额允许的抵免；

"**国际援助协定**"是指联合共和国政府与外国政府或国际公共组织之间关于向联合共和国提供财政、技术、人道主义或行政援助的协定；

"**国际运输服务**"是指除通过公路、铁路、水路或航空运输乘客或货物的辅助运输服务外的以下服务——

  (a) 从联合共和国境外某地前往境外的另一地；

  (b) 从联合共和国境外某地前往坦桑尼亚大陆某地；或者

  (c) 从坦桑尼亚大陆某地前往联合共和国境外某地；

"**部长**"指负责财政的部长；

"**货币**"是指——

  (a) 在联合共和国或其他国家作为法定货币的任何硬币或纸币；

  (b) 作为联合共和国或其他国家使用或流通,或旨在作为货币使用或流通的流通票据；

  (c) 交易媒介、本票、银行汇票、邮政汇票、汇票或类似票据；或者

  (d) 通过信用卡或借记卡,或者以在账户贷记或借记的方式支付的任何款项,

但不包括作为古董收集的收藏品、硬币或纸币；

"**净额**",就某一纳税期而言,是指根据第67条计算的数额;

[第4章第8节]

"**非营利组织**"是指专为以下目的而成立和运作的慈善或宗教组织——

(a) 减轻公众的贫困或痛苦;

(b) 提供一般公共卫生、教育或用水;和

(c) 提供宗教服务;

"**销项税**",就纳税人而言,是指该个人就以下事项应缴纳的增值税——

(a) 作出的应税供应;和

(b) 获得的进口服务的应税供应;

"**合伙**"是指两人或两人以上从事经济活动;

"**个体**"是指——

(a) 个人;

(b) 公司;

(c) 团体;

(d) 政府实体,无论该实体通常是否被视为独立的个体;

(e) 外国政府或其政治分支机构;

[第4章第8节]

(f) 非政府组织;或者

(g) 国际公共组织;

"**预付费电信产品**"是指电话卡、预付卡、充值卡或任何其他形式的电信服务预付款;

"**渐进式或周期性供应**"是指——

(a) 根据渐进式或周期性付款的协议、安排或法律提供的渐进式或周期性供应;

(b) 以租赁、租用、许可或其他财产使用权的方式供应,包括融资租赁项下的供应;或者

(c) 在建筑物或工程的建造、重大改建或扩建过程中直接供应的物资;

"**注册人员**"是指根据本法办理增值税登记的个人;

"**注册门槛**"是指第28条第(4)款规定的金额;

"**个人的亲属**"是指该个人的兄弟、姐妹、祖先或直系后代;

"**住宅房屋**"是指被占用或拟被占用的并且能够作为住宅使用的区域,包括——

(a) 任何车库、储藏室或与房屋相关的其他空间,只要该空间的类型通常被认为是该等住宅房屋的一部分;和

(b) 可合理归属于该房屋的任何土地,

但不包括用于提供商业住宿的房屋或其部分;

"**居民**"是指永久居住在坦桑尼亚大陆的个人;

"**居民公司**"是指在坦桑尼亚注册成立或根据《公司法》获得合规证书的公司,或其管理和控制中心位于坦桑尼亚大陆的公司;

[第212章]

"**居民信托**"是指大多数受托人是坦桑尼亚大陆居民或信托的管理和控制地点位于坦桑

尼亚大陆的信托;

"居民社团"是指符合以下条件的除信托以外的其他社团——

(a) 在坦桑尼亚大陆成立;或者

(b) 其管理和控制地点位于坦桑尼亚大陆。

"常驻政府实体"是指在坦桑尼亚大陆有住所的政府实体;

"销售"是指作为所有人对货物或不动产的处置权的转让,包括交换或易货,但不包括要约或公开出售货物或不动产;

"服务"是指非货物、不动产或货币的任何事物,包括但不限于——

(a) 提供信息或建议;

(b) 授予、转让、终止或放弃权利;

(c) 提供便利、机会或优势;

(d) 为避免或容忍某项活动、某种情况或某种行为的发生而签订协议;和

(e) 签发、转让或放弃许可证、执照、证书、特许权、授权或类似权利;

"与土地直接相关的服务"是指以下服务——

(a) 在土地上实际提供的服务;

(b) 与特定土地有关的专家和房地产经纪人的服务;或者

(c) 与在特定土地上实施或将要实施的建筑工程有关的服务;

"供应"是指任何种类的供应;

"税务决定"具有《税收管理法》规定的相同含义,并且应当包括第90条所述的决定;

[第348章]

"应税部分"是指根据以下公式计算出的税额——

$$\frac{R}{100+R}$$

其中"R"是第5条中规定的增值税税率;

"税务发票"是指根据本法第86条和依据本法制定的法规出具的文件;

"纳税期间"是指自每月的第一日起至该月最后一日止的一个自然月;

"应税进口"是指除免税进口以外的货物进口;

"纳税人"是指注册人员或依本法规定应办理增值税登记的个人;

"应税供应"是指——

(a) 在坦桑尼亚大陆由纳税人在从事或促进其经济活动的过程中作出的供应(豁免供应除外);或者

(b) 向作为买方并在经济活动过程中获得服务的纳税人提供的进口服务,而该服务是由纳税人在坦桑尼亚大陆为促进经济活动的过程中提供的——

(i) 该服务的供应将按零税率以外的税率纳税;和

(ii) 买方将无权获得本应对供应品征收的90%或以上增值税的抵免;

"电信服务"是指公司通过传输、发射或接收任何性质的标志、信号、文字、图像和声音或可理解信息,或者通过电线、光学、视觉或其他电磁手段所提供的任何描述的服务,包括——

(a) 语音、语音邮件、数据服务、音频文本服务、视频文本服务、无线电寻呼等新兴电

信服务;

(b) 固定电话服务,包括提供接入和使用公共交换或非交换电话网络,以传送及交换话音、数据和视频,以及往返国内和国际目的地的入境和出境电话服务;

(c) 蜂窝移动电话服务,包括提供接入和使用交换或非交换网络,以传输语音、数据、视频和增值服务,以及往返国内和国际目的地的入境和出境漫游服务;

(d) 运营商服务,包括提供有线、光纤或无线设施以及用于发起、终止或传输呼叫的任何其他技术,对互连、结算或终止国内或国际电话的收费,对包括电线杆附件在内的共同使用的设施收费,对专用电路、租用电路或专用链路收费,包括语音电路、数据电路或电报电路;

(e) 有偿提供的呼叫管理服务,包括呼叫等待、呼叫转移、来电识别、多路呼叫、呼叫显示、呼叫返回、呼叫屏幕、呼叫阻止、自动回拨、呼叫应答、语音邮件、语音菜单和视频会议;

(f) 专用网络服务,包括在指定点之间提供有线、光纤、无线或任何其他电子通信连接技术,供客户专用;

(g) 数据传输服务,包括提供接入有线或无线设施,以及专门为高效传输数据而设计的服务;和

(h) 通过传真、传呼机、电报、电传和其他电信手段进行的通信服务;

"电信服务提供商"是指获得坦桑尼亚通信监管局或同等国外机构的许可提供电信服务的个体;

"供应时间"是指——

(a) 就货物供应而言,指交付或提供货物的时间;

(b) 就提供服务而言,指提供服务或履行服务的时间;或者

(c) 就不动产的供应而言,指该不动产——

(i) 创建、转移、分配、授予或以其他方式提供给客户的较早时间;或者

(ii) 交付或提供的较早时间;

"信托"是指以特定信托财产的受托人或受托人身份行事的人;

"信托财产"是指由作为和解、信托或遗产受托人的一人或多人持有的财产;

"增值税"是指对应税供应品或应税进口货物征收的税款,包括根据本法规定应缴纳的利息、罚款或罚金;

"增值税申报表"是指纳税人应向主任专员提交的申报表,其中提供了有关该个人或其他人根据本法纳税义务的必要信息;

[第4章第8条]

"凭证"是指邮票、代币、优惠券或类似物品,包括以电子形式发行的物品,持有人可用其兑换商品、服务或不动产,包括预付费的电信产品,但不包括邮票;

"桑给巴尔进项税",就纳税人而言,是指——

(a) 根据适用于坦桑尼亚桑给巴尔的增值税法,对向该纳税人提供的应税供应征收的增值税;和

(b) 根据适用于坦桑尼亚桑给巴尔的增值税法,对个人的应税进口货物征收的增值

税;和

"零税率",就供应或进口而言,是指——

(a) 本法规定为零税率的供应或进口;或者

(b) 根据本法规定,提供接受零税率供应的权利或选择权。

(2) 就本法而言,货物应参考《建立东非共同体关税同盟议定书》附件1规定的税则号进行分类,在解释该附件时,应适用其中所列的一般解释规则。

第二部分
增值税的征收

(a) 征收和豁免

3. 征收增值税

应对应税供应品和应税进口货物征收增值税。

4. 增值税纳税义务人

以下人员应缴纳增值税——

(a) 就应税进口而言,指进口商;

(b) 就在坦桑尼亚大陆进行的应税供应而言,指供应商;和

(c) 就应税的进口服务而言,指买方。

5. 增值税税率和应纳税额

(1) 增值税的应纳税额,按照供应价值或者进口价值乘以增值税税率计算,税率为18%。

(2) 供应或进口为零税率的,则增值税税率为零。

(3) 供应既可免税又是零税率的,则该供应为零税率供应。

(4) 供应既可免税又可按标准税率征税的,则该供应应按本条所规定的标准税率征税。

[2016年第2号法案第91条]

6. 法律规定的豁免和税率

(1) 除本法或附则另有规定,否则——

(a) 一种供应品、一类供应品、进口产品或一类进口产品不得免税或零税率;和

(b) 个人或一类人不得豁免缴纳本法规定征收的增值税。

(2) 尽管有第(1)款的规定,部长仍可通过在《公报》发布的命令,对以下情况给予增值税豁免:

(a) 由与坦桑尼亚联合共和国政府签订履约协议的当地制造商进口仅用于制造长效蚊帐的原材料;

(b) 由政府实体进口或向政府实体提供货物或服务,仅用于实施由以下来源资助的项目——

(i) 政府;

(ii) 通过坦桑尼亚联合共和国政府与另一个政府、自然灾害或灾难的捐赠者或贷款人之间的协议,提供的优惠贷款、非优惠贷款或捐赠款;或者

[第134章]

(ⅲ) 根据《政府贷款、赠款和担保法》的规定,由部长正式批准的在地方政府当局和捐助者之间签订的赠款协议:

但该协议应规定该等货物或服务免征增值税;或者

[第4章第8条]

(c) 为救济自然灾害或灾难而进口或提供货物或服务。

(3) 如果上述货物或服务以任何方式转让、出售或以其他方式处置给无权享有本法赋予的类似特权的其他人,则根据本条授予的豁免将停止生效,增值税应到期缴纳,如同未授予豁免一样。

(4) 部长根据第(2)款发布的命令应指明有资格获得豁免的商品或服务以及豁免的起止日期。

(5) 为本条之目的,根据可能需要的条款和条件,部长可以——

(a) 任命一个技术委员会,该委员会应就豁免的授予和监督向部长提供建议;和

(b) 规定程序,以监督根据本条所授予的豁免的使用情况。

(6) 根据第(5)款任命的委员会应由以下机构的代表组成——

(a) 负责财政和规划的部委;

(b) 总检察长办公室;

(c) 负责地方政府的部委;和

(d) 坦桑尼亚税务局。

(7) 委员会可根据需要,选派具有特殊知识或技能的人就某一特定事项提供专业知识。

(8) 在本条中,"政府资助的项目"是指政府就以下事项资助的项目——

(a) 运输、供水、供气或供电基础设施;

(b) 向公众提供健康或教育服务的建筑物;或者

(c) 残疾人中心。

[2015年第9号法案第34条;2017年第9号法案第34条;2018年第4号法案第67条;2019年第13号法案第101条]

7. 条约

如坦桑尼亚联合共和国政府与《外交和领事豁免及特权法》所列的国际机构签订了经部长批准的协议,依据该协议个人在购买或进口时可享受免税待遇,则根据本法规定,该豁免应通过以下方式实施——

(a) 豁免该个人进口货物的进口;或者

(b) 经本人申请,退还其应税供应的应纳增值税。

[2017年第9号法第35条;第356章]

(b) 进口增值税

8. 进口增值税的缴纳与征收

(1) 应税进口货物应缴纳的增值税,则——

(a) 如果货物是进入坦桑尼亚大陆供国内消费的,应遵守本法规定和《东非海关管理法》适用的程序;或者

(b) 在其他情况下,如果进口货物是为了供坦桑尼亚大陆使用的,则应当在货物进入坦桑尼亚大陆之日并按照本法规定的方式纳税。

(2) 应税进口货物的增值税缴纳义务因本法的实施而产生,不取决于主任专员对应纳增值税税额的评估。

(3) 主任专员应在应税进口货物进口时征收本法规定的增值税。

(4) 除非出现相反的意图,否则——

(a) 就本法而言,《东非海关管理法》的规定应适用于应税进口货物的应缴增值税,如同《东非海关管理法》规定的应缴关税一样;和

(b) 本法中关于进口货物所使用的术语与《东非海关管理法》中的含义相同。

[2005年第1号法案]

9. 进口价值

进口货物的价值为以下各项之和——

(a) 根据《东非海关管理法》征收关税的货物价值,无论该进口货物是否需要缴纳关税;

(b) 进口货物应缴纳的关税金额;和

(c) 除关税和增值税外,该进口货物应缴纳的任何税项、征费、费用或其他财政费用的金额。

[2005年第1号法案;2016年第2号法案第92条;第4章第8条]

10. 退货价值

凡——

(a) 货物在出口后为进行维修、保养、清洁、翻新、改装、处理或其他物理加工而进口的;和

(b) 该货物自出口后其形式或性质未发生改变的,

进口货物的价值应为因维修、保养、清洁、翻新、改装、处理或其他物理加工而增加的价值。

11. 对进口资本货物延期征收增值税

(1) 注册人员可按规定的形式和方式,向主任专员申请批准延期缴纳进口资本货物的增值税。

(2) 主任专员应批准根据本条提出的申请,但须满足以下条件——

(a) 该个人正在从事经济活动;

(b) 该个人的营业额至少占或预计占应税供应的90%;

(c) 该个人妥善保存记录和提交增值税申报表,并遵守本法和其他税法规定的义务;和

(d) 根据第(3)款并无理由驳回该申请。

(3) 如申请人或与申请人相关的个人存在以下情况,主任专员应拒绝根据本条提出的申请——

(a) 根据任何税法的规定,存在未清债务或未清申报;或者

(b) 因逃避缴纳税款、关税或存在违反贸易法律或法规有关的罪行而被坦桑尼亚联合共和国或其他国家的法院定罪。

(4) 如果申请人未能说明延期缴纳进口增值税,所述货物以任何方式转让、出售或以其他

方式处置给另一个无权享受本法赋予的类似特权的人,则根据本法授予的延期缴纳应停止生效,增值税应到期缴纳,如同未授予延期缴纳一样。

(5) 主任专员应在收到申请之日起 14 日内,将批准或驳回申请的决定通知该申请人。

(6) 主任专员批准该申请的,该申请应当自决定所述之日起生效。

(7) 如申请被驳回,主任专员应说明驳回的理由,并给予申请人对该决定提出异议和上诉的权利。

(8) 在以下情况下,主任专员可撤销根据本条作出的批准——
    (a) 该个人不再符合批准要求;或者
    (b) 根据本法或其他税法,该个人可能被罚款或处罚,或被起诉或定罪。

(9) 根据本条获得批准的个人,应将其应税进口产品的应纳税额视为其在货物进入国内消费的纳税期间应缴纳的销项税额。

(10) 就本条而言,"资本货物"是指用于个人经济活动的货物,其有效经济寿命至少为一年,并且不是——
    (a) 消耗品或原材料;和
    (b) 在该个人通常的经济活动中以转售为主要目的而进口的货物,不论货品是否以进口时的形式或状态进口。

[2016 年第 2 号法案第 93 条;2018 年第 4 号法案第 22 条]

(c) 供应品增值税

12. 供应标的和子类别

(1) 除货币外,任何人能够提供的任何物品均为供应标的。

(2) 就本法而言,每项已提供或能够提供的供应均应被认定为——
    (a) 货物供应;
    (b) 不动产的供应;或者
    (c) 服务的供应。

(3) 就本法而言,货物供应包括——
    (a) 出售、交换或以其他方式转让作为所有人的货物处置权,包括根据租赁协议进行的处置;和
    (b) 就货物授予的租赁、租用或其他使用权,包括根据融资租赁提供的货物。

13. 供应的对价

(1) 就本法而言,与供应有关的"对价"是指以下各项金额的总和——
    (a) 任何人就供应、响应供应或诱导供应而直接或间接支付或应付的款项;和

[第 4 章第 8 条]

    (b) 任何人就供应、响应供应或诱导供应而直接或间接以实物支付或应付的任何物品的公允市场价值。

(2) 在不限制第(1)款范围的前提下,供应的对价包括——
    (a) 根据本法征收的任何关税、征费、费用、收费或税收,包括增值税——
        (i) 由供应商在供应时或因供应而支付;和

(ii) 包含在向客户收取的费用中或添加到该费用中；

(b) 参照供应商的成本计算或表示的向客户收取的任何金额；

(c) 自动添加到供应价格中的任何服务费；和

(d) 货物在可退还的集装箱内出售时支付的保证金，且该费用可在归还集装箱时退还。

(3) 供货的对价不应包括供应时允许并计入的价格折扣或返利。

(4) 代理人为付款人实际偿还的费用，不应构成该代理人向付款人所作供应的对价的一部分。

14. 单一和多重供应

如果供应由一个以上要素组成，在确定本法如何适用于供应时，应考虑以下标准——

(a) 每项供应通常应被视为不同且独立的；

(b) 从经济、商业或技术角度看构成单一供应的供应，不得人为分割；

(c) 应确定交易的基本特征，以确定向客户提供的是几项不同的主要供应，还是单一供应；

(d) 如果一个或多个要素构成主要供应，则为单一供应，在此情况下，其他要素为辅助或附属供应，被视为主要供应的一部分；或者

(e) 如果供应本身不构成顾客的目的，而仅仅是为了更好地享受所供应的主要物品的一种手段，则该供应应视为主要供应的辅助或附属。

15. 增值税缴纳时间

对应税供应所征收的增值税应于以下日期（以较早者为准）缴纳——

(a) 供应商开具供货发票的时间；

(b) 收到全部或部分供应的对价的时间；或者

(c) 供应时间。

16. 渐进式、临时出售和自动售货机的例外情况

(1) 尽管第15条有以下规定——

(a) 如累进或定期供应按照第19条的规定被视为一系列单独供应，则对每项供应征收的增值税须按以下时间缴付——

(i) 供应商为供货单独出具发票的，则在出具发票时；

(ii) 在支付供应的部分对价时；

(iii) 在供应的对价到期支付时；或者

(iv) 如果供应商和客户之间存在关联——

(aa) 就定期供应而言，在该供应所涉期间的第一天；或者

(bb) 就累进供应而言，在供应时；

(b) 根据分期付款协议供应应税货物的，在每次支付部分对价时，应就供应的应税货物缴纳增值税；和

(i) 届时应缴纳的增值税额为已缴税额的应税部分；和

(ii) 如果应税供应是通过自动售货机、计价器或其他自动装置（不包括由硬币、纸币或代币操作的付费电话）进行的，则当供应商或其代表从自动

售货机、计价器或其他自动装置中取出硬币、纸币或代币时应缴纳增值税。

(2) 就第(1)款而言,"分期付款协议"指买卖协议,其中——
  (a) 在支付定金后,至少再支付一笔款项;
  (b) 交付货物的时间在支付定金之后;和
  (c) 货物的所有权因交付而转移。

(3) 部长可制定规章,规定根据本条就以下情况缴纳增值税——
  (a) 根据其他法律规定,受法定冷却期约束的应税供应;
  (b) 在供应的总对价确定之前发生的应税供应;
  (c) 根据协议进行的应税供应,而该协议规定在满足某些条件之前保留部分或全部对价;或者
  (d) 后续才知晓其正确的增值税处理方法的应税供应。

17. 应税供应的价值

(1) 在坦桑尼亚大陆进行的应税供应的价值,应为该供应的对价减去与该对价应税部分相等的金额。

(2) 进口服务的应税供应价值,应为该供应的对价。

(3) 非应税供应的价值,应为该供应的对价。

(4) 不支付对价的供应价值,应为公允市场价值。

18. 向相关个体提供供应的例外情况

纳税人向其相关个体提供应税供应,且该供应是无偿或其对价低于公允市场价值的,则该供应的价值应为该供应的公允市场价值减去该公允市场价值的应税金额。

19. 渐进式或周期性供应

(1) 渐进式或周期性供应的每一部分应视为单独供应。

(2) 如渐进式或周期性供应的累进或定期部分不易识别,则应将该供应视为一系列单独的供应,每项供应与每部分对价所涉及的供应比例相对应。

[第4章第8条]

(3) 为确定租赁各部分或者其他财产使用权的供应时间,该供应应视为在租赁或者使用权期间内的连续供应。

20. 经济活动的出售

(1) 在以下情况下,经济活动应作为持续经营的实体出售——
  (a) 向经济活动的购买者提供经济活动持续经营所需的一切物品;和
  (b) 购买者在销售过程中或为销售后进行的经济活动的目的进行收购。

(2) 在不影响第(1)款规定的前提下,经济活动的一部分如果能够单独运作,即属于一项经济活动。

(3) 如果纳税人在坦桑尼亚大陆进行供应,则该纳税人向另一纳税人的出售作为持续经营的经济活动的交易的一部分——
  (a) 该供应应被视为在坦桑尼亚大陆进行的单一供应;和
  (b) 该单一供应应被视为不构成供应。

(4) 为了计算供应商就第(3)款适用的交易而享有的进项税抵免的权利——
    (a) 为交易目的获取货物或服务时产生的任何进项税——
        (i) 如果该供应商在其他情况下只提供应税供应,则应视为与该等供应相关;和
        (ii) 在其他情况下,按照部分进项税抵免公式计算;和
    (b) 根据第70条进行的计算不得包括持续经营的单一供应的价值。

21. 权利、凭证和期权的税务处理

(1) 其中——
    (a) 权利、期权或凭证的供应属于应税供应;和
    (b) 后续供应是在行使权利、期权时提供的,或作为对后续供应的全部或部分付款凭证的回报,后续供应的对价仅限于后续供应或与行使权利或期权有关的额外对价。

(2) 其中——
    (a) 权利、期权或凭证的供应不属于应税供应;
    (b) 后续供应是在行使权利或期权时提供的,或作为对后续供应的全部或部分付款凭证的回报;和
    (c) 后续供应属于应税供应,则后续供应的对价应包括提供权利、期权或凭证而给予的对价。

(3) 就本法而言,提供凭证应视为提供服务。

22. 权利、凭证和期权的偿付

其中——
    (a) 应税供应是在行使权利或期权时提供的,或作为对后续供应的全部或部分付款凭证的回报;和
    (b) 提供该项供应的纳税人收到或将要收到他人就行使权利、期权或接受凭证,或因供应而支付的款项,

纳税义务人应被视为已向付款人提供了应税供应,而收到的款项应被视为该供应的对价。

23. 权利、凭证和期权的进项税抵免

(1) 部长可以规定任何种类的书面证明以代替税务发票,纳税人应持有该证明以支持其在获得凭证或在后续提供的退回凭证中可以享有的进项税抵免。

(2) 在没有上述规定的情况下,任何能够合理计算基本税赋的文件都可用于支持进项税抵免。

24. 电信服务预付款

(1) 本条应——
    (a) 适用于电信服务提供商提供的预付费电信产品服务;
    (b) 适用于由作为分销商、代理商或电信中介提供的有关预付费电信产品服务;和
    (c) 不适用于一个电信服务提供商向另一个电信服务提供商提供的服务。

(2) 电信服务提供商以低于预期零售价的价格向电信中介提供预付费电信产品的,其对价按中介已支付的预期零售价格来计算。

(3) 电信中介购买并转售预付费电信产品时——
  (a) 中介的收购应视为非收购；和
  (b) 中介的供应应视为非供应。
(4) 电信服务提供商通过电信中介机构代理其提供预付费电信产品的,则该供应的对价不会因支付给中介机构的佣金而减少。

25. 雇员实物福利

如果纳税人是雇主,作为雇员工资的一部分或者由于雇佣关系而向雇员提供应税供应的,则该供应应被视为是以与该供应的公允市场价值相等的对价作出的。

26. 已取消的交易

(1) 如果一项供应或供应协议被取消,而供应商保留了先前支付的部分对价,则根据第71条允许或要求的任何调整,应考虑到保留的金额而予以减少。

(2) 如果一项供应或供应协议被取消,供应商因取消行为而向客户追回一笔款项,则追回的款项应视为在追回款项的纳税期间内就该项供应所收回的对价。

(3) 无论取消是否产生不供应的效果,第(1)款和(2)款的规定均应适用,而上述各款中提及的供应商和客户应被视为在交易未被取消的情况下本应成为供应商和客户的人。

27. 债务人财产的出售

(1) 如债权人将债务人的财产提供给第三人以清偿债务人对债权人所负的全部或部分债务——
  (a) 对第三人的供应应被视为由债务人提供,并据此确定其增值税档次;和
  (b) 债权人负有支付与供应有关的增值税的义务,该增值税应优先以下事项予以支付——
    (i) 清偿债务;和
    (ii) 将债务盈余的收益部分返还给债务人或任何其他人。

(2) 非注册人员但根据第(1)款规定而须缴纳增值税的债权人,应按照法规规定的时间和方式缴纳增值税。

(3) 本条适用于根据第92条为债权人行事的代理人。

第三部分
注 册

28. 注册要求

(1) 就任何月份而言,如果有合理理由预期个人在自上月初开始的12个月内的营业额将等于或大于注册门槛,则该人应从该月的第一天起进行增值税登记。

(2) 就任何月份而言,在以下情况下,个人须自该月第一天起进行增值税登记——
  (a) 在截至上月底的12个月内,该个人的营业额等于或大于注册门槛;或者
  (b) 在截至上月底的6个月内,该个人的营业额等于或大于注册门槛的二分之一。

(3) 如主任专员根据向其提交的客观证据,确信该人不符合第(1)款的要求,则第(2)款的规定不应适用于该人。

(4) 注册门槛的金额按条例予以规定。
(5) 就本部分而言,个人的营业额应为以下各项的总和——
  (a) 该个人在该期间进行的经济活动过程中提供或将要提供的供应品总价值;和
  (b) 在该期间向该个人提供或将提供的进口服务的总价值,如果该人在该期间内是纳税人,则该供应属于应纳税供应。
(6) 就本部分而言,在计算个人的营业额时,以下金额不应包括在内——
  (a) 该个人是纳税人的情况下,不属于应税供应的供应价值;
  (b) 该个人出售的资本资产的价值;
  (c) 仅因将一项经济活动或其部分作为持续经营实体出售而产生的供应价值;和
  (d) 仅因永久停止从事某项经济活动而产生的供应价值。

29. 需要注册的其他人员
(1) 尽管有第 28 条的规定,但在以下情况下,个人须进行增值税登记——
  (a) 该个人在坦桑尼亚大陆从事涉及提供专业服务的经济活动,无论该服务是由该个人或其成员、雇员提供;和
  (b) 在坦桑尼亚大陆提供该类服务的人通常符合以下条件——
    (i) 根据任何成文法,被允许、批准、许可或注册提供该类专业服务;或者
    (ii) 属于对提供该类专业服务具有统一的国家注册要求的专业协会。
(2) 从事经济活动的政府实体或机构应当办理增值税登记。
(3) 尽管有第 28 条的规定,主任专员在纳税人满足以下条件的情况下,可将其登记为意向交易商——
  (a) 提供充分的证据,使主任专员确信其有意开展经济活动,包括合同、投标书、建筑规划、商业计划、银行融资;
  (b) 该个人已经注册的,其提供或将提供的供应属于应税供应;和
  (c) 指明预期经济活动开始生产应税供应的期间。

30. 申请注册的时间
(1) 须办理增值税登记的个人应自规定办理登记之日起 30 日内,向主任专员提出登记申请。
(2) 意向交易商的注册申请可随时提出。
(3) 根据本条规定的注册申请可由代表人提出。

31. 申请方式
部长可在规章中规定提出注册申请的方式。

32. 申请的处理
(1) 如主任专员确信申请人符合增值税注册条件的,应为其进行登记。
(2) 主任专员应在收到申请之日起 14 日内将是否注册的决定以书面形式通知注册申请人。
(3) 第(2)款规定的通知应说明,如果主任专员——
  (a) 对该个人进行登记,则应说明登记的生效之日;或者
  (b) 驳回申请,则应说明作出该决定的理由以及该个人对该决定提出异议和上诉权

利的详细情况,包括提交异议通知的时间、地点和方式。

(4)主任专员应向注册人颁发注册证书。

33. 强制注册

如果主任专员确信——

(a) 个人须进行增值税登记,而该个人尚未提出注册申请,则在不违反第30条规定的情况下,主任专员应对该个人进行登记,并在登记完成之日起14日内将登记事宜通知该个人;或者

(b) 存在充分的理由,包括保护政府收入,则无论该个人的营业额如何,均可为其办理增值税登记。

34. 未能处理申请的影响

主任专员未能在规定时间内处理注册申请者的申请,则在其正式注册之前本法规定不适用于该个人。

35. 纳税人识别号和增值税注册号

注册人应在根据本法要求签发的所有文件上使用纳税人识别号和增值税注册号。

36. 注册涵盖分支机构或部门

个人根据本法进行的注册应为单一注册,该注册应涵盖其分支机构或部门从事的所有经济活动。

37. 变更通知

注册人员应在发生以下变更后的14日内以书面形式通知主任专员——

(a) 注册人员的姓名、商业名称或商号;

(b) 该个人的地址或其他联系方式;

(c) 该个人在坦桑尼亚大陆从事经济活动的一个或多个地点;

(d) 该个人从事的一项或多项经济活动的性质;

(e) 该个人作为注册人员的身份;和

(f) 法规规定的其他变更事项。

38. 定价透明度

(1)注册人员就应税供应公布或作出的报价应为包含增值税的价格,并在公告或者报价中写明该价格包括增值税和应纳的增值税额,但供零售的商品或者服务的价格,如果符合以下情况,则无需要单独注明价格所含的增值税额——

(a) 在以下地点和网站(页)的显著位置展示价格包含增值税的通知——

(i) 在提供商品或服务的场所入口处或其附近,或者网站上;和

(ii) 在进行付款的地点或网页;和

(b) 在提供给客户的收据或发票上单独列明其所涉及的供应所收取的增值税总额,并在适用的情况下,确定哪些项目需要缴纳增值税。

(2)部长可制定法规,规定与注册人员或某类注册人员相关的应税供应的任何其他显示价格的方法,但涉及增值税的专属定价方法只能规定用于向注册人员提供的供应。

(3)纳税人就应税供应收取的价款应被视为包括对该供应应缴纳的任何增值税,无论该个人是否注册,或者在确定价格时是否单独声明其应缴纳或有义务缴纳增值税。

39. 申请撤销注册

（1）注册人员永久停止提供应税供应的,应按条例规定的方式申请撤销其注册。

（2）第（1）款规定的申请,应在该个人永久停止提供应税供应之日起的 14 日内提出。

（3）未达到注册门槛的注册人员可以按规定方式申请撤销其注册。

40. 撤销注册申请的决定

如果主任专员确信申请撤销注册的个人无需办理增值税登记,而该个人已办理登记——

（a）大于 12 个月以上的,主任专员应以书面形式通知撤销该个人的注册;或者

（b）不满 12 个月的,如果主任专业确信撤销该个人的注册是适当的,可以书面形式通知撤销该人的注册。

41. 撤销注册的权力

（1）主任专员如确信以下事项,可以发出通知,撤销无须办理增值税登记的个人的注册——

（a）该个人通过提供虚假或误导性信息获得注册;

（b）该个人未从事经济活动;

（c）该个人已停止生产应税供应品;或者

（d）该个人的应纳税营业额低于注册门槛。

（2）个人注册的撤销应自撤销通知中载明的日期起生效。

42. 被撤销注册的人员

被撤销注册的人应——

（a）立即停止作为注册人员;

（b）立即停止使用或签发任何证明其为注册人员身份的文件,包括税务发票和调整票据,并交出增值税登记证书;和

（c）在其注册撤销之日起 30 日内提交最终增值税申报表,并缴纳本法规定的所有税款。

43. 注册人员名单

（1）主任专员应保存并公布最新的注册人员登记册,其中应包括——

（a）注册人的姓名和地址;

（b）注册人从事经济活动所使用的一个或多个企业或公司名称;

（c）注册人的纳税人识别号和增值税登记号;和

（d）注册生效日期。

（2）主任专员应保存一份完整的登记册历史记录,以识别增值税登记人员的身份,并应要求向公众提供该记录,或将历史信息列入已公布的登记册。

第四部分
纳 税 地 点

（a）在坦桑尼亚大陆制造的货物和服务的供应

44. 货物供应

（1）货物在坦桑尼亚大陆交付或提供的,则该货物供应应被视为在坦桑尼亚大陆进行的供应。

（2）就第（1）款而言,在进口坦桑尼亚大陆后,但在进入坦桑尼亚大陆供国内消费前供应的货物,应被视为已在坦桑尼亚大陆境外交付或提供。

45. 货物的出入境

（1）由供应商或根据与供应商签订的合同在坦桑尼亚大陆安装或组装的货物,应被视为在坦桑尼亚大陆进行供应的货物。

（2）货物从坦桑尼亚大陆发运或运输到联合共和国境外某地的,该货物供应应被视为在坦桑尼亚大陆进行的供应。

46. 与不动产有关的供应

（1）提供位于坦桑尼亚大陆的不动产或提供与位于坦桑尼亚大陆的土地直接相关的服务,应被视为在坦桑尼亚大陆提供的供应。

（2）在以下情况下,与不动产直接相关的服务供应应被视为在坦桑尼亚大陆提供的供应——

（a）与该财产相关的土地不在坦桑尼亚大陆境内;和

（b）供应商是——

（i）坦桑尼亚大陆居民;或者

（ii）在坦桑尼亚大陆的固定地点或通过该地点进行经济活动的非居民。

47. 提供与土地直接相关的服务

如果供应商是通过坦桑尼亚大陆的固定地点开展业务的非居民,则与坦桑尼亚大陆以外的土地直接相关的服务供应,应被视为在坦桑尼亚大陆进行的供应。

48. 基本服务的供应

如果水、天然气、石油、电力或热能是通过管道、电缆或其他连续分配网络供应并输送到坦桑尼亚大陆某地,或从坦桑尼亚大陆某地运送到联合共和国境外某地,该供应应被视为在坦桑尼亚大陆进行的供应。

49. 向注册人提供的服务

（1）身为注册人的非居民向身为注册人的客户提供服务,该供应应被视为在坦桑尼亚大陆进行的供应。

（2）如果客户是在坦桑尼亚大陆以外的固定地点或通过该固定地点从事经济活动的非居民,且该供应是在以下情况下进行的,则第（1）款规定无法适用——

（a）以该经济活动为目的;或者

（b）到该固定地点提供。

50. 电信服务

（1）如果坦桑尼亚大陆的个人（电信服务提供商除外）从电信服务提供商处发起供应,无论该个人是否以自己的名义发起供应,该电信服务的供应应被视为在坦桑尼亚大陆进行的供应。

（2）就第（1）款而言,发起电信服务供应的个人应——

（a）控制供应的开始;

（b）支付供应的费用;或者

（c）签订供应合同。

（3）如电信服务提供商因服务类型或客户类别而无法确定第（2）款规定的人员的位置,

则发起电信服务供应的个人应是收到该供应发票的人。

（4）如果在坦桑尼亚大陆发起呼叫的个人是在坦桑尼亚大陆进行全球漫游的非居民,并且该非居民根据与非居民电信服务提供商签订的合同,通过在联合共和国境外设立的某地点支付服务费用,则本条不适用。

[第4章第8节]

51. 向坦桑尼亚大陆未注册人员提供的服务

（1）向非注册人员的客户提供以下任何一项服务,应被视为在坦桑尼亚大陆提供的服务——
　　（a）在坦桑尼亚大陆提供的服务,如果该服务是由居住在坦桑尼亚大陆的个人接受的,并且该个人在坦桑尼亚大陆有效使用或享受该项服务;
　　（b）在坦桑尼亚大陆某地提供的电台或电视广播服务;和
　　（c）向提供服务时居住在坦桑尼亚大陆的个人提供的电子服务。

（2）就本条而言,"电子服务"是指通过电信网络提供或交付的以下任何一项服务——
　　（a）网站、网络托管或程序和设备的远程维护;
　　（b）软件及其更新;
　　（c）图像、文本和信息;
　　（d）数据库访问;
　　（e）自我教育套餐;
　　（f）音乐、电影和游戏,包括游戏活动;和
　　（g）政治、文化、艺术、体育、科学及其他广播和活动,包括广播电视。

52. 向坦桑尼亚大陆未注册人员提供的其他服务

（1）在以下情况下,任何其他服务的供应应被视为在坦桑尼亚大陆的供应——
　　（a）客户是坦桑尼亚大陆居民,且不是注册人员;和
　　（b）供应商是——
　　　　（i）坦桑尼亚大陆居民;或者
　　　　（ii）在坦桑尼亚大陆的某固定地点或通过该地点从事经济活动的非居民;和
　　（c）供应是在该经济活动进行过程中或通过该固定地点提供的。

（2）在坦桑尼亚大陆提供的服务,如果不属于以下情况,则应被视为在坦桑尼亚大陆提供的服务——
　　（a）根据第51条,在坦桑尼亚大陆提供的服务;和
　　（b）供应商是——
　　　　（i）坦桑尼亚大陆居民;或者
　　　　（ii）非居民,并在或通过坦桑尼亚大陆的固定地点进行经济活动。

53. 累进或定期供应

如果累进供应或定期供应是一系列单独的供应,则应当分别确定每次供应的地点。

（b）供联合共和国境外使用的供应

54. 不动产零税率

如果该不动产所涉及的土地在联合共和国境外,则该不动产的供应应为零税率。

55. 货物供应零税率

（1）如果货物出口符合第 2 条规定的"出口"一词的含义,则该货物供应应为零税率。

（2）如果货物是由持许可证的免税供应商提供给游客或访客的,并且该供应商持有在供应时收集的书面证明,证明该货物将被带离联合共和国而未在联合共和国有效使用或享受,则货物供应应为零税率。

（3）第（1）款不适用于在坦桑尼亚大陆再进口的货物。

55A. 向坦桑尼亚桑给巴尔供应货物的零税率

如果当地制造商供应的本地制造货物是提供给根据桑给巴尔增值税法登记的纳税人,且该货物从坦桑尼亚大陆运出且未在坦桑尼亚大陆有效使用或享用,则货物供应应为零税率。

[2016 年第 2 号法案第 94 条]

56. 在联合共和国境外使用的租赁物品

（1）凡在坦桑尼亚大陆以租赁、租用、许可或类似供应方式供应的货物,如果该货物在联合共和国境外使用,并以在境外使用为限,则货物供应应为零税率。

（2）以下条件适用于第（1）款的目的——

（a）在国际领土内租赁货物的使用,如果在此之前货物已在联合共和国境内使用,应被视为完全在联合共和国境内的使用;和

（b）如果货物是运输工具,且租赁、租用、许可或类似供应的总期限等于或少于 30 天,则供应不得为零税率。

57. 用于修理临时进口的货物

在修理、维护、清洁、翻新、改造、处理或以其他方式对临时进口货物造成实际影响的过程中的货物供应,在以下情况下应为零税率——

（a）所供应的货物附于该类临时进口货物,或成为该类临时进口货物的一部分,或因用于修理、维护、清洁、翻新、改造、处理或以其他方式对临时进口货物造成实际影响而无法使用或失去价值;和

（b）临时进口货物——

（i）是根据《东非海关管理法》下的临时进口特别制度进口的,或为履行服务目的而临时带入坦桑尼亚大陆的;

[2005 年第 1 号法案 E.A.C.M]

（ii）在提供服务后被带离坦桑尼亚联合共和国;和

（iii）在坦桑尼亚大陆,除了提供服务或将临时进口货物带入坦桑尼亚大陆或带出联合共和国境外,不得作其他用途。

58. 向非居民担保人提供的货物和服务

如果货物或服务的供应涉及修理或者更换保修期内货物的,则应为零税率,和——

（a）供应是根据与担保人签订的协议提供的并由担保人支付对价,而担保人是非居民,且并非注册人员;和

（b）可以合理地推定,根据本法规定,保修货物在进口时需要缴纳增值税,除非存在无须缴纳增值税的情形。

59. 用于国际运输服务的货物

（1）用于修理、维护、清洁、翻新、改造、处理或以其他方式对从事国际运输服务的飞机或船舶造成实际影响的货物供应，应为零税率。

（2）为飞机或船舶提供的飞机物资或船舶物资，如果是在构成国际运输服务的飞行或航程中用于飞机或船舶上的消费或销售，则应为零税率。

（3）以下服务供应品的税率应为零——
  （a）提供国际运输服务；
  （b）提供国际货物运输保险服务；
  （c）提供维修、维护、清洁、翻新、改造、处理等服务或以其他方式对从事国际运输服务的飞机或船舶造成实际影响的服务；
  （d）向非注册人的非居民提供的以下服务——
    （i）包括国际运输服务中的船舶或飞机的装卸、引航、救助或拖曳服务；或者
    （ii）直接与国际运输服务中的船舶或飞机的营运或管理有关的服务；和
  （e）为经坦桑尼亚大陆过境的货物提供的辅助运输服务，但该服务——
    （i）属于国际运输服务的组成部分；和
    （ii）适用于在港口、机场或申报关税区存放等待运输不超过30日的货物。

（4）就本条而言——

"飞机仓储"是指供飞机的乘客或机组人员使用的物资，或飞机维修用的物资；

"船舶仓储"是指供船舶的乘客、船员使用的物资，或船舶维修用的物资；和

与飞机仓储和船舶仓储有关的"物资"，包括飞机或船舶使用的货物、燃料和备件，以及其他物品或设备，不论是否可供立即装配。

[2017年第4号法案第67条；第4章第8条]

60. 为在联合共和国境外使用而提供的服务

（1）与联合共和国境外土地直接相关的服务供应应为零税率。

（2）在提供服务时，对位于坦桑尼亚联合共和国境外货物实际的服务供应应为零税率。

（3）如果服务是在坦桑尼亚联合共和国以外提供的，提供的服务不是在实际服务提供的时间和地点以外的任何时间和地点实际接受的，则该服务供应应为零税率。

61. 临时进口相关的服务

如果服务包括修理、维护、清洁、翻新、改造、处理或以其他方式对以下物品造成实际影响的，则该服务供应应为零税率——
  （a）是根据《东非海关管理法》下的临时进口特别制度进口，或为履行服务目的而临时带入坦桑尼亚大陆的货品；和
  （b）在提供服务后被运离坦桑尼亚联合共和国，且在坦桑尼亚大陆除能够提供服务或将货物运进坦桑尼亚大陆或带出联合共和国外，不得作任何用途。

[2005年第1号法案；2016年第2号法案第95条]

61A. 服务供应的零税率

（1）在以下情况下，一项服务供应应为零税率——
  （a）供货时客户在坦桑尼亚联合共和国境外，并有效使用或享受该境外的服务；和

(b) 所提供的服务既与位于坦桑尼亚联合共和国境内的土地没有直接关系,也不在供应时对位于联合共和国境内的货物进行实际操作。

(2) 在以下情况下,根据第(1)款的规定,提供的服务不享受零税率待遇——

(a) 提供的是接受随后在坦桑尼亚联合共和国供应的其他物品的权利或选择权;或者

(b) 这些服务是根据与非居民签订的协议而提供的,但服务对象是在联合共和国境内的非注册人员。

[2016年第2号法案第96条]

61B. 零税率的供电服务

坦桑尼亚大陆的一家电力服务供应商向坦桑尼亚桑给巴尔的另一家电力服务供应商提供的电力服务应为零税率。

[2019年第8号法案第48条]

62. 在联合共和国境外使用的知识产权

为在联合共和国境外使用而提供的包括申请、起诉、授予、维护、转让、分配、许可或实施知识产权在内的服务,应为零税率。

63. 运营商之间的电信服务

电信服务提供商向非居民电信服务提供商提供的电信服务应为零税率,包括但不限于涉及在坦桑尼亚大陆终止通话或在坦桑尼亚大陆或通过坦桑尼亚大陆传输信号的服务。

(c) 特 别 规 则

64. 非居民的增值税代表

(1) 在坦桑尼亚境内无固定住所的非居民,在坦桑尼亚境内进行经济活动,并提供该非居民应缴纳增值税的应税供应的,应——

(a) 根据《坦桑尼亚增值税条例》的规定,在坦桑尼亚大陆任命一名增值税代表;

(b) 在主任专员要求的情况下提交担保。

(2) 增值税代表应为居民,并负责完成本法规定的所有事项,其中包括——

(a) 申请注册或注销注册,并履行与注册相关的其他义务;和

(b) 支付根据本法对非居民征收的任何增值税或任何罚款、罚金或利息。

(3) 增值税代表的注册应以委托人的名义进行。

(4) 一个以上非居民的增值税代表,应当为每一个非居民分别办理增值税登记。

65. 国外分支机构提供的服务

(1) 如果纳税人在坦桑尼亚大陆境内的一个固定地点及在坦桑尼亚大陆境外的一个或多个固定地点从事经济活动——

(a) 该个人应被视为两个独立的个人,分别对应于在坦桑尼亚大陆境内和境外开展的经济活动;

(b) 坦桑尼亚大陆境外的个人应被视为向坦桑尼亚大陆境内的个人提供了进口服务,包括坦桑尼亚大陆境内的个人通过坦桑尼亚大陆境外的个人开展的活动或由于坦桑尼亚大陆境外的个人开展的活动而获得的任何服务性质的利益;和

（c）供货时间应在假定已供货的基础上确定。

（2）如在第（1）款所述的供应之日起12个月内,坦桑尼亚大陆境外的个人就该供应向坦桑尼亚大陆境内的个人分摊费用,则该费用的分摊应被视为对价。

（3）如第（1）款所提述的供应是应税供应,则供应的价值——

  （a）在第（2）款规定适用的情况下,应等于所分配的费用金额减去所分配的金额中代表以下情况的部分（如有）——

    （i）支付给该个人在坦桑尼亚大陆境外的雇员的薪金或工资;和

    （ii）该个人在坦桑尼亚大陆境外产生的利息;和

  （b）在任何其他情况下,应假定是由坦桑尼亚大陆境外的非居民向坦桑尼亚大陆境内的联系人提出的。

[2016年第2号法案第97条]

第五部分
退货、付款和退款

（a）退货和付款

66. 增值税申报表

（1）纳税人无论在该纳税期间是否有应缴增值税净额,均应在与之相关的该纳税期间结束后一个月的第20日,按照部长规定的形式和方式提交增值税纳税申报表。

（2）根据本法规定须缴纳增值税的非纳税人,应当在主任专员规定的时间内提交增值税申报表。

（3）已提交增值税纳税申报表的纳税人,可按规定方式提出申请,并在有关报税表的课税期结束后不迟于3年,要求税务专员修改报税表,以改正报税表内任何真正的遗漏或不正确的申报。

（4）凡任何人根据第（3）款提出申请,主任专员可——

  （a）在未对申请人的税务进行审计或调查的情况下,根据申请书中提供的信息对申请作出决定;或者

  （b）修改原申报表或接受提交经修订的申报表。

（5）根据第（4）款,主任专员应在收到申请后90天内作出决定,该决定应以书面形式说明——

  （a）所作修订的详情（如有）;

  （b）作出该决定的理由以及申请人对该决定提出异议和上诉权利的详细情况;和

  （c）提交异议通知的时间、地点和方式。

（6）纳税人如在收到审计或调查通知（如有）前申请修改增值税报税表,则应支付未付税款及适用的逾期付款利息。

（7）就第（1）款而言,如第20天为星期六、星期日或公共假日,增值税应在星期六、星期日或公共假日后的第一个工作日提交。

[2016年第2号法案第98条;2017年第4号法案第68条]

（b）应缴增值税净额

67. 净额的计算和支付

（1）纳税人就某一纳税期间应纳的增值税净额应按以下方式计算——

  （a）将该个人在该纳税期间应缴纳的所有销项税相加；

  （b）减去该纳税期间允许的所有进项税抵免；和

  （c）对由此产生的数额作出如下调整——

    （i）加上该纳税期间需要作出的所有增加调整；和

    （ii）减去该纳税期间允许的所有递减调整。

（2）如果某一纳税期间应缴纳的销项税额为零，其不应妨碍减去进项税抵扣或加减调整。

（3）如果某一纳税期间的净额为正数——

  （a）应由纳税人在缴纳增值税时进行核算和支付；和

  （b）支付净额的法律责任须因本条的施行而产生，并不依赖于主任专员对应缴付款额作出的评估而定。

（4）若某一纳税期间的净额为负数，则应根据第81条的规定结转到一个或多个后续纳税期间，除非根据第82条的规定允许立即退税。

（c）进项税抵免

68. 进项税抵免

（1）在以下情况下，应允许纳税人抵扣其产生的进项税额——

  （a）产生进项税的货物、服务或不动产是该个人在其经济活动过程中为制造应税供应品而取得或进口到坦桑尼亚大陆的；

  （b）在供应的情况下，该个人为供应支付或有义务支付对价；和

  （c）在进口的情况下，该个人支付或有义务支付根据本法对进口征收的增值税或根据坦桑尼亚桑给巴尔适用的增值税法缴纳的进项税，其中相应的货物被转移到坦桑尼亚大陆。

（2）对于应税供应的进口服务，购买方应缴纳的增值税为该个人的销项税和进项税，购买方不得就该供应享受进项税抵免，除非购买方已在要求进项税抵免的同一份增值税申报表中计入销项税。

（3）纳税人不得因以下情况获得进项税抵扣——

  （a）购置货物、服务或不动产，但仅限于其使用的范围内提供娱乐，除非该个人的经济活动涉及在其经济活动的正常过程中的娱乐活动；

  （b）任何个人在体育、社交或娱乐性质的俱乐部、协会或社团中获得会员资格或入会权；

  （c）购置或进口客运车辆，或客运车辆的零部件或为客运车辆提供的维修保养服务，除非该个人的经济活动涉及经营、出租客运车辆或提供客运车辆的运输服务，且该车辆是为此目的而购置的；和

  （d）出口矿产品原料、林产品原料、水产品原料和动物产品原料，但自2017年7月20日起，矿产品原料不得允许进项税额抵免。

[第4章第8条]

(4) 第(3)款第(a)和(b)项的限制不适用于向雇员提供实物福利的购置或进口,其供应应根据第 25 条纳税。

(5) 在将本条适用于术语"调整事件"定义第(b)项所述的调整事件时——

(a) 凡提及"供应",应理解为是指——

(i) 如果增值税以前由供应商入账,则该增值税的价值为发放或出售凭证时支付的附加税;和

(ii) 就供应品应缴纳的增值税而言,如果该凭证的供应品不是应税供应品,则该凭证的供应品应按规定缴纳增值税;和

(b) 第 72 条第(1)款第(b)项第(ii)目的限制不适用。

(6) 如果发生了与进口服务的供应相关的调整事件,则该服务的购买者应被视为该服务的提供者。

[2017 年第 7 号法案第 47 条;2019 年第 8 号法案第 49 条]

69. 进项税抵免的时间

(1) 在允许纳税人抵扣进项税的情况下,根据第 70 条计算抵扣额的纳税期间应为以下两项中的较后一项:

(a) 根据本法就与进项税有关的供应或进口应缴纳增值税的纳税期间;或者

(b) 该个人在该纳税期间未申请进项税抵扣,则可在其后 6 个纳税期间中的任何 1 个纳税期间申请进项税抵扣。

(2) 自税务发票、收据或第(3)款提及的其他证据出具之日起 6 个月后,不得扣除或抵免进项税。

(3) 纳税人不得在第 70 条的计算中包括进项税抵免,除非在为相关纳税期间提交增值税申报表时,该纳税人持有以下资料——

(a) 在由个人进口到联合共和国的情况下,须持有纳税证明、单一行政文件或类似文件,文件上要有进口商的姓名、纳税人识别号和增值税登记号,并经海关正式清关,供坦桑尼亚大陆国内消费;和

(b) 在向坦桑尼亚大陆的个人供应的情况下,须持有供应商根据本法出具的有效税务发票或财政收据。

70. 部分进项税抵免

(1) 本条适用于纳税人在其经济活动过程中获取或进口到坦桑尼亚大陆的货物、服务或不动产所产生的进项税,但仅部分用于提供应税供应品。

(2) 本条所涉及的进项税允许抵扣额应计算如下——

$$\frac{I \times T}{A}$$

[请注意:公式与原文相同]。

其中——

I:为本款涉及并在纳税期间申请抵免的进项税总额;

T:为纳税人在纳税期间提供的所有应税用品的价值;和

A:为纳税人在纳税期间提供的所有供应品的价值。

(3) 根据本条规定允许抵扣的进项税额应为临时性的,并应在每个会计年度结束时对进项税抵扣额进行年度调整,计算方法如下——
  (a) 在该会计年度的 12 个纳税期间中,将第(2)款允许的所有进项税抵免加起来;
  (b) 应用第(2)款中的公式,如同在"I"的定义中提及"纳税期间","A"和"T"指的是相关会计年度;
  (c) 根据第(a)项计算的金额减去根据第(b)项计算的金额,计算调整金额;
  (d) 调整为正数的,纳税人应当在下一个会计年度的第 6 个纳税期间或者规定的更早的纳税期间的增值税纳税申报表中,作与该数额相等的增加调整;和
  (e) 调整额为负数的,允许纳税人在下一个会计年度的第 6 个纳税期间或者规定的更早的纳税期间的增值税纳税申报表中,作与该数额相等的减少调整。
(4) 就本条而言——
  (a) 通过在坦桑尼亚大陆境外的固定地点进行的经济活动所提供的供应品,除非该等供应品是在坦桑尼亚大陆制造,否则不得包括在公式中的 A 或 T 内;
  (b) 如果 T/A 大于 0.90,应允许纳税人抵免本节涉及的所有进项税;和
  (c) 如果 T/A 小于 0.10,纳税人的任何投入均不得抵免本条所涉及的进项税款。

(d) 其 他 调 整

71. 调整事件的后供应调整
(1) 如果调整事件导致供应商先前计入的增值税少于供应品应缴纳的增值税——
  (a) 供应商应——
    (i) 按差额数额进行递增调整;和
    (ii) 在获知该调整事件后的 7 日内向客户发出有效的调整通知单;和
  (b) 如该客户是应纳税人,其应获准作出根据第(1)款第(a)项计算的递减调整。
(2) 如果调整事件使供应商先前计入的增值税超过了该供应商应缴的增值税
  (a) 供应商应——
    (i) 在不违反第 72 条规定的限制条件的情况下,允许作出与差额相等的递减调整;和
    [第 4 章第 8 条]
    (ii) 在获知调整事件后的 7 日内向客户发出有效的调整通知单;和
  (b) 如该客户是应纳税人员,其须作出根据第(3)款计算的递增调整。
(3) 根据第(1)款允许的递减调整,或客户根据第(2)款须作出的递增调整,其金额等于——
  (a) 如果客户有权为原始购置获得全额的进项税收抵免,则为差额的金额;
  (b) 如果客户仅有权抵扣原始购置时的部分进项税,则为差额的适当比例;或者
  (c) 如果客户无权就原始购置获得进项税抵扣,则为零。
  [第 4 章第 8 条]

72. 对调整的限制
(1) 不得根据第 71 条进行递减调整——

（a）就客户而言,除非他在客户就要求调整的纳税期间提交增值税申报表时持有供应商签发的有效调整通知单;和

（b）就供应商而言,除非——

（i）他已向客户发出调整通知,并为自己保留了一份副本记录;和

（ii）如果客户不是注册人员,他已经以现金或作为客户欠供应商的任何金额的抵扣,向客户偿还了超额增值税。

（2）就第（1）条第（b）款第（ii）项而言——

（a）如果供应商退还"调整事件"一词定义的第（a）款第（i）项、第（a）款第（ii）项或第（a）款第（iii）项涵盖的调整事件支付的部分或全部价格,除非有相反证据,否则推定退还金额应包括相当于退还金额应税部分的增值税金额;和

（b）如果供应商因"调整事件"一词定义的第（a）款第（iv）项所涵盖的调整事件而退还一笔金额,除非有相反证据,否则退还的金额将被推定为不再应缴纳的增值税额。

73. 调整期限

（1）纳税人根据第 71 条须作出的递增调整,应在该纳税人意识到调整事件的纳税期间作出。

（2）纳税人根据第 71 条获准的递减调整应为——

（a）就供应商而言,在该供应商发出调整通知书的纳税期间;或者

（b）就客户而言,在客户首次意识到调整事件的纳税期间或其后 6 个纳税期间中的任何一个纳税期间。

[第 4 章第 8 条]

74. 供应后坏账调整

（1）本条适用于应税供应的全部或部分对价尚未支付给供应商的情况。

（2）如果应税供应的全部或部分应付给供应方的对价已逾期超过 18 个月,而供应方已在其账簿中将未付的金额作为坏账注销,则应税供应方应被允许按纳税期间后的未付金额进行递减调整,其中——

（a）首次逾期付款超过 18 个月;或者

（b）在供应商账簿中将这笔债务作为坏账注销。

（3）对于应税供应,应支付给供应商的全部或部分对价逾期超过 18 个月,并且客户就该供应申请进项税额抵免的,客户应当按照首次逾期 18 个月以上的纳税期间未支付的金额进行递增调整。

（4）如果供应商对坏账进行了递减调整,或者客户对逾期债务进行了递增调整,并且客户向供应商支付了部分或全部先前未支付的金额,则应作进一步调整,以确保——

（a）就供应商而言,所缴纳的销项税等于实际收到的对价的应税部分;和

（b）就客户而言,进项税抵免额是实际支付对价中应税部分的适当比例。

（5）根据本节的规定,供应商获准进行递减调整或客户被要求进行递增调整时,不得要求就坏账或逾期债务出具调整说明。

[2017 年第 4 号法案第 69 条]

75. 私人使用申请

（1）将财产用于经济活动以外的其他目的使用或者消费的,被视为将财产用于私人用途。

（2）纳税人在以下情况下,应作出递增调整——

 （a）就购置或进口财产所产生的全部或部分进项税而言,被允许或已经被允许进项税抵免;和

 （b）将同一财产完全用于私人用途,或在将该财产完全用于或部分用于其应税活动,并从某一特定时间起将其适用于这种用途。

（3）递增的调整额应等于以下数额中较小的数额——

 （a）该个人就购置或进口该物品而获准抵免的进项税额;

 （b）如果该财产在用于私人用途之前已用于该人的应税活动,则该财产在首次完全用于私人用途时的公允市场价值的应税部分,减去反映未允许进项税抵扣的部分。

（4）纳税人应就其改装、改进或产生的财产作出递增调整,如果——

 （a）该个人将该财产完全用于私人用途;和

 （b）该个人对该财产的供应本应是应税供应。

（5）根据第（4）款须作出的递增调整金额,须为该财产首次完全用于私人用途时的公允市场价值的应税部分。

（6）根据本条作出的递增调整,应在该财产首次用于私人用途的纳税期间作出。

76. 支付保险金时的调整

（1）在以下情况下,保险人应作出递减调整——

 （a）其根据保险合同向另一人付款;和

 （b）其符合以下所有条件——

  （i）保险合同的供应属于应税供应;

  （ii）该款项并非就提供给保险人的供应或由保险人进口的货物而支付;

[第4章第8条]

  （iii）该项付款并非就提供给他人的供应而缴付,除非该供应属于应税供应,而增值税的税率并非为零;和

  （iv）接受款项的人是居民或非居民,但他们是注册人员:

（2）调整的数额应当与已缴纳税款的部分相等,调整的数额应当反映在已缴纳税款当期的增值税纳税申报表中。

77. 收到保险付款时的调整

（1）在以下情况下,纳税人应作出增加调整——

 （a）某个人根据保险合同获得付款,无论该个人是否是合同的当事人;

 （b）该项付款与发生的损失有关——

  （i）在该个人的经济活动过程中;或者

  （ii）与全部或部分用于该个人经济活动的资产有关;和

 （c）保险合同的供应属于应税供应。

（2）第（1）款所提述的调整须在收到付款的纳税期间作出,而调整的款额须等于所收到

款额的应税部分,或减少至以下程度——
    (a) 造成损失的经济活动涉及制造免税供应品;或者
    (b) 与损失有关的资产被用于制造免税供应品或私人用途;和
    (c) 如果第(a)项和第(b)项均适用,以收到最合适的款额为准。
(3) 在以下情况下,保险人应增加调整额——
    (a) 保险人由于行使保险合同项下的代位求偿权而获得赔偿数额,但加重损害赔偿或惩戒性损害赔偿除外;和
    (b) 保险人根据本条可以就与收回金额有关的付款作出递减调整。
(4) 根据第(3)款作出的调整金额应等于所收回金额的应税部分,该调整应反映在收到该金额的纳税期间的增值税申报表中。

78. 纠正小错误的调整
部长可制定法规以规定条件,在这些条件下,个人可以通过在随后的纳税期间对增值税申报表进行增加调整或减少调整来纠正特定纳税期间增值税申报表中的小错误。

79. 注册时的调整
(1) 在以下情况下,注册人在注册生效前的最后一天结束时,注册人被允许对其拥有的货物作出递减调整——
    (a) 在该个人成为注册人员之前的6个月内,该货物——
        (i) 由该个人进口,而该个人已就进口缴付增值税;或者
        (ii) 已供应给该个人,且该个人持有供应货物的税务发票;
    (b) 该个人在其经济活动过程中获得该货物,其目的是转售;和
    (c) 如果该个人在购置或进口时已注册,则该个人将有权获得进口或购置的进项税抵免。
(2) 允许递减调整的最高数额应等于以下两项中的较小者——
    (a) 个人就进口产品支付的增值税金额,或向该个人供货的供应商应支付的增值税金额;和
    (b) 在该个人成为注册人时,该货物的公允市场价值的应税部分:
(3) 根据本条获准递减调整的人,应在其成为注册人后的前3个纳税期间中的任何一个纳税期间进行调整。
(4) 根据本条作出调整的人,须以书面形式将调整通知主任专员,并提供规则所规定的支持证据。

80. 撤销注册时的调整
(1) 被撤销注册的人如果因购置或进口该财产,或因已纳入该财产的某物而获得进项税抵免,则应在撤销注册时对其手头财产的最终增值税申报表进行递增调整。
(2) 调整额应等于以下两项中的较小者——
    (a) 在撤销前一日该财产的公允市场价值的应税部分;
    (b) 反映该人在购置或进口该财产(如适用)或该财产的投入时未获准进项税抵扣程度的减少的金额。

(e) 退 款

81. 负净额结转

(1) 纳税人应获准对以前纳税期间结转的负净额作出递减调整,其计算方法如下——

 (a) 在任何纳税期间,应首先适用第 67 条,而不考虑本条准许的任何递减调整;

 (b) 如果结果为正数——

  (i) 该纳税人应获准对从以前纳税期间结转的一个或多个负净额中的一部分作出递减调整,以将本期的净额减为正数或减为零;和

  (ii) 以前纳税期间的负净额应按时间顺序计算,最早的先计算,最近的后计算;和

 (c) 不能递减调整的负净额的任何部分应按照第(b)项的规定结转和使用,直至——

  (i) 已减至零;或者

  (ii) 已连续 6 个纳税期结转,且未减至低于条例规定的最低金额。

(2) 在 6 个或 6 个以上纳税期间结转全部或部分负净额的纳税人——

 (a) 在以下情况下,可申请退还未调整的款额——

  (i) 款额等于或大于与第(1)款第(c)项第(ii)目相同的最低款额;或者

  (ii) 该个人在 6 个以上纳税期间结转的所有未经调整款额之和超过该数额;和

 (b) 在任何其他情况下,该个人须继续结转第(1)款下的未调整金额,直至该金额减少至零或因本款第(a)项第(ii)目而产生退款权利为止,以先发生者为准。

(3) 尽管有第(2)款的规定,应税人可选择继续结转未经调整的款额,并按照第(1)款继续适用,直至该人按照第(2)款申请退还该款额为止。

(4) 就本条而言,"最低款额"是指在申报进项税时不考虑的金额。

82. 不结转的退款

(1) 尽管有第 81 条的规定,在以下情况下,纳税人有权获得负净额退款——

 (a) 该个人营业额的 50% 或以上来自或将来自零税率的供应;

 (b) 该个人进项税额的 50% 或以上是在与制造零税率或即将零税率的供应品有关的购置或进口中产生的;或者

 (c) 在任何其他情况下,主任专员确信该个人的业务性质经常导致负净额。

(2) 根据本条有权获得负净额退款的纳税人可以——

 (a) 申请退款;或者

 (b) 选择根据第 81 条将结转该款额,直至该人申请退还本款第(a)项所述款额时为止。

83. 超额退款

(1) 在某一纳税期的退税申报中,纳税人支付的税款超过其增值税税单上显示的净额的,可申请退还多缴的金额。

(2) 如果纳税人在某一纳税期间多缴了应纳税额净额,而多缴的税款是在计算该纳税期的应纳税额净额时产生的,则该纳税人可申请退税,包括——

 (a) 销项税额或递增调整额超出了本应包括在这些计算中的数额;或者

(b) 进项税额或递减调整额少于本应包括在这些计算中的数额。

84. 退款申请

(1) 本条适用于第 81、82 和 83 条规定的退款。

(2) 如任何人有权申请本条所适用的退款,则退款申请须——

 (a) 以条例规定的方式提出,并应附有条例所要求的证明材料;和

 (b) 在根据第 81 或 82 条提出申请的情况下,须在负净额所涉纳税期间结束后 3 年以内提出;或者

 (c) 在根据第 83 条提出申请的情况下,须在多付款项后 3 年内提出申请。

(3) 凡任何人申请与本条相关的退款,主任专员——

 (a) 在有纳税人可信度证明的情况下,可根据所提供的资料对有关申请作出决定,而无须对申请人的税务情况进行审计或调查;和

 (b) 应在收到申请之日起 90 日内对申请作出决定,并将该决定以书面形式通知申请人,说明——

  (i) 允许退还的金额;和

  (ii) 退款的期限。

(4) 如主任专员确信不应予退款,或确信可退还的金额少于申请退还的金额,其应告知——

 (a) 作出决定的理由;

 (b) 申请人对该决定提出异议和上诉的权利;和

 (c) 提交异议通知的时间、地点和方式。

(5) 主任专员如确信存在以下情况,则应退款——

 (a) 该个人有权要求退还所申请的款额;或者

 (b) 较低的金额代表该个人实际享有的退款权利。

(6) 如主任专员确信该个人无权获得退款,则其不得将款项退还该个人。

(7) 如主任专员准许与本条有关的退款,则——

 (a) 除非申请人已提交要求其提交的所有增值税申报表,否则退款将不予支付;和

 (b) 主任专员可将退款首先用于扣减该个人根据本法或其他税法应缴税款的任何未偿债务,包括根据本法或该税法应缴的任何利息、罚金或罚款。

(8) 凡适用第(7)款第(b)项后剩余的款额不超过本条例所规定的最低款额,主任专员可退还该款额,或要求纳税人在主任专员规定的纳税期间将退款作为递减调整。

(9) 凡主任专员根据本条准许退款,则纳税人可经主任专员同意,将退款作为与主任专员商定的纳税期间的递减调整。

[第 4 章第 8 条]

85. 向外交官、国际机构退款

(1) 主任专员可退还因购置或进口而产生的部分或全部进项税给予——

 (a) 国际公共组织、外国政府或条例规定的其他人士,只要该人士根据国际援助协议有权豁免增值税;

 (b) 根据《维也纳外交关系公约》或在坦桑尼亚联合共和国具有法律效力的任何其他国际条约或公约,或根据公认的国际法原则,有权豁免增值税的个人;或者

　　　　(c) 外国在坦桑尼亚大陆设立的外交或领事使团,其与为该特派团的正式目的而进行的交易有关。
　(2) 根据第(1)款提出的退款申请应采用条例规定的格式和方式,并应附有条例要求的证明文件。
　(3) 主任专员应在根据本条提出退款申请之日起的1个税务期间内——
　　　　(a) 就申请作出决定,并将决定通知申请人,说明应退还的金额以及该金额与要求退还的金额之间的差额;和
　　　　(b) 向申请人支付应退还的金额。

[2018年第4号法案第68条]

第六部分
文件和记录

86. 税务发票

　(1) 进行应税供应的注册人应在不迟于根据第15条就该供应缴纳增值税之日,就该供应开具由电子计税设备生成的、按顺序编号的真实无误的税务发票,该发票应包括——
　　　　(a) 按照部长规定的格式和方式颁发;和
　　　　(b) 包括以下信息——
　　　　　　(i) 发布日期;
　　　　　　(ii) 供应商的名称、纳税人识别号和增值税登记号;
　　　　　　(iii) 所供货品的说明、数量和其他相关规格;
　　　　　　(iv) 供应货品的应付对价及包括在该对价内的增值税金额;
　　　　　　(v) 供货价值超过规定的最低限额的,应当提供客户的名称、地址、纳税人识别号码和增值税登记号码;和
　　　　　　(vi) 条例可能规定的任何其他补充信息。
　(2) 不符合第(1)款第(b)项第(v)目规定的税务发票应有效,但不得用于支持进项税抵扣申请或任何退税申请。
　(3) 部长可以制定法规,规定所有或特定种类的供应商或供应品的特殊税务发票要求,包括要求使用经过认证机器创建发票的法规。
　(4) 就每项应税供应应开具一份税务发票原件,如果客户是注册人员,开具税务发票原件的人可以向声称遗失该税务发票的客户提供一份标有税务发票字样的副本。

[2019年第8号法案第50条]

87. 调整通知

　(1) 供应商根据第71条须发出的调整通知单应为——
　　　　(a) 须按条例规定的格式和方式发出;和
　　　　(b) 包括以下信息——
　　　　　　(i) 发布日期;
　　　　　　(ii) 供应商的名称、纳税人识别号和增值税登记号;

（ⅲ）调整事件的性质及其所涉及的供应；

　　（ⅳ）对供应品应缴增值税额的影响；

　　（ⅴ）对供应品应缴增值税的影响超过规定的最低金额的,应当提供客户的名称、纳税人识别号码和增值税登记号码；和

　　（ⅵ）条例规定的任何其他补充信息。

（2）调整通知不应仅仅因不遵守第（1）款第（b）项第（ⅴ）目的要求而无效,但不能用于支持递减调整申请。

（3）部长可制定法规,规定所有或特定种类的供应商或供应的特殊调整票据要求,包括但不限于要求使用经过认证机器创建调整票据的法规。

（4）修订后的税务发票如果符合法规的要求,则可以作为调整通知。

（5）就与供应有关的每项调整事件应开具一份原始调整通知,如果客户是注册人员,开具调整通知原件的人可向声称丢失该调整通知的客户提供一份有标识的副本。

88. 由代理人签发或向代理人签发的文件

（1）如果由代理人或者委托代理人进行应税供应,且代理人和委托人均为注册人员的,需要由委托人出具的文件,包括税务文件,可以由代理人或者向代理人出具,文件中应载明委托人的名称、地址、纳税人识别号和增值税登记号码。

（2）如果向代表委托人的代理人提供应税供应,且代理人和委托人均为注册人,应当向委托人出具的文件,包括电子财政设备开具的税务发票或调整单,可以出具给代理人,文件中应载明委托人的名称、地址、纳税人识别号码和增值税登记号码。

89. 记录和账目

（1）纳税人应保存本法或其他税法规定的所有账目、文件、申报表及其他记录,包括——

　　（a）该个人开具和收到的税务发票和调整通知；

　　（b）与该个人进出口货物有关的海关文件；

　　（c）与向该个人提供进口服务有关的记录,不论该等供应是否属于应税供应；

　　（d）一份增值税账目,在每个纳税期间记录该个人在该期间应缴的所有销项税,或该个人在该期间允许的进项税抵免,以及该个人在该期间要求或有权进行的所有增减调整；和

　　（e）根据本法向主任专员支付的存款记录。

（2）第（1）款提及的记录应在以下情况下保存——

　　（a）自相关纳税期间结束之日起至少5年；或者

　　（b）直至在与该纳税期有关的任何审计、追讨程序、争议、起诉或本法规定的其他程序中作出最终决定的较晚日期。

第七部分
行 政 管 理

90. 税务决定

下列决定应是根据本法作出或被视为已经作出的税务决定——

(a) 对某个人进行增值税登记的决定；
(b) 取消某个人增值税登记的决定；
(c) 不支付退款或不允许递减调整的决定；
(d) 作出评估,包括作出行政处罚评估的决定和关于罚款数额的决定；
(e) 针对允许延迟提交增值税申报表的请求作出的决定；
(f) 针对延期支付本法规定的应付款额的请求,要求申请人提前付款,或要求申请人遵守其他付款安排的决定；
(g) 就本法而言,宣布某个人为纳税人代表的决定；
(h) 不汇出本法项下其他应付款额的全部或部分应付利息的决定；和
(i) 不减免根据本法或与本法有关的全部或部分处罚的决定。

91. 合伙企业或非法人社团的连续性

其中——
(a) 合伙企业或其他个人协会因其一个或多个合伙人或成员退休或退出,或接纳新合伙人或成员而解散或以其他方式停止存在；
(b) 由其余成员,或现有成员和一个或多个新成员组成的新的合伙企业或协会成立；和
(c) 新的合伙企业或协会继续从事已解散的合伙企业或协会所从事的经济活动,

就本法而言,已解散的合伙企业或协会和新的合伙企业或协会应被视为一个整体,除非主任专员另有指示。

92. 纳税人、占有抵押权人死亡或破产

(1) 凡在纳税人死亡或其遗产被扣押后——
(a) 该纳税人以前从事的经济活动由该个人的遗产执行人或受托人进行或代表进行；或者
(b) 因经济活动的终止可作出任何行为,

就本法而言,涉及纳税人遗产的遗嘱执行人或受托人,应视为与该经济活动有关的纳税人。

(2) 抵押权人占有应纳税的抵押人以前抵押的土地或者其他财产,在占有该土地或者其他财产的同时,进行抵押人以前就该土地或者其他财产进行的经济活动的,在进行该经济活动的范围和期间内,其被视为抵押人。

93. 与所得税的相互影响

(1) 本条对所得税具有效力。
(2) 就所得税而言,因供应而应付的任何增值税应被视为不属于供应商因供应而收到对价的一部分。
(3) 供应的应付增值税额以后调整的,计入所得税的金额应当作相应调整。
(4) 个人产生的进项税应包括在计算费用或支出的金额时,无论是收入或资本性质,只要该个人不被允许获得该进项税的进项税抵免。
(5) 计入抵免的进项税额后作调整的,计入所得税的金额应当作相应调整。

第八部分
总　　则

94. 制定条例的权力

（1）部长可制定条例，对任何必要或方便的事项作出规定，以便执行或落实本法的规定。

（2）在不影响第（1）款规定的一般性的前提下，部长可制定条例，以便——

（a）要求某些人或某些类别的人单独或定期提供所需资料；

（b）规定对特定个人或特定类别的人适用支付和追缴增值税的特别方案；

（c）规定纳税人申请财产用于私人用途和应税活动时应进行的调整，以及财产发生重大变化的程度；

（d）规定金融服务供应商计算可合理归因于应税供应的进项税比例的方法；

（e）规定纳税人计算某一进项税额抵免的方法；

（f）规定增值税账户的维护方式；和

（g）规定在坦桑尼亚桑给巴尔制造并由增值税登记人带入坦桑尼亚大陆的货物的增值税核算方式。

（3）在不影响第（1）款规定的前提下，本条例不具有以下效力——

（a）使某项供应或进口获得豁免或零税率；或者

（b）使某人或某类人免于缴纳根据本法征收的税款。

[2016年第2号法案第99条]

95. 废除和保留

（1）废除《增值税法》。

（2）尽管有第（1）款的规定——

（a）根据已废除的《增值税法》作出并仍然有效的法规、规则、命令或通知应继续有效，直至其被根据本法作出的法规、规则、命令或通知撤销、修订或取消为止；

（b）如果坦桑尼亚联合共和国政府在本法生效前与某人签订了有关矿产、天然气或石油勘探的具有约束力的协议，则已废除的法案中有关增值税减免的规定应在协议规定的范围内继续适用；和

（c）根据《出口加工区法》或《经济特区法》授予许可的投资者获准的增值税减免应在已废除的法案规定的范围内继续适用。

[1997年第24号法案]

96. 过渡条款

（1）尽管有第95条的规定，与已废除的《增值税法》相关的空白表格和其他文件可以在本法项下继续使用，并且这些表格和文件中对适用于已废除的《增值税法》的条款和表述都被视为是指本法的相应条款和表述。

（2）在生效日期前的12个月中的任何一个月，根据已废除的《增值税法》提交申报表的任何一个注册人员，均应被视为本法规定的注册人员。

（3）主任专员应在本法生效之日起3个月内，向根据第（2）款成为注册人员的每个人发

出通知,确认该个人的注册,并通知其如不需要进行增值税注册,可以选择取消注册。

(4) 须注册增值税但未自动注册的个人,根据第(2)款的规定,应在生效之日起 30 日内申请注册,并且在注册之前,应像注册人一样遵守本法的规定。

(5) 根据已废除的《增值税法》因以下原因产生的进项税——

(a) 有权对其进口或购置所征收的全部或部分增值税征收进项税的个人;和

(b) 本应在本法生效之日起至结束的纳税期间内允许的进项税抵免,

根据本法,应允许对该个人进行递减调整。

(6) 第(5)款所述的递减调整可在本法生效之日后的前 6 个纳税期间中的任何一个纳税期间申报一次。

(7) 该个人须以规定的格式和方式通知主任专员拟申报的款额、拟申报的纳税期间以及条例规定的其他资料,如主任专员不确信该个人已征收增值税并有权作出递减调整,则其可拒绝全部或部分申报金额。

(8) 有下列情形之一的,依照本法对应税供应征收的增值税,自本法施行之日起缴纳——

(a) 供应是或将在本法生效后提供;

(b) 在此之前,签发了供应发票或已支付有关供应的款项,或两者兼有;和

(c) 未根据被废除的法案就供应缴纳增值税。

(9) 第(8)款应分别适用于被视为单一供应的累进或定期供应的每一部分。

[1997 年第 24 号法案]

附表 [第 6 条第(1)款]

[2016 年第 2 号法案第 100 条;2017 年第 4 号法案第 70 条和第 71 条;2017 年第 9 号法案第 36 条;2018 年第 4 号法案第 69 条;2019 年第 6 号法案第 30 条;2019 年第 8 号法案第 51 条]

第一部分 免征增值税的供应品和进口品

1. 农具

序号	器 具	HS 编码
1.	农用拖拉机	8701.90.00
2.	用于整地或耕种的农业、园林或者林业机械,除草机和压路机及其零部件除外	84.32
3.	收割或脱粒机械,但下列机械除外 HS 编码 8433.11.00、8433.19.00、8433.90.00	84.33
4.	农用液体喷雾器	8424.81.00
5.	农用粉末喷洒器	8424.81.00
6.	铁锹	8201.10.00
7.	铲子	8201.10.00
8.	鹤嘴锄	8201.30.00

续 表

序号	器 具	HS 编码
9.	铁镐	8201.30.00
10.	锄头	8201.30.00
11.	铁叉	8201.90.00
12.	铁耙	8201.30.00
13.	斧头	8201.40.00
14.	拖拉机挂车	8716.10.10
15.	用于农业和林业车辆的新型充气轮胎	4011.61.00
16.	旋耕机	8432.29.00
17.	家禽孵化器	8436.21.00
18.	灌溉设备	8424.81.00
19.	灌溉部件（喷洒系统、化学喷射系统、水消毒系统、雨枪、高压雾化设备、灌溉计算机、灌溉系统过滤器）	8424.90.00
20.	温室系统	9406.00.10
21.	牛科动物精液	0511.10.00
22.	非牛科动物的精液	0511.99.10
23.	大坝衬垫	3920

2. 农业投入

序号	款 项	HS 编码
1.	化肥	第 31 章
2.	农药	3808.99.10 或 3808.99.90
3.	杀虫剂	3808.91.11 至 3808.91.99
4.	杀菌剂	3808.92.10 或 3808.99.90
5.	杀鼠剂	3808.92.10 或 3808.99.90
6.	除草剂	3808.93.10 至 3808.92.90
7.	防发芽产品	3808.93.10 或 3808.93.90
8.	植物生长调节剂	3808.93.10 或 3808.93.90

3. 牲畜、基本农产品和供人类消费的食品

序号	食品项目	HS 编码
1.	活牛	0102.21.00
2.	活猪	0103.10.00
3.	活羊	0104.10.10
4.	活山羊	0104.20.10
5.	活家禽	0105.11.10
6.	未经加工的可食用动物产品	第二章
7.	未经加工的食用鸡蛋	0407.29.00
8.	未经巴氏杀菌或巴氏杀菌的牛奶,含有添加剂和具有长保质期的牛奶除外	04.01
9.	未经巴氏杀菌或巴氏杀菌的羊奶,含有添加剂和具有长保质期的羊奶除外 长寿奶	04.01
10.	未经加工的鱼	03.02
11.	未经加工的食用蔬菜	第7章
12.	未经加工的水果	08.10
13.	未经加工的坚果	08.02
14.	未经加工的鳞茎	0601.10.00
15.	未经加工的块茎	0601.20.00
16.	未经加工的谷物	第10章
17.	小麦或粗面粉	11.01
18.	玉米面粉	11.02
19.	未去梗或者未去皮的烟草	2401.10.00
20.	未经加工的腰果	0801.31.00
21.	未经加工的咖啡	0901.11.00
22.	未经加工的茶叶	0902.10.00 0902.20.00
23.	向日葵的种子	12.06
24.	油料种子	12.07

续 表

序号	食品项目	HS编码
25.	未经加工的除虫菊	1211.90.20
26.	未经加工的棉花	1207.21.00
27.	未经加工的剑麻	5303.10.00
28.	未经加工的甘蔗	1212.93.00
29.	种子及其植物	12.09
30.	用于动物饲养的制剂	23.09
31.	用于孵化的受精卵	0407.11.00 0407.19.00 0407.21.00
32.	黄豆油饼	2304.00.00
33.	棉籽油饼和其他固体残渣	2306.10.00
34.	葵花子油饼和其他固体残渣	2306.30.00
35.	玉米麸	2302.10.00
36.	小麦麸	2302.30.00
37.	赖氨酸	2922.41.00
38.	甲硫氨酸	29390.40.00
39.	霉菌毒素结合剂	3824.10.00
40.	麸皮	2309.90.10
41.	米糠	2306.90.90
42.	棉籽饼	2304.00.00

4. 渔业工具

序号	工具	HS编码
1.	渔网浮标	7020.00.10
2.	渔网	5608.11.00
3.	渔船、工厂船舶和其他加工、保存渔业产品之船舶	8902.00.00
4.	锦纶鱼线	—
5.	舷外发动机	8407.21.00

5. 养蜂工具

序号	工具	HS 编码
1.	蜂箱	任何说明
2.	保护性养蜂外套面纱	6113.40.00
3.	面罩	6307.90
4.	蜂蜜过滤器	—
5.	蜂箱烟熏机	8424.89

6. 日用设备

序号	工具	HS 编码
1.	除草机	8433.30.00
2.	饮料罐和饮料瓶盖	7310.29.20
3.	挤奶机	8434.10.00
4.	均质机、黄油搅拌器、牛奶巴氏杀菌机	8434.20.00
5.	奶油分离器	8421.11.00
6.	牛奶板热交换器	8419.50.00
7.	牛奶软管	3917.31.00, 4009.12.00, 4009.32.00
8.	牛奶泵	8413.60.00, 8413.70.00, 8413.81.00
9.	隔热冷却罐	8419.89.00, 7309.00.00, 7310.00.00
10.	储奶罐	—

7. 药品或医药产品

序号	
1.	经卫生部长批准的人用和兽用基本药品、药物、医疗设备和包装材料。前提是,该包装材料专为包装药品而设计,由当地制造商印制并且其名称出现在包装材料上
2.	向政府提供的补给食品或者维生素

8. 为有特殊需求的人设计的物品

序号	物品	HS 编码
1.	矫形器具,包括拐杖、手术带和支架、夹板和其他骨折器具、人造身体部件、助听器和其他穿戴、携带或植入身体以弥补缺陷或残疾的器具,但不包括 HSC 9021.90.00 项下的其他物品	90.21

续 表

序号	物　　品	HS 编码
2.	盲人或视障人士使用的白色手杖	—
3.	矫正视力眼镜	9004.90.10
4.	隐形眼镜	9001.30.00
5.	玻璃镜片	9001.40.00
6.	其他材料的眼镜片	9001.50.00
7.	白化病患者使用的防晒霜和日晒制剂	33.04
8.	盲文	8469.00.007
9.	残疾人专用三轮车	8713.1.00
10.	残疾人专用机动车	87.03

9. 教育材料

序号	材　　料	HS 编码
1.	字典和百科全书	4901.91.00
2.	印刷书籍	4901
3.	报纸	4902.90.00
4.	用于绘画或着色的儿童图片	4903.00.00
5.	地图和水文图	4905.99.00
6.	考试试题	4911.99.20
7.	教学图表	4911.90.10
8.	考试答题纸	4011.00.90

10. 卫生保健

序号	
1.	医疗、牙科、护理、康复、助产、辅助医疗、眼科或者其他类似服务的供应： (a) 由获准提供以上服务的机构提供或者在该机构内提供；和 (b) 在根据坦桑尼亚法律注册有资格从事该服务的人，或其从事该服务的资格在坦桑尼亚得到承认的人的监督和控制下从事该服务
2.	在寄宿中心或者养老院中为儿童、需要长期护理的老年人、贫困者、体弱者或者残疾人提供服务，这些机构提供的服务要获得相关政府机构的批准

11. 不动产

1.	空置土地出售
2.	租赁、许可、租用或其他形式的供应,但以住宅的占用和居住权利的供应为限
3.	不动产出售,但以该不动产和住宅有关为限,不包括: (a) 新建住宅楼宇的首次出售;或者 (b) 作为住宅使用少于两年的房屋的后续出售

12. 教育服务

1.	由负责教育的部长批准的机构为学生提供的包括教学或者指导在内的服务,包括: (a) 学前、小学或中学; (b) 技术学院、社区学院或大学 (c) 为促进成人教育、职业培训,提高读写能力或者技术教育而设立的教育机构; (d) 为身体或者精神残疾者的教育或者培训而设立的机构;或者 (e) 为训练运动员而设立的机构

13. 中介服务

1.	免费的金融服务供应
2.	飞机保险费
3.	人寿保险或者健康保险
4.	职工赔偿保险

14. 政府实体或机构

1.	由政府实体或者机构进行的非商业活动,但有关活动涉及供应货品、服务或者不动产,并且这些货品、服务或者不动产至少由非政府实体在坦桑尼亚大陆供应或者能够供应的情况除外

15. 石油产品

序号	石油产品	HS 编码
1.	航空汽油	2710.12.30
2.	汽油型喷气燃料	2710.12.40
3.	煤油型喷气燃料(Jet A-1)	2710.19.21
4.	汽油(MSR 和 MSP)	2710.12.10 和 10.12.20

续表

序号	石油产品	HS 编码
5.	柴油（GO）	2710.19.31
6.	煤油（IK）	2710.19.22
7.	沥青	2713.20.00 和 2715.00.00
8.	液化石油和天然气	2711
9.	压缩石油和天然气	2711
10.	石油和烹饪用天然气的压缩或液化气瓶	7311.00.00

16. 供水，但瓶装水、罐装水或者类似的饮用水除外。
17. 以出租车、租赁车辆或者船只以外的任何交通工具运送人员。
18. 向武装部队供应的武器、弹药及其零部件。
19. 殡葬服务，本项所指的殡葬服务包括棺木、裹尸布、运输、殓房和遗体处理服务。
20. 游戏用品。
21. 供应太阳能电池板、组件、太阳能充电控制器、太阳能逆变器、太阳能灯、真空管太阳能集热器和太阳能电池。
22. 包机服务供应。
23. 大豆 12.01。
24. 碎坚果 12.02。
25. 由个体采矿者在采矿站或者由采矿委员会根据《采矿法》指定的矿物和宝石出售处供应的贵金属、宝石和其他宝石。
26. 向当地航空运输运营商供应的珍贵飞机润滑油。HS 编码为 2710.19.51、2710.19.52、3403.19.00 和 3403.99.00。

第二部分 免征增值税的进口产品

项目编号	说　　明
1.	非以销售为目的，无条件赠予国家的进口货物
2.	根据 2004 年《东非海关管理法》附表 5 免除关税的进口行李或个人物品
3.	包括集装箱在内的进口货物，该等货物出口后又由任何人带回坦桑尼亚大陆，没有经过任何制造或者改装过程，也没有永久改变所有权。但以下情况除外—— 在货物出口时，其是根据本法或已废除的《增值税法》认定的零税率的供应对象
4.	装运或者运输到坦桑尼亚联合共和国以转运或者运送到任何其他国家的进口货物
5.	外国政府或国际组织为促进联合共和国的经济发展而免费提供的进口货物
6.	捐赠给非营利组织的进口食品、衣物和鞋子，免费分发给坦桑尼亚大陆有特殊需求的孤儿院或特殊儿童学校

续表

项目编号	说　　明
7.	非营利组织进口的用于抢险救灾的物资，属于资本货物的，应当在灾情结束、完成或者减轻后交由国家灾害委员会处理
8.	宗教组织为提供健康、教育、水、宗教服务而进口的货物，该等服务应满足下列的要求： (a) 不收取费用或者任何其他费用形式的对价；或者 (b) 支付任何对价时，费用或者收费不得超过市场公允价值的 50%
9.	根据联合共和国政府与《外交和领事豁免和特权法》所列国际机构之间签订的协定中豁免的进口货物
10.	根据 2004 年《东非海关管理法》，由注册和许可的勘探者或勘探者进口的专门用于石油、天然气、矿产勘探或者勘探活动的货物，有资格享受关税减免
11.	由当地空运运营商进口的飞机、飞机发动机或者零部件
12.	由已注册的铁路公司、法人或当局进口的铁路机车、货车、有轨电车及其零件和附件
13.	政府进口的消防车
14.	经教育主管部门注册的教育机构进口仅用于教育目的的实验室设备和试剂
15.	天然气经销商进口的 CNG 厂设备、天然气管道、输配管道、CNG 储气梯级、CNG 专用运输车辆、天然气计量设备、CNG 加气装置、气体接收装置、火炬气系统、凝析气罐及龙头设施、系统管道及管架、凝析稳定器
16.	消防设备
17.	本地植物油制造商进口的机器，HS 编码为 8479.20.00、8438.60.00、8421.29.00 及 8419.89.00，只用于在坦桑尼亚大陆制造植物油
18.	由当地纺织品制造商进口的机器，HS 编码为 8444.00.00 8445.11.00、8445.12.00、8445.13.00、8445.19.00、 8445.20.00、8445.30.00、8445.40.00、8445.90.00、 8446.10.00、8446.21.00、8446.29.00、8446.30.00、 84.47、8448.11.00、8448.19.00、8449.00.00、8451.40.00 或者 8451.50.00 只用于在坦桑尼亚大陆制造纺织品
19.	由本地药剂制造商按照第 84 章的规定进口的机器，只用于在坦桑尼亚大陆制造药剂制品
20.	由本地皮革及兽皮制造商进口的机器，HS 编码为 8453.10.00，只用于在坦桑尼亚大陆制造皮革制品
21.	由注册医疗机构（药房、卫生化验所或诊断中心除外）进口的 HS 编码为 8703.90.10 的救护车
22.	HS 编码为 4907.00.90 的印花税票 ［第 4 章第 99 条］
23.	编码为 8470.50.00 的电子收款机

第十五部
海关(管理和关税)法(第403章)
[1952年][2019年修订版](节选)

海关(管理和关税)法
(第 403 章)

[本文件为 2019 年 11 月 30 日版。]

[注:在总检察长办公室的监督下,根据《法律修订法》1994 年第 7 号、《法律修订和年度修订法》第 356 章(R.L.),以及《法律解释和一般条款法》1972 年第 30 号对本法进行了全面修订与合并。本版本为截至 2002 年 7 月 31 日的最新版本。]

[命令编号 1952 年第 2 号令;1955 年第 10 号令;1958 年第 3 号令;1960 年第 5 号令;1961 年第 14 号令;1962 年第 2 号令;1963 年第 2 号令;1964 年第 12 号令;1966 年第 1 号令;1967 年第 10 号令;1969 年第 12 号令;1969 年第 13 号令;1970 年第 10 号令;1976 年第 13 号令;1989 年第 13 号令;1994 年第 16 号令;1996 年第 13 号令;1997 年第 25 号令;1997 年第 27 号令;1998 年第 2 号令;1998 年第 8 号令;1999 年第 12 号令;1999 年第 15 号令;2000 年第 11 号令;2000 年第 15 号令;2001 年第 14 号令;2002 年第 10 号令;2002 年第 18 号令;2008 年第 1 号令;2014 年第 2 号令;EAC. Cap.27; E.A.C.L.N.49/1954; 84/1961; 1/1967; 64/1970]

旨在对海关、转让税及有关事项的管理作出规定的法案。

第三部分
进 口

入境、检查和交付

28. 货物入境

(1)除非海关法律另有规定,任何飞机或者船舶卸载或者准备卸载的全部货物,应当由货主在卸货开始后规定的期限内或者海关官员批准延长的期限内,向海关报关进口,以作以下用途——

(a)国内消费;

(b)仓储;

(c)转运;或者

(d)过境。

(2)货主向海关官员提交报关单时,应当提供完整的货物明细,并且附上证明报关单所述货物的单证。

(3)待卸货物的报关单,可以在进口该等货物的飞机或船舶到达卸货港口前,交由海关官员进行审核;在这种情况下,海关关长可以酌情允许在飞机或船舶到达前对任何货物进行报关。

(4)如果有任何货物在规定的期限届满或者海关官员批准的延长期限届满后仍未报关,那么这些货物应当按照海关官员的要求,由进口该等货物的飞机或者船舶的代理人自费将其移送至海关仓库。

29. 转运货物的入境

（1）除非海关法律另有规定外，从任何飞机、船舶或者车辆卸载或者准备卸载的任何应当缴纳转运税的货物，应由货主按照规定的方式和期限，或者在海关官员批准的延长期限内报关。

（2）如果有任何需要缴纳转运税的货物在规定的期限届满或者海关官员批准的延长期限届满后仍未报关，那么这些货物应当按照海关官员的要求，由转运该货物的飞机、船舶或者车辆的货主自费将其移送至海关仓库。

［1989 年第 13 号法案第 13 条］

第四部分
货 物 仓 储

总　　则

38. 应税货物可以入库

（1）在不违反任何规定的情况下，应缴纳进口税的货物在首次进口时可在政府仓库或保税仓库中储存而无须缴纳关税。

（2）在即将入库的任何货物上岸时，或在上岸后实际可行的情况下，海关官员应详细核算该等货物，并将核算情况记入账簿，在不违反第 43 条和第 49 条规定的情况下，该核算情况应作为确定和支付这些货物关税的依据。

［E.A.C.L.N. 1/1967］

39. 入库程序

（1）任何申报入库并且交付给仓库负责人保管的货物，不论其以前是否已核算，海关工作人员应当按照海关关长的指示，对该货物进行详细核算。

（2）海关官员在进行核算时，如货物属进口物品，则应当在专用账簿中登记进口该等货物的飞机、船舶的名称或车辆的注册号码，或者如货物属邮寄物品，则须登记该等邮寄物品的包裹编号，以及该等货物的货主名称、包裹件数、每件包裹的标记和编号、货物的价值和明细。

（3）核算完毕并且按照海关官员的指示将货物存放在仓库后，海关工作人员应当在账簿底部签字证明该等货物的进口报关和入库已经完成。至此，该等货物应被视为已经正式入库。

（4）在不违反第 41 条规定的情况下，所有申报入库的货物应当立即运送到申报的仓库，并按照进口时的包装存放在仓库内：

但是，按照第 35 条的规定，如果任何货物经许可可以重新包装、分拣、散装、分类、拆卸或者装箱，那么该等货物应当按照核算时的包装存放在仓库内。

（5）任何人违反第（4）款的规定，即属犯罪，涉案的货物应当被没收。

［E.A.C.L.N. 1/1967］

40. 未入库货物的移送

（1）任何申报入库的货物，如果货主未按照规定及时入库的，海关官员可以将其移送到申报的仓库。

(2) 如果任何货物被移送到保税仓库的,仓库管理人应当支付该货物的移送费用,并对该货物享有留置权,以保证费用的偿付。

41. 入库货物的进口报关

(1) 已经入库的货物可以申报以下用途——

 (a) 国内消费;

 (b) 出口;

 (c) 转移至另一仓库;

 (d) 作为飞机或者船舶的仓库;或者

 (e) 重新入库。

(2) 任何已经申报入库的货物,在实际入库之前,可以申报国内消费、出口或者转移至另一个仓库或者作为飞机或者船舶的仓库;在这种情况下,该等货物应被视为已经入库,并可以按照申报的用途交付国内消费、出口、转移至另一个仓库或者作为飞机或者船舶的仓库,如同实际入库一样。

第十七部分
海 关 关 税

194A. 进口时缴纳关税

从事采矿作业的人员,或该人员为进行任何此类采矿作业而分包的任何人员,在该矿山开始商业生产一周年后,有权在缴纳不超过5%的关税后进口炸药、燃料、润滑油、工业用品和其他用品、机械、车辆和其他基本设备以及此类设备的备件。前提是在与负责矿产的部长协商后,此类设备已被验证符合海关关长的要求且是合理必要的,并仅用于该矿产作业。

[1997年第27号法案第17条]

194B. 一周年后免征关税

从事非矿山采矿作业的采矿作业的人员,或该人员为此类采矿作业而分包的任何人员,在任何矿山开始商业生产一周年后,有权免税进口炸药、燃料、润滑油、工业用品和其他用品、机械、车辆和其他基本设备以及此类设备的备件。前提是在与负责矿产的部长协商后,此类设备已被验证符合海关关长的要求且是合理必要的,并仅用于该矿产作业。

[1997年第27号法案第17条]

194C. 在出售或转让任何物品时支付的关税

任何人出售或转让由从事采矿作业的任何人进口到坦桑尼亚共和国而未支付关税的任何物品,或者从事该等采矿作业而被分包的任何人将货物出售或转让给坦桑尼亚共和国境内的任何人,应在出售或转让之日就其价值(如有)缴纳关税:

但是,如果该销售或转让是通过根据《采矿法》出售或转让任何权益的方式发生的,则不应支付该等关税。

[第123章]

[1997年第27号法案第17条;第123章]

第十六部
货物和服务付款的预扣税业务指南[2019年]

坦桑尼亚税务局

根据《所得税法》第332章,货物和服务付款的预扣税

2019年第01号业务指南

2019年2月

货物和服务付款的预扣税

1.0 税法
本业务指南根据《税收管理法》(第438章)第9条(经不时修订)发布。

2.0 目的
发布本业务指南(PN)的目的是为公众和坦桑尼亚税务局(TRA)官员提供指导,以便根据《所得税法》第332章第83条的规定,实现商品和服务预扣税管理(WHT)的一致性。它解释了法律和行政方面的问题,包括货物和服务预扣税的处理和计算程序。

3.0 释义
在本业务指南中,除非上下文另有规定,否则——

"法案" 指《所得税法》(第332章)和《税收管理法》(第438章)。

除非上下文另有要求,本业务指南中使用的定义和表述与本法中的含义相同。

4.0 本业务指南的应用
本业务指南涉及以下方面:

服务

i. 根据《所得税法》第83条第(i)款第(c)项第(ii)目,应归属于支付服务费而须缴纳预扣税的服务类别。

ii. 计算服务费时应包括的付款

iii. 付款来源规则

iv. 对特定类型的人适用

v. 预扣款项的计算

vi. 适用于预扣的程序

货物

对任何人向公司及其机构提供货物的付款征收预扣税。

5.0 适用概念

5.1 预扣税
预扣税是指就提供的货物或服务向另一人"支付"一定金额的人必须预扣的税款。这是一种在源头扣除的税,因为付款人有义务预扣税款。

5.2 款项
本法将为此目的支付的款项定义为:

"付款包括资产或货币的转让、负债的转移或者减少、服务的提供、货币或资产的使用或者可供使用以及在他人身上创造资产"。

5.3 预扣税款人
预扣税款人是指收到或者有权收到需要预扣所得税款项的人。

5.4 扣缴义务人

扣缴义务人是指被要求从支付给预扣税款人的款项中代扣所得税的人。

5.5 "专业服务"

"专业服务"是指得到任何公认的专业机构颁发执照的从业人员所提供的服务,并应包括其他具有独立商业性质的服务或者活动,包括咨询、法律、建筑、工程、监理、会计和审计、医疗、艺术、调查、戏剧表演、体育、展览、私人保安服务、私人调查和学科顾问,或者举行或提供的任何娱乐活动,但根据雇佣合同收取酬金的除外。

5.6 "公司"

"公司"是指根据坦桑尼亚联合共和国或者其他地方的任何现行法律成立、注册或登记的任何公司或法人团体、非法人协会或者其他团体、政府、政府的政治分支机构、公共当局、公共机构、公共国际组织和单位信托,但不包括合伙企业;

6.0 预扣税类型

最终预扣税是指扣缴义务人在计算收入年度的应纳所得税时不能申请任何税收抵免的税种。

非最终预扣税是指扣缴义务人有权获得税收抵免的税款,抵免金额相当于该金额产生的收入年度所支付的税款。

注:本业务指南仅涵盖与非最终预扣税相关的预扣税。

7.0 预扣税义务

本法规定,居民在向其他居民或者非居民付款时,必须按照《所得税法》附表 1 第 4 条第(c)款规定的税率预扣税款。

7.1 在下列情况下——

(a) 服务

就下列所支付的款项预扣税款:

ⅰ. 支付给非居民的来源地为坦桑尼亚联合共和国的服务费

ⅱ. 支付给居民的专业服务费

(b) 货物

(1) 任何居民法人就居民在经营业务过程中提供的货物进行支付时,应按附表 1 第 4 条第(c)款规定的 2% 的税率预扣所得税。

(2) 本法适用于其预算全部或者大部分由政府预算补助金资助的居民法人。

就本业务指南而言,水电供应应视为货物,因此不受服务项下预扣义务的限制。

注:水电不可转让,这是任何服务的关键属性之一。

7.2 第 83 条规定的豁免付款

1. 个人付款,但在经营业务时支付的款项除外;

2. 免税付款。

7.3 付款来源

服务费支付的来源是在坦桑尼亚联合共和国境内提供服务所产生的费用:

ⅰ. 在坦桑尼亚联合共和国,无论付款地点在哪里,只要服务是在坦桑尼亚联合共和国提供的,就认为付款的来源地是坦桑尼亚联合共和国。在下列情况下,服务是在坦桑尼亚联合共和国提供的:

(a) 在坦桑尼亚联合共和国境内开展活动,或者

(b) 活动成果的针对对象、使用对象或者受益对象是坦桑尼亚联合共和国居民。

ii. 付款人为坦桑尼亚联合共和国政府,即联邦政府和桑给巴尔革命政府。

8.0 适用于特定类型人

预扣税适用于居民(包括非居民的国内常设机构)向居民支付的款项。

向居民支付款项时,预扣税为非最终预扣税。扣缴义务人应享有与所得年度已缴税款抵扣额相等的税收抵免。

向合伙企业支付的款项中所扣除的税款应按比例分配给合伙人,并视为合伙人在其收入年度已缴纳的税款。

9.0 预扣款项的计算依据

预扣税税基

I. 税款应按支付的总额计算,不扣除费用或者津贴

II. 预扣税应按不含增值税的金额计算

例 1:

ABC 有限公司向达累斯萨拉姆市政委员会提供咨询服务的发票金额如下:

说 明	金额(坦桑尼亚先令)
服务费	10 000 000
增值税	1 800 000
总计	11 800 000

因此

I. W/Tax(预扣税)服务支付总额为 10 000 000 坦桑尼亚先令

II. W/Tax 为 5% * 10 000 000

WHT(预扣税)= 500 000 坦桑尼亚先令

10.0 包括福利和设施的情况

如果向扣缴义务人提供服务并支付现金,同时提供福利和设施,则预扣税基应包括支付的福利或者设施的金额。如果未支付福利,则应按支付时的市场价值计算。此外,如果提供了服务,并以服务费和报销的形式向扣缴义务人支付了款项,那么预扣税基将是全额,即服务费加报销金额。

例 2:

Kinondoni 区议会聘请 FLG 咨询公司开展咨询工作。合同条款包括由客户支付 4 名 FLG 工作人员在一家五星级酒店住宿 20 天的报销费用。合同报价为 150 000 000 先令,外加报销费用。客户共支付了 16 000 000 先令,作为 FLG 工作人员的住宿报销费用。

说 明	金额(坦桑尼亚先令)
咨询费	150 000 000
报销	16 000 000
总计	166 000 000

W/Tax 税基

咨询费　150 000 000 坦桑尼亚先令

报销　　16 000 000 坦桑尼亚先令

W/Tax 税基 166 000 000 坦桑尼亚先令

WHT 计算 = 166 000 000 * 5%

WHT = 8 300 000 坦桑尼亚先令

11.0　混合供应品(货物和服务)的预扣税基

如果开具的发票同时涉及货物和服务供应,则必须将货物价值和服务价值的应付金额分开。但是,如果不分开,则全部金额将被视为服务供应。

例3：

XYZ 受雇为教育部进行一项调查。合同还包含在需要时提供书籍和文具。工作完成后,XYZ 开具了一张发票,详情如下：

说　　明	金额(坦桑尼亚先令)
勘测费	70 000 000
书籍和文具	30 000 000
增值税	18 000 000
总计	118 000 000

I. W/Tax 的收费如下：

（a）货物 W/Tax（2% * 30 000 000）

　　　　　= 600 000 坦桑尼亚先令

（b）服务 W/Tax（5% * 70 000 000）。

　　　　　= 3 500 000 坦桑尼亚先令

注：如果未将货物和服务价值应付金额的相关数值分开,则需按全部金额的5%(5% * 100 000 000) = 5 000 000 坦桑尼亚先令缴纳预扣税。

12.0　建筑工程预扣税基

I.《所得税法》第83条第(3)款与2016《财政法》一并解读,规定了在确定预扣税基时要对建筑工程进行分摊。

II. 如果付款涉及建筑工程,则应按照材料和服务3∶2的比例分别支付预扣税。

例4：

姆盖尼承包商获得了在多多马为财政部建造新办公室的合同。根据完工率开具的发票中,有一笔金额如下：

说　　明	金额（坦桑尼亚先令）
工作价值	600 000 000
增值税	108 000 000
总计	708 000 000

根据建筑工程完工率计算的预扣税

材　　料	服　　务
3	2
3/5 * 600 000 000	2/5 * 600 000 000
360 000 000	240 000 000

货物 W/Tax-(2% * 360 000 000)

WHT = 7 200 000 坦桑尼亚先令

服务 W/Tax-(5% * 240 000 000)

WHT = 12 000 000 坦桑尼亚先令

13.0 预扣税适用程序

预扣税或视为预扣税的报表和付款——第 84 条

I. 付款时间

（a）预扣税款应在每个月扣款日结束后 7 天内支付给税务局局长

（b）通过税收网关系以电子方式缴纳预扣税款

II. 提交预扣税款报表

每个扣缴义务人应在每 6 个月期限结束后的 30 天内，通过填写规定的 **ITX 230.01. E.——预扣税报表表格**，向税务局局长提交当月预扣所得税的报表——

（a）扣缴义务人在此期间支付的应予扣缴的款项；

（b）扣缴义务人的姓名和地址；

（c）从每笔付款中预扣的所得税；和

（d）税务局局长可能规定的任何其他信息。

注：扣缴义务人如未按照法律规定预扣所得税，则必须在预扣税款的同时，以同样的方式支付本应预扣的税款。所有报税表均可以通过以下网址下载：www.tra.go.tz

14.0 预扣凭证的签发——《所得税法》第 85 条

扣缴义务人必须在扣缴月份结束后的 30 天内，编制并向所有扣缴义务人分别送达每个月的扣缴证明。但是，由于在线支付模块的引入，扣缴人和被扣缴人都可以通过税收门户系统查看和打印证书。

15.0 扣缴义务人的税收抵免

预扣税款是对扣缴义务人收入年度总税款的税收抵免。

扣缴义务人代扣代缴税款时,其有权获得与代扣代缴或视为代扣代缴税款相等的税额抵免。在扣缴税款时,税收抵免是针对被扣缴人当年的纳税义务。

16.0 未预扣的后果——《所得税法》第 84 条

扣缴义务人未依法预扣所得税的,必须以同样的方式,在预扣税款的同时支付应预扣的税款及利息。

扣缴义务人如未扣缴所得税,但将本应扣缴的税款支付给了税务局,则有权向扣缴义务人追回同等数额的税款。

17.0 未按期申报的后果——《税收管理法》第 438 章第 78 条

未遵守申报要求的,将依据《税收管理法》第 438 章的规定,受到包括利息和罚款在内的处罚,具体如下——

如果扣缴义务人未按期提交纳税申报表(预扣税款和已付税款明细),则应按每月或当月的部分时间缴纳罚款,罚金金额为以下两者中的较高者:

I. 每份纳税申报表应纳税额减去期初已缴纳税款金额的 2.5%;或者

II. 对于法人团体,罚款金额为 225 000 坦桑尼亚先令;对于个人,罚款金额为 75 000 坦桑尼亚先令。

18.0 向税务局提交合同文件

为了遵守 2011 年第 7 号《公共采购法》第 109 条规定,该法于 2013 年通过第 446 号政府公告发布,规定:"会计主管应确保将所有合同的副本在签订合同之日起 30 日内送交主管机关、总检察长、财务总监和审计长、内部审计长或者政府资产管理部门(视情况而定)以及坦桑尼亚税务局。"

第六编
反商业贿赂法规

第十七部
预防和反腐败法(第329章)
[2007年][2019年修订版](节选)

预防和反腐败法
（第 329 章）

2007 年 7 月 1 日生效

[本文件为 2019 年 11 月 30 日版。]

[注：在总检察长办公室的监督下，根据《法律修订法》1994 年第 7 号、《法律修订和年度修订法》第 356 章（R.L.），以及《法律解释和一般条款法》1972 年第 30 号对本法进行了全面修订与合并。本版本为截至 2002 年 7 月 31 日的最新版本。]

[政府公告 2007 年第 153 号；法案编号 2007 年第 11 号法案；2018 年第 7 号法案；2019 年第 11 号法案]

鉴于腐败是民主、良政和人权之原则的障碍，对社会的和平、安宁和安全构成威胁；

鉴于政府已决心采取长期措施，以确保坦桑尼亚仍然是一个遵守自由、平等、正义、兄弟情谊以及和平之原则的无腐败国家，在这些原则下，所有人都是平等的，每个人都有权拥有和保护通过合法手段获得的财产；

鉴于全球化和通信信息技术的发展所带来的科技变革，本局有必要改组，制订预防及打击腐败的现代战术和策略，并检查现行的法律架构，以使本局能有效地管制腐败及腐败行为；

鉴于有必要就预防、调查和打击腐败及有关罪行作出全面的规定，并确保本局独立开展业务和有效履行职能；

因此，现由坦桑尼亚联合共和国议会颁布如下：

第三部分
腐败及相关犯罪

15. 腐败交易

（1）任何人自行或伙同他人腐败的——

　　（a）为自己或他人向任何人索取，从任何人处接受或获得或试图获得任何利益，作为对任何代理人的引诱、报酬或其他，无论该代理人与上述第一人是否为同一人，且无论该代理人是否有权作出或不作出或已经作出或未作出任何与其委托人相关的事务或业务，或者

　　（b）为自己或者他人利益，给予、许诺或提供任何利益给任何人作为对任何代理人的引诱、报酬或其他，无论该代理人是否是获得该好处的人，且无论该代理人是否有权作出或不作出或已经作出或未作出任何与其委托人相关的事务或业务，

即构成腐败罪。

（2）被判犯有本条所规定罪行的人，应被处以 50 万先令以上 100 万先令以下的罚款，或 3 年以上 5 年以下的监禁，或两者并罚。

(3) 除第(2)款规定的处罚外,如该人符合以下情况,法院应——
  (a) 该人是代理人,则命令其以法院指示的方式向其委托人付以下款项——
    (i) 其所收取的任何利益或其中任何部分的金额或金钱价值;
    (ii) 其所收取的任何利益的金额或金钱价值的一部分,而余下的全部或部分应予没收;或者
  (b) 不论该人是否为代理人,命令将其所获得的任何利益的金额或价值,或其中任何部分上缴政府。

16. 合同中的腐败交易

(1) 任何人向公职人员提供利益作为对其的引诱或酬劳,使该公职人员在以下方面给予帮助、利用影响力、已经给予帮助或已经利用影响力,以促进、执行或获得——
  (a) 与公共机构签订的关于执行任何工作、提供任何服务、从事任何事情、提供任何物品、材料或物质的任何合同;
  (b) 根据与公共机构签订的合同要求执行任何工作、提供任何服务、从事任何事情或提供任何物品、材料或物质的任何分包合同,

即构成腐败罪。

(2) 任何公职人员给予帮助、利用影响力、已经给予帮助或已经利用影响力,以促进、执行或获得第(1)款第(a)和(b)项所述合同或分包合同中所规定或以其他方式规定的价款,对价或其他款项的支付,从而索取或收受任何好处以作为对上述行为的报酬,即属犯罪。

(3) 被判定犯有本条所规定的罪行的人,应被处以 100 万先令以上 300 万先令以下的罚款,或 3 年以上 5 年以下的监禁,或两者并罚。

(4) 除本条规定的处罚外,如该人符合以下情况,法院应——
  (a) 该人代理人,则命令其以法院指示的方式向其委托人付以下款项——
    (i) 其所收取的任何利益或其中任何部分的金额或金钱价值;或者
    (ii) 其所收取的任何利益的金额或金钱价值的一部分,而余下的全部或部分应予没收;
  (b) 不论该人是否为代理人,命令将其所获得的任何利益的金额或价值,或其中任何部分上缴政府。

17. 采购中的腐败交易

(1) 任何人——
  (a) 为与公共或私人机构签订的任何合同提供任何利益,作为撤回投标或不邀请投标的诱因或奖励,以执行任何工作、提供任何服务、做任何事情或提供任何物品、材料或物质;或者
  (b) 为达成(a)款所指的合同,索取或接受任何好处作为诱因或报酬或其他以撤回投标或不邀请投标,

即构成犯罪。

(2) 被判定犯有本条所规定罪行的人,应被处以 1 500 万先令以下的罚款或 7 年以下的监禁,或两者并罚。

(3) 除本条规定的处罚外,如该人符合以下情况,法院应——

(a) 该人是代理人,则命令其以法院指示的方式向其委托人付以下款项——
　　(i) 其所收取的任何利益或其中任何部分的金额或金钱价值;或者
　　(ii) 其所收取的任何利益的金额或金钱价值的一部分,而余下的全部或部分应予没收;
(b) 不论该人是否为代理人,命令将其所获得的任何利益的金额或价值,或其中任何部分上缴政府。

18. 拍卖中的腐败交易

(1) 任何人——
(a) 向他人提供任何利益,以引诱或奖励他人在由任何公共或私人机构或代表任何公共或私人机构举行的拍卖中不投标或曾经不投标;或者
(b) 索取或接受任何利益作为诱因或报酬,作为其拒绝或曾经拒绝在由任何公共或私人机构或代表任何公共或私人机构举行的拍卖中投标的诱因或报酬,
则构成本法规定的腐败罪,
(2) 被判定犯有本条所规定罪行的人,应被处以1 500万先令以下的罚款或7年以下的监禁,或两者并处罚。
(3) 除本条规定的处罚外,如该人符合以下情况,法院应——
(a) 该人是代理人,则命令其以法院指示的方式向其委托人付以下款项——
　　(i) 其所收取的任何利益或其中任何部分的金额或金钱价值;或者
　　(ii) 其所收取的任何利益的金额或金钱价值的一部分,而余下的全部或部分应予没收;
(b) 不论该人是否为代理人,命令将其所获得的任何利益的金额或价值,或其中任何部分上缴政府。

21. 贿赂外国公职人员

(1) 任何人直接或间接地向外国公职人员或国际公共组织的官员承诺、提议或给予该外国公职人员本人或其他个人或实体不正当利益,以使该外国公职人员在履行公务时作为或不作为,以获取或保留与当地或国际经济活动或商业交易有关的业务或其他不正当利益,即属犯罪,应被处以1 000万先令以下的罚款或7年以下的监禁,或两者并处罚。

(2) 任何外国公职人员或国际公共组织的官员,故意为自己或他人或实体直接或间接地索取或接受不正当利益,以便其在执行公务时作为或不作为,即属犯罪,一经定罪,应被处以1 000万先令以下的罚款或7年以下的监禁,或两者并处罚。

22. 使用旨在误导委托人的文件

任何人故意向任何代理人提供,或代理人故意欺骗或欺诈委托人使用任何收据、账目或其他文件,例如凭证、发票、电子生成的数据、与委托人事务或业务有关的会议记录,且该收据、账目或其他文件载有任何虚假、错误或在重要细节上有缺陷的陈述,并且故意误导委托人,即属犯罪,一经定罪,应被处以700万先令以下的罚款或5年以下的监禁,或两者并处罚。

23. 获取利益的人

(1) 在没有合法对价或本人明知或有理由相信对价不充足的情况下,从以下人员处为自己或为他人索取、接受或获得或同意接受或试图获得利益的——

(a) 其知道或有理由相信曾经、正在、可能或将要与自己有任何事务或交易上的关联的任何人,或与其本人及其下属的任何官员的官方职能有关的任何人;或者

(b) 其知道或有理由相信与其有利害关系或亲缘关系的任何人,或代表该有关人士行事、或与该有关人士有上述联系的任何人,

即属犯罪,一经定罪,应被处以1 000万先令以下的罚款或7年以下的监禁,或两者并罚。

(2) 除根据第(1)款判处的刑罚外,法院还应命令将公职人员获得的任何利益的货币价值或其任何部分上缴政府。

24. 代表被告获得的利益

在被告或被告以外的任何人知情的情况下接受任何利益,而法院在考虑到该其他人与被告的关系或任何其他情况后,确信该人已因代表被告,或因其与被告的关系或因被告的官方职务而获得利益,该利益应视为被告已接受。

25. 性或任何其他方面的利益

任何拥有权力或权威的人,在行使其权力时,要求或向任何人强加性利益或任何其他利益,作为提供就业、晋升、权利、特权或任何优惠待遇的条件,即属犯罪,一经定罪,应被处以500万先令以下的罚款或3年以下的监禁,或两者并罚。

26. 政府官员提供财产账目

(1) 任何经总干事书面授权的本局官员均可通过书面通知向任何公职人员发出通知,要求该公职人员在规定的时间内,以通知中指定的方式,提供该公职人员或其代理人所拥有或其在担任公职期间所曾经拥有的全部或任何类别的财产的完整和真实记录,本局官员还可通过同一或随后的通知,要求该公职人员如实说明他是如何获得这些财产。

(2) 在对任何罪行的起诉中,被告根据第(1)款发出的通知所作的任何书面陈述或说明均可作为证据。

(3) 公职人员如不遵守根据本条规定向他发出通知的要求,或故意提供与财产有关的虚假账目,即属犯罪,一经定罪,应被处以500万先令以下的罚款或3年以下的监禁,或两者并罚。

(4) 在就第(3)款所指罪行提出的检控中,如有证据证明该本局官员已根据第(1)款发出通知,此证据即为其已获授权的确凿证据。

(5) 就本条而言——

"代理人"是指公职人员的丈夫、妻子或子女,公职人员的任何债务人,或为公职人员或代表公职人员行事的任何其他人,包括拥有由公职人员全部或部分获得或曾经获得的财产所有权的任何人;

"公职人员"包括在根据第(1)款发出通知之日的5年内担任过公职的人。

27. 拥有来历不明的财产

(1) 任何作为或曾经作为公职人员的人,有下列行为即属犯罪——

(a) 维持高于其目前或过去合法收入的生活水平;

(b) 拥有与其目前或过去合法收入不成比例的财产,

除非他向法院作出令人满意的解释,说明他如何能够维持这样的生活水平,或说明他如何拥有这些财产。

(2) 在对第(1)款第(b)项所述罪行进行的法律程序中,在考虑到与被告的亲密关系以及

其他情况后,法院有理由认为任何人正在或曾经以信托或以其他方式为被告持有财产,已从被告处获得该财产作为礼物,在没有相反证据的情况下,该财产应推定为由被告控制。

(3)在符合本条规定的情况下,被判犯有本条所规定罪行的人,一经定罪,应被处以1 000万先令以下的罚款或7年以下的监禁,或两者并罚。

[第4章第8节]

(4)除根据第(3)款判处的刑罚外,法院还应命令没收以下金钱收益或财产——

  (a)被认定为被告所有的;和

  (b)其数额或货币价值不超过金钱收益或财产的数额或价值,而该金钱收益或财产的获得没有得到令法院满意的解释。

(5)总干事应在定罪之日后28天内就第(4)款下的命令提出任何申请,但该命令不得针对被定罪人以外的人持有的财产提出——

  (a)除非该人已获合理通知可作出该命令,并有机会说明不应作出该命令的原因;或者

  (b)如该人在任何法律程序中令法庭信赖其有理由——

    (i)在财产归其占有的情况下,以善意行事;和

    (ii)就财产作出的行为,致使在这种情况下作出的命令是不公正的。

(6)第(5)款的任何规定均不得解释为限制法院拒绝依据以第(4)款而非第(5)款规定作出命令的自由裁量权。

(7)根据第(4)款作出的命令,可在法院认为对该案件的所有情况作出适当考虑的条件下作出。

(8)法院可就同一罪行根据第(4)款的两项作出命令,但不得根据这两项规定就同一金钱收益或财产作出命令。

(9)根据第(4)款作出的命令,可就接管该命令所适用的财产,以及由政府或代表政府处置此类财产作出规定。

30. 协助和教唆

任何人协助或教唆他人实施本法规定的罪行,即属犯罪。一经定罪,应被处以200万先令以下的罚款或2年以下的监禁,或两者并罚。

31. 滥用职权

任何人在实施或不实施行为时故意滥用职权、违反法律、履行职责或利用职务之便为自己或他人或实体谋取不正当利益,即属犯罪,一经定罪,应被处以500万先令以下的罚款或3年以下的监禁,或两者并罚。

32. 串谋

任何人与他人共谋实施本法规定的犯罪,即构成同类犯罪,一经定罪,应被处以500万先令以下的罚款或3年以下的监禁,或两者并罚。

33. 利用影响力交易

(1)任何人直接或间接向公职人员或任何其他人承诺、提供或给予不正当利益,以该公职人员或该其他人滥用其实际或假定的影响力,以从行政部门或公共当局为该行为的最初教唆者或任何其他人获取不正当利益,即属犯罪,一经定罪,应被处以300万先令以下的罚款或2

年以下的监禁,或两者并罚。

(2)任何公职人员或任何其他人直接或间接为自己或他人索取或接受不正当利益,以使该公职人员或其他人滥用其实际或假定的影响力,以期从行政部门或公共当局获取不正当利益,即属犯罪,一经定罪,应被处以 300 万先令以下的罚款或 2 年以下的监禁,或两者并罚。

34. 腐败所得的转移

(1)任何人——

 (a)明知财产是腐败或相关犯罪所得,仍将其转换、转移或处置,以隐瞒或掩饰该等财产来源或帮助任何参与犯罪的人逃避法律制裁;或者

 (b)在明知财产是腐败或相关犯罪所得的情况下获取、拥有或使用,

即属犯罪,一经定罪,应被处以 1 000 万先令以下的罚款或 7 年以下的监禁,或两者并罚。

(2)如果检察长有理由相信任何人非法收受或获得利益或财产,其可向该人或该利益、财产、收益或货币价值或收益或货币价值的任何部分归其所有的其他人发出通知,该利益或财产被认为是由涉嫌非法收受或获得该利益或财产的人或该人的代理人转移的,并指示通知的收件人不得转让、处置或分拆对该通知中指定的财产或货币价值的占有。

(3)在不违反第(1)款规定的情况下,检察长可依据法律规定向可获得本条所规定的金钱或财产的任何其他人发出通知。

(4)根据第(2)款发出的每一份通知,应自通知书发出之日起 6 个月内有效,并对收件人具有约束力,或者,如果本法或任何其他成文法规定的与利益或财产有关的罪行作出裁决之前,不得对任何此类人员提起诉讼。

(5)任何已根据第(2)及(3)款送达通知的人,如违反该通知,将该通知所指明的金钱或财产转让、处置或分拆,即属犯罪,一经定罪,应被处以 1 000 万先令以下的罚款或 7 年以下的监禁,或两者并罚。

(6)在对本条所定罪行提起的任何诉讼中,如果被告令法院确信以下情况,即为无罪辩护——

 (a)通知中指明的款项或其他财产已交付给该局的一名官员或通知中指示的其他人;

 (b)通知中指明的款项或其他财产已提交法院,并已由该法院保留;或者

 (c)该通知随后由检察长以书面形式撤回。

[2018 年第 7 号法案第 89 条]

35. 腐败推定

在根据本法进行的诉讼中,如果证明公职人员由持有或寻求从公职人员处获得合同的人或其代理人提供、承诺或给予、或索取、接受或获得或同意接受或获得利益,则该利益应视为已提供、承诺或给予、索取、接受或取得或同意接受或取得作为第 18 条所提述的诱因或报酬,除非有相反的证明。

36. 冒充官员

任何谎称自己——

 (a)根据本法或与预防和反腐败有关的任何其他法律的任何授权或授权令,担任官员或拥有官员的任何权力;或者

（b）能够促使一个机构作出或不作出与该机构职责有关的任何事情，

即属犯罪，一经定罪，应被处以200万先令以下的罚款或1年以下的监禁，或两者并罚。

37. 泄露身份罪

（1）任何人在明知或怀疑正在对根据本法或任何其他与腐败有关的法律所指控或涉嫌实施的罪行进行调查时，在没有合法授权或合理理由的情况下，向以下人员披露以下信息——

（a）向受调查的人披露其被调查的事实或该调查的任何细节；或者

（b）向公众、部分公众或任何特定的人披露当事人的身份或当事人是调查对象的事实或此类调查的任何细节，

即属犯罪，一经定罪，应被处以10万先令的罚款或1年监禁，或两者并罚。

（2）第（1）款不适用于以下情况的调查披露——

（a）已对当事人发出逮捕令；

（b）当事人已被逮捕，无论是否有逮捕令；

（c）根据本法向当事人送达的通知已要求当事人提供书面陈述；和

（d）当事人已被传唤，或其陈述已被记录。

（3）在不影响第（1）款所述"合理理由"一般性的前提下，就披露第（1）款所提述的任何内容，相关人员须有合理的辨解，但仅限于披露以下内容——

（a）总干事、主任或任何本局官员的非法活动、滥用职权、严重失职或其他严重不当行为；或者

[第4章第8节]

（b）对公共秩序或坦桑尼亚联合共和国安全，或公众健康或安全构成的严重威胁。

38. 资产冻结

（1）当某人在任何法院被指控或即将被指控犯有腐败罪或任何其他相关罪行时，法院可根据检察长的申请，在法院认为符合命令期限条件或其他条件的情况下，命令——

（a）将所有到期或欠下的或属于被告的或为被告持有的款项和其他财产扣押在命令中指定的任何人手中；和

（b）禁止被告或命令中指定的任何其他人转让、质押或以其他方式处置所扣押的任何资金或其他财产。

（2）法院可就第（1）款作出的任何命令，指明应支付给被告或由被告领取的金钱或薪金、工资、抚恤金或其他福利，并注明支付或收取款项的来源、方或情形。

（3）在根据第（1）款作出命令时，法院可授权——

（a）在检察长提出命令请求之前，偿还被告的债权人善意欠下的债务；或者

（b）被告出售、转让或处置任何财产，而法庭确信该等出售、转让或处置对于该财产主张权益的任何其他人财产权的保障是必要的。

（4）根据本条作出的命令应立即生效，检察长应——

（a）安排在下一期政府《公报》和至少两份在坦桑尼亚广泛发行的日报上发布该命令的通知；和

（b）将该命令通知——

（i）所有公证人；

(ⅱ) 银行、金融机构和现金交易商；和

(ⅲ) 可能持有或被赋予属于被告财产或代表被告持有财产的任何人。

（5）除根据第（1）条规定的任何相反条件外，根据本条发出的命令应继续有效，直至

（a）检察长决定不进行控诉；或者

（b）对指控的终局裁决。

（6）凡根据本条发出的命令停止生效或被撤销，检察长应安排在政府《公报》和至少两份在坦桑尼亚广泛发行的日报上发布公告。

（7）任何违反根据本条的命令而作出的付款、转让、质押或其他财产处置，均属无效。

39. 提供信息的义务

（1）凡知悉或意识到他人实施或意图实施本法项下的犯罪行为的人，都应向本局提供信息。

（2）根据本条提供和处理信息的程序应符合本条例的规定。

GROUP ONE
INVESTMENT LAWS AND REGULATIONS

TITLE ONE
INVESTMENT REGULATIONS [2023]

THE UNITED REPUBLIC OF TANZANIA

Supplement No.27   21st July, 2023

SUBSIDIARY LEGISLATION

To The Gazette of the United Republic of Tanzania No.27 Vol. 104 Dated 21st July, 2023

Printed by The Government Printer, Dodoma by Order of Government

GOVERNMENT NOTICE No.477 published on 21/7/2023

THE TANZANIA INVESTMENT ACT, (CAP. 38)

REGULATIONS

(*Made under sections 5(4) and 35*)

THE TANZANIA INVESTMENT REGULATIONS, 2023

PART I
PRELIMINARY PROVISIONS

1. Citation
These Regulations may be cited as the Tanzania Investment Regulations, 2023.

2. Interpretation
In these Regulations, unless the context requires otherwise —

"**Board**" means the Board of the Tanzania Investment Centre established under section 9 of the Act;

"**National Investment Steering Committee**" means the National Investment Steering Committee established under section 5(1) of the Act;

"**Technical Committee**" means the Technical Committee established under section 5(3) of the Act;

"**Centre**" means the Tanzania Investment Centre established under section 4 of the Act;

"**person**" includes —
  (a) a natural person, and heirs, executors, administrators, or other representative of such person, and any corporation or other entity which is given, or is recognised as having legal personality under the law of any country or territory;
  (b) the government of any country or territory, public authority in Tanzania or elsewhere and any international organization or body, whether or not its members include Tanzania and whether or not having legal personality;

"**connected person**" means a person who is connected with an individual who is —
  (a) that individual's parent, spouse, brother, sister or child;
  (b) a person acting in his capacity as the trustee of any trust, the principal beneficiary of the trust, his spouse or any of his children or a body corporate which he controls;
  (c) partner of that individual; or
  (d) directly or indirectly controlling or is controlled by the individual;

"**Secretariat**" means secretariat of the National Investment Steering Committee;

"**Act**" means the Tanzania Investment Act; [Cap. 38] and

"**Minister**" means the Minister responsible for investments.

PART II
RESPONSIBILITIES OF THE BOARD

3. Responsibilities of Board

Subject to the provisions of the Act, the Board shall —

(a) keep the functions of the Centre under constant review to ensure that it achieves its objectives;

(b) constantly monitor the national investment situation as well as world investment climate and to propose measures to be adopted to make the investment environment in Tanzania more competitive;

(c) submit to the Minister quarterly progress reports on the activities of the Centre; and

(d) approve code of ethics and conduct for the staff of the Centre.

4. Cessation of membership

A member of the Board appointed according to the provisions of the Act shall cease to be a member if —

(a) he is incapable by reason of mental disorder, illness or injury;

(b) by notice in writing to the appointing authority, that he intends to resign, the resignation shall take effect on the date on which the notice is received by the appointing authority;

(c) he is convicted of criminal offence involving dishonesty;

(d) he becomes bankrupt or makes any arrangement or composition with his or her creditors;

(e) having been given proper notice of each meeting, he is absent from three consecutive meetings of the Board without prior written permission of the Chairman, or in the case of the Chairman without the prior written permission of the Minister; or

(f) the appointing authority is of the opinion that the member is incapable of performing his duties or his termination is necessary for the effective performance of the functions of the Board.

5. Filling of vacant position

Where a member of the Board ceases to be a member on the reasons prescribed under these Regulations, appointing authority may appoint a person to be a member of the Board to fill the vacant on the remaining period of the Board.

6. Quorum

The quorum at the meeting of the Board shall consist of not less than five members.

7. Decisions of Board

Decisions of the Board shall be arrived by consensus provided that, where consensus cannot be obtained, decision shall be made by votes where each member shall have one vote and in the event of equality of votes, the Chairman shall have a casting vote in addition of his deliberative vote.

8. Circular resolutions

Subject to the provisions of the Act, a resolution in writing signed by a quorum of the Board shall be as valid and effective as if the same had been passed at a meeting of the Board duly convened and held.

9. Defect in appointment of member

Any acts done at a meeting of the Board, or of a Committee of the Board shall be valid notwithstanding that it be afterwards discovered that there was a defect in the appointment of any member or that any of them were disqualified from holding office or from voting in the decision.

10. Conflict of interest

Where an individual is a member of the Board, a member of a Committee of the Board, the Executive Director, a member of the staff of the Centre, a consultant or other person engaged by the Board has a pecuniary interest or other beneficial interest in or material to any matter including a direct or indirect interest in any person or in an undertaking or property or contract or investment made or proposed to be made or any other matter which has to be considered by the Board or committee of the Board, the individual shall —

(a) declare the nature of the interest to the Board at a meeting of the Board prior to any consideration of the matter;

(b) request his statement be recorded in the minutes of the meeting concerned;

(c) not be present during any deliberations of the Board with respect to the matter; and

(d) not act in relation to the matter.

11. Beneficial interest

(1) For the purposes of regulation 10, a person shall be regarded as having beneficial interest where —

(a) he or a connected person, or his employee or his nominee is a member or apartner of a company or any other body which has a beneficial interest in, or material to, a matter referred to in regulation 10;

(b) he or a connected person is in partnership with or is in the employment of a person who has a beneficial interest in or material to, a matter referred to in regulation 10; or

(c) he or a connected person is a party to any arrangement or agreement whether or not enforceable concerning a matter referred to in regulation 10.

(2) Where a question arises as to whether or not a course of conduct, if pursued by a person, would be a failure by him or her to comply with the requirements of regulation 10, the question shall be determined by the Board and particulars of such determination shall be recorded in the minutes of the meeting concerned.

(3) Where a person referred to in this regulation fails to make a disclosure in accordance with regulation 10, the appointing authority shall decide the appropriate action to be taken including removal from office or termination of his position.

12. Secretary to Board

(1) Secretary to the Board, shall keep accurate records of all formal proceedings and decisions of the Board.

(2) Notwithstanding the generality of subregulation (1), the Secretary shall —
   (a) maintain accurate documents, records and resolutions of the Board;
   (b) file reports noting the date of submission;
   (c) issue written notice of meetings;
   (d) prepare agenda for Board meetings;
   (e) maintain a roster of Board members;
   (f) prepare minutes of meetings;
   (g) ensure documents for Board meetings are available to members at reasonable time;
   (h) maintain accurate lists of all committees established by the Board; and
   (i) notify persons chosen as members of committees.

PART III
IMPLEMENTATION OF FUNCTIONS OF THE NATIONAL INVESTMENT STEERING COMMITTEE AND TECHNICAL COMMITTEE

13. Implementation of Functions of National Investment Steering Committee

In performing its functions specified under the Act, the National Investment Steering Committee may —
   (a) build common understanding in the Government for the purpose of facilitating of matters relating to implementation investment;
   (b) issue directives with respect to removing different obstacles which hamper investment in the country;
   (c) receive and deal with complaints or sectoral obstacles which hinder delivery of quality services on investment matters and to promptly resolve administrative challenges;
   (d) receive, issue directives and approve major investment projects which have major impacts to the national economy based on the amount of capital, employment generation and technology used in the project.

14. Technical Committee

Subject to section 5(3) of the Act, the Technical Committee shall comprise of the following members:
   (a) Permanent Secretary from the Ministry responsible for investment matters, who shall be a Chairman;
   (b) Deputy Permanent Secretary from the Ministry responsible for Finance (policy), who shall be a Vice-Chairman;
   (c) Commissioner responsible for Policy Analysis from Ministry responsible for finance;
   (d) Commissioner for Land;
   (e) Director of Contracts and Treaties from the Office of the Attorney General;
   (f) Commissioner for large Taxpayers from the Tanzania Revenue Authority;
   (g) Director of Investment Development from the Ministry responsible for investment matters;

(h) Director of Industry Development from the Ministry responsible for Industrial matters; and

(i) any person from the sector from which the matter under discussion relates, who may be invited by Chairperson.

15. Meetings of Technical Committee

(1) The Technical Committee shall meet at least once after every three months.

(2) The Technical Committee shall regulate its own procedures for conducting its meetings.

(3) The quorum for the meeting of Technical Committee shall be at least half of its members.

16. Functions of Technical Committee

(1) The Technical Committee shall perform the following functions:

(a) receive and process various matters from the Secretariat aiming at improving investment environment and to advise the National Investment Steering Committee;

(b) receive and process applications for additional fiscal and non-fiscal benefits from Secretariat and advise the National Investment Steering Committee; and

(c) perform any other function as may be directed by the National Investment Steering Committee.

(2) During processing of applications under subregulation (1)(b), the Technical Committee may invite and hear the applicant, and taking into account conditions stated under section 19(2) and (3) of the Act at the time of giving its recommendations.

PART IV
PROCEDURES FOR SUBMITTING VARIOUS MATTERS BEFORE THE NATIONAL INVESTMENT STEERING COMMITTEE

17. Application for strategic investment and related matters

(1) Application for strategic and special strategic investment for additional fiscal and non-fiscal benefits shall, upon payment of prescribed fee under the Second Schedule to these Regulations, be submitted to the Secretary of the National Investment Steering Committee in Form No.1 set out in the First Schedule to these Regulations.

(2) The application under subregulation (1) shall be accompanied by the following documents:

(a) copy of certificate of incentives;

(b) analysis of the project showing actual costs, profits to the nation and investor, additional benefits requested from the National Investment Steering Committee in order to enable him to implement the project effectively; and

(c) brief statement showing key issues within the investor's application as prescribed in paragraph (b).

(3) Applications under subregulation (1) shall not be granted if they do not meet conditions stated under the Act.

(4) Without prejudice to the provisions of subregulation (2), application for strategic investment in areas with challenges shall identify challenges facing the project and proposals on

how to overcome such challenges.

(5) For the purpose of these Regulations, challenges in peripheral areas of the country includes shortage of infrastructure and trained manpower.

18. Other submissions

Submission of other matters relating to investment, other than investment disputes, for the decision of or direction of National Investment Steering Committee, shall be made through Form No.2 set out in the First Schedule to these Regulations.

19. Procedure for decision making

(1) After receipt of application in accordance with regulations 17 and 18, the Secretary to the National Investment Steering Committee shall submit the same to the Technical Committee which shall process and make recommendations to the National Investment Steering Committee within fourteen days after the last meeting of processing such application.

(2) Upon receipt of recommendations from the Technical Committee, the National Investment Steering Committee shall make decision whether to accept or to reject the recommendations of the Technical Committee, and where the recommendations are accepted, direct the Secretariat to communicate such decision to the respective Ministries, Department and Agencies or person concerned.

PART V
CERTIFICATE OF INCENTIVES, REHABILITATION AND EXPANSION

20. Application for certificate of incentives

(1) A business enterprise person may, upon payment of fees prescribed in the Second Schedule to these Regulations and complying with the requirements of the Act, submit application for certificate of incentives to the Centre by using Form No.3 set out in the First Schedule to these Regulations.

(2) After receiving the application under subregulation (1), the Centre shall process and may —

(a) accept the application and certify the business enterprise; or

(b) reject the application.

(3) Where the Centre has accepted the application and certify the business enterprise under subregulation (2), it shall issue certificate of incentives to the certified enterprise.

(4) Where the Centre rejects the application under subregulation (2), it shall notify the applicant the reasons for rejection.

21. Certificate to be conclusive evidence

A Certificate of incentives issued by the Centre in respect of a business enterprise shall be conclusive evidence that all the requirements of the Act and these Regulations have been complied with.

22. Change of name, shareholding or control

Where a certified business enterprise changes its name or ownership or equity control relating to shareholders, the Centre shall, upon receipt of confirmation of change effected as per statutory requirements under the Companies Act or the Business Names (Registration) Act or any other relevant law, issue an amended certificate of incentives to meet the circumstances of the case.

[Cap. 212; Cap. 213]

23. Change not to affect benefits

Subject to the minimum capital requirement under the Act, any changes referred to in regulation 22 shall not affect any rights or obligations of the enterprise.

24. Procedure for extension of time for additional benefits

(1) A strategic investor or special strategic investor granted additional benefits may, before the expriry of the initial period, apply for extension of time of the benefits by submitting a letter to the Secretary to the National Investment Steering Committee stating the reasonable grounds for the applications.

(2) Secretary to the National Investment Steering Committee shall submit applications made under subregulation (1) to the National Investment Steering Committee which shall decide and Secretary to the National Investment Steering Committee shall communicate in writings such decision to the applicant.

(3) In making the decision on application made under subregulation (1), the National Investment Steering Committee shall, among other things, consider whether there were delays in granting of land for investment, approval for investment capital and other relevant licenses and permits for investment.

25. Extension of time for certificate of incentives

(1) A business enterprise granted certificate of incentives may apply for an extension of time of the certificate by way of a letter submitted to the Centre specifying reasons for such extension, before expiry of the previous time granted.

(2) The Centre shall, when considering the extension of time of the certificate subject to this regulation, among other things, consider if there were delays in acquiring land for the project, capital or permits or various licenses.

(3) The Centre shall process the application under subregulation (1) within seven working days from the date of receipt of such application and communicate the decisions in writing to the applicant.

26. Procedure for revocation of certificate of incentives

(1) The Centre may revoke a certificate of incentives after satisfying itself that the investor has breached the provisions of the Act subject to the reasons provided under section 20(3) of the Act.

(2) The Centre shall, after identifying the reasons for revocation of the certificate of incentive as provided under subregulation (2), before revoking the certificate, give a notice to the holder of the certificate to remedy the identified anomalies within the time specified in the notice.

(3) Where the holder of the certificate fails to remedy the anomaly within the time specified in the notice under subregulation (2), the Centre shall issue a seven days' notice of intention to revoke such certificate and require him to state the reasons as to why his certificate should not be revoked upon the expiry of such notice.

(4) Where the holder of certificate fails to submit his defence or where his defence is not accepted by the Centre, the Centre shall revoke the certificate and notify the reasons of such decision to the holder of the certificate.

PART VI
PROMOTION, FACILITATION AND COORDINATION OF INVESTMENT MATTERS

27. Investment promotion program

(1) The Centre shall implement the functions of investment promotion under the Act.

(2) In implementing the function under subregulation (1), the Centre shall prepare and submit to the Board an investment promotion program for approval.

(3) Upon approval of the program, the Board shall take all necessary steps to ensure that the investment promotion program is implemented.

28. Implementation of program

(1) For purposes of implementing the investment promotion program, the Centre shall —
   (a) market the country as an investment destination to potential local and foreign investors by disseminating information, organization of public relations activities and advertising investment opportunities to build and improve the image of Tanzania as a favorable investment destination;
   (b) keep under review the progress made in the attainment of the objectives and purposes of the Act and to publish reports and provide information for the purpose of enhancing investor's and public awareness of such progress and of the challenges and remedies that exist in relation to the investment climate in Tanzania; and
   (c) develop professional knowledge, skills and other technical capacity to advise the Government on investment promotion and related matters.

29. Monitoring and evaluation of projects

(1) The Centre shall have the responsibility of conducting monitoring and evaluation of registered projects.

(2) In implementing the responsibility provided under subregulation (1), the Centre shall develop the monitoring and evaluation framework and prepare a report once in every three months.

(3) During conducting monitoring and evaluation, the Centre shall consider conditions provided under section 19(2) and (3) of the Act.

(4) The Centre shall inform the National Investment Steering Committee on the development in implementation of strategic investment and special strategic investment projects.

30. Investor's annual report

(1) Every business enterprise with certificate of incentives granted under the Act, shall be responsible to submit to the Centre annual report concerning development of the project.

(2) A newly certified business enterprise shall submit annual report twelve months from the date of issuance of certificate of incentives.

(3) An existing registered business enterprise shall submit annual report twelve months from the last date of submitting annual report of the previous year.

(4) A report prescribed under this regulation, shall be prepared in the manner prescribed in

Form No.4 of the First Schedule to these Regulations.

31. Stationing of land officers and issuance of derivative titles to investors

(1) Pursuant to the provisions of sections 6(1)(e) and 18(2) of the Act, the land officers who shall be stationed at the Centre shall be charged with the duty of making fast track arrangements with respect to land for purposes of investment under the Act.

(2) The land officers stationed at the Centre shall receive and process application for derivative titles for land designated for investment purposes and shall advise the Executive Director to issue such derivative titles to investors in accordance with the Land Act. [Cap.113]

(3) The Executive Director, shall within seven working days after receipt of the advice of the land officers and upon being satisfied that the advice is in conformity to the law, issue to an investor a derivative title for designated land.

32. Residence and work permits, etc.

Subject to the provisions of sections 6(1)(f) and 18(1) of the Act, Centre shall upon application by the investor assist the investors to secure residence and work permits, certificates of registration of business and requisite licenses within seven working days of receipt of such an application.

33. Stationed officers

Subject to the provisions of section 18(2) of the Act, officers from different Ministries, Department and Agencies stationed at the Centre, shall coordinate and facilitate the processing of various licenses and permits on the basis of applications channeled through the Centre, so as to secure issuance of the permits within seven working days of receipt of such applications.

34. Access to guarantees and transfer of profits

The Centre shall automatically issue, a certificate of incentives to any investor holding a mineral right granted under the Mining Act or a license granted under the Petroleum Act to enable them enjoy the guarantee of transfer of capital, profits and dividends provided for under section 28 of the Act; and guarantees against expropriation as provided for under section 29 of the Act read together with section 2(3) of the Act.

[Cap.123; Cap.392]

PART VII
MISCELLANEOUS PROVISIONS

35. Appeals

(1) A person who is disatisfied with any decision rendered by the Centre relating to —

 (a) rejection of application for certificate of incentives;

 (b) rejection of application relating to rehabilitation or expansion of business enterprises;

 (c) rejection of application for extension of time of certificate of incentives; or

 (d) revocation of certificate of incentives,

may appeal by writing a letter to the Minister within twenty-one days from the date on which the decision was made.

(2) After receipt of appeal, the Minister may cofirm or reverse or vary the decision or issue

specific directives in respect of the decision made by the Centre.

(3) The decision by the Minister made under subregulation (2) shall be final.

36. Review

(1) An investor who is disatisfied with the decision of the National Investment Steering Committe on grant of incentives or other matter submitted under regulation 18 may, within twenty-one days from the date of receipt of such decision, apply for review by way of a letter to the National Investment Steering Committee stating the reasons for the review.

(2) Application for review to the National Investment Steering Committe, shall be submitted to the Secretary to the National Investment Steering Committe.

(3) After receipt the application, Committee shall delibarate and makes decision which shall be final.

37. Coordination of investment disputes

(1) Subject to the provisions of section 33 of the Act, the Centre shall receive and resolve, within thirty days from its receipt, disputes relating to investment registered by the Centre submitted to it.

(2) An investor facing any dispute shall be required to submit the statement of the dispute in writing to the Centre within twenty-one days from the date the dispute arose, together with the relief sought.

(3) Upon receipt of the submission under subregulation (2), the Centre shall make an effort to convene a meeting with responsible parties for the purpose of resolving the dispute amicably and timely.

38. Offences and penalty

A person who contravenes the provisions of these Regulations, commits an offence and upon conviction shall be liable for penalty as provided for in the Act.

39. Revocation

The Tanzania Investment Regulations, 2002 are hereby revoked.

[GN. No.381A of 2002]

40. Saving provisions

Notwithstanding the revocation of the Tanzania Investment Regulations of 2005, all acts done under the revoked Regulations shall continue to be valid as if made under these Regulations until they are invalidated under these Regulations.

FIRST SCHEDULE

FORMS

FORM NO. 1

(*Made under regulation 17(1)*)

APPLICATION FORM FOR STRATEGIC AND SPECIAL STRATEGIC INVESTOR STATUS

To: Executive Director,

    Tanzania Investment Centre,

P. O. Box 938,
DAR ES SALAAM

1. Specify names of the Directors or shareholders (for a company) for a sole trader name of the owner who apply for Strategic/Special Strategic Investor Status
   _____

2. Specify place and location of the registered office of the company
   _____

3. Attach copies of the following documents:
   (a) Certificate of Incentives; and
   (b) A summary of the Project showing it meets requirements for registration under the Act, it includes project financing structure and the implementation period and operating date

4. State amount of the intended capital investment of the Company in terms of Tanzanian shillings or United States dollars _____

5. Declaration of payment of application fees

   I/We enclose a cheque/cash made payable to the Tanzania Investment Centre nonrefundable of TShs./US $ _____. Being the Strategic/Special Strategic Investor

   I, _____ of Post Office Number _____ do solemnly and sincerely declare that I am a director/duly authorized agent

   of _____

   AND that all the requirements of the Tanzania Investment Act, 2022 in respect of matters precedent to the registration of the business enterprise under the Act and incidental thereto have been complied with, AND I make this solemn declaration conscientiously believing the same to be true.

   Declared at _____
   This ____ day of ____ year ____
   Before me:

   _____
   Commissioner for Oaths

Attach only where applicable, otherwise indicate "N/A"

APPLICATION SUMMARY AND ADDITIONAL INFORMATION

Company Name: _____
Certificate of Incentives Number: _____ And Date: _____
Post Box: _____
Town: _____
Sector: _____   Sub-Sector: _____

Investment Financing Plan in Million US $ /Tshs.

Foreign Equity   Local Equity   Foreign Loan   Local Loan

....

Project Objectives ....

....

....

Capacity: ....

Direct Employment: Foreign: .... Local: .... Total: ....

Indirect Employment: ....

Implementation Period: ....

Project Location

Site/Plot/Block No.: ....

Street: .... District: .... Region: ....

(Attach sketch map showing project location)

Shareholders   Nationality   %

....

....

....

Investment Breakdown US $ /Tshs.

Land/Building   ....

Plant   ....

Vehicles   ....

Furniture & Fittings   ....

Pre-expenses   ....

Others   ....

Working Capital   ....

TOTAL   ....

Contact Details:

Name: .... Title: ....

Telephone: .... Fax: ....

Email: ....

Additional Specific Fiscal and Non Fiscal Incentives Requested

S/N	Name of Incentive	Name of Items/Goods/ Service	Unit of Measure	Estimated Quantity	Estimated Value of the Incentive (US $)	Incentive Implementation Period	Justify the Incentive
1.							
2.							

Continued

S/N	Name of Incentive	Name of Items/Goods/ Service	Unit of Measure	Estimated Quantity	Estimated Value of the Incentive (US $)	Incentive Implementation Period	Justify the Incentive
3.							
4.							
5.							
6.							
7.							
8.							

FORM NO. 2

(*Made under regulation 18*)

SUBMISSION OF INVESTMENT RELATED MATTERS FOR DECISION AND CONSIDERATION OF NATIONAL INVESTMENT STEERING COMMITTEE

To Executive Director and Secretary to the National Investment Steering Committee, Tanzania Investment Centre,

P. O. Box 938,

DAR ES SALAAM

1. Write name of the business enterprise or Government entity that submit an investment matter which requires National Investment Steering Committee guidance.

   ....

2. Write investment related matter/issue that requires intervention of National Investment Steering Committee

   ....

3. Attach copies of the following documents in the submission:

   (a) A copy of the detailed write-up elaborating the matter,

   (b) responsible ministry or sector, department or agency,

   (c) action taken and proposed National Investment Steering Committee interventions;

4. Declaration of the Applicants

   I, ... of Post Office Number .... do solemnly and sincerely declare that I am a director/duly authorized agent of ....

   ....
   Applicant

5. Contact Details:

   Name: .... Title: ....

Telephone: .... Fax: ....

Email: ....

SUBMISSION SUMMARY

Na	Details on the Matter	Responsible Institution	Effects to the investment climate or the business enterprise	Action taken	Proposed National Investment Steering Committee interventions

FORM NO. 3

(Made under regulation 20(1))

APPLICATION FORM FOR CERTIFICATE OF INCENTIVES

To: Executive Director,

Tanzania Investment Centre,

P. O. Box 938

DAR ES SALAAM

1. Write names of the Director/Directors/Agent of ....
2. State the name and location of the registered office of the company or business enterprise

   ....

3. Attach copies of the following documents:
   (a) The Memorandum and Articles of Association/or partnership agreement
   (b) Certificate of Incorporation/Registration
   (c) A copy of the Project Profile or Feasibility Study showing the implementation period, program of implementation and operative date
   (d) Evidence of financing and evidence of land ownership for the project
4. Name the location of the project

   ....

5. Write the Principal Officers of the Company are;
   (a) ....
   (b) ....
   (c) ....
6. Write the authorized share capital of the Company in Tshs. or US $

   ....

7. Write the intended capital investment of the project in Tshs or US $

   ....

8. Enclose a cheque/cash for proof of payment of non-refundable registration fees;

9. Declaration

I, _____ of Post Office Number _____ _____ do solemnly and sincerely declare that I am a director/duly authorized agent of _____ AND that all the requirements of the Tanzania Investment Act, 2022 in respect of matters precedent to the registration of the business enterprise under the Act and incidental thereto have been complied with, AND I make this solemn declaration conscientiously believing the same to be true.

Declared at _____ }
_____ } Applicant
The _____ day of _____ year _____ }

Before me:

_____
Commissioner for Oaths

Attach only where applicable, otherwise indicate "N/A"

APPLICATION SUMMARY AND ADDITIONAL INFORMATION

Name of Business Enterprise: _____
Registration type _____
Registration Number: _____ Registration Date: _____
Post Box: _____
Town: _____
Sector: _____ Sub-Sector: _____
Investment Financing Plan in Million US $/Tshs.

Foreign Equity	Local Equity	Foreign Loan	Local Loan
_____	_____	_____	_____

Objectives of the Project: _____
_____
_____
Project Capacity: _____
Employment: Foreign: _____ Local: _____ Total: _____
Implementation Period: _____
Project Location
Site/Plot/Block No.: _____
Street: _____ District: _____ Region: _____
(Attach sketch map showing project location)

Shareholders	Nationality	%
_____	_____	_____

....
....

Investment Breakdown   US $/Tshs.

Land/Building _____

Plant _____

Vehicles _____

Furniture & Fittings _____

Pre-expenses _____

Others _____

Working Capital _____

TOTAL _____

Contact Details:

Name: _____   Title: _____

Telephone: _____   Fax: _____

Email: _____

FORM NO. 4

(Made under regulation 30(4))

INVESTOR'S ANNUAL REPORT

To: Executive Director,

Tanzania Investment Centre,

P. O. Box 938,

DAR ES SALAAM

1. The report should show

    (a) Planned Activities for the period

    (b) Achievements made on the project implementation to date:

    (i.e. from the date the project was approved to the date of writing the report)

    (c) Describe the status of activities that have already been undertaken e.g. construction of buildings, acquisition of supplies, installation of equipment, etc.

2. The report to provide updated information on the following aspects;

S/No.	Information	Description	Current Project Status
1.	Shareholder's Information	Current Shareholders names, nationality and percentage of ownership	

Continued

S/No.	Information	Description	Current Project Status
2.	Company Communication Information	Email address	
		Mobile Number	
		Land Line Telephone Number	
		Physical Address (Plot No., Block No, Street, District and Region)	
3.	Contact Person	Name	
		Position	
		Communication Details (Email, Mobile and telephone)	
4.	Incorporation	Certificate of Incorporation No.	
5.	TIN information	TIN Certificate No.	
6.	Project Objective	Project Core Activity	
7.	Capacity	Project Capacity per Year	
8.	Direct Employment	Foreign-Men	
		Foreign-Women	
		Local-Men	
		Local-Women	
9.	Indirect employment	Estimated Total No.	

S/No.	Information	Description	Current Project Status
		Type/areas of Indirect Employment	

3. Report to show Project Financial Expenditure (USD):

	Foreign (USD)	Local (USD)	Total (USD)
Land and Buildings			
Plant and machinery			
Vehicles/Aircrafts			
Furniture			
Office equipment			
Insurance Cover			
Pre-operational expenses			

Continued

	Foreign (USD)	Local (USD)	Total (USD)
Working sub-total capital			
TOTAL			

4. Report to show Project Financing

Explain how the project is being financed e.g. equity, loans, sources of loans, conditions, etc. See table below.

	Amount (USD)	Source Country
Local Equity		Tanzania
Local Loans		Tanzania
Foreign Equity		
Foreign Loans		
Total Investment		

5. Report to show Problems and Solution

Explain problems, which the management is encountering in executing the project and the steps being taken to solve them.

6. Report to show Future Plans

Explain future plans for the next coming six months and planned financial Commitments.

7. Report to show Recommendations and any other comments

SECOND SCHEDULE

(*Made under regulations 17(1) and 20(1)*)

Schedule of Fees

	Service Issued	Applicable Fee US $ or its equivalent to TShs.
1.	Application for Certificate of Incentives	1 200
2.	Application for Strategic and Special Strategic Investor Status	3 000
3.	Application for Expansion and Rehabilitation of investment project	1 200
4.	One Stop Shop Services	10% of the fee charged by the issuing Authority

Dodoma,

4th July, 2023

ASHATU K. KIJAJI,
Minister of Investment, Industry and Trade

TITLE TWO
IMMIGRATION ACT (CHAPTER 54)
[1998] [Revised Edition 2016] (Excerpts)

THE UNITED REPUBLIC OF TANZANIA
CHAPTER 54
THE IMMIGRATION ACT
[PRINCIPAL LEGISLATION]
REVISED EDITION OF 2016

This Edition of the Immigration Act, Chapter 54, incorporates all amendments made up to and including 15th November, 2016 and is printed under the authority of section 4 of the Laws Revision Act, Chapter 4.

Dar es Salaam,	GEORGE M. MASAJU
20th December, 2016	*Attorney General*

THE IMMIGRATION ACT
(CHAPTER 54)

An Act to provide for the control of immigration into the United Republie and for matters relating to immigration.

[1st February, 1998]

[G.N. No.51 of 1998]

PART IV
PROHIBITED IMMIGRANT

27. Deportation

(1) Any person, other than a citizen of Tanzania, whose deportation is recommended by the Commissioner General consequent upon his conviction for an offence against any of the provisions of this Act may be deported from Tanzania pursuant to an order under the hand of the Minister.

(2) The Minister may make an order requiring:

    (a) any prohibited immigrant (other than a prohibited immigrant who is the holder of a valid pass or other authorisation issued to him under this Act);

    (b) any person whose entry into Tanzania was, or presence within Tanzania is, unlawful; or

    (c) any person, other than a citizen of Tanzania, whose conduct or continued presence in Tanzania is, in the opinion of the President, likely to be a danger to peace and good order in Tanzania or is for any other reason undesirable, to be deported from and remain out of Tanzania, either indefinitely or for the period specified in the order.

(3) Any order made under subsection (1) or (2) shall be carried into effect in such manner as the Minister may direct.

(4) A person against whom a deportation order is made may, if the Minister so directs, while awaiting deportation and while being conveyed to the place of departure, be kept in custody, and while so kept shall be deemed to be in lawful custody.

(5) Where any person is brought before a court under the provisions of this Act and the court is informed that an application for an order under this section has been made in respect of him, the court may direct that, that person be detained in custody for any period not exceeding twenty eight days.

(6) A deportation order shall remain in force for the period specified therein, unless sooner varied or revoked by the Minister, or, if no period is so specified, until varied or revoked by the Minister.

(7) Where a deportation order under this section is made against a person serving a sentence of

imprisonment the order shall, if the President so directs, be implemented notwithstanding that the full term of imprisonment has not been served, and any such direction by the President shall be sufficient authority for the release of that person from prison for the purpose of his deportation.

[Act No.8 of 2015 s.3]

PART V
CONDITIONS OF ENTRY AND RESIDENCE

28. Prohibition on entry without passport, permit or pass

(1) Subject to subsections (2) and (3), no person to whom this section applies shall enter Tanzania from any place outside Tanzania or remain in Tanzania unless —

(a) he is in possession of a passport with a visa;

(b) he is the holder of or his name is endorsed upon, a residence permit issued under the provisions of this Act; or

(c) he is the holder of, or his name is endorsed upon, a pass issued under the provisions of this Act.

(2) Notwithstanding subsection (1), the Commissioner General may, in any particular case allow any person to enter Tanzania without a passport, subject to such conditions as he may impose.

(3) The Minister may exempt any person or category of persons from the requirement of possessing a passport.

(4) Where any permit or pass or any endorsement on a permit or pass is cancelled and no further permit or pass is issued or endorsement made, the presence in Tanzania of the former holder of that permit or pass or of the person whose name was endorsed on that permit or pass, as the case may be, shall not be unlawful by reason only of the provisions of subsection (1) before the date or during the period commencing with, the expiry or cancellation, as may be provided for in relation to permits, passes or endorsements, on permits, passes or endorsements of the relevant category, by regulations made under section 48, unless the Minister directs otherwise.

(5) The provisions of paragraphs (a) and (b) of subsection (1) shall apply to every person other than —

(a) the envoy or other representative of a foreign sovereign power accredited to Tanzania, and members of the official staff and the domestic staff of such envoy or representative;

(b) a consular officer or consular employee of a foreign sovereign power appointed to Tanzania and recognised as such by the Government of Tanzania;

(c) the wife and dependant children of an envoy or other representative of a foreign sovereign power accredited to Tanzania, or of a member of the official staff of the envoy or other representative or of a consular officer or consular employee of a foreign sovereign power appointed to Tanzania and recognised as such by the Government of Tanzania;

(d) a person in the service of the Government of Tanzania or the Revolutionary

Government of Zanzibar and stationed in Tanzania who has in his possession a valid passport and satisfies the immigration officer as to his identity and occupation, and the wife and dependant children of such person; except that any person so engaged in the service of the Government of Tanzania or the Revolutionary Government of Zanzibar, may be called upon to provide security either by bond or cash deposit for any expenses which may be incurred by the Government or his employer for repatriating him, his wife and dependant children to his country of origin;

(e) any other person in respect of whom the Minister has given directions that he shall be exempt from the provisions of paragraphs (a) and (b) of subsection (1) of this section.

(6) The wife or any dependant child of any person exempted under subsection (5) shall not engage in any employment, business, trade or profession in Tanzania without first obtaining a residence permit issued or deemed to have been issued to him for that purpose.

(7) Where:

(a) any person to whom paragraph (a) of subsection (5) refers ceases to hold that office;

(b) any person to whom paragraph (d) of subsection (5) refers ceases to be in the service of the Government of Tanzania or the Revolutionary Government of Zanzibar, or ceases to be stationed in Tanzania; or

(c) the Minister gives directions that any exemption granted under paragraph (e) of subsection (5) is revoked or withdrawn, then, on the expiration of one month from the cessation, revocation or withdrawal of the exemption, as the case may be, or such longer period as the Minister may allow, the presence in Tanzania of such person and, in the case of a person to whom paragraph (a), (b), (d) or (e) of subsection (5) refers, of his wife and dependant children, shall, unless otherwise authorised under this Act, be unlawful.

(8) The Minister may, after consulting and obtaining the consent of the President of Zanzibar, by order published in the *Gazette*, make additional provisions regulating the entry into and exit from Zanzibar for visitors to Tanzania.

[Act Nos.15 of 2004 s.25; 8 of 2015 s.3]

29. Rates payable for visa

(1) The rates payable for visa granted under this Act shall be as set out in the Schedule to this Act.

(2) The Minister may by Notice published in the *Gazette*, repeal or amend the Schedule.

[Act No.15 of 2004 s.25]

30. Prohibition on employment, study, etc., without permit

(1) No person shall engage in paid employment under an employer resident in Tanzania except under a permit issued in accordance with the provisions of the Non-Citizens (Employment Regulation) Act.

(2) No person shall for gain or reward engage in any prescribed trade, business, profession or other occupation except in accordance with the terms of an appropriate permit issued in accordance with the Non-Citizens (Employment Regulation) Act.

(3) No person shall commence any course of study at an educational institution in Tanzania unless he is the holder of a valid appropriate permit issued in accordance with this Act.

[Cap.436; Act Nos.1 of 2015 s.28; 8 of 2015 s.3]

31. Establishment, composition and functions of the Alien Immigrants Board

(1) There is hereby established a Board to be known as the Alien Immigrants Board.

(2) The Board shall be composed of the following members:

(a) a Chairman, being a senior officer in the Ministry responsible for immigration, appointed by the President;

(b) the Commissioner for Labour in the Union Government or his representative, who shall be the Secretary of the board;

(c) the Commissioner for Labour in the Revolutionary Government of Zanzibar or his representative;

(d) six senior public officers, one each from the Union Government and the Revolutionary Government of Zanzibar representing the following institutions namely —

(i) the Ministry responsible for trade and industry;

(ii) the institution responsible for planning matters;

(iii) the institution responsible for the Civil service.

(3) The functions of the Board shall be:

(a) to advise the Commissioner General and other relevant authorities on factors to be considered before the Commissioner General or the authority concerned makes a decision to issue business licences or Class B residence permits to alien immigrants;

(b) to advise the Commissioner General and other relevant authorities on conditions for, and ways of, controlling and monitoring entry, residence or mobility of any alien immigrant who applies for and is issued with a business licence or Class B residence permit under paragraph (a);

(c) to advise the Commissioner General and other relevant authorities on whether or not the business or employment vacancy in which an alien immigrant proposes to be engaged cannot be gainfully filled by citizens of Tanzania;

(d) to advise the Commissioner General generally on any measures for the more effective carrying out of the provisions of this section.

(4) The Minister may by regulations published in the *Gazette* prescribe the tenure of members and proceedings of the Board and otherwise in relation to the Board.

(5) The Minister may amend, vary or revoke the regulations made under subsection (4) of this section.

[Act No.8 of 2015 s.3]

32. Classes of residence permits Act Nos.

(1) There shall be three classes of residence permits to be known respectively as Class A permits, Class B permits and Class C permits.

(2) A residence permit may be issued for any period not exceeding three years and may be renewed for any period not exceeding two years by an endorsement of renewal effected on it by the

Commissioner General but so that the total period of the validity of the original permit and of its renewals shall not in any case exceed five years.

(3) The power to issue any class of permit shall be vested in the Commissioner General.

(4) Subject to this Act and in particular the provisions of this Part, any person who is granted a certificate of incentives pursuant to the Tanzania Investment Act, shall be entitled to an initial automatic immigrant quota of up to five persons during the start period of the investment.
[Cap.38]

(5) In issuing permits pursuant to the application submitted by the Tanzania Investment Centre on behalf of a holder of certificate of incentives, the Commissioner General shall, having due regard to the immigrant quota under subsection (4) and within fourteen days from the date of receipt of the application, issue the permit or indicate to the Centre his reasons for refusal to grant a permit.

(6) Notwithstanding subsection (4) and (5), the immigration quota in respect of mining and petroleum operations shall be determined by the investor depending on the nature of the operations.

(7) Subject to subsections (4) and (5), the Tanzania Investment Centre shall make any application for an additional person within the immigrant quota to the Commissioner General who may authorise any additional person whom he shall deem necessary after taking into consideration the availability of qualified Tanzanians, complexity of the technology employed by the business enterprise and agreements reached with the investor.

[27 of 1997 s.25; 8 of 2015 s.3]

33. Class "A" residence permit

(1) A person, other than a prohibited immigrant, who intends to enter or remain in Tanzania and engage in any trade, business, profession, agriculture, animal husbandry, prospecting of minerals or manufacture may, if the Commissioner General thinks fit after taking into consideration the conditions of the work permit issued by the Labour Commissioner to that effect, be granted a class A permit if:

(a) such person or some other person on his behalf furnishes security by depositing with an immigration officer such sum as in the opinion of the immigration officer, is sufficient to cover the cost of returning him, his wife and dependant children, if any, to his country of origin or, in the discretion of the immigration officer, to some other country into which he may be admitted, together with a further sum not exceeding twenty-five per centum of such first-named sum; or

(b) he furnishes security by entering into a bond with one or more sureties to be approved by the immigration officer for an amount calculated in accordance with paragraph (a).

(2) A person to whom a Class A permit has been granted shall be permitted to enter or remain in Tanzania subject to such conditions relating to:

(a) the area within which he may reside;

(b) the kind of occupation or business if any, in which he may engage, and the restrictions prohibitions or limitations subject to which he may engage therein; and

(c) the duration of his residence in Tanzania, as may be specified in the permit by the

Commissioner General.

(3) Where any person to whom a Class A permit has been granted —
   (a) fails or ceases to be engaged in the trade, business, profession or other occupation specified in the permit, or
   (b) engages on any terms, in any trade, business profession or occupation other than the trade, business, profession specified in the permit, the permit shall immediately cease to be valid and the presence of that person in Tanzania shall, subject to the other provisions of this Act, be unlawful.

(4) A person, other than a prohibited immigrant, who resides in Tanzania for ten or more years and whose contribution to the economy or the well being of Tanzania and Tanzanians through investment in trade, business, profession, agriculture, animal husbandry, prospecting of minerals or manufacture is immense or of great value may, the Commissioner General after taking into consideration conditions of the work permit issued by the Labour Commissioner to that effect, he may, subject to the other conditions set out in this section, be granted a class A permit for another period to be determined by the Commissioner General.

[Act Nos.1 of 2015 s.28; 8 of 2015 s.3]

34. Class "B" residence permit

(1) A person, other than prohibited immigrant, who has been offered a specified employment in Tanzania and in respect of whom the Commissioner General is satisfied that he possesses the qualifications or skill necessary for that employment and that his employment will be of benefit to Tanzania may, if the Commissioner General thinks fit after taking into consideration conditions of the work permit issued by the Labour Commissioner to that effect, be granted a Class B permit subject to the condition that the employer shall, before entry into Tanzania of that person and his dependants, if any, or before he is granted the permit, give security for the permit and for any other purposes as the Commissioner General may determine.

(2) A person to whom a Class B permit is granted shall be permitted to enter or remain in Tanzania subject to any conditions in respect of any of the matters referred to in paragraphs (a), (b) and (c) of subsection (2) of section 33, or any other matter, which the Commissioner General may specify.

(3) Where any person to whom a Class B permit has been granted:
   (a) fails or ceases to be engaged in the employment specified in the permit; or
   (b) is engaged, on any terms, in any employment other than the employment specified in the permit, the permit shall immediately cease to be valid and the presence of that person in Tanzania shall, subject to the other provisions of this Act, be unlawful.

(4) Where the presence of a person in Tanzania becomes unlawful by virtue of the provisions of subsection (3), the employer specified in the permit of that person shall, within a period of thirty days from the date on which the holder fails or ceases to be employed by that employer, report that failure or cessation to an immigration officer; and any employer who refuses or fails to comply with this subsection shall be guilty of an offence.

[Act Nos.1 of 2015 s.28; 8 of 2015 s.3]

35. Class "C" residence permit

(1) A person, other than prohibited immigrant, who is not granted a Class A or Class B permit may, if the Commissioner General thinks fit, be granted a Class C permit subject to any condition in respect of matters referred to in paragraphs (a) and (b) of subsection (1) of section 33, or any other matter, as may be specified by the Commissioner General.

(2) A person to whom a Class C permit is granted shall be permitted to enter or remain in Tanzania subject to such conditions as may be specified by the Commissioner General.

[Act No.8 of 2015 s.3]

36. Permits to be issued subject to conditions

(1) Each residence permit issued under this Act shall be subject to the conditions prescribed from time to time in respect of the class of that residence permit.

(2) Every residence permit, irrespective of its class, issued under this Act shall be subject to the condition that if at any time its holder is notified by the Commissioner General that the permit has been revoked in accordance with section 41, that holder shall, within the time specified by the Commissioner General, leave Tanzania.

(3) A residence permit issued under this Act to any person intending to visit or to remain in Zanzibar for the duration of the validity of the permit shall be subject to the further condition that the holder shall comply with the provisions of any order made under subsection (8) of section 28.

(4) Where it is proved that any person to whom a residence permit was issued has contravened, failed or refused to comply with, any condition subject to which the permit was, or was deemed to have been, issued, then the permit shall expire and the presence of that person in Tanzania shall become unlawful; and if the security furnished —

(a) was furnished by way of deposit, that deposit may be forfeited, or

(b) by way of bond, then the Commissioner General may sue for and recover the amount secured by the bond.

[Act No.8 of 2015 s.3]

37. Appeals to the Minister

Any person aggrieved by any decision of the Commissioner General refusing an application for a residence permit or varying the conditions or period of validity specified in the permit, may appeal to the Minister against the decision and the decision of the Minister on that appeal shall be final and shall not be subject to any inquiry by any court of law.

[Act No.8 of 2015 s.3]

38. Variation of conditions of permits

Subject to the provisions of this Act relating to any permit or class of permits, the Commissioner General may, on his own motion or on application in the prescribed manner by the holder of a permit issued under this Act, vary the conditions and the period of validity, specified in the permit.

[Act No.8 of 2015 s.3]

39. Dependants of person granted permits

(1) Subject to any conditions prescribed in that behalf, the Commissioner General may, on

application being made in that behalf in the prescribed form by the holder of or the applicant for a residence permit, endorse on the residence permit the name or names of the wife and the dependent children of the holder or applicant accompanying him to or resident in Tanzania.

(2) An endorsement made under subsection (1) shall, unless the Minister in any particular case directs otherwise, expire with effect from the expiration of one month or such further period as the Commissioner General may, on application made to him in that behalf in his discretion allow, from the death of the holder of the residence permit or the date when the wife or child ceases to be a dependant of the holder, or the date when the person whose name is so endorsed ceases to be the wife or, as the case may be, a child, within the meaning of this Act, of the holder, and the presence of that wife or as the case may be, that child, in Tanzania shall unless otherwise authorised under this Act, thereupon be unlawful.

[Act No.8 of 2015 s.3]

40. Effect of fraud

(1) Where:
- (a) the Commissioner General is satisfied, in the performance of his functions; or
- (b) it is proved in any proceedings under this Act, that any permit, pass, certificate or other authority issued under this Act was obtained by, or issued in consequence of, any fraud or misrepresentation or the concealment or non-disclosure, whether intentional or inadvertent, of any material particular, that permit, pass, certificate or other authority shall be and be deemed to have been, void with effect from the date when it was issued.

(2) Where a permit pass, certificate or other authority issued under this Act becomes, or is deemed to have been void, by virtue of the provisions of subsection (1) the presence of its holder in Tanzania shall be, and be deemed to have been, unlawful from the date when that permit, pass, certificate or authority was issued and the provisions of section 27 of this Act shall apply to him.

[Act No.8 of 2015 s.3]

41. Revocation and surrender of permits

(1) The Commissioner General may, by a written notice under his hand, revoke any permit issued under this Act if he is satisfied that the holder:
- (a) has contravened any of the provisions of this Act or has failed to comply with any requirement made under this Act;
- (b) obtained any permit by means of any representation which was false in any material particular or by means of concealment of any material information;
- (c) has failed to observe any conditions specified in the permit;
- (d) has become or is likely to become a charge on the United Republic in consequence of his failure to support himself and any of his dependants who is in Tanzania.

(2) A notice revoking a permit issued under this Act shall be served in person on the holder of the permit and shall specify:
- (a) the permit to be revoked;

(b) the date, not being less than three days after the service of the notice, on which the revocation shall take effect; and

(c) the ground or grounds on which the revocation is made, and the permit shall cease to be valid on the date specified under paragraph (b).

(3) Every permit issued under this Act to a person who is a prohibited immigrant shall be of no force and effect and shall be deemed never to have been so issued.

(4) Every permit issued under this Act to a person who after being issued with it becomes a prohibited immigrant shall cease to be of force and effect at the time when the holder becomes a prohibited immigrant.

(5) Where a person issued with a permit of one class of residence permit is subsequently granted a permit of another class, he shall surrender the former permit to an immigration officer for cancellation.

(6) Where any person to whom a Class A, Class B or Class C permit has been granted leaves Tanzania permanently, the permit shall be cancelled by an immigration officer and that person shall surrender the permit to an immigration officer for cancellation.

(7) Any person who contravenes or refuses or fails to comply with any of the provisions of this section shall be guilty of an offence.

[Act No.8 of 2015 s.3]

TITLE THREE
LAND ACT (CHAPTER 113)
[2001] [Revised Edition 2019] (Excerpts)

Tanzania
Land Act
(Chapter 113)

Commenced on 1 May 2001

[*This is the version of this document at 30 November 2019.*]

[*Note: This Act has been thoroughly revised and consolidated under the supervision of the Attorney General's Office, in compliance with the Laws Revision Act No.7 of 1994, the Revised Laws and Annual Revision Act (Chapter 356 (R.L.)), and the Interpretation of Laws and General Clauses Act No.30 of 1972. This version is up-to-date as at 31st July 2002.*]

[*G.N. No.484 of 2001; Acts Nos.4 of 1999; 2 of 2002; 2 of 2004; 12 of 2004; 11 of 2005; 12 of 2008; 17 of 2008; 3 of 2009; 2 of 2010; 7 of 2016; 1 of 2018; 4 of 2018; 17 of 2018*]

An Act to provide for the basic law in relation to land other than the village land, the management of land, settlement of disputes and related matters.

PART V
RIGHTS AND INCIDENTS OF LAND OCCUPATION

19. Rights to occupy land

(1) The rights to occupy land which a citizen, a group of two or more citizens whether formed together in an association under this Act or any other law or not, a partnership or a corporate body, in this Act called "right holders" may enjoy under this Act are hereby declared to be —

(a) granted right of occupancy;

(b) a right derivative of a granted right of occupancy, in this Act called a derivative right;

(2) A person or a group of persons, whether formed into a corporate body under the Companies Act or otherwise who is or are non-citizens, including a corporate body the majority of whose shareholders or owners are non-citizens, may only obtain —

[Cap.212]

(a) a right of occupancy for purposes of investment approved under the Tanzania Investment Act;

[Cap.38]

(b) a derivative right for purposes of investment approved under the Tanzania Investment Act or issued under the Export processing Zones Act; or

[Cap.373]

(c) an interest in land under a partial transfer of interest by a citizen for purposes of investment approved under the Tanzania Investment Act or issued under the Export processing Zones Act in a joint venture to facilitate compliance with development conditions.

(3) The provisions of subsection (2) shall not apply to —

(a) a not-for-profit foreign or local corporation or organization of the relief of poverty or distress of public or provision of health or other social services for the advancement of religion or education under an agreement to which the Government of United Republic is a party, and where no such agreement exists, the Minister is satisfied that such corporation or organization is established solely for the purpose of the relief of poverty or distress for the public, or for provision of health or other social services or for the advancement of religion or educations;

(b) a foreign Government, an institution wholly owned by a foreign Government, an International Institution or organization.

(4) Subject to the provisions of subsection (3), the provisions of sections 47, 48 and 49 shall apply *mutatis mutandis* where there is a breach of agreement.

[Acts Nos.2 of 2004 s.3; 12 of 2004 Sch.]

20. Occupation of land by non-citizen restricted

(1) For avoidance of doubt, a non-citizen shall not be allocated or granted land unless it is for investment purposes under the Tanzania Investment Act.

(2) Land to be designated for investment purposes under subsection (1), shall be identified, gazetted and allocated to the Tanzania Investment Centre which shall create derivative rights to investors.

(3) For the purposes of compensation made pursuant to this Act or any other written law, all lands acquired by non-citizens prior to the enactment of this Act, shall be deemed to have no value, except for unexhausted improvements for which compensation maybe paid under this Act or any other law.

(4) For the purposes of this Act, anybody corporate of whose majority shareholders or owners are non-citizens shall be deemed to be non citizens or foreign companies.

(5) At the expiry, termination or extinction of the occupancy or derivative right granted to a non-citizen or a foreign company, reversion of interests or rights in and over the land shall vest in the Tanzania Investment Centre or any other authority as the Minister may describe in the *Gazette*.

[Cap.38; Act No.2 of 2004 s.4]

TITLE FOUR
VILLAGE LAND ACT (CHAPTER 114)
[2001] [Revised Edition 2019] (Excerpts)

Tanzania
Village Land Act
(Chapter 114)

Commenced on 1 May 2001

[*This is the version of this document at 30 November 2019.*]

[*Note: This Act has been thoroughly revised and consolidated under the supervision of the Attorney General's Office, in compliance with the Laws Revision Act No.7 of 1994, the Revised Laws and Annual Revision Act (Chapter 356 (R.L.)), and the Interpretation of Laws and General Clauses Act No.30 of 1972. This version is up-to-date as at 31st July 2002.*]

[*G.N. No.486 of 2001; Acts Nos.5 of 1999; 2 of 2010*]

An Act to provide for the management and administration of land in villages, and for related matters.

PART IV
VILLAGE LANDS

A: Management and Administration

17. Occupation of village land by non-village organization

(1) A non-village organisation to which this Part applies is —

(a) a government department or any office or part of it;

(b) a public corporation or other parastatal body or any office, part, division or its subsidiary body;

(c) a corporate or other body, a majority of whose members or shareholders are citizens registered or licensed to operate under any law for the time being in force in Tanzania applicable to that corporate or other body which does not consist of a majority of the members of the village; or any similarly composed subsidiary of that corporate or other body.

(2) Where, at the commencement of this Act, any nonvillage organisation occupies village land under a granted right of occupancy, that granted right of occupancy shall, notwithstanding that it exists in village land, continue to be a granted right of occupancy for the remainder of its term.

(3) Subject to the provisions of the Land Act, relating to disposition of a right of occupancy the Commissioner shall continue to be responsible for the management of the right of occupancy to which this section applies.

[Cap.113]

(4) Where the Commissioner is satisfied that a village council is managing the village land in an efficient manner, he may, in writing delegate his functions of managing a right of occupancy to which this section applies to that village council subject to any conditions which he shall think fit to include in the instrument of delegation.

(5) On and after the coming into operation of this Act, a non-village organisation which wishes to obtain a portion of village land for the better carrying on of its operations may apply to the village council for that land, and the village council shall recommend to the Commissioner for the grant or refusal of such grant.

(6) Any association of persons formed in accordance with customary law for the purpose of occupying, using and managing land or any association which has come together and is recognised with the community of which it is a part as an association of persons formed to occupy, use and manage land in an urban or peri-urban area, shall, if the persons forming the association registers it in accordance with the provisions of the Trustees Incorporation Act, be recognised as such by this Act and according the provisions of that Act shall apply in relation to such associations.

[Cap.318]

TITLE FIVE
BUSINESS LICENSING ACT (CHAPTER 208)
[1972] [Revised Edition 2002] (Excerpts)

Tanzania
Business Licensing Act
(Chapter 208)

Published in Tanzania Government *Gazette*

Commenced on 1 September 1972

[*This is the version of this document at 31 July 2002.*]

[*Note: This Act has been thoroughly revised and consolidated under the supervision of the Attorney General's Office, in compliance with the Laws Revision Act No.7 of 1994, the Revised Laws and Annual Revision Act (Chapter 356 (R.L.)), and the Interpretation of Laws and General Clauses Act No.30 of 1972. This version is up-to-date as at 31st July 2002.*]

[*Acts Nos.25 of 1972; 10 of 1973; 16 of 1974; 7 of 1976; 20 of 1978; 8 of 1979; 12 of 1979; 9 of 1980; 25 of 1980; 12 of 1981; 9 of 1982; 10 of 1987; 13 of 1989; 17 of 1990; 13 of 1991; 18 of 1991; 3 of 1993; 10 of 1993; 16 of 1994; 13 of 1996; 25 of 1997; 8 of 1998; 12 of 1999; 11 of 2000; 14 of 2001; 10 of 2002; 18 of 2002*]

An Act to provide for the licensing of businesses and for related matters.

3. Prohibition on carrying on business without licence

(1) No person shall carry on in Tanzania, whether as a principal or agent, any business unless —

    (a) he is the holder of a valid business licence issued to him in relation to such business; and

    (b) such business is being carried on at the place specified in the licence.

(2) No person shall carry on business at two or more places, unless he is the holder of a separate business licence issued to him in relation to such business for each of such places:

Provided that, in any such case, if a valid business licence exists in respect of any of the places of business (hereinafter referred to as "the principal place of business") the holder shall be deemed not to have contravened the provisions of this subsection —

    (a) If such person holds in relation to such business a subsidiary licence in respect of the other place of business or if he carries on such business at two or more other places, each of such other places; or

    (b) if no licence fee is prescribed for any subsidiary licence in relation to such business.

(3) Without prejudice to the provisions of any other written law to the contrary, nothing in this section shall be construed as prohibiting the carrying on, whether by the same person or by different persons, of two or more businesses at the same place if each such business is carried on under the authority of a valid business licence:

Provided that regulations made under this Act may provide that any business specified in such regulations shall not be carried on at any place where any other business or any business of a class or description specified in the regulations is also being carried on.

(4) The licensing authority shall have the power to close business premises of any trader who is found to carry on business without a licence, and in doing so the licensing authority may request the assistance of a police officer or any other authorised agent.

[Cap.77]

10. Temporary licences for non-residents

(1) This section shall apply to persons belonging to specified professions and to building contractors.

(2) No person to whom this section applies and who is not ordinarily resident in the United Republic shall, in Tanzania —

- (a) in the case of a person belonging to a specified profession, render any professional services which he is qualified to render by virtue of being a member of such profession;
- (b) in the case of a building contractor, carry out any work of, or relating to, the construction of a building;
- (c) in the case of a commercial traveller, carry on the business of a column of the said Schedule, unless such person is —
  - (i) the holder of a valid business licence in respect of the specified profession or, as the case may be, the business of a building contractor; or
  - (ii) exempted by or under this Act from the requirement to take out such licence; or
  - (iii) the holder of a valid temporary licence granted to him in relation to the business of such specified profession or, as the case may be, the business of a building contractor.

(3) A temporary licence may be issued to any person to whom this section applies on payment of a fee —

- (a) in the case of a specified profession, of five hundred shillings;
- (b) in the case of a building contractor, of seven hundred and fifty shillings;
- (c) in the case of a commercial traveller, of one hundred and twenty shillings.

(4) Every temporary licence granted under this section shall be valid for a period of thirty days from the date of issue or such longer period as the Permanent Secretary may in any case direct.

(5) The holder of a temporary licence shall be entitled, during the period of validity of such licence, to carry on the business specified in such licence and any auxiliary business to the same extent as the holder of a corresponding business licence.

[Cap.77 s.9]

19. Offences

(1) Any person who —

- (a) carries on business without being the holder of a valid licence or, in cases to which section 10 applies, a valid temporary licence authorising him to carry on such business;
- (b) carries on business at any place not specified in a valid business licence or a subsidiary

licence granted to him in respect of such a business in contravention of the provisions of section 3;

(c) fails to exhibit, as required by section 16, any business licence granted to him;

(d) fails to comply with the provisions of section 17;

(e) fails to surrender a business licence granted to him when called upon to do so under section 14;

(f) in or in relation to any application for a licence makes any statement which is false in any material particular;

(g) being the holder of a business licence to which conditions have been annexed under this Act, fails to comply with any such condition;

(h) fails to comply with the provisions of section 18A;

(i) with intent to evade the payment of the full licence fee wilfully does or omits to do any act or thing,

shall be guilty of an offence and shall be liable on conviction to —

(i) in the case of an offence under paragraph (a) to (i), a fine of —

(aa) not less than one hundred thousand shillings but not exceeding five hundred thousand shillings for a business of national and international character; and

(bb) not less than fifty thousand shillings but not exceeding three hundred thousand shillings for a business whose licence is issued and governed by the local authorities,

or to imprisonment for a term not exceeding two years or to both.

(ii) in the case of an offence under paragraph (h), shall be liable to pay in addition to the licence fee a penalty of three hundred *per centum* (300%) of such fee.

(2) In any proceedings for an offence under paragraph (a) of section (1), if the accused satisfies the court that the date on which allegedly he committed the offence was within twenty-one days from the date on which the business licence previously held by him expired or, as the case may be, the date on which he first commenced business, the maximum penalty to which he may be sentenced shall be a fine of fifty thousand shillings for those businesses of national and international character and to ten thousand shillings for those businesses whose licences are issued and governed by the local authorities.

[s.17]

TITLE SIX
BUSINESS LAWS (MISCELLANEOUS AMENDMENTS) ACT [1930] [Revised Edition 2012] (Excerpts)

THE UNITED REPUBLIC OF TANZANIA
ACT SUPPLEMENT
NO.3 27th July, 2012

To The Gazette of the United Republic of Tanzania No.30 Vol.93 dated 27th July, 2012

Printed by the Government Printer, Dares Salaam by Order of Government

THE BUSINESS LAWS (MISCELLANEOUS AMENDMENTS) ACT, 2012

An Act to amend laws which regulates the conduct of business with a view to create more condusive climate for doing business in Tanzania.

ENACTED by Parliament of the United Republic of Tanzania.

PART II
AMENDMENT OF THE BUSINESS NAMES (REGISTRATION) ACT, (CAP.213)

3. Construction

This Part shall be read as one with the Business Names (Registration) Act, hereinafter referred to as "the principal Act".

[Cap.213]

4. Amendment of the long title

The principal Act is amended in the long title by repealing and substituting for it the following:

"An Act to provide for the registration of firms, individuals and corporations carrying on business under a business name and to provide for other related matters."

5. Amendmant of section 1

The principal Act is amended by repealing section 1 and replacing for it the following:

"1. Short title

This Act may cited as the Business Names Act."

6. Amendmant of section 2

The principal Act is amended in section 2, by —

(a) inserting the words "every trade and" between the words "includes" and "profession" appearing in the definition of the term "business";

(b) adding in its appropriate alphabetical order the following new definitions:

"carrying on business" includes establishing a place of business and soliciting or procuring any order from any person in Tanzania;

"the Registrar" means the Registrar or any of the Deputy Registrars performing the functions of registration of business names under this Act;

"Minister" means the Minister responsible for trade;

"corporation" means any legal person that possess a corporate personality status;

"correspondence address" includes e-mail, fax, website and telephone numbers; and

"surname" in relation to a peer or person usually known by a title different from his surname, means that title.

7. Amendment of section 3

The principal Act is amended in section 3, by —

(a) deleting subsection (1) and substituting for it the following:

"(1) The Minister may appoint a Registrar, Deputy Registrar and such Assistant Registrars as may, from time to time, be required for the purposes of this Act."; and

(b) inserting the words "and Assistant" between the words "Deputy" and "Registrar".

8. Amendment of section 6

The principal Act is amended in section 6(1), by —

(a) deleting the words "send by post" appearing in subsection (1);

(b) adding the phrase "its postal and any other correspondence address" at the end of paragraph (a); and

(c) deleting the phrase "twenty one years, it shall be sufficient for him to state his age as full age" appearing in the proviso and substituting for it the phrase "eighteen years, it shall be sufficient for him to state his age as full age and that the use of general terms to describe nature of business shall be avoided."

9. Amendment of section 8

The principal Act is amended in section 8, by deleting the words "twenty-eight" and substituting for them the word "twenty one".

10. Amendment of section 9

The principal Act is amended in section 9 as follows:

(a) in subsection (1), by —

(i) deleting paragraph (b) and substituting for it the following new paragraph (b):

"(b) which is expressing or implying the sanction, approval or patronage of the Government;";

(ii) deleting a "full stop" appearing in paragraph (d) and substituting for it a "semi-colon" and adding immediately thereafter the word "and";

(iii) adding immediately after paragraph (d) the following new paragraph (e):

"(e) which in the opinion of the Registrar, is undesirable;".

(b) in subsection(3), by deleting the words "twenty-eight" and substituting for them the word "five working days"; and

(c) in subsection(4), by deleting the phrase "whose decision shall be final".

11. Amendment of section 11

The principal Act is amended in section 11, by deleting the words "twenty-eight" and substituting for them the word "fourteen".

12. Amendment of section 12

The principal Act is amended in section 12, by —

(a) deleting subsection (1) and substituting for it the following new subsection:

"(1) Where a business name sought to be registered under this Act is in contravention of section 9(1) or is by inadvertence or otherwise, registered, the Registrar may submit, by correspondence address, a notice addressed to the person in relation to whom the name is registered at the place shown in the register where business is carried on under that name:

(a) stating the Registrar's proposal to cancel or refuse the registration of that name upon expiration of a period of not more than twenty one days; and

(b) stating the reasons for the proposed cancellation or refusal.";

(b) deleting the phrase "whose decision shall be final" appearing in subsection (2).

13. Amendment of section 13

The principal Act is amended in section 13, by deleting the words "two hundred" and substituting for them the words "fifty thousand".

14. Amendment of section 18

The principal Act is amended in section 18, by deleting the words "five thousand" and substituting for them the words "fifty thousand".

15. Amendment of section 20

The principal Act is amended in section 20, by —

(a) deleting the word "post" appearing in subsection (1) and substituting for it the words "correspondence address"; and

(b) adding immediately after subsection (4) the following new subsections:

"(5) Upon removal from register, any firm, individual or corporation, that firm, individual or corporation shall, within twenty one days, from the date of the expiration of the notice of removal from the register, surrender to the Registrar, any certificates issued under this Act.

(6) Upon receipt of a certificate in terms of subsection (4), the Registrar shall cancel that certificate."

16. Addition of section 25

The principal Act is amended by adding immediately after section 24 the following new section:

"25. Forms

Every certificate issued under this Act shall be in the form set out in the Second Schedule to this Act."

TITLE SEVEN
PUBLIC PRIVATE PARTNERSHIP ACT
(CHAPTER 103) [2011] [Revised Edition 2019]

THE UNITED REPUBLIC OF TANZANIA
CHAPTER 103
THE PUBLIC PRIVATE PARTNERSHIP ACT
[PRINCIPAL LEGISLATION]
REVISED EDITION OF 2019

This Edition of the Public Private Partnership Act, Chapter 103, has been revised up to and including 30th November, 2019 and is printed under the authority of section 4 of the Laws Revision Act, Chapter 4.

Dodoma,   ADELARDUS L. KILANGI
30th November, 2018   *Attorney General*

THE PUBLIC PRIVATE PARTNERSHIP ACT
(CHAPTER 103)

An Act to provide for the institutional framework for the implementation of public private partnership agreements between the public sector and private sector entities; to set rules, guidelines and procedures governing public private partnership procurement, development and implementation of public private partnerships and to provide for other related matters.

[26th May, 2011]

[G.N. No.156A of 2011]

Acts Nos.
18 of 2010
3 of 2014
9 of 2018
GN. No.
483 of 2018

PART I
PRELIMINARY PROVISIONS

1. Short title

This Act may be cited as the Public Private Partnership Act.

2. Application

This Act shall apply to Mainland Tanzania in respect of projects undertaken in partnership between the public sector and private sector.

3. Interpretation

In this Act, unless the context otherwise requires:

"**accounting officer**" means a Permanent Secretary or a Chief Executive of a Contracting authority and includes accounting officers of a local government authority;

"**affordable**" in relation to an agreement, means that the contracting party shall meet any financial commitment to be incurred in relation to that agreement;

"**agreement**" means a public private partnership agreement entered into in terms of this Act;

"**asset**" includes an existing asset of a relevant Contracting authority or a new asset to be acquired for the purposes of entering into an agreement;

"**contingent liability**" means a legal or contractual obligation to make payment depending on the outcome of uncertain future event arising from project transaction including all other contingent liabilities that may be borne by the Government in relation to or associated with public private partnership projects;

"**contracting authority**" means any Ministry, government department or agency, local government authority, public or statutory corporation;

"**Executive Director**" means the Executive Director for the PPP Centre appointed under section 6;

"**Facilitation Fund**" means the Public Private Partnership Facilitation Fund established under section 10A;

"**local government authorities**" shall have the meaning ascribed to it under the Local Government (District Authorities) Act and the Local Government (Urban Authorities) Act; [Caps.287 and 288]

"**Minister**" means the Minister responsible for public private partnership;

"**Ministry**" means the Ministry responsible for public private partnership;

"**PPP agreement**" means a written contract defining terms of the public private partnership agreement concluded between a contracting authority and one or more private parties;

"**PPP Centre**" means the Public Private Partnership Centre established under section 4;

"**private party**" in relation to an agreement, means a party to the agreement other than a Contracting authority;

"**project**" means a project or service to be implemented under an agreement entered into under this Act;

"**private sector**" means a sector other than a public sector including non-profit making non-governmental organisations;

"**public private partnership**" or known in its acronym as "**PPP**" means a contractual arrangement between a contracting authority and a private party in which the private party —

 (a) undertakes to perform for contracting authority function on behalf of the contracting authority for a specified period;

 (b) assumes substantial financial, technical and operation risks in connection with the performance on behalf of the contracting authority function or use of government property; or

 (c) receives a benefit for performing on behalf of contracting authority function or from utilizing the public property, either by way of:

  (i) consideration to be paid by the contracting authority which derives from a revenue fund, or where the contracting authority is a central government or local government authority, from revenues of such authority;

  (ii) charges or fees to be collected by a private party or its agent from users or customers; or

  (iii) a combination of such consideration and such charges or fees;

"**Public Private Partnership Steering Committee**" means the Private Public Partnership Steering Committee established under section 7;

"**public sector**" means a government ministry, department or agency, local government authority and any other person acting on behalf of the government ministry, department or agency or local government authority;

"**request for proposals**" means the specific terms of the project requirement, the procedures for submission of bids, the criteria for the evaluation of bids and includes a model agreement;

"**Sector Ministry**" means a ministry responsible for the Contracting authority;

"**small scale PPP project**" means a PPP project approved under this Act of an amount not exceeding twenty million US dollars.

[Acts Nos.3 of 2014 s.2; 9 of 2018 s.2]

PART II
ESTABLISHMENT AND ADMINISTRATION OF THE PPP CENTRE

4. PPP Centre

(1) There is established a PPP Centre to be known as the Public Private Partnerships Centre.

(2) There shall be such other number of departments as the Executive Director may, upon approval of the authority responsible for establishment in the public service, determine.

(3) The centre shall be a body corporate with perpetual succession and common seal and shall, in its own name, be capable of —

(a) acquiring and holding movable property, to dispose of property and to enter into a contract or other transactions;

(b) suing and being sued; and

(c) doing or suffering to do all other acts and things which bodies corporate may lawfully do or suffer to do, for the proper performance of its functions under this Act.

(4) The PPP Centre shall deal with promotion and co-ordination of all matters relating to public private partnership projects.

(5) The projects referred to under subsection (4) shall, subject to subsections (6) and (7), be undertaken in productive and social sectors, including but not limited to the following sectors:

(a) agriculture;

(b) infrastructure;

(c) industry and manufacturing;

(d) exploration and mining;

(e) education;

(f) health;

(g) environment and waste management;

(h) information and communication technology (ICT);

(i) trade and marketing;

(j) sports, entertainment and recreation;

(k) natural resources and tourism; and

(l) energy.

(6) Every contracting authority shall, at the beginning of every budget cycle, submit to the PPP Centre concept note and prefeasibility study of potential public private partnership projects:

Provided that —
- (a) the potential public private partnership project complies with the national development priorities; and
- (b) the concept note and prefeasibility study of potential public private partnership projects is approved by the respective Minister.

(6A) The PPP Centre shall, within twenty one working days, analyse the potential public private partnership project received in terms of subsection (6) and forward to the Public Private Partnership Steering Committee.

(7) For the purposes of subsection (6), the Minister shall, at least two months before the beginning of the financial year, ask each contracting authority to submit to the PPP Centre a concept note and prefeasibility study of potential public private partnership projects.

(8) In this section, the term "budget cycle" shall have the meaning ascribed to it under the Budget Act.

[Acts Nos.3 of 2014 s.4; 9 of 2018 s.4; GN. No.483 of 2018]

5. Functions of PPP Centre

(1) The functions of the PPP Centre shall be to —
- (a) mobilize resources for project development and Government support to public private partnership projects;
- (b) develop a mechanism to ensure that all ministries, Government departments and agencies and local government authorities integrate public private partnership into their sector strategies and plans;
- (c) develop operational guidelines for contracting authorities;
- (d) design and implement a fair, transparent, competitive and cost effective procurement process;
- (e) deal with fiscal risk allocation and other financial matters of all public private partnership projects;
- (f) advise contracting authorities on all matters relating to public private partnership projects;
- (g) provide technical assistance to ministries, Government departments, agencies, local government authorities and private sector in planning, managing and appraising public private partnership projects;
- (h) examine requests for proposals to ensure conformity with the approved feasibility study;
- (i) monitor, review and evaluate implementation of Public Private Partnership Facilitation Fund;
- (j) ensure relevance and adequacy of proposals submitted to it by contracting authorities;
- (k) monitor and evaluate the performance of the public private partnership projects and prepare periodic performance reports;
- (l) design and implement programmes for public private partnership capacity building to public and private sectors;

(m) develop and implement programmes intended to promote public awareness on public private partnership issues; and

(n) undertake research on public private partnership matters.

(2) Without prejudice to the generality of subsection (1), the PPP Centre shall analyse projects submitted by contracting authorities within thirty working days from the date of receipt.

(3) The PPP Centre shall, upon completion of analysis under subsection (2), submit the feasibility study, selection of preferred bidder and PPP agreements to the Public Private Partnership Steering Committee for approval.

(4) The PPP centre be a One Stop Center, and in so being, it shall, for effective discharge of its functions seek recommendations from the Ministries responsible for investment, finance, planning or any other ministry, department or agency.

(5) Nothing in this section shall prevent the contracting authorities from undertaking necessary technical analysis relevant for project within their jurisdiction.

(6) The Minister shall, for the purpose of ensuring investment in PPP projects and in consultation with the Minister responsible for investment, prepare programmes for development and maintenance of favourable environment for investment through public private partnership arrangement.

[Acts Nos.3 of 2014 s.5; 9 of 2018 s.5]

6. Executive Director

(1) The PPP Centre shall be headed by a Executive Director who shall be appointed on competitive basis in accordance with the Public Service Act.

(2) A person shall be qualified for appointment as Executive Director if that person —

(a) possesses at least a degree in the field of project management, accounting, law, engineering, economics or other related fields; and

(b) has knowledge and experience on the development, formation or implementation of projects or undertakings of a public or private nature.

(3) There shall be appointed to the PPP Centre such persons who are qualified and possess knowledge and experience on the formation, development or implementation of projects or undertakings of a public or private nature.

(4) The appointment of persons to the PPP Centre shall be made on competitive basis in accordance with the Public Service Act.

[Act No.3 of 2014 s.6; Cap.298]

7. Public Private Partnership Steering Committee

(1) There shall be a Public Private Partnership Steering Committee comprised of —

(a) the Permanent Secretary of the Ministry who shall be the Chairman;

(b) the Permanent Secretary Prime Minister's office;

(c) the Permanent Secretary of the Ministry responsible for lands;

(d) the Deputy Attorney General;

(e) a representative of authority responsible for national planning;

(f) the Executive Director of the Tanzania Investment Centre;

(g) the Executive Director of the Tanzania Private Sector Foundation;

(h) the Commissioner General of Tanzania Revenue Authority;

(i) the Permanent Secretary, Ministry responsible for Local Government;

(j) two persons from private sector nominated by the Minister on recommendation of Tanzania Private Sector Foundation.

(2) The Permanent Secretary of the sector Ministry whose project is the subject of deliberation shall attend meetings of the Public Private Partnership Steering Committee.

(3) The Public Private Partnership Steering Committee may co-opt any other person who has knowledge and experience in the subject matter of the deliberation.

(4) The Executive Director shall be the Secretary to the Public Private Partnership Steering Committee.

(5) The Public Private Partnership Steering Committee shall meet at least once in every three months.

(6) Notwithstanding subsection (5), the Public Partnership Steering Committee may meet as often as it may be necessary for effective discharge of its functions.

[Acts Nos.3 of 2014 s.7; 9 of 2018 s.6]

7A. Functions of Public Private Partnership Steering Committee

(1) The functions of the Public Private Partnership Steering Committee shall be to —

(a) review policy, legislation, plans and strategies pertaining to the promotion, facilitation and development of public private partnership and to advise the Minister accordingly;

(b) advise the Minister on matters relating to implementation of the National Public Private Partnership Programme;

(c) approve feasibility study, detailed project report and design, selection of preferred bidder, public private partnership agreement or any amendment to the agreement;

(d) approve allocation of project development funds from the Facilitation Fund; and

(e) assign to contracting authorities terms and conditions for utilisation of the Facilitation Fund.

(2) Subject to the recommendation made by the PPP Centre, the Public Private Partnership Steering Committee shall, within twenty one working days, approve feasibility studies, detailed project report and design, selection of preferred bidder, agreements and amendment to agreements.

(3) Subject to the recommendation made by the PPP Centre, the Public Private Partnership Steering Committee shall approve feasibility studies, selection of preferred bidder agreements and amendment to agreements.

[Acts Nos.3 of 2014 s.8; 9 of 2018 s.7]

7B. Public funding and other support of PPP project

(1) Notwithstanding the provisions of section 7A, the Public Private Steering Committee shall, where a project requires public funding, any other government support or determination of matters of policy, refer the matter to the Minister for determination.

(2) The Minister shall, within twenty one working days from the date of receipt of matters from the Public Private Partnership Steering Committee in terms of subsection (1) —

(a) in the case of matters requiring public funding, process the matter in the manner prescribed under the Government Loans, Guarantees and Grants Act; [Cap.134]

(b) in the case of matters requiring any government support or determination of matters of policy, make determination and direct the Public Private Partnership Steering Committee accordingly.

(3) Notwithstanding subsection (2), the Minister shall, where a matter has not been determined within twenty one working days, notify the Public Private Partnership Steering Committee with reasons thereof.

[Act No.9 of 2018 s.8]

7C. Powers of Minister generally

(1) The Minister shall, through the official *Gazette*, newspaper of wide circulation or public media, notify the general public of all approved projects under this Act.

(2) The Minister shall monitor and manage fiscal risks and other financial matters relating to the implementation of PPP projects in accordance with the respective agreement.

(3) Subject to the provisions of this Act, the Minister shall issue directives to accounting officers of contracting authorities on the analysis and approval or disapproval of small scale PPP projects.

[Act No.9 of 2018 s.9]

PART III
PARTICIPATION OF THE PUBLIC AND PRIVATE PARTY

8. Roles of Public and Private sector

(1) The public sector shall facilitate the implementation of the public private partnership projects by:

(a) identifying projects;

(b) carrying out feasibility studies;

(c) monitoring and evaluation;

(d) risk sharing; and

(e) putting in place an appropriate enabling environment, including:

(i) favourable policies;

(ii) implementation strategies;

(iii) the legal and institutional framework.

(2) The private sector, shall play the role of identifying and implementing public private partnership projects by:

(a) carrying out feasibility studies;

(b) mobilizing resources;

(c) risk sharing;

(d) monitoring and evaluation; and

(e) providing technical experience and managerial skills.

(3) The public sector and private sector shall, have the duty to prepare a communication

strategy for awareness creation and consensus building for acceptance by all stakeholders of public private partnerships and their outcomes benefits and associated costs and risks.

9. Responsibilities of contracting authority

(1) The contracting authority shall for the purpose of this Act:

(a) identify, appraise, develop, manage and monitor a project to be implemented under this Act;

(b) undertake or cause to be undertaken a feasibility study where it considers that the project is suitable for implementation under an agreement; and

(c) submit the proposed project together with the feasibility study to the PPP Centre for consideration.

(2) The contracting authority shall make consultation with the relevant regulatory authorities prior to submission of feasibility study of the proposed project to the PPP Centre.

(3) Sections 7A and 7B shall not be construed as removing or abrogating powers of the contracting authority or accounting officer for assuming overall responsibility on matters assigned to it under this section.

[Act No.3 of 2014 s.9]

10. Feasibility Study

(1) Every contracting authority shall undertake or cause to be undertaken a feasibility study where it considers that a project may be implemented under Public Private Partnership agreement for purposes of assessing whether the proposed project is feasible.

(2) The feasibility study shall:

(a) identify and define the activity which the Government intends to outsource from a private party;

(b) assess the projected impact of intended outsourcing of the activity to a private party on the staff, assets, liabilities and revenues of the Government;

(c) asses the need for the Government in relation to such activity including:

(i) options available to the Government to satisfy those needs;

(ii) the advantages and disadvantages of each option;

(d) demonstrate comparative advantage in terms of strategic and operational benefits for implementation under the agreement;

(e) describe, in specific terms:

(i) the nature of the contracting authority's functions, the specific functions to be considered in relation to the project and the expected inputs and deliverables;

(ii) the extent to which those functions can lawfully and effectively be performed by a private party in terms of an agreement;

(f) demonstrate that the agreement shall:

(i) be affordable to the Contracting authority;

(ii) provide value for money;

(iii) transfer appropriate technical, operational or financial risks to the private party;

(g) assess the capacity of the contracting authority to effectively implement the agreement, including the ability to monitor and regulate project implementation and the performance of the private party in terms of the agreement; and

(h) assess the capacity, resources and ability of the private party to implement the project.

(3) For the purposes of subsection (2), the feasibility study shall include technical and socio-economic impact analysis.

(4) The assessment under paragraph (c) of subsection (2) shall indicate comparative projections of:

(a) the full costs to the Government or the activity if that activity is not outsourced through Public Private Partnership agreement; and

(b) the full costs to the Government for the activity if that activity is outsourced through a Public Private Partnership agreement.

(5) Without prejudice to the provisions of subsection (2), the Minister may, by regulations, prescribe additional or detailed contents of a concept note and feasibility study as may be required under a PPP project.

(6) Where the project which is to be undertaken is of such a nature or type for which an environmental impact assessment is required under Part VI of the Environmental Management Act, to be carried on, the contracting authority shall ensure that the environmental impact assessment certificate is obtained by the private party before undertaking the project. [Cap.191]

[Act No.9 of 2018 s.10]

10A. Facilitation Fund

(1) There shall be a Facilitation Fund to be known as the Public Private Partnership Facilitation Fund.

(2) The PPP Centre shall open a bank account into which shall be kept all moneys constituting the Facilitation Fund.

(3) The Executive Director shall be the accounting officer of the Facilitation Fund.

(4) The use of funds from the Facilitation Fund shall require approval of the Public Private Partnership Steering Committee.

[Acts Nos.3 of 2014 s.10; 9 of 2018 s.11]

10B. Sources of funds

(1) The sources of funds of the Facilitation Fund shall be such sums of moneys appropriated by Parliament for that purpose, and any other funds mobilized from any of following sources —

(a) development partners, public entities, parastatal organizations and social security funds; and

(b) funds previously advanced to contracting authorities wholly or partially recovered by the Facilitation Fund in accordance with agreements for project support.

(2) Upon approval by the Public Private Partnership Steering Committee, the Facilitation Fund shall be used for —

(a) financing wholly or partly the feasibility studies and other project preparation costs as may be required by a contracting authority;

(b) providing resources to enhance the viability of projects which have high economics benefits that have demonstrated to be of limited financial viability; and

(c) any such other purposes as may be prescribed in the regulations.

(3) The provisions of subsection (2) shall not be construed as limiting or preventing contracting authorities from using own funds to finance feasibility studies and other project preparation costs.

[Acts Nos.3 of 2014 s.10; 9 of 2018 s.2]

10C. Books of accounts, records and annual reports

(1) The PPP Centre shall keep books of accounts and maintain proper records of operations of the Facilitation Fund in accordance with acceptable accounting standards.

(2) The PPP Centre shall, at any time, and at the end of each financial year, have the accounts of the Fund audited by the Controller and Auditor General.

(3) The PPP Centre shall submit to the Minister audited report and annual report containing detailed information regarding activities of the Facilitation Fund during the previous year ending on the 30th June.

(4) The Minister shall cause to be tabled to the National Assembly statement of audited accounts and report of the PPP Centre.

(5) The Minister shall prepare and submit to the Cabinet annual report on implementation of the Public Private Partnership programme.

[Act No.3 of 2014 s.10]

11. Agreement

(1) Notwithstanding the provisions of any other written laws, a contracting authority may enter into an agreement with a private party for the performance of one or more of the functions of that contracting authority.

(2) For the purposes of subsection (1), the accounting officer of a contracting authority shall, for the purposes of advising the Minister responsible for contracting authority, form a multi disciplinary negotiating team possessing knowledge, skills and experience on the subject matter of the proposed project.

(3) Without prejudice to subsection (2), the negotiating shall ensure that the agreement is made in writing and —

(a) specifies the responsibilities of the contracting of authority and the private party;

(b) specifies the relevant financial terms;

(c) ensures for the management of performance of the private party;

(d) provides for undertaking by the Contracting authority to the private party in obtaining licences and permits which may be necessary for the implementation of the project;

(e) provides for the return of assets, if any, to the contracting authority, at the termination or expiry of the agreement;

(f) specifies the roles and risks undertaken by either party;

(g) provides for the payment to the private party, by way of compensation from a revenue fund of charges or fees collected by the private party from users or customers of the service provided by it;

(h) specifies payment of the private party to the contracting authority;

(i) provides for remedies in the event of default by either party;

(j) imposes financial management duties on part of the private party, including procedures relating to internal financial control, budgeting, transparency, accountability and reporting;

(k) provides for the termination of the agreement in case of breach of terms and conditions by either party;

(l) provides for the conditions for the provision of service, where necessary;

(m) provides for the period of execution; and

(n) contains such other information as may be necessary.

(4) Without prejudice to the provisions of subsection (3), the agreement shall contain conditions that ensures that:

(a) the private party undertakes to perform a contracting authority's function on behalf of the contracting authority for a specified period;

(b) the private party is liable for the risks arising from the performance of its functions;

(c) the environmental impact assessment certificate has been issued in respect of the project;

(d) government facilities, equipment or other state resources which are necessary for the project and are transferred or made available to the private party on a timely basis; and

(e) the public and private assets are clearly specified.

(5) Every agreement entered into under this Act shall be governed and construed in accordance with the laws of Mainland Tanzania.

(6) The rights, obligation and controlling interests of the private party in any project performed under the agreement shall not be transferred or assigned to a third party without the prior written consent of the contracting authority.

(7) The contracting authority shall ensure that an agreement involving public private partnership project is executed under procedures stipulated and through institutions specified under this Act.

[Act No.3 of 2014 s.11]

12. Land acquisition

Where the project requires acquisition of land for its implementation, the acquisitionshall be carried out in accordance with the Land Act, the Village Land Act, the Land Use Planning Act, the Land Acquisition Act and any other relevant laws.

[Caps.113, 114, 116 and 118]

13. Duration and extension of agreement

(1) The duration of an agreement shall be provided for in the agreement and shall not be extended unless:

(a) there is a delay in completion or interruption of operations due to circumstances beyond any party's control;

(b) there was an increase in costs arising from requirements of the Co-ordination Unit or contracting authority which were not foreseen or included in the agreement; and

(c) the service is required and the contracting authority has no capacity or immediate intention to take over and run the project.

(2) A violation of the provisions of subsection (1) by either of the parties to an agreement shall render a defaulting party liable for any pecuniary loss incurred by the other party.

14. Vetting of agreements

Every agreement intended to be entered into under this Act shall be submitted to the Office of the Attorney General for a legal opinion.

15. Procurement process

(1) All public private partnership projects under this Act shall be procured through an open and competitive bidding process.

(2) Notwithstanding subsection (1), the Minister may exempt procurement of an unsolicited project from competitive bidding process where it meets the following criteria:

(a) the project shall be of priority to the Government at the particular time and broadly consistent with the government strategic objectives;

(b) the private proponent does not require Government guarantee or any form of financial support from the Government;

(c) the project shall have unique attributes that justify departing from a competitive tender process;

(d) the project is of significant size, scope and requires substantial financing as per conditions provided in the regulations;

(e) the project shall demonstrate value for money, affordability and shall transfer significant risks to the private proponent;

(f) the project has wide social economic benefits including improved services, employment and taxation; and

(g) the proponent commits to bear cost of undertaking a feasibility study.

(3) Upon approval of project concept for unsolicited proposals, the private proponent shall make a commitment to undertake the project by depositing a refundable amount of not exceeding three percent of the estimated cost of the project to be conducted.

(4) The Minister may make regulations prescribing procedure for deposit and refund of commitment deposits under subsection (3).

(5) All solicited and unsolicited projects shall be procured in a manner prescribed in the regulations made under this Act.

(6) The regulations under this section, shall among other things, prescribe the following —

(a) inclusion of local firms and experts in consultancy contracts;

(b) use of local goods and experts in works and non-consultancy services;

(c) preference to local goods in process of evaluation;

(d) capacity building of local firms; and

(e) any other matter relating to empowerment of local company and Tanzanian citizens.

[Acts Nos.3 of 2014 s.12; 9 of 2018 s.12]

16. Unsolicited bids

(1) The private party shall undertake a feasibility study in respect of unsolicited project proposals and submit the feasibility study to the relevant contracting authority.

(2) The feasibility study undertaken under subsection (1) shall take into consideration technical, financial, social environmental impact, economic or any other relevant issues as may be required under this Act.

(3) Without prejudice to the generality of subsection (2), the feasibility study of unsolicited project proposalshall:

    (a) specify the proposed project activities;

    (b) prescribe environmental issues;

    (c) explain the significance and benefits of the proposed project to the government; and

    (d) explain the financial capacity and ability of the private party in the implementation and management of the proposed project.

(4) The Minister shall make regulations prescribing procedures for handling public private partnership project proposals initiated through unsolicited bids under this Act.

[Act No.3 of 2014 s.13]

17. Project officers

(1) As soon as a contracting authority initiates a project that may be a public private partnership, the accounting officershall appoint a person with appropriate skills and experience, either from within or outside the contracting authority, as a project officer for the project.

(2) The project officer shall be responsible for:

    (a) assisting the accounting officer in monitoring the performance of the private party and ensure that the agreement is properly implemented; and

    (b) any other duties or powers delegated to him by the accounting officer under this Act.

18. Signing of Agreements

(1) The agreements entered into under this Act shall be signed by the accounting officer of the relevant contracting authority after it has been considered and approved by the Public Private Partnership Steering Committee and vetted by the Office of the Attorney General.

(2) The accounting officer shall sign an agreement upon fully satisfying himself that the agreement has complied with the provisions of this Act and any other relevant laws.

(3) Any person who contravenes any provision of this section commits an offence.

[Acts Nos.3 of 2014 s.14; 9 of 2018 s.12]

19. Responsibilities of accounting officers

The accounting officer who has entered into an agreement shall in addition to any other responsibilities under this Act, take all necessary and reasonable steps to ensure that:

    (a) the outsourced activity is effectively and efficiently carried out in accordance with the agreement;

    (b) any public property which is placed under the control of the private party, in terms of the agreement, is appropriately protected against forfeiture, theft, loss, wastage and misuse; and

(c) the Contracting authority has adequate contract management and monitoring capacity.

20. Amendment of Agreements

Subject to section 7B, an agreement may be reviewed and amended by parties if the review or amendment is consented to by the Public Private Partnership Steering Committee and vetted by the Attorney General.

[Act No.9 of 2018 s.13]

21. Enjoyment of benefits

(1) A project undertaken ill accordance with the provisions of this Act which ought to qualify for benefits granted to similar investment under the Tanzania Investment Act, shall be entitled to such benefits granted under that Act.

(2) The benefits referred to under subsection (1) shall not apply to tax incentives.

[Cap.38]

22. Dispute resolutions

Any dispute arising during the course of the agreement shall —
 (a) be resolved through negotiation; or
 (b) in the case of mediation or arbitration, be adjudicated by judicial bodies or other organs established in the United Republic and in accordance with laws of Tanzania.

[Act No.9 of 2018 s.14]

PART IV
MISCELLANEOUS PROVISIONS

23. Monitoring and evaluation

(1) All public private partnership projects under this Act shall be monitored by the Ministry, Sector Ministries, Government Departments; Agencies or local government authorities under which they are carried out.

(2) The purpose of monitoring under sub-section (1) shall be to incorporate coherent oversight and regular review mechanisms that would include:
 (a) measurable performance targets;
 (b) meaningful incentives and rewards; and
 (c) effective penalties.

(3) The Ministry, sector ministry, Department, Agency or local government authority shall, as much as practicable, involve other relevant stakeholders for better implementation and conduct of monitoring and evaluation.

23A. Periodic performance reports

(1) An accounting officer shall submit to the PPP Centre mid-year performance report on the implementation of public private partnership projects in the manner prescribed in the Regulations.

(2) The PPP Centre shall consolidate mid-year performance reports of contracting authorities and submit the report to the Minister.

[Act No.9 of 2018 s.15]

24. Conflict of Interest

(1) Where a member of the Public Private Partnership Steering Committee, an officer of the PPP Centre or the contracting authority has any pecuniary interest, direct or indirect, in any project, proposed projector other matter, and is involved or participating in a process at which the project, proposed project or other matter is the subject of consideration, he shall, as soon as practicable after the commencement of that process, disclose that fact and shall not take part in or be present at the consideration or discussion of, or involved in any question relating to the project, proposed project or that other matter.

(2) Subject to this subsection, for the purposes of this section a person shall be treated as having direct or indirect pecuniary interest in a project or other matter, if:

(a) he or his nominee is a member of a company or other body, or is the holder of shares or debentures in a company with which the project is made or proposed to be made or he has a direct or indirect pecuniary interest in the project, proposed project or matter under consideration; or

(b) he is a partner or in the employment of a person with whom the project is made or proposed to be made or who has a direct or indirect pecuniary interest in the project, proposed project or other matter under consideration.

(3) In this section a direct or indirect interest of a spouse or any members of the family of an officer of the PPP Centre or the contracting authority shall, if known to that officer, be deemed to be a direct or indirect interest of the officer of the PPP Centre or the contracting authority.

(4) A person who contravenes the provision of this section, commits an offence.

[Acts Nos.3 of 2014 s.16; 9 of 2018 s.2; Cap.4 s.8]

25. Empowerment of citizens

Public private partnerships agreements shall endeavour to provide opportunity for empowerment of the citizens of Tanzania as provided for under the National Economic Empowerment Act.

[Cap.386]

25A. Projects relating to natural wealth and resources

The public private partnership project that relates to natural wealth and resources shall take into account the provisions of the Natural Wealth and Resources (Permanent Sovereignty) Act and the Natural Wealth and Resources Contracts (Review and Re- Negotiation of Unconscionable Terms) Act.

[Acts Nos.5 of 2017; 6 of 2017; 9 of 2018 s.16]

26. Duty to take care and exercise due diligence

Every public officer performing any functions, discharging any duty or exercising any power under this Act or any other written law related to a public private partnershipshall be under the obligation to take reasonable care and exercise due diligence in the performance of the functions and discharge of duties and exercise of powers in accordance with the provisions of this Act and any other relevant laws.

27. General penalty

Any person who commits an offence under this Act to which no specific penalty is prescribed shall be liable to a fine not less than five million shillings and not exceeding fifty million shillings or to imprisonment for a term of not less than three months and not exceeding three years or both.

[Act No.9 of 2018 s.16]

28. Regulations

(1) The Minister may make regulations for better carrying out of the provisions of this Act.

(2) Without prejudice to subsection (1), the Minister may make regulations prescribing:

 (a) levying of fees and charges;

 (b) investment opportunities and promotion;

 (c) functions of local government authorities under this Act and clear linkages of roles between the implementing ministries and appropriate bodies at the local government;

 (d) evaluation, operation and management of projects under this Act;

 (e) the management of, and terms and conditions for accessing the Facilitation Fund;

 (f) procedures for procurement of private parties and matters incidental thereto;

 (g) the manner in which the empowerment of citizens of Tanzania may be implemented including provision of goods and services by Tanzanian entrepreneurs, training and technology transfer, employment of Tanzanians and corporate social responsibility;

 (h) process and procedure for scrutiny and analysis of projects that require provision of Government support;

 (i) the manner in which the Empowerment of the citizens of Tanzania may be implemented; and

 (j) any other matter in the promotion and furtherance of objectives of this Act.

(3) Notwithstanding the provisions of subsections (1) and (2), the Minister may make rules and guidelines for the better implementation of this Act.

[Act No.3 of 2014 s.17; 9 of 2018 s.17]

29. Saving provisions

All existing agreements or memoranda of understanding entered into by any contracting authority with the private party before the commencement of this Act, shall not be affected by the coming into force of this Act.

TITLE EIGHT
PUBLIC PRIVATE PARTNERSHIP
(AMENDMENT) ACT [2023]

THE UNITED REPUBLIC OF TANZANIA
No.6   14ᵗʰ July, 2023
ACT SUPPLEMENT

To the Gazette of The United Republic of Tanzania No.28 Vol. 104 dated 14ᵗʰ July, 2023
Printed by the Government Printer, Dodoma by Order of Government

THE UNITED REPUBLIC OF TANZANIA
NO. 4 OF 2023

An Act to amend the Public Private Partnership Act.

ENACTED by the Parliament of the United Republic of Tanzania.

PART I
PRELIMINARY PROVISIONS

1. Short title

This Act may be cited as the Public Private Partnership (Amendment) Act, 2023 and shall be read as one with the Public Private Partnership Act, hereinafter referred to as the "principal Act".

[Cap.103]

PART II
AMENDMENT OF VARIOUS PROVISIONS

2. Amendment of section 2

The principal Act is amended in section 2 by deleting subsection (2) and substituting for it the following:

> "(2) Notwithstanding any provision to the contrary, the provisions of this Act shall not prejudice the implementation of an agreement that provides for special arrangement for development of a strategic project in the United Republic where such agreement has been approved by the Cabinet:
>
> Provided that, the agreement shall, prior to submission to the Cabinet for approval, be vetted by the Attorney General."

3. Amendment of section 3

The principal Act is amended in section 3 —

(a) by inserting in their appropriate alphabetical order the following new definitions:

> "'special purpose vehicle' means a private company established by a successful private party prior to the execution of an agreement for the purpose of implementing a PPP project and such company may have other parties including a public entity as members, whose liabilities and financial risk exposure are limited by shares;
>
> 'standard document' includes standard request for qualification, standard request for proposal and standard PPP agreement;
>
> 'strategic project' means a strategic project determined as such by the authority responsible for national planning";

(b) in the definition of the term "public sector", by deleting the words "and any other person acting on behalf of the government ministry, department, agency or local government authority" and substituting for them the words "regional secretariat or any other public institution and any other person acting on behalf of the government ministry, department, agency, local government authority or regional secretariat"; and

(c) in the definition of the term "request for proposals", by deleting the words "a model agreement" and substituting for them the words "standard documents".

4. Amendment of section 4

The principal Act is amended in section 4 —

(a) in subsection (3)(a), by adding the words "and immovable" between the words "movable" and "property";

(b) by deleting subsection (6) and substituting for it the following:

"(6) Every contracting authority shall, at the beginning of every budget cycle, submit to the Minister a prefeasibility study of potential public private partnership projects for consideration in the National Development Plan:

Provided that —

(a) the potential public private partnership project complies with the national development priorities; and

(b) the prefeasibility study of potential public private partnership project is approved by the respective Minister.";

(c) by deleting subsection (6A) and substituting for it the following:

"(6A) The Minister shall, within seven working days, upon receipt of prefeasibility study of potential public private partnership project from the contracting authority, cause such study to be forwarded to the PPP Centre for analysis.";

(d) by adding immediately after subsection (6A) the following:

"(6B) The PPP Centre shall, within twenty-one working days, analyse the prefeasibility study of potential public private partnership project received in terms of subsection (6A) and forward it to the Public Private Partnership Steering Committee for notification.";

(e) by deleting subsection (7); and

(f) by renumbering subsection (8) as subsection (7).

5. Amendment of section 5

The principal Act is amended in section 5 by deleting subsection (2) and substituting for it the following:

"(2) Without prejudice to the generality of subsection (1), the PPP Centre shall, within thirty working days from the date of receiving the prefeasibility study of potential public private partnership project, request for proposal, evaluation reports for selection of preferred bidder and PPP agreements submitted by contracting authorities, analyse them."

6. Amendment of section 7

The principal Act is amended in section 7(6) by adding the word "Private" immediately after the word "Public".

7. Amendment of section 7B

The principal Act is amended in section 7B by adding immediately after subsection (3) the following:

> "(4) For the purpose of this section, 'public funding' means government financial support that constitutes fiscal commitment or contingent liabilities in relation to a PPP project."

8. Amendment of section 9

The principal Act is amended in section 9(1) by adding immediately after paragraph (c) the following:

> "(d) submit after every three months to the PPP Centre implementation report of the recommendations issued by the PPP Centre."

9. Amendment of section 13

The principal Act is amended in section 13(1) by deleting the words "Co-ordination Unit or" appearing in paragraph (b).

10. Amendment of section 15

The principal Act is amended by in section 15 —

(a) by deleting subsections (3) and (4) and substituting for them the following:

> "(3) Upon recommendation from the PPP Steering Committee, the Minister may exempt procurement of solicited project from competitive bidding process where the project meets criteria prescribed under subsection (2) and any of the following conditions are satisfied:
>
> (a) the project deliverable is of an urgent need, and any other procurement method is impracticable:
>
> Provided that, the circumstances giving rise to the urgency were not foreseeable by the contracting authority;
>
> (b) the private party possesses the intellectual property rights to the key approaches or technologies required for the project; or
>
> (c) a particular private party has exclusive rights in respect of the project, and no reasonable alternative or substitute is available.
>
> (4) Upon exemption of an unsolicited project from competitive bidding process, the Government and the private proponent shall commence negotiations of terms and conditions of the agreement.";

(b) in subsection (6), by —

(i) adding immediately after paragraph (c) the following:

> "(d) timeframe within which negotiation of terms and conditions of an agreement shall commence;

(ii) renaming paragraphs (d) and (e) as paragraphs (e) and (f) respectively."

11. Addition of section 18A

The principal Act is amended by adding immediately after section 18 the following:

"18A. Establishment of special purpose vehicle

(1) The private party shall, before the signing of the PPP agreement, establish a special purpose vehicle in accordance with the Companies Act for the purpose of undertaking the project. [Cap.212]

(2) A special purpose vehicle established under subsection (1) may include a public entity as a minority shareholder provided that the public entity shall —

(a) hold shares not exceeding 25 percent of equity contribution in the special purpose vehicle;

(b) demonstrate financial capacity on the contribution of equity in the special purpose vehicle; and

(c) demonstrate capacity to bear and mitigate risk associated with the implementation of the project."

12. Amendment of section 21

The principal Act is amended in section 21, by —

(a) deleting subsection (2); and

(b) designating the contents of subsection (1) as section 21.

13. Repeal and replacement of section 22

The principal Act is amended by repealing section 22 and replacing for it the following:

"22. Settlement of disputes

(1) Where the dispute arises during the implementation of the PPP agreement, efforts shall be made to amicably settle the dispute through negotiations.

(2) A dispute which is not amicably settled through negotiations may, by mutual agreement between the parties, be submitted for arbitration —

(a) in accordance with arbitration laws of Tanzania;

(b) in accordance with the rules of procedure for arbitration of the International Centre for Settlement of Investment Disputes; or

(c) within the framework of any bilateral or multilateral agreement on investment protection entered into by the Government of the United Republic and the Government of the country where the investor originates."

14. Amendment of section 23

The principal Act is amended in section 23, by —

(a) adding the words "and evaluated" immediately after the word "monitored" appearing in subsection (1); and

(b) adding the words "and evaluation" immediately after the word "monitoring" appearing in subsection (2).

15. Amendment of section 23A

The principal Act is amended in section 23A, by —

(a) adding the words "and annual" immediately after the word "mid-year" appearing in subsections (1) and (2); and

(b) adding the words "to the PPP Steering Committee before being submitted" between the words "report" and "to the Minister" appearing in subsection (2).

16. Amendment of section 28

The principal Act is amended in section 28(2)(b) by adding the word "PPP" before the word "investment".

17. Addition of section 28A

The principal Act is amended by adding immediately after section 28 the following:

"28A. Inconsistency with other laws

Where there is any inconsistency between the provisions of this Act and the provisions of any other written law in relation to development, procurement and implementation of public private partnerships, the provisions of this Act shall prevail."

Passed by the National Assembly on the 13th June, 2023

NENELWA J. MWIHAMBI
Clerk of the National Assembly

GROUP TWO
LABOUR LAWS AND REGULATIONS

TITLE NINE
EMPLOYMENT AND LABOUR RELATIONS
ACT (CHAPTER 366) [2006] [Revised Edition 2019]

THE UNITED REPUBLIC OF TANZANIA
CHAPTER 366
THE EMPLOYMENT AND LABOUR RELATIONS ACT
[PRINCIPAL LEGISLATION]
REVISED EDITION 2019

This Edition of the Employment and Labour Relations Act, Chapter 366, has been revised up to and including 30th November, 2019 and is printed under the authority of section 4 of the Laws Revision Act, Chapter 4.

Dodoma, 30th November, 2019	ADELARDUS L. KILANGI *Attorney General*

THE EMPLOYMENT AND LABOUR RELATIONS ACT
(CHAPTER 366)

An Act to make provisions for core labour rights, to establish basic employment standards, to provide a framework for collective bargaining, to provide for the prevention and settlement of disputes, and to provide for related matters.

[20th DECEMBER, 2006]

[G.N. No.1 of 2007]

Acts Nos.
6 of 2004
8 of 2006
21 of 2009
2 of 2010
17 of 2010
24 of 2015
4 of 2016

PART I
PRELIMINARY PROVISIONS

1. Short title

This Act may be cited as the Employment and Labour Relations Act.

2. Application

(1) This Act shall apply to all employees including those in the public service of the Government of Tanzania in Mainland Tanzania but shall not apply to members, whether temporary or permanent, in the service of:

 (i) the Tanzania Peoples Defence Forces;

 (ii) the Police Force;

 (iii) the Prisons Service; or

 (iv) the national Service.

(2) The Minister may, after consultation with the Council and the relevant Minister responsible for the service or services excluded under subsection (1) of this section, by notice published in the *Gazette*, determine the categories of employees employed in the said services who may be excluded services to whom this Act may apply.

(3) The provisions of sections 5, 6 and 7 shall apply to members of the forces and services referred to in subsection (1).

3. Objects

The principal objects of this Act shall be —

(a) to promote economic development through economic efficiency, productivity and social justice;

(b) to provide the legal framework for effective and fair employment relations and minimum standards regarding conditions of work;

(c) to provide a framework for voluntary collective bargaining;

(d) to regulate the resort to industrial action as a means to resolve disputes;

(e) to provide a framework for the resolution of disputes by mediation, arbitration and adjudication;

(f) to give effect to the provisions of the Constitution of the United Republic of Tanzania, 1977, in so far as they apply to employment and labour relations and conditions of work; and

(g) generally to give effect to the core Conventions of the International Labour Organisation as well as other ratified conventions.

4. Interpretation

In this Act, unless the context requires otherwise —

"**arbitrator**" means an arbitrator appointed under section 19 of the Labour Institutions Act;

"**basic wage**" means that part of an employee's remuneration paid in respect of work done during the hours ordinarily worked but does not include —

(a) allowances, whether or not based on the employee's basic wage;

(b) pay for overtime worked in terms of section 19 (5);

(c) additional pay for work on a Sunday or a public holiday; or

(d) additional pay for night work, as required under section 20(4);

"**child**" means a person under the age of 14 years; provided that for the employment in hazardous sectors, child means a person under the age of 18 years;

"**collective agreement**" means a written agreement concluded by a registered trade union and an employer or registered employers' association on any labour matter;

"**Commission**" means the Commission for Mediation and Arbitration established under section 12 of the Labour Institutions Act; [Cap.300]

"**complaint**" means any dispute arising from the application, interpretation or implementation of —

(a) an agreement or contract with an employee;

(b) a collective agreement;

(c) this Act or any other written law administered by the Minister;

(d) Part VII of the Merchant Shipping Act; [Cap.72]

"**Council**" means the Labour, Economic and Social Council established under section 3 of the Labour Institutions Act; [Cap.300]

"**dispute**" —

(a) means any dispute concerning a labour matter between any employer or registered employers' association on the one hand, and any employee or registered trade union on the other hand; and

(b) includes an alleged dispute;

"**dispute of interest**" means any dispute except a complaint;

"**employee**" means an individual who —

(a) has entered into a contract of employment; or

(b) has entered into any other contract under which —

(i) the individual undertakes to work personally for the other party to the contract; and

(ii) the other party is not a client or customer of any profession, business, or undertaking carried on by the individual; or

(c) is deemed to be an employee by the Minister under section 98(3);

"**employer**" means any person, including the Government and an executive agency, who employs an employee;

"**employers' association**" means any number of employers associated together for the purpose, whether by itself or with other purposes, of regulating relations between employers and their employees or the trade unions representing those employees;

"**employment**" means the performance of a contract of employment by parties to the contract, under emoployer-employee relationship;

"**Essential Services Committee**" means the Essential Services Committee established under section 29 of the Labour Institutions Act; [Cap.300]

"**federation**" means either an association of trade unions or an association of employers' associations;

"**Labour Commissioner**" means the Labour Commissioner appointed under section 43(1) of the Labour Institutions Act; [Cap.300]

"**Labour Court**" means the Labour Division of the High Court established under section 50 of the Labour Institutions Act;

"**Labour matter**" means any matter relating to employment or labour relations;

"**lockout**" means a total or partial refusal by one or more employers to allow their employees to work, if that refusal is to compel them to accept, modify or abandon any demand that may form the subject matter of a dispute of interest;

"**mediator**" means a mediator appointed under section 19 of the Labour Institutions Act; [Cap.300]

"**Minister**" means the Minister for the time being responsible for labour;

"**operational requirements**" means requirements based on the economic, technological, structural or similar needs of the employer;

"**organisation**" means a trade union or an employers' association;

"**protest action**" means a total or partial stoppage of work by employees for the purpose of promoting or defending the socio-economic interests of workers but not for a purpose —

(a) referred to in the definition of strike; or

(b) a dispute in respect of which there is a legal remedy;

"**registered organisation**" means a registered trade union or registered employers' association;

"**Registrar**" means the Registrar appointed under section 43(2) of the Labour Institutions Act; [Cap.300]

"**reinstatement**" means that the contract of employment has revived with all its incidents and that the employee is entitled to all his rights during the period of absence from actual service;

"**remuneration**" means the total value of all payments, in money or in kind, made or owing to an employee arising from the employment of that employee;

"**strike**" means a total or partial stoppage of work by employees if the stoppage is to compel their employer, any other employer, or an employers' association to which the employer belongs, to accept, modify or abandon any demand that may form the subject matter of a dispute of interest;

"**specific task**" means a task which is occasional or seasonal and is non-continuous in nature;

"**trade union**" means any number of employees associated together for the purpose, whether by itself or with other purposes, of regulating relations between employees and their employers or the employers' associations to which the employers belong.

[Cap.300; Act No.24 of 2015 s.4]

PART II
FUNDAMENTAL RIGHTS AND PROTECTIONS

Sub-Part A: Child Labour

5. Prohibition of child labour

(1) No person shall employ a child under the age of fourteen years.

(2) A child of fourteen years of age may only be employed to do light work, which is not likely to be harmful to the child's health and development; and does not prejudice the child's attendance at school, participation in vocational orientation or training programmes approved by the competent authority or the child's capacity to benefit from the instruction received.

(3) A child under eighteen years of age shall not be employed in a mine, factory or as crew on a ship or in any other worksite including non-formal settings and agriculture, where work conditions may be considered hazardous by the Minister.

(3A) For the purpose of subsection (3), "ship" includes a vessel of any description used for navigation. [Cap 4 s.8]

(4) No person shall employ a child in employment —

    (a) that is inappropriate for a person of that age;

    (b) that places at risk the child's well-being, education, physical or mental health, or spiritual, moral or social development.

(5) Notwithstanding the provisions of subsection (3), any written law regulating the provisions of training may permit a child under the age of eighteen to work —

    (a) on board a training ship as part of the child's training;

    (b) in a factory or a mine if that work is part of the child's training;

    (c) in any other worksites on condition that the health, safety and morals of the child are fully protected and that the child has received or is receiving adequate specific instruction or vocational training in the relevant work or activity.

(6) The Minister shall make regulations —
- (a) to prohibit, or place conditions on the employment and training of children under eighteen years of age;
- (b) to determine the forms of work referred to in sub-section (4) of this Act and to make provision for the regular revision and updating of the list of hazardous forms of work.

(7) It is an offence for any person —
- (a) to employ a child in contravention of this section;
- (b) to procure a child for employment in contravention of this section.

(8) In any proceedings under this section, if the age of the child is in issue, the burden of proving that it was reasonable to believe, after investigation, that the child was not under age for the purposes of this section shall lie on the person employing or procuring the child for employment.

(9) Without prejudice to the provisions of this section, every employer shall ensure that every child lawfully employed under this Act is protected against discrimination or acts which may have negative effect on the child taking into consideration age and evolving capacities.

[Act No.21 of 2009 s.172]

Sub-Part B: Forced Labour

6. Prohibition of forced labour

(1) Any person who procures, demands or imposes forced labour, commits an offence.

(2) For the purposes of this section, forced labour includes bonded labour or any work exacted from a person under the threat of a penalty and to which that person has not consented but does not include [Cap.192]—
- (a) any work exacted under the National Defence Act, for work of a purely military character;
- (b) any work that forms part of the normal civic obligations of a citizen of the United Republic of Tanzania;
- (c) any work exacted from any person as a consequence of a conviction in a court of law, provided that the work is carried out under the supervision and control of a public authority and that the person is not hired to, or placed at, the disposal of private persons;
- (d) any work exacted in cases of an emergency or a circumstance that would endanger the existence or the well-being of the whole or part of the population;
- (e) minor communal services performed by the members of a community in the direct interest of that community after consultation with them or their direct representatives on the need for the services.

Sub-Part C: Discrimination

7. Prohibition of discrimination in the work-place

(1) Every employer shall ensure that he promotes an equal opportunity in employment and

strives to eliminate discrimination in any employment policy or practice.

(2) An employer shall register, with the Labour Commissioner, a plan to promote equal opportunity and to eliminate discrimination in the work place.

(3) The Labour Commissioner may require an employer —

    (a) to develop a plan prescribed in subsection (2); and

    (b) to register the plan with the Commissioner.

(4) No employer shall discriminate, directly or indirectly, against an employee, in any employment policy or practice, on any of the following grounds:

    (a) colour;

    (b) nationality;

    (c) tribe or place of origin;

    (d) race;

    (e) national extraction;

    (f) social origin;

    (g) political opinion or religion;

    (h) sex;

    (i) gender;

    (j) pregnancy;

    (k) marital status or family responsibility;

    (l) disability;

    (m) HIV/Aids;

    (n) age; or

    (o) station of life.

(5) Harassment of an employee shall be a form of discrimination and shall be prohibited on any one, or combination, of the grounds prescribed in subsection (4).

(6) it is not discrimination —

    (a) to take affirmative action measures consistent with the promotion of equality or the elimination of discrimination in the workplace;

    (b) to distinguish, exclude or prefer any person on the basis of an inherent requirement of a job; or

    (c) to employ citizens in accordance with the National Employment Promotion Services Act. [Cap.243]

(7) Any person who contravenes the provisions of subsections (4) and (5), commits an offence.

(8) In any proceedings —

    (a) where the employee makes out a *prima facie* case of discrimination by the employer on any of the grounds prescribed in subsection (4), it shall be the duty of the employer to prove —

        (i) that the discrimination did not take place as alleged; or

        (ii) that the discriminatory act or omission is not based on any of those grounds;

(b) employer shall prove a defence in terms of subsection (6) if the discrimination did take place on a ground stipulated in subsection (5); or

(c) the Labour Court or arbitrator, as the case may be, shall take into account any plan registered with the Labour Commissioner under this section.

(9) For the purposes of this section —

(a) "employer" includes an employment agency;

(b) "employee" includes an applicant for employment;

(c) an "employment policy or practice" includes any policy or practice relating to recruitment procedures, advertising and selection criteria, appointments and the appointment process, job classification and grading, remuneration, employment benefits and terms and conditions of employment, job assignments, the working environment and facilities, training and development, performance evaluation systems, promotion transfer, demotion, termination of employment and disciplinary measures.

(10) For the avoidance of doubt every employer shall take positive steps to guarantee equal remuneration for men and women for work of equal value.

8. Prohibition of discrimination in trade unions and employer associations

(1) No trade union or employers' association shall discriminate, directly or indirectly, against any of the grounds prescribed in subsection (4) of section 7 —

(a) in its admission, representation or termination of membership;

(b) in any employment policy or practice prescribed in sub-section (9) of section 7; or

(c) in any collective agreement.

(2) Any person who contravenes the provisions of subsection (1), commits an offence.

Sub-Part D: Freedom of Association

9. Employee's right to freedom of association

(1) Every employee shall have the right —

(a) to form and join a trade union; or

(b) to participate in the lawful activities of the trade union.

(2) Notwithstanding the provisions of subsection (1) —

(a) a magistrate may only form or join a trade union that restricts its membership to judicial officers;

(b) a prosecutor may only form or join a trade union that restricts its membership to prosecutors or other court officials;

(c) a senior management employee may not belong to a trade union that represents the non-senior management employees of the employer.

(3) No person shall discriminate against an employee on the grounds that the employee —

(a) exercises or has exercised any right under this Act or any other written law administered by the Minister;

(b) belongs to or has belonged to a trade union; or

(c) participates or has participated in the lawful activities of a trade union.

(4) No person shall discriminate against an official or office bearer of a trade union or federation for representing it or participating in its lawful activities.

(5) Any person who contravenes the provisions of subsections (3) and (4), commits an offence.

(6) For the purposes of this section —
    (a) "employee" includes an applicant for employment;
    (b) "senior management employee" means an employee who, by virtue of that employee's position —
        (i) makes policy on behalf of the employer; and
        (ii) is authorized to conclude collective agreements on behalf of the employer.

10. Employer's right to freedom of association

(1) Every employer shall have the right —
    (a) to form and join an employer's association; or
    (b) to participate in the lawful activities of an employer's association.

(2) No person shall discriminate against an employer on the grounds that the employer —
    (a) exercises or has exercised a right under the Act;
    (b) belongs or has belonged to an employer's association; or
    (c) participates or has participated in the lawful activities of an employer's association.

(3) No person shall discriminate against an official or office bearer of an employer's association or federation for representing it or participating in its lawful activities.

(4) Any person who contravenes the provisions of subsections (2) and (3), commits an offence.

11. Rights of trade unions and employers' associations

Every organisation has the right to —
    (a) determine its own constitution;
    (b) plan and organise its administration and lawful activities;
    (c) join and form a federation;
    (d) participate in the lawful activities of a federation;
    (e) affiliate with, and participate in the affairs of any international workers' organisation or international employers' organisation or the International Labour Organisation, and to contribute to, or receive financial assistance from those organisations.

PART III
EMPLOYMENT STANDARDS

Sub-Part A: Preliminary

12. Application of this Part

(1) Subject to the provisions of subsection (2), the provisions of Sub-Parts A to D and F shall not apply to seafarers whose terms and conditions of employment are regulated under the Merchant

Shipping Act. [Cap.72]

(2) Notwithstanding the provisions of subsection (1), the provisions of this Part apply to seafarers who work on fishing vessels and shall be to the extent that in the event there is any conflict between the provisions of this Act and the Merchant Shipping Act and its regulations, the provisions of this Act shall prevail.

(3) Where the provisions of any written law relating to vocational training regulates an employment standard stipulated in section 13(1), the provisions of that other law shall apply. [Cap.72]

13. Employment standards

(1) Provisions of this Act on wage determination that stipulate a minimum term and condition of employment shall be an employment standard.

(2) An employment standard constitutes a term of a contract with an employee unless —

(a) a term of the contract contains a term that is more favourable to the employee;

(b) a provision of an agreement alters the employment standard to the extent permitted by the provisions of this Part;

(c) a provision of any collective agreement, a written law regulating employment, wage determination or exemption granted under section 100 alters the employment standard.

14. Contracts with employees

(1) A contract with an employee shall be of the following types —

(a) a contract for an unspecified period of time;

(b) a contract for a specified period of time for professionals and managerial cadre;

(c) a contract for a specific task.

(2) A contract with an employee shall be in writing if the contract provides that the employee is to work within or outside the United Republic of Tanzania.

[Act No.24 of 2015 s.5]

15. Written statement of particulars

(1) Subject to the provisions of subsection (2) of section 19, an employer shall supply an employee, when the employee commences employment, with the following particulars in writing, namely —

(a) name, age, permanent address and sex of the employee;

(b) place of recruitment;

(c) job description;

(d) date of commencement;

(e) form and duration of the contract;

(f) place of work;

(g) hours of work;

(h) remuneration, the method of its calculation, and details of any benefits or payments in kind; and

(i) any other prescribed matter.

(2) If all the particulars referred to in subsection (1) are stated in a written contract and the employer has supplied the employee with that contract, then the employer may not furnish the

written statement referred to in section 14.

(3) If an employee does not understand the written particulars, the employer shall ensure that they are explained to the employee in a manner that the employee understands.

(4) Where any matter stipulated in subsection (1) changes, the employer shall, in consultation with the employee, revise the written particulars to reflect the change and notify the employee of the change in writing.

(5) The employer shall keep the written particulars prescribed in subsection (1) for a period of five years after the termination of employment.

(6) If in any legal proceedings, an employer fails to produce a written contract or the written particulars prescribed in subsection (1), the burden of proving or disproving an alleged term of employment stipulated in subsection (1) shall be on the employer.

(7) The provisions of this section shall not apply to an employee who works less than 6 days in a month for an employer.

16. Informing employees of their rights

Every employer shall display a statement in the prescribed form of the employee's rights under this Act in a conspicuous place.

Sub-Part B: Hours of work

17. Application of this Sub-Part

(1) The provisions of this Sub-Part shall not apply to employees who manage other employees on behalf of the employer and who report directly to a senior management employee specified in section 9(6)(b).

(2) The provisions of sections 19(1), 19(3), 23(1), 24(1) and 25(1) shall not apply to work in an emergency which cannot be performed by employees during their ordinary hours of work.

18. Interpretation

For the purposes of this Sub-Part —

(a) "day" means a period of 24 hours measured from the time when the employee normally starts work, and "daily" has a corresponding meaning;

(b) "overtime" means work over and above ordinary hours of work;

(c) "week" means a period of seven days measured from the day the employee normally starts the working week and "weekly" has a corresponding meaning.

19. Hours of work

(1) Subject to the provisions of this Sub-Part, an employer shall not require or permit an employee to work more than 12 hours in any day.

(2) Subject to this Sub-Part, the maximum number of ordinary days or hours that an employee may be permitted or required to work are —

(a) six days in any week;

(b) 45 hours in any week; and

(c) nine hours in any day.

(3) Subject to this Sub-Part, an employer shall not require or permit an employee to work

overtime —

(a) except in accordance with an agreement; and

(b) more than 50 overtime hours in any four week cycle.

(4) An agreement under subsection (3) may not require an employee to work more than the 12-hour limit contained in subsection (1).

(5) An employer shall pay an employee not less than one and one-half times the employee's basic wage for any overtime worked.

20. Night work

(1) In this section, "night" means the hours after twenty hours and before six hours.

(2) It is prohibited for an employer to require or permit —

(a) pregnant employees to work at night —

(i) two months before the expected date of confinement; or

(ii) before that date if the employee produces a medical certificate that she is no longer fit to perform night work;

(b) mothers to work at night —

(i) for a period of 2 months after the date of birth;

(ii) before that date if the mother requests to work and produces a medical certificate that her and the baby's health shall not be endangered;

(iii) after that date if the mother produces a medical certificate that she is not yet fit to perform night work or that the baby's health does not permit the employee to work night shift;

(c) children under the age of 18 years;

(d) an employee who is medically certified as unfit to do night work.

(3) An employer shall transfer any employee working night shift who becomes certified as unfit to do night work unless it is impracticable.

(4) An employer shall pay an employee at least 5% of that employee's basic wage for each hour worked at night and if the hours worked are overtime hours, the 5% shall be calculated on the employee's overtime rate.

(5) For the purposes of this section, a medical certificate means a certificate issued by a registered medical practitioner or any other medical practitioner accepted by the employer, which acceptance may not be unreasonably withheld.

21. Compressed working week

(1) A written agreement shall require or permit an employee to work up to twelve hours in a day, inclusive of any meal interval, without receiving overtime pay.

(2) An agreement under subsection (1) shall not require or permit an employee to work —

(a) more than 5 days in a week;

(b) more than 45 hours in a week;

(c) more than 10 hours overtime in a week.

22. Averaging hours of work

(1) Notwithstanding the provisions of section 19 or 24, a collective agreement shall provide for

the averaging of the ordinary and overtime hours of work over an agreed period.

(2) A collective agreement in subsection (1) shall not require or permit an employee to work more than an average of —

(a) 40 ordinary hours of work per week calculated over the agreed period;

(b) ten hours overtime per week calculated over the agreed period.

(3) A collective agreement prescribed in subsection (1) shall not permit averaging for a period longer than a year.

23. Break in working day

(1) Subject to this Part, an employer shall give an employee who work continuously for more than five hours a break of at least 60 minutes.

(2) An employer may require an employee to work during a break only if the work cannot be left unattended or cannot be performed by another employee.

(3) An employer shall not be obliged to pay an employee for the period of a break unless the employee is required to work, or to be available for work, during the break.

24. Daily and weekly rest periods

(1) An employer shall allow an employee —

(a) a daily rest period of at least 12 consecutive hours between ending and recommencing work;

(b) a weekly rest period of at least 24 hours between the last ordinary working day in the week and the first ordinary working day of the next week.

(2) A daily rest period may be reduced to 8 hours if —

(a) there is a written agreement to that effect; and

(b) the ordinary working hours are interrupted by an interval of at least three hours; or

(c) the employee lives on the premises of the workplace.

(3) A weekly rest period may, by written agreement, provide for —

(a) a rest period of at least 60 consecutive hours every two weeks; or

(b) a reduced weekly rest period by 8 hours if the rest period in the following week is extended equivalently.

(4) An employee may only work during the weekly rest period referred to in subsection (1) if the employee has agreed to do so and provided that the employer shall pay the employee double the employee's hourly basic wage for each hour worked during the period.

25. Public holidays

If an employee works on a public holiday specified in the Public Holidays Act, the employer shall pay the employee double the employee's basic wage for each hour worked on that day.

[Cap.93]

Sub-Part C: Remuneration

26. Calculation of wage rates

(1) The provisions of this section apply, when, for any purpose of this Act, it is necessary to determine the applicable hourly, daily, weekly or monthly rate of pay.

(2) The hourly, daily, weekly or monthly wage rates shall be determined in accordance with the Table provided for in the First Schedule.

(3) Where an employee is employed on a basis other than time worked, that employee shall be considered, for the purposes of this section, to be paid on a weekly basis and that employee's basic weekly wage shall be calculated on the amount earned —

   (a) over the immediately proceeding 13 weeks; or

   (b) if the employee has been in employment for less than 13 weeks, that period.

27. Payment of remuneration

(1) An employer shall pay to an employee any monetary remuneration to which the employee is entitled —

   (a) during working hours at the place of work on the agreed pay day;

   (b) in cash, unless the employee agrees otherwise, in which case the payment shall be made either by —

      (i) cheque payable to the employee; or

      (ii) direct deposit into an account designated by the employee in writing; and

   (c) in a sealed envelope, if the payment is made in cash or by cheque.

(2) Each payment prescribed in subsection (1) shall be supported by a written statement of particulars in the prescribed from which —

   (a) shall accompany the payment if the payment is in cash or by cheque; or

   (b) shall be given to the employee in a sealed envelope if the payment is by direct deposit.

(3) Remuneration shall be due and payable at the end of contract period provided the employer may pay an advance before the due day on a mutually agreed day and, if such day is not agreed, at least once on completion of half the contract period; such advance shall not be considered a loan and shall not attract interest. [Cap 4 s.8]

(4) Notwithstanding the provisions of subsection (1), the Minister may by regulations, provide for the partial payment of remuneration in the form of allowance in kind, but in no case alcoholic beverages or noxious drugs, in industries or occupations in which payment in the form of such allowance is customary or desirable, and any such allowance in kind shall be for the personal use of the employee and his or her family, and the value attributed to such allowance shall be fair and reasonable.

(5) Any employer who contravenes the provisions of this section, commits an offence.

28. Deductions and other acts concerning remuneration

(1) An employer shall not make any deduction from an employee's remuneration unless —

   (a) the deduction is required or permitted under a written law, collective agreement, wage determination, court order or arbitration award; or

   (b) subject to subsection (2), the employee in writing agrees to the deduction in respect of a debt.

(2) A deduction under subsection (1)(b) may be made to reimburse an employer for loss or damage only if —

   (a) the loss or damage occurred in the course of employment and was due to the fault of the employee;

(b) the employer has submitted to the employee, in writing, the cause, the amount and calculation of the debt;

(c) the employer has given the employee a reasonable opportunity to challenge the cause, amount or calculation;

(d) the total amount of the debt does not exceed the actual amount of the loss or damage;

(e) the total deductions from the employee's remuneration under this subsection do not exceed one quarter of the employee's remuneration in money.

(3) An agreement to make a deduction under subsection (1)(b) in respect of goods or services purchased by the employee shall specify the cause, amount and calculation of the debt.

(4) An employer who deducts an amount from an employee's remuneration under subsection (1) for payment to another person shall pay the amount to the person in accordance with any requirements specified in the agreement, law, determination, court order or arbitration award.

(5) An employer shall not require or permit an employee to —

(a) repay any remuneration except for overpayments previously made by the employer resulting from an error in calculating the employee's remuneration; or

(b) acknowledge receipt of an amount greater than the remuneration actually received.

(6) Notwithstanding the provisions of any other law on bankruptcy or winding up of an employer's business, the claim of an employee or those claiming on behalf of the employee of any remuneration to which the employee is entitled under this Act, shall be the claim that which have accrued in respect of the twenty six weeks immediately preceding the date on which the declaration of bankruptcy or winding-up is made.

(7) Any person who contravenes the provisions of this section, commits an offence.

Sub-Part D: Leave

29. Application of this Sub-Part

(1) Subject to the provisions of subsection (2), an employee with less than six months service shall not be entitled to paid leave under the provisions of this Part.

(2) Notwithstanding the provisions of subsection (1) —

(a) an employee employed on a seasonal basis is entitled to paid leave under the provisions of this Part;

(b) an employee, with less than six months service and who has worked more than once in a year for the same employer, shall be entitled to paid leave under the provisions of this Part if the total period worked for that employer exceeds six months in that year.

30. Interpretation in this Sub-Part

(1) For the purpose of this Sub-Part —

(a) "day" includes any rest period prescribed in section 24;

(b) "leave cycle" means —

(i) in respect of annual leave, a period of 12 months consecutive employment with

an employer following —
- (aa) subject to subsection (2), an employee's commencement of employment; or
- (bb) the completion of the last 12 months leave cycle.;

(ii) in respect of all other forms of leave conferred under this Sub-Part, a period of 36 months' consecutive employment with an employer following —
- (aa) subject to subsection (2), an employee's commencement of employment; or
- (bb) the completion of the last 36 months leave cycle;

(c) "paid leave" means any leave paid under this Part and calculated on an employee's basic wage.

(2) Notwithstanding the provisions of subsection (1)(b)(i)(aa) and (ii)(aa), an employer and employee may agree to a standard leave cycle provided that an employee's entitlement to paid leave under this Sub-Part is not prejudiced.

31. Annual leave

(1) An employer shall grant an employee at least 28 consecutive days' leave in respect of each leave cycle, and such leave shall be inclusive of any public holiday that may fall within the period of leave.

(2) The number of days referred to in subsection (1) may be reduced by the number of days during the leave cycle which, at the request of the employee, the employer granted that employee paid occasional leave.

(3) An employer may determine when the annual leave is to be taken provided that it is taken no later than —
- (a) six months after the end of the leave cycle; or
- (b) twelve months after the end of the leave cycle if —
  - (i) the employee has consented; and
  - (ii) the extension is justified by the operational requirements of the employer.

(4) An employer shall pay an employee the remuneration the employee would have been paid had the employee worked during the period of leave before the commencement of the leave.

(5) An employer shall not require or permit an employee to take annual leave in place of any leave to which the employee is entitled under this Part.

(6) With the consent of an employee, the employer may require or permit such employee to work for the employer during a period of annual leave on condition that such employee shall not work for a continuous period of two years.

(7) Subject to subsections (6) and (8) an employer shall pay the employee one month salary *in lieu* of annual leave to which that employee is entitled or was called upon to work.

(8) An employer shall pay an employee a *pro rata* amount for annual leave accrued —
- (a) subject to the provisions of subsection (9), at the termination of employment; or
- (b) at the expiry of each season in respect of an employee employed on a seasonal basis.

(9) An employee is not entitled to be paid any *pro rata* amount for accrued annual leave if the employee has not taken the leave within the periods and circumstances prescribed in subsection (3).

(10) The *pro rata* amount of annual leave referred to in subsection (8) shall be calculated at

the rate of one day's basic wage for every 13 days the employee worked or was entitled to work.

[Act No.24 of 2015 s.6]

32. Sick leave

(1) An employee shall be entitled to sick leave for at least 126 days in any leave cycle.

(2) The sick leave referred to in subsection (1) shall be calculated as follows —

(a) the first 63 days shall be paid full wages;

(b) the second 63 days shall be paid half wages.

(3) Notwithstanding the provisions of subsection (2), an employer shall not be required to pay an employee for sick leave if —

(a) the employee fails to produce a medical certificate; or

(b) the employee is entitled to paid sick leave under any law, fund or collective agreement.

(4) For the purposes of this section, "medical certificate" means a certificate issued by a registered medical practitioner or any other medical practitioner accepted by the employer, which acceptance may not be unreasonably withheld.

33. Maternity leave

(1) An employee shall give notice to the employer of her intention to take maternity leave at least 3 months before the expected date of birth and such notice shall be supported by a medical certificate.

(2) An employee may commence maternity leave —

(a) at any time from four weeks before the expected date of confinement;

(b) on an earlier date if a medical practitioner certifies that it is necessary for the employee's health or that of her unborn child.

(3) No employee shall work within six weeks of the birth of her child unless a medical practitioner certifies that she is fit to do so.

(4) Subject to the provisions of subsections (2) and (3), the employee may resume employment on the same terms and conditions of employment at the end of her maternity leave.

(5) No employer shall require or permit a pregnant employee or an employee who is nursing a child to perform work that is hazardous to her health or the health of her child.

(6) Subject to the provisions of subsections (7) and (8), an employee shall be entitled, within any leave cycle, to at least —

(a) 84 days paid maternity leave; or

(b) 100 days' paid maternity leave if the employee gives birth to more than one child at the same time.

(7) Notwithstanding the provisions subsection (6)(a), an employee is entitled to an additional 84 days paid maternity leave within the leave cycle if the child dies within a year of birth.

(8) An employer is only obliged to grant paid leave for 4 terms of maternity leave to an employee in terms of this section.

(9) Where an employee performs work that is hazardous to her health or that of her child, her employer shall offer her suitable alternative employment, if practicable, on terms and conditions that are no less favourable than her terms and conditions.

(10) Where an employee is breast-feeding a child, the employer shall allow the employee to

feed the child during working hours up to a maximum of two hours per day.

(11) For the purposes of this section, "medical certificate" means a certificate issued by a registered medical practitioner, including a midwife, or any other medical practitioner accepted by the employer, which acceptance may not be unreasonably withheld.

34. Paternity and other forms of leave

(1) During any leave cycle, an employee shall be entitled to —
- (a) at least 3 days paid paternity leave if —
  - (i) the leave is taken within 7 days of the birth of a child; and
  - (ii) the employee is the father of the child;
- (b) at least 4 days paid leave for any of the following reasons —
  - (i) the sickness or death of the employee's child;
  - (ii) the death of the employee's spouse, parent, grandparent, grandchild or sibling.

(2) Before paying an employee for leave under this section, an employer may require reasonable proof of the event prescribed in subsection (1).

(3) For the purpose of clarity —
- (a) the 3 days referred to in subsection (1)(a) are the total number of days to which the employee is entitled irrespective of how many of the employee's children are born within the leave cycle;
- (b) the 4 days referred to in subsection (1)(b) are the total number of days to which the employee is entitled irrespective of how many of the events prescribed in that paragraph occur within the leave cycle, but the employee may take more days as may be authorised by the employer for the event and other subsequent events within the same leave cycle provided that such extra days will be without pay.

Sub-Part E: Unfair termination of employment

35. Application of this Sub-Part

The provisions of this Sub-Part shall not apply to an employee with less than 6 months' employment with the same employer, whether under one or more contracts.

36. Interpretation

For purposes of this Sub-Part —
- (a) "termination of employment" includes —
  - (i) a lawful termination of employment under the common law;
  - (ii) a termination by an employee because the employer made continued employment intolerable for the employee;
  - (iii) a failure to renew a fixed term contract on the same or similar terms if there was a reasonable expectation of renewal;
  - (iv) a failure to allow an employee to resume work after taking maternity leave granted under this Act or any agreed maternity leave; and
  - (v) a failure to re-employ an employee if the employer has terminated the employment of a number of employees for the same or similar reasons and has

offered to reemploy one or more of them;

(b) "terminate employment" has a meaning corresponding to "termination of employment".

37. Unfair termination

(1) It shall be unlawful for an employer to terminate the employment of an employee unfairly.

(2) A termination of employment by an employer is unfair if the employer fails to prove —

  (a) that the reason for the termination is valid;

  (b) that the reason is a fair reason —

    (i) related to the employee's conduct, capacity or compatibility; or

    (ii) based on the operational requirements of the employer, and

  (c) that the employment was terminated in accordance with a fair procedure.

(3) It shall not be a fair reason to terminate the employment of an employee —

  (a) for the reason that the employee —

    (i) discloses information that the employee is entitled or required to disclose to another person under this Act or any other law;

    (ii) fails or refuses to do anything that an employer may not lawfully permit or require the employee to do;

    (iii) exercises any right conferred by agreement, this Act or any other law;

    (iv) belongs, or belonged, to any trade union; or

    (v) participates in the lawful activities of a trade union, including a lawful strike;

        [Cap.4 s.8]

  (b) for reasons —

    (i) related to pregnancy;

    (ii) related to disability; and

    (iii) that constitute discrimination under this Act.

(4) In deciding whether a termination by an employer is fair, an employer, arbitrator or Labour Court shall take into account any Code of Good Practice published under section 99.

(5) No displinary action in form of penalty, termination or dismissal shall lie upon an employee who has been charged with a criminal offence which is substantially the same until final determination by the Court and any appeal thereto.

38. Termination based on operational requirements

(1) In any termination for operational requirements (retrenchment), the employer shall comply with the following principles, that is to say, he shall —

  (a) give notice of any intention to retrench as soon as it is contemplated;

  (b) disclose all relevant information on the intended retrenchment for the purpose of proper consultation;

  (c) consult prior to retrenchment or redundancy on —

    (i) the reasons for the intended retrenchment;

    (ii) any measures to avoid or minimize the intended retrenchment;

    (iii) the method of selection of the employees to be retrenched;

    (iv) the timing of the retrenchments; and

(v) severance pay in respect of the retrenchments;

(d) give the notice, make the disclosure and consult, in terms of this subsection, with —

(i) any trade union recognized in terms of section 67;

(ii) any registered trade union which members in the workplace not represented by a recognised trade union;

(iii) any employees not represented by a recognized or registered trade union.

(2) Where in the consultations held in terms of sub-section (1) no agreement is reached between the parties, the matter shall be referred to mediation under Part VIII of this Act.

(3) Where the mediation has failed, the dispute shall be referred for arbitration which shall be concluded within thirty days during which period no retrenchment shall take effect and, where the employees are dissatisfied with the award and are desirous to proceed with revision to the Labour Court under section 91(2), the employer may proceed with their retrenchment.

[Acts Nos.17 of 2010 s.8; 24 of 2015 s.7]

39. Proof in unfair termination proceedings

In any proceedings concerning unfair termination of an employee by an employer, the employer shall prove that the termination is fair.

40. Remedies for unfair termination

(1) Where an arbitrator or Labour Court finds a termination is unfair, the arbitrator or Court may order the employer —

(a) to reinstate the employee from the date the employee was terminated without loss of remuneration during the period that the employee was absent from work due to the unfair termination; or

(b) to re-engage the employee on any terms that the arbitrator or Court may decide; or

(c) to pay compensation to the employee of not less than twelve months remuneration.

(2) An order for compensation made under this section shall be in addition to, and not a substitute for, any other amount to which the employee may be entitled in terms of any law or agreement.

(3) Where an order of reinstatement or re-engagement is made by an arbitrator or Court and the employer decides not to reinstate or re-engage the employee, the employer shall pay compensation of twelve months wages in addition to wages due and other benefits from the date of unfair termination to the date of final payment.

[Cap.4. s.8]

Sub-Part F: Other incidents of Termination

41. Notice of termination

(1) Where a contract of employment can be terminated on notice, the period of notice shall not be less than —

(a) seven days, if notice is given in the first month of employment; and

(b) after that —

(i) 4 days, if the employee is employed on a daily or weekly basis; or

(ii) 28 days, if the employee is employed on a monthly basis.

(2) An agreement may provide for a notice period that is longer than that required in subsection (1) provided that, the agreed notice period is of equal duration for both the employer and the employee.

(3) Notice of termination shall be in writing, stating —
- (i) the reasons for termination; and
- (ii) the date on which the notice is given.

(4) Notice of termination shall not be given —
- (a) during any period of leave taken under this Act; or
- (b) to run, concurrently with any such period of leave.

(5) Instead of giving an employee notice of termination, an employer may pay the employee the remuneration that the employee would have received if the employee had worked during the notice period.

(6) Where an employee refuses to work during the notice period, an employer may deduct, from any money due to that employee on termination, the amount that would have been due to the employee if that employee had worked during the notice period.

(7) Nothing in this section shall affect the right of —
- (a) an employee to dispute the lawfulness or fairness of a termination of employment under this Act or any other law;
- (b) an employer or an employee to terminate employment without notice for any cause recognised by law.

[Cap.4 s.8]

42. Severance pay

(1) For the purposes of this section, "severance pay" means an amount at least equal to 7 days' basic wage for each completed year of continuous service with that employer up to a maximum of ten years.

(2) An employer shall pay severance pay on termination of employment if —
- (a) the employee has completed 12 months continuous service with an employer; and
- (b) subject to the provisions of subsection (3), the employer terminates the employment.

(3) The provisions of subsection (2) shall not apply —
- (a) to a fair termination on grounds of misconduct;
- (b) to an employee who is terminated on grounds of capacity compatibility or operational requirements of the employer but who unreasonably refuses to accept alternative employment with that employer or any other employer; or
- (c) to an employee who attains the age of retirement or an employee whose contract of service has expired or ended by reason of time.

(4) The payment of severance pay under this section shall not affectan employee's right to any other amount payable under this or any other written law.

[Act No.2 of 2010 s.13]

43. Transport to place of recruitment

(1) Where an employee's contract of employment is terminated at a place other than where the

employee was recruited, the employer shall either —
- (a) transport the employee and his personal effects to the place of recruitment;
- (b) pay for the transportation of the employee to the place of recruitment; or
- (c) pay the employee an allowance for transportation to the place of recruitment in accordance with subsection (2) and daily subsistence expenses during the period, if any, between the date of termination of the contract and the date of transporting the employee and his family to the place of recruitment.

(2) An allowance prescribed under subsection (1)(c) shall be equal to at least a bus fare to the bus station nearest to the place of recruitment.

(3) For the purposes of this section, "recruit" means the solicitation of any employee for employment by the employer or the employer's agent.

44. Payment of termination and certificates of employment

(1) On termination of employment, an employer shall pay an employee —
- (a) any remuneration for work done before the termination;
- (b) any annual leave pay due to an employee under section 31 for leave that the employee has not taken;
- (c) any annual leave pay accrued during any incomplete leave cycle determined in accordance with section 31(1);
- (d) any notice pay due under section 41(5); and
- (e) any severance pay due under section 42;
- (f) any transport allowance that may be due under section 43.

(2) On termination, the employer shall issue to an employee a prescribed certificate of service.

PART IV
TRADE UNIONS, EMPLOYERS ASSOCIATIONS AND FEDERATIONS

45. Obligation to register

(1) A trade union or employers' association shall register itself under this Part within 6 months of its establishment.

(2) A federation may register if it meets the requirements for registration of a federation in terms of section 46(3).

(3) It is an offence for a trade union or employer's association to operate as a union or association —
- (a) after 6 months have expired of its establishment if it has not applied for registration under this Part; or
- (b) unless it is registered under this Part.

46. Requirements for registration

(1) The requirements for registration as a trade union are:
- (a) it is a bona fide trade union;
- (b) it is an association not for gain;

(c) it is independent of any employer or employer's association;

(d) it has been established at a meeting of at least 20 employees;

(e) it has adopted a constitution and rules that comply with provisions of section 47;

(f) it has adopted a name that does not resemble the name of another union so as to mislead or create confusion; and

(g) it has an address in the United Republic of Tanzania.

(2) The requirements for registration as an employers' association are:

(a) it is a bona fide employees association;

(b) it is an association not for gain;

(c) it has been established at a meeting of at least four employers;

(d) it has adopted a constitution and rules that comply with provisions of section 47;

(e) it has adopted a name that does not resemble the name of another employer association so as to mislead or create confusion; and

(f) it has an address in the United Republic of Tanzania.

(3) The requirements for registration as a federation are:

(a) it is a bona fide federation;

(b) it is a federation not for gain;

(c) it has been established at a meeting of at least five registered organizations of the same kind;

(d) it has adopted a constitution and rules that comply with section 47;

(e) it has adopted a name that does not resemble the name of another organization or federation so as to mislead or create confusion;

(f) it comprises registered organizations only; and

(g) it has an address in the United Republic of Tanzania.

47. Constitutional requirements

(1) The constitution and rules of a trade union, employers' association or federation shall —

(a) state that it is an organization not for gain;

(b) prescribe the qualifications for membership and the grounds and procedure for termination of membership;

(c) prescribe the membership fee or any method of determining the fee;

(d) prescribe rules for the convening and conduct of meetings, including the quorum required, and the minutes to be kept of, those meetings;

(e) establish the manner in which decisions are made;

(f) establish the office of secretary and define its functions;

(g) provide for office bearers, officials and define their respective functions;

(h) prescribe a procedure for the nomination and election of office bearers;

(i) prescribe a procedure for the appointment or nomination or election of officials;

(j) establish the circumstances and manner in which office bearers, officials and trade union representatives may be removed from office;

(k) establish the circumstances and manner in which a ballot shall be conducted;

(1) provide for the conduct of a ballot of the members in respect of whom —
- (i) in the case of a trade union, the union may call upon to strike;
- (ii) in the case of an employers' association, the association may call upon to lock out;
- (iii) in the case of a federation of trade unions, the federation may call upon to engage in protest action;

(m) provide for banking and investing of money;

(n) establish the purposes for which its money may be used;

(o) provide for acquiring and controlling of property;

(p) prescribe a procedure for the amendment of the constitution and rules;

(q) prescribe a procedure for affiliation, or amalgamation —
- (i) in the case of trade unions, with other registered unions;
- (ii) in the case of employer associations, with other registered associations;
- (iii) in the case of federations, with other federations;

(r) prescribe a procedure for affiliation to an international workers' association or an international employers' association;

(s) prescribe a procedure to dissolve the organisation or federation;

(t) any other prescribed matter.

(2) A constitution or rules of a registered organisation shall not —
- (a) conflict with —
  - (i) the basic rights and duties set out in Part III of the Constitution of the United Republic of Tanzania, 1977;
  - (ii) the provisions of this law or any other written law; or
- (b) evade any obligation imposed by any law.

48. Process of registration

(1) Any organisation or federation may apply for registration, by submitting to the Registrar —
- (a) a prescribed form that has been properly completed and signed by the secretary of the organisation or federation;
- (b) a certified copy of the attendance register and minutes of its establishment meeting prescribed in section 46(1)(d), (2)(c) or (3)(c); and
- (c) a certified copy of its constitution and rules.

(2) Notwithstanding the provisions of subsection (1), the Registrar may require further information in support of the application.

(3) Where the Registrar is satisfied that the organisation or federation has complied with the requirements of sections 46 and 47, he shall register the organisation or federation.

(4) Where the Registrar is not satisfied that the organisation or federation complies with the requirements of sections 46 and 47, he —
- (a) may give the applicant an opportunity to rectify its application within a stipulated period;
- (b) may refuse the application and send the applicant a written notice of the decision and

the reasons.

(5) After registering an organisation or federation, the Registrar shall —
- (a) enter the name of the organisation or federation in the appropriate register;
- (b) issue a certificate of registration to the organisation or federation.

49. Effect of registration

(1) On registration, an organization or federation shall be a body corporate —
- (a) with perpetual succession and a common seal;
- (b) with the capacity, in its own name, to —
  - (i) sue and be sued;
  - (i) contract; and
  - (iii) hold, purchase or otherwise acquire and dispose of movable or immovable property.

(2) A registered organisation or federation shall not be an association in restraint of trade.

(3) The fact that a person is a member of a registered organisation or federation shall not make that person liable for any of the obligations or liabilities of the union or organisation.

(4) A member; office bearer, official of a registered organisation or federation shall not be personally liable for any loss suffered by any person as a result of an act performed or omitted in good faith while performing their functions for or on behalf of the organisation or federation.

(5) A duly issued certificate of registration is sufficient proof that a registered organisation or federation is a body corporate.

(6) For the purposes of this section, "office bearer" in relation to a trade union includes a trade union representative prescribed in section 62.

50. Change of name or constitution

(1) Any change of name or change to the constitution and rules of a registered organisation or federation shall have effect only when the Registrar approves the change under this section.

(2) A registered organization or federation may apply for the approval of a change of name or to its constitution and rules by submitting to the Registrar —
- (a) the prescribed form duly completed and signed by the secretary;
- (b) a copy of the resolution containing the wording of the change; and
- (c) a certificate signed by the secretary stating that the resolution was passed in accordance with the constitution rules.

(3) Notwithstanding the provisions of subsection (2), the Registrar may require further information in support of the application.

(4) The Registrar shall —
- (a) consider the application and any further information supplied by the applicant;
- (b) if satisfied that the change to the constitution and rules complies with the requirements prescribed in sections 46 and 47, approve the change by issuing the prescribed certificate approving the change; and
- (c) if satisfied that the change of name does not resemble the name of another union so as to mislead or create confusion, approve the change by issuing a new certificate of registration reflecting the new name.

(5) Where the Registrar refuses to approve a change, he shall give written notice of that decision and the reasons for the refusal.

51. Accounts and audits

(1) Every registered organisation and federation shall, to the standards of generally accepted accounting practice, principles and procedures —
- (a) keep books and records of its income, expenditure, assets and liabilities;
- (b) for each financial year ending on 31 December, prepare financial statements in the prescribed form;
- (c) arrange an annual audit of its books and records of accounts and its financial statements by a registered auditor;
- (d) by 31 March of the following year, submit the financial statements and auditor's report to —
  - (i) a meeting of members or their representatives as provided for in the constitution of the organisation or federation; and
  - (ii) the Registrar.

(2) Every registered organisation and federation shall make its financial statements and auditor's report available to members for inspection at its offices.

52. Duties of registered organizations and federations

(1) In addition to the records required by section 51, every registered organisation or federation shall keep for five years —
- (a) a list of its members in the prescribed form;
- (b) the minutes of its meetings;
- (c) the ballot papers.

(2) Every registered organisation or federation shall provide to the Registrar —
- (a) by 31 March of the following year, an annual statement certified by the secretary showing the total number of members as of 31 December of the previous year;
- (b) within 30 days of a request from the Registrar, a written explanation of anything relating to the statement of membership, the auditor's report or the financial statements:

Provided that, the Registrar shall not inquire into the financial affairs of any organisation unless there are serious grounds for believing that the organisation has infringed the law or that the funds of the organization have been embezzled or otherwise misused;
- (c) within 30 days of any appointment or election of its national office bearers, the names and work addresses of those office bearers;
- (d) 30 days before a new address for service of documents will take effect, notice of that change of address.

53. Non-compliance with constitution

(1) Where a federation or registered organisation fails to comply with its constitution, the Registrar or member of the federation or registered organisation may apply to the Labour Court for any appropriate order including —
- (a) setting aside any decision, agreement or election;

(b) requiring the organisation or federation or any official thereof to —
  (i) comply with the constitution;
  (ii) take steps to rectify the failure to comply;
(c) restraining any person from any action not in compliance with the constitution.

(2) Before the Labour Court hears an application prescribed in subsection (1), it shall satisfy itself that —
  (a) the organisation's or federation's internal procedures have been exhausted; or
  (b) it is in the best interests of the organisation or federation that the application be heard notwithstanding that any internal procedures have not been exhausted.

54. Amalgamation of registered organizations and federations

(1) Any registered —
  (a) trade union may resolve to amalgamate with one or more registered trade unions; and
  (b) employer's association may resolve to amalgamate with one or more registered employer's associations;
  (c) federation may resolve to amalgamate with one or more federations to form a confederation.

(2) The amalgamating organisations or federations may apply to the Registrar for registration of the amalgamated organisation or federation and the provisions of section 48, relating to registration process shall *mutatis mutandis* apply in relation to the application.

(3) After the Registrar has registered the amalgamated organization or federation, he shall cancel the registration of each of the amalgamating organisations or federations by removing their names from the appropriate register.

(4) The registration of an amalgamated organisation or federation shall become effective from the date the Registrar enters its name in the appropriate register.

(5) Where the Registrar has registered an amalgamated organization or federation —
  (a) all the assets, rights, obligations and liabilities of the amalgamating organisations or federations shall devolve upon and vest in the amalgamated organisation or federation; and
  (b) the amalgamated organisation or federation shall succeed the amalgamating organisations or federations in respect of —
    (i) any right that the amalgamating organisations or federations enjoyed;
    (ii) any fund established under this Act or any other law;
    (iii) any collective agreement or other agreement; and
    (iv) any written authorisation by a member for the periodic deduction of levies or subscriptions due to the amalgamating organisations.

55. Cancellation of registration

(1) The Registrar may apply to the Labour Court for an order to cancel the registration of a registered organisation or federation if that organisation or federation fails to comply with —
  (a) the requirements for registration; or
  (b) the provisions of this Part.

(2) Where the Labour Court may make any appropriate order including —
- (a) cancelling the registration of an organisation or federation;
- (b) giving the organisation or federation an opportunity to remedy any failure to comply.

(3) Where the registration of an organisation or federation is cancelled —
- (a) all the rights enjoyed by it under this Act shall cease; and
- (b) the organization or federation shall be dissolved in accordance with the provisions of section 56.

56. Dissolution of trade union or employers association

(1) The Registrar may apply to the Labour Court for the dissolution of any organisation that contravenes the provisions of section 45.

(2) An organisation or federation may apply to the Labour Court for its dissolution.

(3) Where the Labour Court makes an order for cancelling the registration of an organisation or federation under section 55(2), it may in addition make an order dissolving the organisation or federation.

(4) In accordance with the laws relating to bankruptcy, any interested person may apply to the Labour Court for dissolution of a registered organisation or federation on any ground of bankruptcy.

(5) The laws of bankruptcy, shall apply to an application prescribed in subsection (3) and any reference to a court in those laws shall be interpreted as referring to the Labour Court.

(6) In granting an order of dissolution under this section, the Labour Court may —
- (a) appoint any suitable person as a liquidator on any appropriate conditions;
- (b) decide where any residue of assets shall vest if the constitution and rules fail to do so.

57. Appeals from decisions of Registrar

Any person aggrieved by a decision of the Registrar made under this Part may appeal to the Labour Court against that decision.

58. Publication in *Gazette*

(1) The Registrar shall publish a notice in the *Gazette* stating the following facts, that —
- (a) an organisation or federation has been registered;
- (b) the registration of any organisation or federation has been cancelled;
- (c) a change of a name or amalgamation affecting any registered organisation or federation has been registered;
- (d) a registered organisation or federation has been dissolved.

(2) Where the notice referred to in subsection (1) deals with registration of an organisation or federation, it shall contain a statement to the effect that, any person may view the constitution of that organisation or federation at the Registrar's office.

PART V
ORGANISATIONAL RIGHTS

59. Interpretation

For the purposes of this Part —

"authorised representative" means an office bearer or official of a trade union or any other person authorized to represent the trade union;

"employer's premises" includes any premises under the control of the employer where work is done or the employees are accommodated;

"labour laws" includes this Act and any other law relating to labour matters;

"registered trade union" includes two or more trade unions acting jointly;

"representative trade union" means a registered trade union that is the most representative trade union.

60. Access to employer's premises

(1) Any authorised representative of a registered trade union shall be entitled to enter the employer's premises in order to —

    (a) recruit members;

    (b) communicate with members;

    (c) meet members in dealings with the employer;

    (d) hold meetings of employees on the premises;

    (e) vote in any ballot under the union constitution.

(2) A registered trade union may establish a field branch at any workplace where ten or more of its members are employed.

(3) The employer shall provide a union recognised in terms of section 67 reasonable and necessary facilities to conduct its activities at the workplace.

(4) The rights under this section shall be subject to any conditions as to time and place that are reasonable and necessary to safeguard life or property or to prevent undue disruption of work.

61. Deduction of trade union dues

(1) An employer shall deduct dues of a registered trade union from an employee's wages if that employee has authorised the employer to do so in the prescribed form.

(2) The employer shall remit the deductions to the trade union within seven days after the end of the month in which the deductions are made.

(3) Where the employer fails to remit the union dues within the time specified in subsection (2), without reasonable grounds, the employer shall be liable to pay the union the equivalent of five percent of the total amount due for each day the dues remain unremitted.

(4) An employee may revoke an authorisation by giving one month's written notice to the employer and the trade union.

(5) Where an employee revokes any authorization under subsection (3), the employer shall cease to make any deductions after the expiry of the notice.

(6) With each monthly remittance, the employer shall give a registered trade union —

    (a) a list in the prescribed form of the names of the members in respect of whom deductions are required to be made;

    (b) a copy of any notice of revocation under subsection (3).

62. Trade union representation

(1) A registered trade union shall be entitled to —

(a) one trade union representative for one to nine members;
(b) three representatives for ten to twenty members;
(c) ten representatives for twenty one to one hundred members;
(d) fifteen representatives for work places with more than one hundred members.

[Cap 4 s.8]

(2) In workplace with more than one hundred members, at least five of the trade union representatives shall represent women employees, if any, who are employed and belong to the union.

(3) The constitution of a registered trade union shall govern the election, terms of office and removal from office of a trade union representative.

(4) Trade union representatives shall perform the following functions —
   (a) to represent members in grievance and disciplinary hearings;
   (b) to make representations on behalf of members in respect of rules;
   (c) to consult on productivity in the workplace;
   (d) to represent the trade union in enquiries and investigations conducted by inspectors in terms of any labour laws;
   (e) to monitor employer compliance with labour laws;
   (f) to perform trade union functions under the union's constitution;
   (g) to further good relations;
   (h) to perform any function or role agreed to by the employer.

(5) Trade union representatives shall be entitled to reasonable paid time off to perform any of the functions referred to in subsection (4).

(6) The employer shall disclose to the trade union representatives any information relevant to the performance of their functions.

(7) The provisions of section 70 relating to disclosure of relevant information shall *mutatis mutandis* apply to any disclosure prescribed in subsection (6).

(8) The rights under this section are subject to any reasonable conditions to ensure the orderly exercise of the rights and that work is not unduly interrupted.

63. Leave for trade union activities

The employer shall grant reasonable paid leave to —
   (a) trade union representatives referred to in section 62 to attend training courses relevant to their functions;
   (b) office bearers of —
      (i) a registered trade union, to perform the functions of their officer;
      (ii) a registered federation, to which the representative union belongs, to perform the functions of their office.

64. Procedure for exercising organizational right

(1) Any registered trade union may notify an employer in the prescribed form that it seeks to exercise a right conferred under this Part.

(2) Within 30 days of the receipt of a notice under subsection (1), the employer shall meet

with the trade union to conclude a collective agreement granting the right and regulating the manner in which the right is to be exercised.

(3) Where there is no agreement or the employer fails to meet with the trade union within 30 days, the union may refer the dispute to the Commission for mediation.

(4) Where the mediation fails to resolve the dispute, the trade union may refer the dispute to the Labour Court which shall make appropriate orders.

(5) Any dispute over the interpretation or application of an order made under this section shall be referred to the Labour Court for decision.

65. Termination of organizational rights

(1) Where a trade union materially breaches the terms and conditions for the exercise of organisational rights, the employer —

    (a) may refer the issue to the Commission for mediation;

    (b) if the mediation fails to resolve the issue, may apply to the Labour Court to —

        (i) terminate any of the organisational rights granted to the trade union under a collective agreement; or

        (ii) withdraw an order made under section 64.

(2) A Labour Court making a decision under this section may make any appropriate order including —

    (a) requiring the union to take measures to ensure compliance with the conditions for the exercise of a right;

    (b) suspending the exercise of a right for a period of time;

    (c) terminating the organisational rights contained in a collective agreement or order made under section 64.

PART VI
COLLECTIVE BARGAINING

66. Interpretation

For the purposes of this Part —

    (a) a "bargaining unit" —

        (i) means any unit of employees in respect of which a registered trade union is recognised, or is entitled to be recognised, as the exclusive bargaining agent in terms of this Part;

        (ii) includes a unit of employees employed by more than one employer;

    (b) a "recognised trade union" means a trade union recognised by a collective agreement or in respect of an order made by the Labour Court under the provisions of section 67;

    (c) a "registered trade union" includes two or more registered trade unions acting jointly.

67. Recognition as exclusive bargaining agent of employees

(1) A registered trade union that represents the majority of the employees in an appropriate bargaining unit shall be entitled to be recognised as the exclusive bargaining agent of the

employees in that unit.

(2) An employer or employers' association may not recognise a trade union as an exclusive bargaining agent unless the trade union is registered and represents the majority of the employees in the bargaining unit.

(3) A registered trade union may notify the employer or employers' association in the prescribed form that it shall seek recognition as the exclusive bargaining agent within an appropriate bargaining unit.

(4) Within thirty days of the notice prescribed in subsection (3), an employer shall meet to conclude a collective agreement recognising the trade union.

(5) Where there is no agreement or the employer fails to meet with the trade union within the thirty days, the union may refer the dispute to the Commission for mediation, and the period of thirty days may be extended by agreement.

(6) If the mediation fails to resolve the dispute, the trade union or the employer may refer the dispute to the Labour Court for decision.

(7) The Labour Court may decide any dispute over the representativeness of the trade union by arranging any appropriate person to conduct a ballot of the affected employees.

(8) In determining the appropriateness of a bargaining unit, the Labour Court shall —
 (a) consider the following:
  (i) the wishes of the parties;
  (ii) the bargaining history of the parties;
  (iii) the extent of union organisation among the employees of the employer or employers;
  (iv) the employee similarity of interest;
  (v) the organisational structure of the employer or employers;
  (vi) the different functions and processes of the employer or employers and the degree of integration;
  (vii) the geographic location of the employer or the employers;
 (b) promote orderly and effective collective bargaining with a minimum of fragmentation of an employer's organisational structure.

(9) Any dispute over the interpretation or application of an order made under this section shall be referred to the authority or the court which made the order for interpretation and other necessary orders.

(10) Any order made pursuant to this section shall be enforced like any other order issued by the Labour Court.

(11) Nothing in this section precludes registered trade unions, employers and registered employers' associations from establishing their own collective bargaining arrangements by collective agreement.

[Act No.17 of 2010 s.9]

68. Duty to bargain in good faith

(1) An employer or employers' association shall bargain in good faith with a recognised trade union.

(2) A recognised trade union shall bargain in good faith with the employer or employers' association that has recognised it or is required to recognize it under the provisions of section 67.

69. Withdrawal of recognition

(1) Where a recognised trade union ceases to represent the majority of the employees in the bargaining unit, the employer shall —

(a) give the trade union notice to acquire a majority within three months;

(b) withdraw exclusive recognition, if it fails to acquire that majority at the expiry of the three months.

(2) Where a recognised trade union has ceased to represent the majority in the bargaining unit, any other trade union may fill the prescribed forms for purpose of being recognized as an execusive bargaining unit.

(3) Where a party to a collective agreement prescribed in section 67(10), or a party subject to a recognition order, materially breaches the agreement or order, the other party may apply to Labour Court to have recognition withdrawn by [Cap.4 s.8]—

(a) terminating the recognition agreement;

(b) rescinding the recognition order.

(4) The Labour Court may decide any dispute over the representativeness of the trade union by arranging any appropriate person to conduct a ballot of the affected employees.

(5) The Labour Court may make any appropriate order including —

(a) giving the trade union an opportunity to become representative;

(b) altering the bargaining unit;

(c) suspending recognition for a period of time;

(d) withdrawing recognition.

[Act No.17 of 2010 s.10]

70. Obligation to disclose relevant information

(1) An employer that has recognised a trade union under this Part shall allow the union to engage effectively in collective bargaining.

(2) An employer shall not be obliged to disclose information that —

(a) is legally privileged;

(b) the employer cannot disclose without contravening a law or an order of court;

(c) is confidential and, if disclosed, may cause substantial harm to an employee or the employer;

(d) is private personal information relating to an employee without that employee's consent.

(3) A trade union that receives confidential or private personal information under this section —

(a) shall not disclose the information to any person other than its members and advisors;

(b) shall take reasonable measures to ensure that the information disclosed is kept confidential.

(4) Where there is a dispute over disclosure of information, any party to the dispute may refer the dispute to the Commission for mediation. [Cap.4 s.8]

(5) Where the mediation fails, any party may refer the dispute to the Labour Court for decision.

(6) In making any decision, the Labour Court may —

(a) hold the proceedings in camera;

(b) take into account any previous breaches of confidentiality by the trade union or its members;

(c) order an employer to disclose any confidential information if, on balance, the effect of the non-disclosure may seriously impede the union's ability —

(i) to bargain effectively;

(ii) to represent employees effectively;

(d) order the disclosure of information on terms designed to limit any harm that may be caused by disclosure;

(e) order the trade union to pay damages for any breach of confidentiality;

(f) suspend or withdraw the right to disclosure.

71. Binding nature of collective agreements

(1) Collective agreements shall be in writing and signed by the parties.

(2) A collective agreement shall be binding on the last signature unless the agreement states otherwise.

(3) A collective agreement shall be binding on —

(a) the parties to the agreement;

(b) any members of the parties to the agreement;

(c) any employees who are not members of a trade union party to the agreement if the trade union is recognised as the exclusive bargaining agent of those employees under section 67.

(4) A collective agreement shall continue to be binding on employers or employees who were party to the agreement at the time of its commencement and includes resigned members from that trade union or employer association.

(5) A collective agreement becomes binding on employers and employees who become members of the parties to the agreement after its commencement.

(6) Unless a collective agreement provides otherwise, any party to an agreement may terminate the agreement on reasonable notice and shall give reasons for the termination.

(7) The parties to a collective agreement shall be required to lodge a copy of the agreement with the Labour Commissioner and shall be a rebuttable presumption that the copy so registered is authentic and may be executed as a decree of the Court.

[Acts Nos.8 of 2006 Sch.; 17 of 2010 s.11]

72. Agency Shop agreements

(1) An agreement that compels an employee to become a member of a trade union is not enforceable.

(2) A recognised trade union and employer may conclude a collective agreement providing for an agency shop.

(3) The requirements for a binding agency shop agreement are:

(a) the agreement applies to employees in the bargaining unit only;

(b) employees who are not members of the trade union are not compelled to become members;

(c) any agency fee deducted from the remuneration of an employee, who is not a member, is equivalent to, or less than, the union dues deducted by the employer from the remuneration of a member;

(d) the amount deducted from both members and non-members shall be paid into a separate account administered by the trade union;

(e) the monies in that account may only be used to advance or defend the socioeconomic interests of the employees in that workplace and shall not be used to pay —

(i) an affiliation fee to a political party; or

(ii) any contributions to a political party of person standing for political office.

(4) Notwithstanding the provisions of any law or contract, an employer may deduct an agency fee under an agency shop agreement that complies with the provisions of this section from an employee's wages without the consent of that employee:

Provided that, such deduction complies with the terms and conditions prescribed in the regulations.

(5) A trade union party to an agency shop agreement shall —

(a) appoint a registered auditor to audit the account prescribed in subsection (3)(d) annually;

(b) submit the auditor's report to the Labour Commissioner and to the Registrar within thirty days of the date of the report; and

(c) permit any interested person to inspect the report at the union's offices during office hours.

(6) A report by an auditor appointed by a trade union under this section shall include an opinion on whether the provisions of this section have been complied with.

(7) An agency shop agreement shall be —

(a) suspended for so long as the trade union is not representative;

(b) terminated once recognition is withdrawn under section 69.

(8) Where an agency shop agreement is suspended or terminated, the provisions of this section shall continue to apply in respect of any money remaining in the account prescribed in subsection (3)(d). [Cap.4 s.8]

(9) For the purposes of this section, "agency shop" means a union security arrangement in terms of which employees in a bargaining unit, who are not members of the recognised trade union, are required to pay an agency fee to the trade union.

[Act No.24 of 2015 s.8]

73. Workers participation agreement

(1) A recognised trade union and an employer or an employers' association may conclude a collective agreement establishing a forum for workers participation in a workplace.

(2) Where a registered trade union, employer or employers' association wishes to establish a

forum for workers' participation in any workplace, the union, employer or association may request the assistance of the Labour Commissioner to facilitate discussions between the union, employer or association.

(3) The Labour Commissioner shall facilitate any discussion concerning the establishment of a forum for workers participation in any workplace taking into account any code of good practice published by the Council on workers participation.

[Act No.24 of 2015 s.9; Cap.4 s.8]

74. Disputes concerning collective agreements

Unless the parties to a collective agreement agree otherwise —

 (a) a dispute concerning the application, interpretation or implementation of a collective agreement shall be referred to the Commission for mediation; and

 (b) if the mediation fails, any party may refer the dispute to the Labour Court for a decision.

PART VII
STRIKES AND LOCKOUTS

75. Right to strike and to lockout

(1) Subject to the provisions contained in this Part —

 (a) every employee has the right to strike in respect of a dispute of interest; and

 (b) every employer has the right to lockout in respect of a dispute of interest.

76. Restrictions on right to strike or lockout

(1) No person shall take part in a strike or a lock out or in any way conduct himself in a manner contemplating or in furtherance of a strike or lockout if —

 (a) subject to the provisions of subsection (2), that person is engaged in an essential service referred to in section 77;

 (b) that person is engaged in a minimum service prescribed in section 79;

 (c) that person is bound by an agreement that requires the issue in dispute to be referred to arbitration;

 (d) that person is bound by a collective agreement or arbitration award that regulates the issue in dispute;

 (e) that person is bound by a wage determination that regulates the issue in dispute during the first year of that determination;

 (f) that person is a magistrate, a prosecutor or other court personnel;

 (g) the issue in dispute is a complaint;

 (h) the procedures prescribed in sections 80, 81 and 82 have not been followed.

(2) Notwithstanding the provisions of subsection (1)(a), a person engaged in an essential service may strike or lockout if —

 (a) there is a collective agreement providing for minimum services during a strike or lockout; and

 (b) that agreement has been approved under section 77 by the Essential Services

Committee.

(3) The following conduct associated with strikes and lockouts is prohibited:

(a) picketing —

(i) in support of a strike; or

(ii) in opposition to a lawful lockout;

(b) use of replacement labour in a lockout or a lawful strike;

(c) locking employers in the premises;

(d) preventing employers from entering the premises.

(4) For the purposes of this section, "replacement labour" means taking into employment any person to continue or maintain production during a strike or a lockout, but It does not include the deployment of an employee to do the work of an employee on strike or subject to a lockout provided that the deployment is with the consent of that employee. [Cap.4 s.8]

77. Essential services

(1) For the purposes of this section, "service" includes any part of service.

(2) The following services are essential services:

(a) water and sanitation;

(b) electricity;

(c) health services and associated laboratory services;

(d) fire-fighting services;

(e) air traffic control and civil aviation telecommunications;

(f) any transport services required for the provision of these services.

(3) In addition to the services designated in subsection (2), the Essential Services Committee may designate a service as essential if the interruption of that service endangers the personal safety or health of the population or any part of it.

(4) Before the Essential Services Committee designates an essential service under subsection (3), it shall —

(a) give notice in the prescribed manner of the investigation inviting interested parties to make representations;

(b) conduct an investigation in the prescribed manner;

(c) make any written representations available for inspection;

(d) hold a public hearing at which the interested parties may make oral representations; and

(e) consider those representations.

(5) Where the Essential Services Committee designates a service as an essential service, it shall publish a notice to that effect in the *Gazette*. [Cap.4 s.8]

(6) The Essential Services Committee may vary or cancel a designation made under this section in accordance with the procedure set out in subsections (4) and (5) *mutatis mutandis*.

(7) Any party to a dispute as to whether or not a service is an essential service or an employer or an employee is engaged in an essential service shall refer the dispute to the Essential Services Committee for determination.

(8) The party who refers the dispute to the Essential Services Committee shall satisfy the Committee that a copy of the dispute has been served on all the other parties to the dispute.

(9) The Essential Services Committee shall determine the dispute as soon as possible.

78. Disputes of interest in essential services

(1) Unless a collective agreement provides otherwise —
- (a) any party to a dispute of interest in an essential service may refer the dispute to the Commission for mediation.
- (b) if the mediation fails, any party to the dispute may refer the dispute to arbitration by the Commission.

(2) The provisions of subsection (1) shall apply if —
- (a) the parties are bound by a collective agreement providing for minimum services during a strike or lockout; and
- (b) the Essential Services Committee has approved that agreement in terms of section 79(2).

79. Minimum services during strike or lockout

(1) The parties to a collective agreement may agree to the provision of minimum services during a strike or a lockout.

(2) Any party to a collective agreement that provides for minimum services during a strike or lockout in an essential service may apply in the prescribed manner to the Essential Services Committee for approval of that agreement.

(3) An employer may apply in the prescribed manner to the Essential Services Committee for the designation of a minimum service if —
- (a) a minimum service is necessary to prevent damage to property, machinery or plant during a strike or lawful lockout; and
- (b) there is no collective agreement providing for minimum services during a strike or lockout.

80. Procedure for engaging in lawful strike

(1) Subject to the provisions of this section, employees may engage in a lawful strike if —
- (a) the dispute is a dispute of interest;
- (b) the dispute has been referred in the prescribed form to the Commission for mediation;
- (c) the dispute remains unresolved at the end of period of mediation provided under section 86(4) read with subsections (1) and (2) of section 87;
- (d) the strike is called by a trade union, a ballot has been conducted under the union's constitution and a majority of those who voted were in favour of the strike; and
- (e) after the applicable period referred to in paragraph (c), they or their trade union have given forty eight hours notice to their employer of their intention to strike.

(2) Where the dispute relates to the unilateral alteration of terms and conditions of employment, the employees and the trade union, may require the employer in the referral of the dispute under subsection (1) [Cap.4 s.8] —
- (a) not to implement any proposed change to terms and conditions; or
- (b) if the employer has implemented the change, to restore the terms and conditions of

employment that applied before the change.

(3) Where the employer does not comply with the requirement referred to in subsection (2) within forty eight hours of service of the referral on the employer, the employees and trade union may strike without complying with paragraphs (c) to (e) of subsection (1). [Cap.4 s.8]

(4) Nothing in this section prevents a trade union and an employer or employers' association from agreeing to their own strike procedure in a collective agreement, in which case the provisions of that agreement shall apply and the provisions of subsections (1) to (3) shall not apply.

81. Procedure for engaging in secondary strike

(1) "secondary strike" means a strike that is —
   (a) in support of a lawful strike (the "primary strike") by other employees against their employer (the "primary employer"); or
   (b) in opposition to a lockout (the "primary lockout") imposed by another employer (the "primary employer") against its employees.

(2) A trade union may only call a secondary strike if —
   (a) fourteen days notice of the commencement of the secondary strike has been given to the secondary employer;
   (b) there is a relationship between the secondary and primary employer that may permit the exercise of pressure;
   (c) the secondary strike is proportional taking into account —
      (i) the effect of the strike on the secondary employer;
      (ii) the possible effect that the strike may have on resolving the dispute giving rise to the primary strike or primary lockout.

(3) Employees engaged in the following services are prohibited from engaging in a secondary strike:
   (a) the essential services referred to in section 77 in respect of which there is no approved collective agreement as prescribed in section 79(2); or
   (b) agreed or determined minimum services as prescribed in section 79.

(4) Nothing in this section shall prevent a trade union and an employer or an employers' association from agreeing to their own requirements and procedure in a collective agreement, in which case the provisions of that agreement shall apply and the provisions of subsections (1) and (2) shall not apply.

82. Procedure for engaging in lawful lockout

(1) Subject to the provisions of subsection (2), an employer may engage in a lawful lockout if —
   (a) the dispute is a dispute of interest;
   (b) the dispute has been referred in the prescribed form to the Commission for mediation;
   (c) the dispute remains unresolved at the end of the period of medication prescribed in sections 86 and 87;
   (d) after the applicable period referred to in paragraph (c) the employer or employers' association has given forty eight hours notice to the employees or their trade union of

the intention to lockout.

(2) Nothing in this section shall prevent a trade union and an employer or an employers' association from agreeing to their own procedure in a collective agreement, in which case the provisions of that agreement shall apply and the provisions of subsection (1) shall not apply.

83. Nature of protection of lawful strike or lockout

(1) Notwithstanding the provisions of any law, including the common law, a lawful strike or lawful lockout shall not be —

(a) a breach of contract;

(b) a tort;

(c) a criminal offence.

(2) An employer shall not terminate the employment of an employee for —

(a) participating in a lawful strike; or

(b) not acceding to an employer's demand in a lockout.

(3) No civil or criminal proceedings shall be instituted against any person for participating in a lawful strike or lawful lockout.

(4) Notwithstanding the provisions of subsection (1), an employer shall not be obliged to remunerate an employee for services that the employee does not render during a lawful strike or lawful lockout, however —

(a) the employer shall continue to make its contribution and the employee's contributions to any funds that the employee is required to belong to by law or under the contract of employment during the strike or lockout;

(b) if the employer provides accommodation, the provision of food or other basic amenities of life, the employer shall continue to provide that accommodation, food or amenities during the strike or lockout;

(c) after the end of the strike or lockout, the employer may —

(i) deduct any of the employee's contributions referred to in paragraph (a) from the employee's remuneration;

(ii) deduct the agreed monetary value of the accommodation, food or amenities from the employee's remuneration with the consent of the employee.

(5) Where an employee does not consent to the deduction prescribed in subsection (4)(c)(ii), the employer may refer the dispute to mediation.

(6) Where the dispute referred to in subsection (5) is not resolved, the employer may refer it to the Labour Court for a decision.

(7) Nothing in subsection (4) shall prevent a trade union or employer or employers' association from concluding a collective agreement that regulates the matters dealt with in that subsection differently.

84. Strikes and lockouts not in compliance with this Part

(1) Where a strike or lockout is not in compliance with this Act, or a trade union or employer or employers' association engages in prohibited conduct, the Labour Court shall have exclusive jurisdiction —

(a) to issue an injunction to restrain any person from —
  (i) participating in an unlawful strike or lockout;
  (ii) engaging in any prohibited conduct;
(b) to order the payment of just and equitable compensation for any loss attributable to the strike, lockout or conduct, having regard to —
  (i) the degree of fault;
  (ii) the cause of the strike, lockout or conduct;
  (iii) any prior history of non-compliance;
  (iv) the ability to pay;
  (v) the extent of the harm;
  (vi) the interests of collective bargaining;
  (vii) the duration of the strike, lockout or conduct.

(2) The Labour Court may not issue an injunction unless fourty eight hours notice of the application has been given to the respondent.

(3) Notwithstanding the provisions of subsection (2), the Court may grant a shorter period on good cause and only if the respondent is given a reasonable opportunity to be heard.

(4) Other than in exceptional circumstances, the Labour Court may not make an order of compensation that may cause a trade union, employer or employer's association to become bankrupt.

85. Protest action

(1) Subject to the provisions of subsection (2), an employee may take part in protest action if —
  (a) the protest action has been called by a registered trade union or registered federation of trade unions;
  (b) the union or federation has served a notice on the Council stating —
    (i) the reasons for the protest action; and
    (ii) the duration and form of the protest action;
  (c) thirty days have elapsed from the date the notice was served; and
  (d) the union or federation has given at least fourteen days notice of the commencement of the protest action.

(2) Employees engaged in the following services are prohibited from engaging in protest action:
  (a) the essential services referred to in section 77 in respect of which there is no approved collective agreement as prescribed in section 79(2); or
  (b) agreed or determined minimum services as prescribed in section 79.

(3) The Council shall convene a meeting within thirty days of the notice to —
  (a) resolve the matter giving rise to the protest action; and
  (b) if unable to resolve the matter, secure an agreement with the trade unions or federation of trade unions calling for the protest action on the duration and form of the protest action in order to minimise the harm that may be caused by the protest

action.

(4) In order to achieve the objects prescribed in subsection (3), the Council may —

(a) establish a tripartite committee to perform its functions under subsection (3);

(b) appoint a mediator after consultation with the Commission to mediate;

(c) apply to the Labour Court for a declaratory order prescribed in subsection (5).

(5) Any person who is likely to be, or has been, affected by the protest action may apply to the Labour Court for —

(a) an order restraining any person from taking part in protest action or in any conduct in contemplation or furtherance of an action that does not comply with the provisions of subsections (1) and (2);

(b) a declaratory order on the proportionality of any proposed action taking into account —

(i) the nature and the duration of the protest action;

(ii) the importance of the reasons for the protest action; and

(iii) the steps taken by the union or the federation to minimise the harm caused by the protest action.

(6) Subject to the provisions of subsection (7), any person who takes part in protest action that complies with this section enjoys the protections conferred on lawful strikes in terms of section 83.

(7) The protections conferred by subsection (6) on persons engaged in lawful protest action shall not apply to persons who do not comply with any declaratory order issued under paragraph (b) of subsection (5).

PART VIII
DISPUTE RESOLUTION

Sub-Part A: Mediation

86. Referral of disputes for mediation under this Act

(1) Disputes referred to the Commission shall be in the prescribed form.

(2) The party who refers the dispute under subsection (1), shall satisfy the Commission that a copy of the referral has been served on the other parties to the dispute.

(3) On receipt of the referral made under subsection (1) the Commission shall —

(a) appoint a mediator to mediate the dispute;

(b) decide the time, date and place of the mediation hearing;

(c) advise the parties to the dispute of the details stipulated in paragraphs (a) and (b).

(4) Subject to the provisions of section 87, the mediator shall resolve the dispute within thirty days of the referral or any longer period to which the parties agree in writing.

(5) The mediator shall decide the manner in which the mediation shall be conducted and if necessary may require further meetings within the period referred to in subsection (4).

(6) In any mediation, a party to a dispute may be represented by —

(a) a member or an official of that party's trade union or employers' association;

(b) an advocate; or

(c) a personal representative of the party's own choice.

(7) Where the mediator fails to resolve a dispute within the period prescribed in subsection (4), a party to the dispute may —

(a) if the dispute is a dispute of interest, give notice of its intention to commence a strike or a lockout in accordance with sections 80 or 82;

(b) if the dispute is a complaint —

(i) refer the complaint to arbitration; or

(ii) refer the complaint to the Labour Court.

(8) Notwithstanding the failure to resolve a dispute within the period stipulated in subsection (4), the mediator shall remain seized with the dispute until the dispute is settled and may convene meetings between the parties to the dispute in order to settle the dispute at any time before or during any strike, lockout, arbitration or adjudication.

[Act No.8 of 2006 Sch.]

87. Consequences of not attending mediation hearing

(1) Where the employees or a trade union refer a dispute of interest to the Commission under section 86, the mediator may —

(a) extend the period stipulated under section 86(4) by a further thirty days if the employees or union fail to attend the hearing arranged by the Commission;

(b) shorten the period stipulated in section 86(4) if the employer or employers' association party to the dispute fail to attend the hearing.

(2) Where an employer or an employers' association refers a dispute of interest to the Commission under section 86, the mediator may —

(a) extend the period stipulated under section 86(4) by a further thirty days if the employer or employer's association fails to attend the hearing arranged by the Commission;

(b) shorten the period stipulated in section 86(4) if the employees or trade union party to the dispute fail to attend the hearing.

(3) In respect of a complaint referred under this Act, the mediator may —

(a) dismiss the complaint if the party who referred the complaint fails to attend a mediation hearing;

(b) decide the complaint if the other party to the complaint fails to attend a mediation hearing.

(4) The decision made under this section may be enforced in the Labour Court as a decree of a court of competent jurisdiction.

(5) The Commission may reverse a decision made under this section —

(a) application is made in the prescribed manner; and

(b) the Commission is satisfied that there are good grounds for failing to attend the hearing.

Sub-Part B: Arbitration
88. Resolving disputes by compulsory arbitration

(1) For the purposes of this section, a dispute means —
  (a) a dispute of interest if the parties to the dispute are engaged in an essential service;
  (b) a complaint over —
    (i) the fairness or lawfulness of an employee's termination of employment;
    (ii) any other contravention of this Act or any other labour law or breach of contract or any employment or labour matter falling under common law, tortious liability and vicarious liability;
    (iii) any dispute referred to arbitration by the Labour Court under section 94(3)(a)(ii).

(2) Where the parties fail to resolve a dispute referred to mediation under section 86, the Commission shall [Cap.4 s.8]—
  (a) appoint an arbitrator to decide the dispute;
  (b) determine the time, date and place of the arbitration hearing; and
  (c) advise the parties to the dispute of the details stipulated in paragraph (a) or (b).

(3) Nothing in subsection (2) shall prevent the Commission from —
  (a) appointing an arbitrator before the dispute has been mediated;
  (b) determining the time, date and place of the arbitration hearing, which date may coincide with the date of the mediation hearing;
  (c) advising the parties to the dispute of the details stipulated in paragraphs (a) and (b).

(4) The arbitrator —
  (a) may conduct the arbitration in a manner that the arbitrator considers appropriate in order to determine the dispute fairly and quickly;
  (b) shall deal with the substantial merits of the dispute with the minimum of legal formalities.

(5) Subject to the discretion of the arbitrator as to the appropriate form of the proceedings, a party to the dispute may give evidence, call witnesses, question witnesses, and present arguments.

(6) Where the parties to the dispute consent, the arbitrator may suspend proceedings and resolve the dispute through mediation. [Cap.4 s.8]

(7) A mediator may, by an agreement between the parties or on application by the parties, draw a settlement agreement in respect of any dispute pending before him, which shall be signed by the parties and the mediator, and such agreement shall be deemed to be a decree of the Court.

(8) Where a party fails to —
  (a) attend any arbitration proceedings convened by arbitrator, the matter may be heard ex-parte as provided for under rule 28 of the Labour Institutions (Mediation and Arbitration Guidelines) Rules; [G.N. No.67 of 2007] or
  (b) comply with any direction made by the arbitrator, the arbitrator shall proceed to make the award.

(9) In any arbitration hearing, a party to a dispute may be represented by —

    (a) member or official of that party's trade union or employers' association;

    (b) an advocate; or

    (c) a personal representative of the party's own choice.

(10) An arbitrator may make any appropriate award but may not make an order for costs unless a party or a person representing a party acted in a frivolous or vexatious manner.

(11) Within thirty days of the conclusion of the arbitration proceedings, the arbitrator shall issue an award with reasons signed by the arbitrator.

[Acts Nos.8 of 2006 Sch.; 17 of 2010 s.12]

89. Effect of arbitration award

(1) An arbitration award made under this Act shall be binding on the parties to the dispute.

(2) An arbitration award made under this Act may be served and executed in the Labour Court as if it were a decree of a court of law.

90. Correction of arbitration award

An arbitrator who has made an award under section 88(10) may, on application or on his own motion, correct in the award any clerical mistake or error arising from any accidental slip or omission.

[Act No.17 of 2010 s.13]

91. Revision of arbitration award

(1) Any party to an arbitration award made under section 88(10) who alleges a defect in any arbitration proceedings under the auspices of the Commission may apply to the Labour Court for a decision to set aside the arbitration award —

    (a) within six weeks of the date that the award was served on the applicant unless the alleged defect involves improper procurement;

    (b) if the alleged defect involves improper procurement, within six weeks of the date that the applicant discovers that fact.

(2) The Labour Court may set aside an arbitration award made under this Act on grounds that —

    (a) there was a misconduct on the part of the arbitrator;

    (b) the award was improperly procured;

    (c) the award is unlawful, illogical or irrational.

(3) The Labour Court may stay the enforcement of the award pending its decision.

(4) Where the award is set aside, the Labour Court may —

    (a) determine the dispute in the manner it considers appropriate;

    (b) make any order it considers appropriate about the procedures to be followed to determine the dispute.

[Act No.17 of 2010 s.14]

92. Application of Arbitration

The Arbitration Act, does not apply to an arbitration conducted by the Commission.

[Act Cap.15]

93. Voluntary arbitration

(1) Nothing in this Act prevents agreement to submit a dispute to arbitration.

(2) The provisions of the Arbitration Act, shall apply to any agreed submission of a dispute to arbitration provided that [Cap.4 s.8]—

(a) notwithstanding the provisions of section 3 of the Arbitration Act, any dispute may be submitted to arbitration;

(b) any reference to the High Court in the Arbitration Act shall be interpreted as referring to the Labour Court.

(3) A voluntary arbitration preferred under section 14(1)(b)(ii) of the Labour Institutions Act shall be dealt with by the Commission as if it were a compulsory arbitration referred to under subsections (2) to (9) of section 88. [Cap.300]

[Act No.17 of 2010 s.15; Cap.15]

Sub-Part C: Adjudication

94. Jurisdiction of Labour Court

(1) Subject to the Constitution of the United Republic of Tanzania, 1977, the Labour Court shall have exclusive jurisdiction over the application, interpretation and implementation of the provisions of this Act and over any employment or labour matter falling under common law, tortious liability, vicarious liability or breach of contract and to decide —

(a) appeals from the decisions of the Registrar made under Part IV;

(b) reviews and revisions of —

(i) arbitrator's awards made under this Part;

(ii) decisions of the Essential Services Committee made under Part VII;

(c) reviews of decisions, codes, guidelines or regulations made by the Minister under this Act;

(d) complaints, other than those that are to be decided by arbitration under the provisions of this Act;

(e) any dispute reserved for decision by the Labour Court under this Act; and

(f) applications including —

(i) a declaratory order in respect of any provision of this Act; or

(ii) an injunction.

(2) The Labour Court may refuse to hear a complaint if —

(a) the complaint has not been referred to mediation by the Commission under section 86; or

(b) the provisions of that section have not been complied with; and

(c) the application is not urgent.

(3) Where a party refers a dispute to the Labour Court, the Court may —

(a) if it is a dispute that is required to be referred to the Labour Court in terms of this Act —

(i) decide the dispute; or

(ii) refer the dispute to the Commission to be decided by arbitration;
(b) if it is a complaint that is required to be referred to arbitration —
(i) refer the complaint to the Commission for it to be dealt with under section 88;
(ii) decide the complaint provided that it may make an appropriate order as to costs.

[Acts Nos.8 of 2006 Sch.; 17 of 2010 s.16]

Sub-Part D: Dispute Procedure in Collective Agreements

95. Dispute resolution procedures in collective agreements

(1) Nothing in this Part shall prevent a trade union on the one hand and an employer or employers' association on the other hand from concluding a collective agreement providing for the resolution of disputes not within the provisions of this Part.

(2) A collective agreement may depart from the provisions of this Part provided that the disputes are mediated or arbitrated in an independent, neutral, expedited and professional manner.

(3) A person bound by a collective agreement prescribed in this section may not refer a dispute to the Commission for Mediation and Arbitration under the provision of this Part:

Provided that, any dispute which is not resolved shall be referred by any party to the dispute or the mediator or arbitrator to the Labour Court for adjudication, decision and execution.

(4) Subject to the Provisions of subsection (3), any resolution made or award passed by the mediator or arbitrator respectively, shall be binding on the parties and shall be executed as a decree of the Labour Court.

(5) On application, the Labour Court, may set aside a provision of a collective agreement that does not comply with subsection (2).

[Act No.8 of 2006 Sch.]

PART IX
GENERAL PROVISIONS

96. Records to be kept by employers and employees

(1) Every employer and employee shall keep a record of the following information —
(a) the written particulars prescribed in section 15 and any changes to those particulars;
(b) any remuneration paid to the employee.

(2) Every employer shall retain the record of an employee prescribed in subsection (1) for a period of five years after the termination of that employee.

(3) An employer shall keep a record of the prescribed details of anystrike, lockout or protest action involving its employees.

(4) The Labour Commissioner, in the prescribed manner, may require information based on the records referred to in this section from an employer.

(5) An employer shall submit to the Labour Commissioner any information required in terms of subsection (4).

(6) Subject to the provisions of section 101, the Labour Commissioner may —

(a) compile, analyse and tabulate statistics collected from the information submitted under this section; and

(b) upon the Minister's direction publish those statistics.

97. Service of documents

(1) A document required to be served on a registered organization or federation in any civil or criminal proceedings shall be deemed to be duly served if it is —

(a) delivered to the registered office of the organisation or federation;

(b) delivered by registered post to its postal address; or

(c) served personally on an officer of the organisation or federation.

(2) For the purposes of this section, a "document" includes any notice, referral, submission, application or other document required to be served under this Act.

98. Regulations

(1) The Minister may, in consultation with the Council, make regulations and prescribe forms for the purpose of carrying out or giving effect to the principles and provisions of this Act.

(2) In particular and without prejudice to the generality of the powers conferred by subsection (1), the Minister may make regulations for or in respect of all or any of the following matters:

(a) all matters stated or required in this Act to be prescribed;

(b) the prohibition or regulation of employment of children under the age of eighteen years;

(c) the registration of plans for eliminating discrimination in the workplace;

(d) the form and manner in which written particulars of employment are to be given to an employee;

(e) regulating the payment of wages including payment of any money due to a deceased employee to the heirs or estate of that employee;

(f) the form and content of information and documentation to be supplied by the employer to its employees;

(g) regulating the procedure of registration of organisations and federations, the registers to be kept and the certificate of registration;

(h) the authorisation of access by trade union officials to employer premises for the purpose of recruiting, meeting and representing members;

(i) the deduction of trade union dues including authorisation and remittance of money to the registered trade union;

(j) the procedure for the recognition of registered trade unions;

(k) the lodgement of collective agreements with the Labour Commissioner;

(l) the procedure for investigations by the Essential Services Committee into essential services and minimum services;

(m) the books, records, accounts and other documents to be kept under this Act;

(n) the information to be furnished by an employer to the Labour Commissioner;

(o) the returns to be rendered by the employer to the Labour Commissioner;

(p) the fees to be charged for registration or any other service or matter prescribed or permitted by this Act;

(q) occupational safety and health standards and the working environment secured by an appropriate system of inspection; and

(r) generally for all matters incidental to or connected with the matters or subjects specifically mentioned in this Act.

(3) The Minister, after consultation with the Council, may, by notice in the *Gazette*, deem any category of persons to be employees for the purposes of this section, any provisions of this Act or any other written law in respect of which the Minister is responsible.

99. Guidelines and codes of good practice

(1) The Minister, after consulting the Council, may —

(a) issue codes of good practice;

(b) issue guidelines for the proper administration of this Act;

(c) change or replace any code or guideline.

(2) Any code of good practice or guideline or any change to, or replacement of, a code or guideline shall be published in the *Gazette*.

(3) Any person interpreting or applying this Act shall take into account any code of good practice or guideline published under this section, and where that person departs from the code or guideline, he shall justify the grounds for departure.

100. Exemptions

(1) The Minister may exempt any employer or class of employers from any employment standard contained in sections 19, 20, 23 to 25, 27, 31 to 34, 41, 42 and 43.

(2) Before the Minister grants an exemption under this section —

(a) the employer or employers' organisation shall satisfy the Minister that they have consulted with the employees affected by the exemption or their registered trade union;

(b) he shall notify the affected employers and employees or their registered organisations of any proposed exemption and request representations to be submitted within a reasonable period;

(c) he shall take into account any representations made by the employees or their registered trade union;

(d) he shall strike a fair balance between the interests of the employers and their employees, taking into account any applicable International Labour Organisation Convention or recommendation.

(3) An exemption granted under subsection (1) shall —

(a) be in the prescribed form signed by the Minister, and the form shall include a statement of the employers, or category of employers affected by the exemption;

(b) include any conditions under which the exemption is granted;

(c) state the period of the exemption, which may be made retrospective to a date not earlier than the date of the application for exemption; and

(d) if the exemption is granted to a class of employers, be published in the *Gazette*.

(4) An exemption granted under this section may be amended or withdrawn by the Minister.

(5) If the exemption is published in the *Gazette* under subsection (3)(d), the Minister may amend or withdraw the exemption only by notice in the *Gazette* from a date stated in that notice.

(6) Any person who is aggrieved by the grant, amendment or withdrawal of an exemption or its terms or period, may apply for the review of the decision in the Labour Court.

101. Confidentiality

(1) Subject to the provisions of subsection (2), it is an offence for any person to disclose any information relating to the financial or business affairs of another person if that information was acquired in the performance of any function or the exercise of any power under this Act.

(2) Subsection (1) does not apply if the information is disclosed incompliance with this Act —

(a) to enable a person to perform a function or exercise a power under this Act;

(b) in accordance with any written law;

(c) for the purpose of the proper administration of this Act;

(d) for the purposes of the administration of justice.

102. Penalties

(1) A District Court and a Resident Magistrate's Court have jurisdiction to impose a penalty for an offence under this Act.

(2) Any person convicted of any of the offences referred to in sections 5 and 6, may be sentenced to —

(a) a fine not exceeding five million shillings;

(b) imprisonment for a term of one year; or

(c) both such fine and imprisonment.

(3) Any person convicted of any of the offences referred to in sections 7, 8 and 9 may be sentenced to a fine not exceeding five million shillings.

(4) Any person convicted of any of the offences referred to in sections 27, 28, 45(3) and 101 shall be sentenced to a fine not exceeding one million shillings.

(5) Any person aggrieved by the decision of a court under this section may appeal to the High Court.

102A. Inconsistency with written laws

In case of conflict between this Act and any other written law relating to employment standards, the standards stipulated under this Act shall prevail.

[Act No.24 of 2015 s.10]

103. Repeal and amendment of laws and savings provisions

(1) The laws specified in the Second Schedule are repealed subject to the savings and transitional provisions set out in the Third Schedule.

(2) Each of the laws specified in the Second Schedule are amended to the extent specified in that Schedule.

(3) The Third Schedule governs the transition from the administration of the laws repealed under paragraph (1) to the administration of the matters in this Act.

FIRST SCHEDULE

(*Made under section 26(1)*)

Table for calculation of comparable wage rates

For the purpose of this Table —

"ordinary hours" do not include overtime hours;

"ordinary days" mean the days the employee ordinarily works in a week excluding any day falling within the weekly rest period stipulated in section 24;

"rate" is based on the employee's basic wage.

Table — Calculation of comparable wage rates

Basis of payment	To calculate hourly rates	To calculate daily rates	To calculate weekly rates	To calculate monthly rates
Employees whose basic wage is set by the hour		Multiply the hourly rate by the number of ordinary hours of work each day	Multiply the hourly rate by the number of ordinary hours of work each week	Calculate the weekly rate, then Multiply the calculated weekly rate by 4 333
Employees whose basic wage is set by the day	Divide the daily rate by the number of ordinary hours of work each day		Multiply the daily rate by the number of ordinary days of work each week	Calculate the weekly rate, then Multiply the calculated weekly rate by 4 333
Employees whose basic wage is set by the week	Divide the weekly rate (or calculated weekly rate) by the number of ordinary hours of work each week	Divide the weekly rate (or calculated weekly rate) by the number of ordinary days of work each week		Multiply the weekly rate (or calculated weekly rate) by 4 333
Employees whose basic wage is set by the month	Divide the monthly rate by 4 333 times the number of hours ordinarily worked each week	Divide the monthly rate by 4 333 times the number or days ordinarily worked each week	Divide the monthly rate by 4 333	

SECOND SCHEDULE

(*Made under section 103(1)*)

Citation of law	Extent of repeal
Employment Ordinance (Cap.366)	The whole
Regulation of Wages and Terms of Employment Ordinance (Cap.300)	The whole
Wages and Salaries (General Revision) Act, 1974 (Act No.22 of 1974)	The whole

Continued

Citation of law	Extent of repeal
Trade Union Act, 1998 (Act No.10 of 1998)	The whole
Security of Employment Act (Cap.574)	The whole
Severance Allowances Act (Cap.487)	The whole
Industrial Court of Tanzania Act, 1967 (Act No.41 of 1967)	The whole

THIRD SCHEDULE

(Made under section (103)(2), (3))
Savings and Transitional provisions

1. Interpretation

In this Schedule, unless the context requires otherwise —

"employers organisation" means an employer's organisation registered under the Trade Unions Act;

"federation" means a federation registered under the Trade Unions Act;

"repealed laws" means the laws repealed under section 103 (1) and listed in the Second Schedule; [Cap 4. s.8]

"trade union" means a trade union registered under the Trade Unions Act;

"Trade Unions Act" means the Trade Unions Act, 1998. [Act No.10 of 1998]
[Act No.10 of 1998]

2. Existing trade unions employer's organization and federations

(1) A trade union, employer's organisation or federation registered under the repealed laws immediately before the commencement of this Act, shall be deemed to be registered under this Act.

(2) As soon as practicable after the commencement of this Act, the Registrar shall —
- (a) enter the names and details of the trade unions, employers' organisations and federations into the appropriate registers prescribed under section 48 (5)(a) of this Act;
- (b) issue a certificate in terms of section 48 (5)(b) of this Act to the trade unions, employers' organisations and federations referred to in paragraph (a).

(3) If any provision of the constitution of a trade union, employers' organisation or federation does not comply with the requirements of sections 46 and 47 of this Act, the trade union, employers organisation or federation shall rectify its constitution and submit the rectifications to the Registrar within 6 months of the commencement of this Act.

(4) The provisions of section 50, shall apply *mutatis mutandis* in respect of a rectification under subparagraph (3).

(5) If a trade union, employers' organisation or federation fails to comply with sub-paragraph (3) or fails to make the requisite changes, the Registrar shall apply to the Labour Court to cancel the registration of the trade union, employers' organisation or federation because of its failure to

comply with the provisions of this paragraph read together with sections 46 and 47 of this Act.

(6) Section 55, shall apply *mutatis mutandis* in respect of an application brought under subparagraph (5).

3. Pending applications for registration

(1) Any pending application for registration, alteration of name or constitution in terms of the repealed laws shall be dealt with as if the application had been made under this Act.

(2) When dealing with an application referred to in subparagraph (1), the Registrar may —

(a) condone any technical non-compliance with this Act;

(b) require the applicant to amend its application in order to comply with this Act.

4. Organizational rights and recognition

(1) For the purposes of this paragraph —

(a) "organisational rights" means any of the following rights:

(i) the right to trade union representation in the workplace including the right to a committee or a field branch;

(ii) the right to facilities for trade union representatives in the workplace;

(iii) the right to disclosure of information;

(iv) the right to deduction of trade union dues and levies;

(v) the right of access to the employer premises for the purposes of recruitment of members, meeting with members and representing members;

(b) "recognition" means any agreement or practice in terms of which a trade union is recognised under the repealed laws for the purposes of negotiating terms and conditions of employment.

(2) A trade union shall retain any organisational rights conferred by —

(a) any of the repealed laws for a period of three years;

(b) any collective agreement in force at the commencement of this Act until the agreement's expiry, except that, if the agreement expires within two years of the commencement of this Act, the agreement shall be extended for a further year as if the repealed laws had not been repealed.

(3) Any dispute referred to a labour officer under the repealed laws before the commencement of this Act shall be dealt with as if the repealed laws had not been repealed.

(4) Where a trade union is recognised at the commencement of this Act, the employer shall continue to recognise the trade union for a period of three years unless another trade union is recognised as the exclusive bargaining agent under section 67.

(5) Any dispute over any organisational rights or recognition conferred under there repealed laws shall be decided by the Labour Court as if the repealed laws had not been repealed.

5. Negotiated or voluntary agreements

(1) Any negotiated or voluntary agreement concluded before the commencement of this Act, whether or not the agreement has been registered by the Industrial Court under the repealed laws, shall be binding until its expiry provided that —

(a) if the agreement is due to expire after a year from the commencement of this Act, the agreement expires at the end of the year.

(b) subject to paragraph 4(2)(b), any renewal of any such agreement shall be done in terms of this Act.

(2) Any dispute arising from the application, interpretation or implementation of an agreement stipulated in sub-paragraph (1) shall be decided by the Labour Court as if the repealed laws had not been repealed.

6. The Employment Ordinance

Notwithstanding the repeal of the Employment Ordinance, the provisions of sections 100 and 102 relating to "provision of medicine and medical treatment" and "burial of deceased employees and dependants" shall continue to apply until they are repealed by another law.

7. Industrial Court awards

(1) Subject to sub-paragraph (3), any trade dispute stipulated in the repealed laws that arose before the commencement of this Act shall be dealt with as if those laws had not been repealed.

(2) Subject to sub-paragraph (3), any trade dispute referred to the Industrial Court under section 4 of the Industrial Court of Tanzania Act or referred to the Court as a trade enquiry under section 8 of that Act before the commencement of this Act shall be dealt with as if those laws had not been repealed.

(3) Notwithstanding sub-paragraphs (1) and (2), a strike or a lockout that commences after the commencement of this Act shall be dealt with in terms of this Act.

(4) Any revision or interpretation of an award made by the Industrial Court shall be done as if the repealed laws had not been repealed.

(5) Any award made by the Industrial Court under the repealed laws shall remain in force until the expiry of the award.

8. References to conciliation boards

Any reference concerning a summary dismissal or disciplinary penalty that takes place before the commencement of this Act shall be dealt with as if the repealed laws had not been repealed. [Cap.4 s.8]

9. Disputes referred to labour officers

Any dispute contemplated in the repealed laws arising before the commencement of this Act shall be dealt with as if the repealed laws had not been repealed.

10. References to Minister

Any reference to the Minister stipulated under the repealed laws shall be dealt with as if the repealed laws had not been repealed.

11. Maters before ordinary courts

(1) Any offence committed under the repealed laws before the commencement of this Act shall be dealt with as if the repealed laws had not been repealed.

(2) Any claim arising under the repealed laws before the commencement of this Acts shall be dealt with as if the repealed laws had not been repealed.

(3) Any suit or other civil proceedings commenced before the commencement of this Act shall be dealt with as if the repealed laws had not been repealed.

12. Minister may authorize Commission to perform functions of conciliation board and Industrial Court

(1) The Minister may, after consultation with the Commission, authorize the Commission by notice in the *Gazette* to perform the functions of conciliation boards or the industrial court in terms of paragraph 7 or 8 —

(a) in respect of the whole or any specified part of Mainland Tanzania;

(b) with effect from a date specified in the *Gazette*.

(2) The authorisation of the Commission under sub-paragraph (1) shall not affect the competence of a conciliation board or the industrial court in terms of paragraph 7 or 8 to decide or finalise any matter that is partly heard at the date specified in the *Gazette*.

13. Disputes originating from repealed laws

(1) All disputes originating from the repealed laws shall be determined by the substantive laws applicable immediately before the commencement of this Act.

(2) All disputes pending and all applications for executions filed arising from the decision of the Minister in the subordinate courts prior to the commencement of this Act shall proceed to be determined by such courts.

(3) All disputes pending —

(a) revision of the defunct Industrial Court of Tanzania shall be determined by a panel of three Judges of the Labour Court; and

(b) hearing before the Industrial Court of Tanzania shall be determined by the Labour Court.

(4) All appeals and applications for judicial review originating from the industrial Court of Tanzania pending in the High Court shall be determined by the High Court.

(5) The Commission shall have powers to mediate and arbitrate all disputes originating from the repealed laws brought before the Commission and all such disputes shall be deemed to have been duly instituted under section 86 of the Act.

(6) All references pending decision of the Minister shall —

(a) in the case of references which were returned by the High Court to the Minister for retrial, be determined and finalized by the Minister; and

(b) in the case of references pending the decision of the Minister be forwarded together with their respective complete records to the Labour Court for determination.

(7) The date of the decision of the Minister shall be the date indicated in the prescribed form.

(8) Notwithstanding the provisions of any other written laws, for the purposes of computation of limitation of time, the period between the date of decision and the date of receipt of the decision shall be excluded.

[Acts Nos.11 of 2010 s.42; 4 of 2016 s.24]

14. Minimum wages

(1) Notwithstanding the repeal of the Regulation of Wages and Terms of Employment Ordinance —

(a) the Minister may, within 3 years of the commencement of this Act —

(i) establish a minimum wage board under section 4 of the Ordinance; and

(ii) make, with the approval of the President, a wages regulation order under section 10 fixing a basic minimum wage;

(b) the relevant provisions of the Ordinance shall apply to a board established and an order made in terms of paragraph (a).

(2) Subject to subsection (3), a Wages Regulation Order published under the Regulation of Wages and Terms of Employment Ordinance, shall remain in force after the commencement of this Act.

(3) Where a wage determination is published under the Labour Institutions Act, any applicable wages regulations order stipulated in sub-paragraph (1) shall cease to apply to the employers and employees subject to the determination. [Cap.300; Cap.4 s.8]

[Ord No.15 of 1951]

15. Subsidiary legislation

Any subsidiary legislation made under the repealed laws shall remain in force until they are —

(a) repealed by the Minister; or

(b) replaced by subsidiary legislation made under this Act.

16. Hours of work domestic and security workers

Notwithstanding the provisions of section 19, the hours of work of domestic workers and security workers shall be a maximum of —

(a) 54 ordinary hours for the first year after the commencement of this Act;

(b) 51 ordinary hours for the second year after the commencement of this Act;

(c) 48 ordinary hours for the third year after the commencement of this Act; and

(d) 45 hours thereafter.

17. Written particulars

Each employer shall submit the written particulars contemplated in section 15 of this Act and applicable to an employee in employment at the commencement of this Act within a year of the commencement of this Act.

TITLE TEN
MINIMUM WAGE ORDINANCE (CHAPTER 300) [2022]

THE UNITED REPUBLIC OF TANZANIA

Supplement No.45 *25th November, 2022*

SUBSIDIARY LEGISLATION

To The Gazette Of The United Republic Of Tanzania

No 45 Vol.103 Dated 25th November, 2022

Printed By The Government Printer, Dodoma By Order Of Government

GOVERNMENT ANNOUNCEMENT NO.687 dated 25/11/2022

LABOR INSTITUTIONS ACT, (CHAPTER 300)

COMMAND

(Issued under section 39(1))

MINIMUM WAGE ORDER 2022

1. Name and take effect

This Order shall be known as the Minimum Order of Salary Year 2022 and will come into effect on January 1, 2023.

2. Usage

This decree will apply to all employees and employers in private sector.

3. Translation

In this Decree, unless the context otherwise requires —

"**agriculture**" shall include the production of crops, forestry activities, breeding and breeding of insects, pre-processing of agricultural produce and animals carried out by, or on behalf of, the operator of such activity including the use and repair of machinery, equipment, tools and agricultural machinery, including processing, storage, operation or transportation in agricultural activities involving Cooperatives related to agricultural production;

"**good standing agreements**" means a written agreement reached by a registered trade union and an employer or a registered employers' association on any matter of work;

"**business and industry**" includes the conduct of business, the provision of professional services or any similar activities for the purpose of earning income, unless they will not include mining and agriculture activities;

"**contractors**" includes civil engineers, buildings, machinery, electricians and special contractors;

"**domestic worker**" means any person who does domestic work in homes or households for wages;

"**employee**" has the meaning interpreted in the Employment Law no Relations at Work; [Chapter 366]

"**employer**" has the meaning assigned to it in the Employment and Relations Act At work; [Chapter 366]

"**energy**" includes all processes related to production or supply of energy from any source;

"**international companies**" means international organizations or international business companies involved in business in various countries;

"**mining activities**" shall have the meaning as

interpreted under the Mining Law, and shall not include any activity related to the production of salt or limestone; [Chapter 123]

"**big businessman**" means any person who engages in economic activities with high production and high profits;

"**private sector**" means any sector except the public sector;

"**small company**" means all companies except large or international companies;

"**large or tourist hotels**" means all hotels that are run at a high level with high profits including camps that provide accommodation and other services to tourists.

4. Sectors and areas

(1) Based on the provisions of this Decree, the sectors and areas of the minimum wage are established in the order set out in the First Table of this Decree.

(2) The calculation of comparable wage rates based on hours, days, weeks, fortnights or months, will be determined as specified in the First Table issued under section 26(1) of the Employment and Labor Relations Act. [Chapter 366]

(3) The minimum wage specified in the Second Table shall be considered the minimum wage paid to an employee in the relevant sector or area, and the employer may pay the employee more than the minimum unless he does not pay the employee less than the level set in the sector or the area concerned.

(4) Minimum wage rates may be improved through collective agreements or otherwise.

5. Employment standards

(1) Subject to the provisions of this Order, the employment rates applicable to all workers in each specified sector or area shall be as specified under Part III of Employment and Labor Relations Act, or as implemented in employment contracts and contracts of better conditions. [Chapter 366]

(2) In addition to annual leave with pay, an employee shall be entitled to leave allowance once in every two years of continuous service with the same employer.

(3) The employee shall be entitled to other allowances as agreed upon in the discussion between the employer and the employee.

(4) Notwithstanding the generality of this paragraph, the truck driver shall be entitled to an allowance for travel distance, overstaying outside the work station, loading and unloading as agreed upon in the negotiations between the drivers and the employers.

6. Employees who get better interests

If at the time this Order comes into force, any employee who receives a higher wage and better working conditions than those provided under this Order, that employee will continue to receive a higher wage and better working conditions, if employed by the same employer.

7. Canceled

Minimum Wage Ordinance 2013 is deleted.

[TS. And. 196 of 2013]

FIRST TABLE

(Made under paragraph 4(1))

MINIMUM WAGE SECTORS AND REGIONS

(a) Agricultural sector;

(b) Health sector;

(c) Telecommunication industry;

(d) Domestic and hotel work;

(e) Personal protection services;

(f) Energy sector;

(g) Transportation industry;

(h) Construction industry;

(i) Mining industry;

(j) Private school services;

(k) Business and industrial sector;

(l) Fishing and marine services industry;

(m) Other industry.

SECOND TABLE

(Made under paragraph 4(3))

MINIMUM WAGES

	Sectors and Areas	Time	Level (TZS)
1.	The agricultural sector	Weather Day A week Two weeks The month	718 5 385 32 310 64 620 140 000
2.	The health industry	Weather Day A week Two weeks The month	1 000 7 501 45 003 90 007 195 000
3.	Communication industry		
	(a) Communication services	Weather Day A week Two weeks The month	2 564 19 232 115 394 230 787 500 000
	(b) Advertising and media, postal and parcel delivery services	Weather Day A week Two weeks The month	1 154 8 654 51 927 103 854 225 000

Continued

	Sectors and Areas	Time	Level (TZS)
4.	Domestic and hotel work (a)		
	domestic workers employed by diplomats and big businessmen	Weather Day A week Two weeks The month	1 282 9 616 57 697 115 393 250 000
	(b) domestic workers employed by qualified officers	Weather Day A week Two weeks The month	1 026 7 693 46 157 92 315 200 000
	(c) domestic workers, except those employed by diplomats, big businessmen and eligible officials who do not live in the employer's household	Weather Day A week Two weeks The month	615 4 616 27 694 55 389 120 000
	(d) domestic workers other than at home who are not specified in paragraphs (a), (b) and (c) above	Weather Day A week Two weeks The month	308 2 308 13 847 27 694 60 000
	(e) large or tourist hotels	Weather Day A week Two weeks The month	1 539 11 539 69 236 138 472 300 000
	(f) hotels for floors	Weather Day A week Two weeks The month	923 6 924 41 542 83 083 180 000
	(g) restaurants, lodges and bars	Weather Day A week Two weeks The month	769 5 770 34 618 69 236 150 000
5.	Private security services (a) large		
	and international companies	Weather Day A week Two weeks The month	1 139 8 539 51 235 102 469 222 000

Continued

Sectors and Areas		Time	Level (TZS)
	(b) small companies	Weather Day A week Two weeks The month	759 5 693 34 156 68 313 148 000
6.	Energy sector (a)		
	international companies	Weather Day A week Two weeks The month	3 036 22 771 136 626 273 252 592 000
	(b) small companies	Weather Day A week Two weeks The month	1 154 8 654 51 927 103 854 225 000
7.	Transport industry (a) air		
	transport services	Weather Day A week Two weeks The month	2 000 15 001 90 007 180 014 390 000
	(b) cargo delivery and distribution services	Weather Day A week Two weeks The month	1 846 13 847 83 083 166 167 360 000
	(c) land transport services	Weather Day A week Two weeks The month	1 539 11 539 69 236 138 472 300 000
8.	Construction industry		
	(a) Contractors Class I	Weather Day A week Two weeks The month	2 154 16 155 96 931 193 861 420 000

Continued

	Sectors and Areas	Time	Level(TZS)
	(b) Contractors Class II – IV	Weather Day A week Two weeks The month	1 846 13 847 83 083 166 167 360 000
	(c) Contractors Class V – VII	Weather Day A week Two weeks The month	1 641 12 309 73 852 147 704 320 000
9.	Mining industry (a)		
	with mining and prospecting licenses	Weather Day A week Two weeks The month	2 564 19 232 115 394 230 787 500 000
	(b) holders of small-scale mining licences	Weather Day A week Two weeks The month	1 539 11 539 69 236 138 472 300 000
	(c) business license holders	Weather Day A week Two weeks The month	2 308 17 309 103 854 207 708 450 000
	(d) licensed brokers	Weather Day A week Two weeks The month	1 282 9 616 57 697 115 393 250 000
10.	Private school services (primary, primary and secondary) Hours	Weather Day A week Two weeks The month	1 062 7 962 47 773 95 546 207 000
11.	Business and industry sector (a) business		
	and industry	Weather Day A week Two weeks The month	769 5 770 34 618 69 236 150 000

Continued

	Sectors and Areas	Time	Level(TZS)
	(b) financial institutions	Weather Day A week Two weeks The month	3 036 22 771 136 626 273 252 592 000
12.	Fishing and marine services industry	Weather Day A week Two weeks The month	1 221 9 155 54 927 109 855 238 000
13.	Other industries not specified in this Order	Weather Day A week Two weeks The month	769 5 770 34 618 69 236 150 000

Dodoma,

16 November, 2022

JOYCE L. WHAT I HAD

Minister of State, Prime Minister's Office, Labour,

Youth, Employment and the Disabled

GROUP THREE
SPECIAL ECONOMIC LAWS AND REGULATIONS

TITLE ELEVEN
EXPORT PROCESSING ZONES ACT
(CHAPTER 373) [2002] [Revised Edition 2012]

THE UNITED REPUBLIC OF TANZANIA
THE EXPORT PROCESSING ZONES ACT
CHAPTER 373 OF THE LAWS
[PRINCIPAL LEGISLATION]

REVISED EDITION OF 2012

THE UNITED REPUBLIC OF TANZANIA
THE EXPORT PROCESSING ZONES ACT

CHAPTER 373 OF THE LAWS
[PRINCIPAL LEGISLATION]
REVISED EDITION OF 2012

This Edition of the Export Proccssing Zones Act, Cap.373, replaces the Revised Edition of 2006, incorporates all amendments made up to and including 31 Dccember, 2012 and is printed under the authority of section 4 of the Laws Revision Act, Cap.4 and published under Government Notice No 206 of 2013

Dar es Salaam,
21st June, 2013

FREDERICK M. WEREMA,
Attorney General

CHAPTER 373
THE EXPORT PROCESSING ZONES ACT

An Act to make provisions for establishment, development and management of the Export Processing Zones; for the creation of international competitiveness for export growth and to provide for related matters

[1st July, 2002]
[G.N. No.316 of 2002]

Acts Nos.
11 of 2002,
3 of 2006
2 of 2011

PART I
PRELIMINARY PROVISIONS

1. Short title and application

(1) This Act may be cited as the Export Processing Zones Act.

(2) [Omitted].

(3) This Act shall apply to Mainland Tanzania.

2. Interpretation

In this Act, unless the context requires otherwise —

"**Act**" means the Export Processing Zones Act;

"**Authority**" means the Export Processing Zones Authority established under section 12 of this Act;

"**Board**" means the Board established under section 14 (1) of the Act;

"**Commissioner-General**" means the Commissioner-General of the Tanzania Revenue Authority as defined under the Tanzania Revenue Authority Act; [Cap.399]

"**customs territory**" means the area in the United Republic of Tanzania which is not within an area declared to be an Export Processing Zone;

"**Export Processing Zone**" means an area of land which has been so established or so declared in accordance with section 3(1) of the Act;

"**foreign market**" means any market other than those located in the customs territory;

"**investor**" means a company incorporated in the United Republic which makes application for, and is licensed by the Authority to manufacture and export industrial products from the Export Processing Zones to foreign markets and includes a person who provides infrastructure necessary for development of an area established or declared to be the Export Processing Zone;

"**joint venture**" means an association whether incorporated or unincorporated, between a foreign investor and a local co-operative or parastatal organisation, a foreign investor and a local private investor, a domestic private investor and a local parastatal and co-operative organisation, a foreign investor and another foreign investor, for purposes of making an investment jointly in an Export Processing Zone;

"**licence**" means an official permit granted by the Authority upon application by an investor to conduct business transactions within an Export Processing Zone;

"**manufacture**" means any operation or process to change the form of any material for value of use and includes assembling, processing, packaging and re-packaging;

"**Minister**" means the Minister responsible for industries;

"**single factory**" means an industrial estate which may be granted an Export Processing Zone status but which is not located in an Export Processing Zone estate;

"**tax relief period**" means the period specified in the licence during which an investor may not be required to pay tax and duties in relation to any business transaction carried by him.

[Acts Nos.3 of 2006 s.2; 11 of 2002; G.N. No.90 of 1969]

PART II
ESTABLISHMENT OR DECLARATION OF EXPORT PROCESSING ZONES

3. Establishment or declaration of EPZ

(1) The Minister may, upon the advice of the Board and in consultation with relevant authorities and on the recommendation of the Authority, by notice published in the *Gazette* —

    (a) establish or declare any area of land to be an Export Processing Zone; and

    (b) determine the location, extent, and physical characteristics or boundaries of an Export

Processing Zone contemplated in paragraph (a).

(2) Where the Minister has consulted relevant authorities pursuant to subsection (1) and the latter have, within a period of thirty days, not responded or given reason why any such area of land should not be established or declared to be the Export Processing Zone, it shall be presumed that such authorities have consented to the establishment or declaration of Export Processing Zone in the area of land in question.

(3) The Export Processing Zone established or declared as such may consist of a developed, partly developed or underdeveloped area of land or may comprise of a single factory unit or group of factory units.

[Act No.3 of 2006 s.2]

4. Objects and purposes of establishment of Export Processing Zone

The objects and purposes for which an Export Processing Zone may be established or declared are—

   (a) to attract and promote investment for export-led industrialisation with a view to diversifying and facilitating Tanzania's exports and promoting international competitiveness;

   (b) to create and expand foreign exchange earnings;

   (c) to create and increase employment and the development of skilled labour;

   (d) to attract and encourage transfer of new technology;

   (e) to foster linkages of the local economy with the international market; and

   (f) to promote processing of local raw materials for export.

PART III
LICENSING

5. Restriction on entering into, residing in, etc., the Export Processing Zones

(1) No person shall —

   (a) unless he is the holder of a licence granted by the Authority —

      (i) conduct any business or undertake a retail trade in an Export Processing Zone in respect of any goods manufactured in, or imported into, such Export Processing Zone; or

      (ii) remove any goods manufactured in an Export Processing Zone for any purpose other than conveyance to another Export Processing Zone or for export into a foreign market or for purposes of processing such goods only; or

      (iii) use any goods manufactured in an Export Processing Zone for consumption in such Export Processing Zone or in any other Export Processing Zone; or

   (b) unless authorised in writing by the Authority —

      (i) subject to the provisions of subsection (2), enter into an Export Processing Zone; or

      (ii) reside in an Export Processing Zone.

(2) The provisions of paragraph (b) (i) shall not apply to or in respect of —

(i) members of the Police Force; or

(ii) members of the public service; including customs officers or officers of the local government authorities; or

(iii) any person employed by an investor or an institution or company charged or authorised by law to supply any public utility, acting in the course of their respective duties and functions.

(3) The Authority may, by notice in writing addressed to he Investor, or any person who is in an Export Processing Zone

(a) impose conditions relating to the regulation, restriction or prohibition of entry of goods or categories of goods, into an Export Processing Zone;

(b) order such investor or person in an Export Processing Zone to, within a period of time prescribed in the notice, which shall not be less than fourteen days —

(i) remove from the Export Processing Zone any article, item or thing; or

(ii) discontinue any activity or operation in such Export Processing Zone, as the Authority may specify in such notice.

(4) An addressee who receives a Notice in accordance with the preceding subsection may, within seven days after receipt of such notice, make written representations to the Authority relating to any condition imposed by, or order contained in, such notice.

(5) Any person who contravenes the provision of subsection (1) or fails to comply with a notice issued pursuant to subsection (4) commits an offence and is liable on conviction —

(a) if such a person is a natural person, to a fine not exceeding fifteen million shillings or to imprisonment for a term not exceeding four years or to both;

(b) if such a person is not a natural person, to a fine not exceeding fifty million shillings.

[Act No.3 of 2006 s.2]

6. Authority to issue licence

(1) The Authority shall be responsible for the issuance of a licence to any person who wishes to carry on business or activity in an Export Processing Zone.

(2) The licence issued pursuant to subsection (1) shall operate as if it were a licence issued by competent authorities under the repealed Business Licensing Act and the National Industries (Licensing and Registration) Act. [Act No.25 of 1972; Cap.46]

(3) For the purposes of this section, the Authority shall consult the relevant authorities responsible for administration of the Busincss Activities Registration Act and the National Industries (Licensing and Registration) Act with a view to have a co-ordinated record of persons or company carrying on business in Tanzania. [Cap.208; Cap.46]

[Act No.3 of 2006 s.2]

7. Canccllation and suspension of a licence

(1) The Authority may, after issuing a thirty days written notice to the holder of the licence, cancel or suspend a licence if it is satisfied that the holder —

(a) without reasonable cause stated in writing, fails to establish the business or activity for which a licence was granted, within the time stipulated in a licence or any period which may be prescribed by the Authority; or

(b) suspends its activities in an Export Processing Zone for a period of more than six months without the prior consent of, or notification to, the Authority;

(c) without reasonable cause stated in writing, fails to comply with the terms of a licence or the provisions of this Part or any regulation or, upon request of extension of time made to the Authority and accepted by the licensee, fails to continue with the business for such period of time as may be prescribed in a licence or by the Authority in a notice to the holder of a licence.

(2) The Authority shall cancel the licence issued to the investor for carrying on a business or activity in an Export Processing Zone where such a liccnce holder has —

(a) failed to pay tax or evaded payment of tax in respect of any transaction eligible for taxation; or

(b) failed to comply with any of the provisions of this Act or of any regulation made under this Act or the condition subject to which such certificate was issued; or

(c) assigned to another person a licence without obtaining the prior approval of the Authority; or

(d) obtained such licence on the basis of fraud or deliberate submission of false or misleading information or statements.

(3) The holder of a licence may, within twenty-one days after receipt of the notice in terms of subsection (1), make written representations to the Authority, and the Authority shall take into consideration of such representation when deliberating on whether or not to cancel or suspend a licence.

[Act No.3 of 2006 s.2]

8. No variation of a licence

(1) The Authority shall not vary a licence and conditions attached to it, except where the holder has requested the Authority in writing to do so and such variation is necessary for purposes of causing the holder to better carry out the business or activity for which such a licence was issued.

(2) Where variation of a licence relates to extension of the tax relief period, such variation shall not extend the tax relief period originally granted to an investor.

[Act No.3 of 2006 s.2]

9. Appeal against a decision of the Authority

(1) Any person who is aggrieved by a decision of the Authority to reject an application for a licence, cancel or suspend a licence may appeal to the Minister who may confirm, vary or set aside the decision of the Authority.

(2) A person who is dissatisfied with the decision of the Minister made in pursuant to subsection (1) may, within thirty days from the date on which the decision of the Minister was made, appeal to the High Court.

[Act No.3 of 2006 s.2]

10. Prohibition of other activities

(1) No person shall, during the tax relief period, carry on any trade or business other than the trade or business in relation to which a licence was granted.

(2) Without prejudice to subsection(1), no person shall carry on the business of retail sales of articles produced or assembled in an Export Processing Zone except as may be determined and authorised by the Authority.

[Act No.3 of 2006 s.2]

11. Authority to determine certain goods or articles to be processed in Export Processing Zones

(1) The Authority shall determine the rightful products to be processed, produced or the type of services to be supplied in the Export Processing Zones.

(2) No goods or articles specified or referred to in this subsection shall, subject to the provisions of subsection (3), be manufactured, processed, produced or supplied and no such goods or articles shall be brought into, or be allowed to remain in an Export Processing Zone —

(a) firearms or ammunition, or other war materials as provided in the Arms and Ammunitions Act;

(b) dangerous explosives and other hazardous substances;

(c) drugs and narcotics.

[Act No.3 of 2006 s.2]

PART IV
EXPORT PROCESSING ZONES AUTHORITY

12. Establishment of the Authority

(1) There is hereby established an autonomous Government agency to be known as the Export Processing Zones Authority.

(2) The Authority shall be a body corporate and shall —

(a) have perpetual succession and a common seal;

(b) in its corporate name be capable of suing and be sued;

(c) subject to this Act, be capable of purchasing or otherwise acquiring, and or, alienating movable and immovable property.

[Act No.3 of 2006 s.4]

13. Objectives and functions of the Authority

(1) The Authority shall initiate, develop and manage the operations of the publicly owned export processing zones and for that purpose shall carry out duties and perform the functions as stipulated under this section.

(2) For purposes of initiating, developing and managing operations of the Export Processing Zones, the Authority shall —

(a) in consultation with the Minister responsible for lands and Minister responsible for local government authorities, acquire land in its name and lease or issue derivative rights to investors or erect thereon industrial and commercial buildings and lease such buildings to investors for undertaking thereon the Export Processing Zones licenced businesses;

(b) provide basic infrastructure for purposes of operations in the Export Processing Zones;

(c) provide within the Export Processing Zones utilities and a system of sewerage, drainage and removal of refuse and waste for the benefit of export processing zones investor and other users;

(d) prepare national and international programmes for appropriate promotion of the Export Processing Zones;

(e) ensure the provision of security and surveillance, property and equipment maintenance and availability of restaurants and food services;

(f) provide commercial information for the benefit of investors in the Export Processing Zones; and

(g) provide any other public utility as may be necessary for the betterment of operators and investors with the Export Processing Zones or consumers of products or services from the Export Processing Zones.

(3) In discharging the duties and performing the functions referred to in subscction (2), the Authority shall have powers to subcontract any person to execute any duty or perform any function provided for under subsection (2), and in particular, may license or enter into joint venture with private investors to develop Export Processing Zones' infrastructure.

(4) The Authorily may charge rent, dues and impose fees and charges for services rendered or facilities provided in the Export Processing Zones.

(5) The Authority may, in discharging the powers and duties conferred by this Act, provide such other services, perform such other duties and functions and exercise such powers as may be necessary to attain the spirit of this Act.

[Acts Nos.3 of 2006 s.4; 2 of 2011 s.5]

14. Establishment of the Export Processing Zones Authority's Board

(1) There is established for the Authority a Board to be known as the Export Processing Zones Authority Board.

(2) The Board shall consist of the following members —

(a) the Minister responsible for industries who shall be the Chairman;

(b) the Attorney-General;

(c) the Permanent Secretary of the Ministry responsible for finance;

(d) the Permanent Secretary of the Ministry responsible for water;

(e) the Permanent Secretary of the Ministry responsible for energy;

(f) the Permanent Secretary of the Ministry responsible for local government authorities;

(g) the Executive Secretary of the Planning Commission;

(h) the Commissioner General of the Tanzania Revenue Authority;

(i) the Commissioner for Lands;

(j) the Chairman of the Tanzania Private Sector Foundation; and

(k) the President of the Tanzania Chamber of Commerce, Industry and Agriculture.

(3) The Board may co-opt any other person to attend meetings of the Board.

(4) The Board may, from time to time, establish such committees as it may deem expedient to

discharge such duties and perform such functions as it may direct.

[Acts Nos.3 of 2006 s.4; 2 of 2011 s.6]

15. Functions and powers of the Board

(1) The Board shall be responsible for the performance of the functions and management of the affairs of the Authority.

(2) For the proper discharge of the functions of the Authority, the Board shall subject to any directions on matters of general policy which the Minister may give in that behalf, have the responsibility and power —

    (a) to develop Export Processing Zones' policies and to give general policy directions in relations to the development and operations of the Export Processing Zones;

    (b) to approve plans and programmes related to the establishment and development of Export Processing Zones;

    (c) to advise the Minister pursuant to section 3 of this Act;

    (d) to determine priority sectors to be promoted in a particular Export Processing Zones;

    (e) to approve specific financing requirements for the development of the Export Processing Zones;

    (f) to approve the budgets of the Authority;

    (g) to approve structure and manning levels of the Authority; and

    (h) to approve operational policies and staff remunerations.

(3) The Board shall have powers to regulate its own procedures.

[Acts Nos.3 of 2006 s.4; 2 of 2011 s.7]

(4) The Chairman shall preside at all meetings of the Board that he is present.

(5) Where the Chairman is absent, the members present shall elect one of their members to be the Chairman of that meeting.

(6) The decision of the Board shall be by majority votes of the members present and voting, in the cvent of an equality of votes, the Chairman of the meeting shall have a casting vote.

17. Director General and other employees

(1) The Board shall, after consultation with the Minister, appoint a Director General of the Authority on such terms and conditions as the Board may determine.

(2) The Director General shall be the Chief Executive Officer of the Authority and shall be directly responsible to the Board for the day to day administration of the affairs of the Authority.

(3) The Director General shall be the Secretary of the Board and may participate in its deliberations, but shall not be entitled to vote on any resolution or other matters before the Board.

(4) The Board may appoint or employ senior officers of the Authority on such terms and conditions as the Board may approve.

[Acts Nos.3 of 2006 s.4; 2 of 2011 s.4]

18. Sources of funds

(1) The sources of funds for the Authority shall include —

    (a) sums of money as may be appropriated by the Parliament for that purpose;

    (b) returns on investments in the Export Processing Zones' infrastructure and industrial shed;

(c) borrowing;

(d) such donations, grants or bequeathed as the Authority may receive from person or organisation associated with its duties in the Export Processing Zones as provided for in this Act;

(e) Proceeds from the rent and other services charges derived from the activities in the Export Processing Zones; and

(f) any other moneys received by or made available to the Authority for the purposes of performing its functions under this Act.

[Act No.3 of 2006 s.4]

19. Use of the authority funds

(1) The funds of the Authority shall be used for —

(a) initiating, developing and managing Export Processing Zones infrastructure in accordance with the provisions of this Act;

(b) providing utilities in the Export Processing Zones;

(c) rehabilitating and maintaining Export Processing Zones' infrastructure; and

(d) discharging liabilities arising out of implementation of this Act.

(2) Notwithstanding the provisions of subsection(1), the Authority shall retain all the moneys accrued for its continuous use in carrying out its functions.

[Act No.3 of 2006 s.4]

20. Management and auditing of the funds of the Authority

(1) The funds of the Authority shall be managed in accordance with the provisions of the Public Finance Act.

(2) The funds of the Authority shall be audited by the Controller and Auditor General or an Auditor appointed by him to act on his behalf.

(3) The Authority shall prepare an annual report on the implementation of the Export Processing Zones operations and submit the same to the Minister, who shall lay the report before the National Assembly.

[Act No.3 of 2006 s.4; Cap.348]

PART V
INVESTMENT INCENTIVES

21. Incentives granted for investments in the Export Processing Zones

(1) An investor in the Fixport Processing Zones shall be entitled to the following incentives —

(a) subject to compliance with applicable conditions and procedures, accessing the Export credit guarantee scheme;

(b) remission of customs duty, value added tax and any other tax charged on raw materials and goods of capital nature related to the production in the Export Processing Zones;

(c) exemption from any payment of corporate tax for an initial period of ten years and thereafter a corporate tax shall be charged at the arte specified in the Income Tax Act;

(d) exemption from payment of withholding tax on dividends and interest for the first ten years;

(e) exemption from payment of all taxes and levies imposed by local government authorities for products produced in the Export Processing Zones for a period of ten years;

(f) exemption from pre-shipment or destination inspection requirements;

(g) on-site customs inspection of goods in the Export Processing Zones;

(h) provisions of business visa at the point of entry to key technical, management and training staff for a maximum of two months, thereafter the requirements to obtain a residence permit, according to the Immigration Act, shall apply; [Cap.54]

(i) remission of customs duty, value added tax and any other tax payable in respect of importation of one administrative vehicle, ambulances, fire fighting equipment vehicles and up to two buses for employees transportation to and from the Export Processing Zones;

(j) treatment of goods destined into Export Processing Zones as transit cargo;

(k) exemption from value added tax on utility and wharfage charges;

(l) entitlement to an initial immigrant quota of up to five persons during the start up period and thereafter any application fro an extra person shall be submitted to the Authority which shall, in consultation with the Immigration Department and Commissioner for Labour, authorise any additional persons dcemed necessary taking into consideration the availability of qualified Tanzanians, complexity of the technology employed by the investor and agreements reached with the investor;

(m) access to competitive, modern and reliable services available within the Export Processing Zones; and

(n) unconditional transferability through any authorised dealer bank in freely convertible currency of —

(i) net profit or dividends attributable to the investment;

(ii) payments in respect of loan servicing where foreign loan has been obtained;

(iii) royalties, fees and charges in respect of any technology transfer agreement;

(iv) the remittance of proceeds (act of all taxes and other obligations) in the event of sale or liquidation of the business enterprises or any interest attributable to the investment; and

(v) payments of emoluments and other benefits to foreign personnel employed in Tanzania in connection with the business enterprise.

(2) The provision of paragraph (e) of subsection (1) shall not apply in relation to the goods manufactured and sold or otherwise off-loaded in the customs territory.

(3) The Authority may, subject to such conditions relating to the grant of investment incentives, recommend to the Board, variation, addition, alteration or general amendments to the

types of investment incentives to be granted to the persons who are doing business in the Export Processing Zones.

(4) where the Board is satisfied that the variation, addition, alteration or general amendments to the types of investment incentives be made, it shall submit proposals to the Minister responsible for finance who shall proceed to make the variation, addition, alteration or general amendments as may be neccssary.

[Acts Nos.3 of 2006 s.6; 2 of 2011 s.4; Cap.332; Cap.4 s.8(k)]

22. Restriction on exportation of goods into cusloms territory by Export Processing Zones Investment

(1) Goods which are subject to the exemption from taxes within an Export Proccssing Zones shall not be taken out of the zone except —

(a) as export outside the customs territory;

(b) as exports into the customs territory subject to —

(i) necessary permits being obtained from the customs authority;

(ii) payment of all applicable import duties, levies and other charges;

(iii) compliance with all customs procedures; and

(iv) the per centum of such exports not exceeding twenty per centum of the total annual production of the investors within the establishment.

(2) The Board may, depending on the nature of the industry or goods and market circumstances, authorise an investor to sell in the customs territory the amount exceeding that prescribed under subsection(1).

(3) All goods off-loaded for sale into the customs territory shall be liable to all applicable duties and taxes.

[Acts Nos.3 of 2006 s.7; 2 of 2011 s.4]

23. Work Permits for technical staff

(1) The Government shall provide work permits for management and technical staff for skills that are not locally available, the number of which shall be determined by the Authority after consultation with the Ministry responsible for Labour.

(2) Subject to the provisions of subsection (1), the Authority shall make recommendations to the Government with a view to exempt from payment of training levy, an investor who has trained local employees, the quantum of which shall be fifty percent of the said training levy.

[Act No.3 of 2006 s.5]

24. Authority may enter into contractual agreement

(1) The Authority may cnter into a contractual agrcement not inconsistent with this Act, with an investor on the grant of such investment incentives and the conduct of business within the Export Processing Zones.

(2) The contractual agreement entered into pursuant to subsection(1) may contain provisions binding on the United Republic in relation to a special licence or business transactions that may be conducted under a special licence —

(a) which guarantee special provisions for the payment of taxes, fees and other fiscal import;

(b) relating to the circumstances or the manner in which the Authority may exercise any discretion conferred on it by this Act or regulations made under this Act;

(c) relating to environmental matters, including matters which are project specific and not covered by any regulations of general application. Provisions intended to define the scope and, as may be appropriate in any particular case, limit the extent of the obligations or liabilities of the holder of a special licence.

(3) Where this Act or regulations confer on the Minister or the Authority a discretion to do anything, the Minister or, as the case may be, the Authority shall exercise such discretion subject to and in accordance with relevant stipulations contained in the contractual agreement entered into pursuant to the provisions of this section.

(4) The Authority shall refer the proposed contractual agreement to the Minister for purposes of obtaining approval in relation to the business transactions or project which the investor proposes to enter into.

[Act No.3 of 2006 s.5]

PART VI
APPLICATION AND DISAPPLICATION OF OTHER LAWS

25. Disapplication

[Disapplication of the Tanzania Investment Act.]

[Act No.3 of 2006 s.5]

26. Exemption of the Stamp Duty Act

No instrument executed in or outside an Export Processing Zone which relates to the transfer, hypothecation or lease of any movable or immovable properly and no any act to be performed or done in such an Export Processing Zone, or any document, certificate, instrument, report or record relating to any activity, action, operation, enterprise, project, undertaking or venture including —

(a) a mortgage bond;

(b) customs and excise documents;

(c) a hire purchase agreement or financial lease;

(d) an agreement of partnership;

(e) power of attorney;

(f) a deed of transfer;

(g) bills of exchange; or

(h) promissory notes.

shall be subject to any duty imposed under the Stamp Duty Act. [Cap.189]

[Cap.189; Act No.3 of 2006 s.5]

27. Application of Urhan Plauning

For the purposes of the Urban Planning Act and the rules relating to buildings in the Export

Processing Zones, a reference to a local government authority in any provision of those laws with regards to planning consent and building permit, shall be construed as a reference to the Authority.

[Act No.3 of 2006 Ss. 2&5]

28. Application of labour laws

The existing labour laws applicable in the United Republic shall apply *mutatis muandis* in the Export Processing Zones.

[Act No.3 of 2006 Ss. 2&5]

PART VII
ACQUISITION.COMPENSATION AND DISPUTES SETTLEMENT

29. Acquisition and compensation Acts

(1) No interest in or right over any property within the Export Processing Zones may be acquired by the Government except in accordance with the Constitution of the United Republic and the Land Acquisition Act.

(2) Where any property is acquired in accordance with subsection (1), the Government shall, subject to the provisions of section 25, pay the owner of such property just and prompt compensation in a freely convertible currency. [Act No.3 of 2006 Ss. 2&5]

[Cap.2; Cap.118]

30. Setlement of drputes

(1) If a person to whom the Export Processing Zone licence is to be issued pursuant to this Act so elects, a licence concerned may provide that any dispute between the holder of such licence and the Authority in respect of —

(a) any issue relating to the amount of, or any other matter in connection with any compensation payable in case of acquisition as provided under section 23; or

(b) the validity or continued validity of such licence; or

(c) any other dispute arising under this Act, shall be settled by arbitration —

(i) in accordance with the rules and procedures for arbitration of the International Centre for Settlement of Investment Disputes; or

(ii) within the framework of any bilateral or multilateral agreement on investment protection to which the Government of the United Republic and the country in which the investor is a national are signatories; or

(iii) in accordance with the rules and procedures for arbitration of the International Chamber of Commerce; or

(iv) in accordance with any other international machinery for the settlement of investment disputes by the parties.

(2) A licence referred to in subsection (1) which makes provision for arbitration shall constitute the consent of the holder of a licence and the Government to submit to arbitration.

(3) Any award in any arbitration contemplated in this section shall be final and binding on the

Government and the holder of the licence, and shall be enforceable, in the case of a foreign award, in accordance with the Convention on The Recognition and Enforcement of Foreign Arbitral Awards.

[Act No.3 of 2006 Ss.2&5]

31. Non-limitation for scttlement of disputes

Nothing in section 24 shall be construed —

(a) in the case where a licence referred to in subsection (1) of section 24 does not make provision for the settlement of disputes, as restricting or limiting the right of a holder of such licence to any other remedy available; or

(b) in the case where a licence referred to in subsection (1) of section 24 does make provision for settlement of disputes, as precluding a holder of such licence or the Authority from entering into an agrecment providing that any particular dispute specified or contemplated in such agreement shall not be settled otherwise than as provided in such licence.

[Act No.3 of 2006 Ss. 2&5]

32. Minister may make Regulations

The Minister may, in consultation with the Authority, make regulations generally for the better carrying out of the purposes of this Act.

[Act No.3 of 2006 Ss. 2&5]

PART VIII
OFFENCES

33. Offences relating to licences and foreign currency

Any person who —

(a) in or in connection with an application for granting of a licence; or

(b) for purposes of obtaining or retaining any foreign currency, makes any false statement which he or she knows to be false or have reason to believe not to be true, or knowingly furnishes any false information,

commits an offence and is liable on conviction to a fine not excceding fifteen million shillings or to imprisonment for a term not exceeding four years or to both.

[Act No.3 of 2006 s.5]

34. Offence for transhipment of products etc.

(1) No person shall trans-ship any products to any other country purporting that such products were produced or manufactured in an Export Proccssing Zone for purposes of gaining any advantage accorded to Tanzania in terms of a trade quota under any bilateral, multilateral or regional agrecment or protocol.

(2) A person who contravenes subsection (1) commits an offence and shall be liable on conviction to —

(a) if such a person is a natural person, to a fine not exceeding twenty million shillings or to imprisonment for a term not exceeding five years or to both;

(b) if such a person is not a natural person, to a fine not exceeding one billion shillings, closure and forfeiture of his enterprise or business.

[Act No.3 of 2006 s.5]

35. Offences for manufacture, processing, ctc. of prohibited goods or articles

(1) Any person who commits an offence against subsection (1) of section 11 shall be liable on conviction to a fine not exceeding fifty million shillings or to imprisonment for a term not exceeding fifteen years.

(2) The trial Court may, in addition to a sentence imposed pursuant to subsection (1), order forfeiture to the Government of the goods or articles with respect to which an offence was committed.

[Act No.3 of 2006 s.5]

GROUP FOUR
MINING AND ENVIRONMENT PROTECTION LAWS AND REGULATIONS

TITLE TWELVE
MINING ACT (CHAPTER 123)
[2010] [Revised Edition 2019] (Excerpts)

Mining Act
(Chapter 123)

Commenced on 1 November 2010

[This is the version of this document at 30 November 2019.]

[Note: This Act has been thoroughly revised and consolidated under the supervision of the Attorney General's Office, in compliance with the Laws Revision Act No.7 of 1994, the Revised Laws and Annual Revision Act (Chapter 356 (R.L.)), and the Interpretation of Laws and General Clauses Act No.30 of 1972. This version is up-to-date as at 31st July 2002.]

[G.N. No.396 of 2010; Acts Nos.14 of 2010; 17 of 2010; 23 of 2015; 4 of 2017; 7 of 2017; 9 of 2017; 4 of 2018; 6 of 2019; 14 of 2019]

An Act to re-enact with substantial amendments the provisions that regulate the law relating to prospecting for minerals, mining, processing and dealing in minerals, to granting, renewal and termination of mineral rights, payment of royalties, fees and other charges and any other relevant matters.

Part II
GENERAL PRINCIPLES

6. Authority required for prospecting or mining

(1) A person shall not on or in any land to which this Act applies, prospect for minerals or carry on mining operations or processing operations except under the authority of a mineral right granted or deemed to have been granted, under this Act.

(2) The activities carried on by the Agency in the course of geological mapping shall not be treated for the purpose of subsection (1) as prospecting for minerals or mining operations.

(3) Any person who contravenes subsection (1), commits an offence and on conviction is liable —

(a) in the case of an individual, to a fine of not exceeding ten million shillings but not less than five million shillings or to imprisonment for a term not exceeding three years or both;

(b) in the case of a body corporate, to a fine of not less than fifty million shillings.

(4) Any minerals obtained in the course of unauthorized prospecting or mining or processing operations including equipment involved in such operations and any minerals possessed without a proper permit shall be forfeited to the Government by the Commission and auctioned through relevant Government Asset Auctioning Procedures.

[Act No.23 of 2015 s.30]

7. Mineral rights and exclusivity

(1) The following mineral rights maybe granted under this Act —

(a) under Division A of Part IV —
  (i) a prospecting licence;
  (ii) a gemstone prospecting licence;
(b) under Division B of Part IV —
  (i) a special mining licence;
  (ii) a mining licence;
(c) under Division C of Part IV — primary mining licence;
(d) under division D of Part IV —
  (i) a processing licence;
  (ii) a smelting licence;
  (iii) a refining licence.

(2) The licensing authority may, upon consent of the mineral right holder, grant more than one mineral right over the same mining area as follows —

(a) a mining licence or primary mining licence for building materials maybe granted in an area subject to a mineral right for minerals other than building materials;

(b) a primary mining licence for gemstones maybe granted in an area subject to a prospecting licence for minerals other than gemstones.

(3) Notwithstanding the foregoing provision of this section, nothing in this Act shall prevent any person engaged in the construction of tunnels, road, dams, aerodromes and similar public works of an engineering nature from utilizing as building materials any minerals derived from a source approved by the Minister in writing.

(4) The Minister shall not, for the purposes of subsection (3), approve a source in a mining area.

(5) The Minister may, at any time withdraw the approval given under subsection (3).

[Act No.23 of 2015 s.31; Cap.4 s.8]

8. Restriction on grant of mineral rights

(1) Mineral rights shall not be granted to —

(a) an individual who —
  (i) is under the age of eighteen years;
  (ii) not being a citizen of the United Republic, has not been ordinarily resident in the United Republic for a period of four years or such other period as maybe prescribed;
  (iii) is an un-discharged bankrupt, having been adjudged or, otherwise declared bankrupt under any written law whether under the laws of the United Republic or elsewhere, or enters into any agreement or scheme of composition with creditors, or takes advantage of any law for the benefit of debtors; or
  (iv) has been convicted, within the previous ten years, of an offence of which dishonesty is an element, or of any offence under this Act, any related or similar Act, or any similar written law in force outside the United Republic and has been sentenced to imprisonment or to a fine exceeding twenty million shillings.

(b) a company—
- (i) which has not established a physical and postal address in the United Republic for the purpose of serving legal notices and other correspondences;
- (ii) unless, such company is incorporated under the Companies Act and intends to carry out the business of mining under a mining licence;
- (iii) which is in liquidation other than a liquidation that forms part of a scheme for the reconstruction or amalgamation of the holder;
- (iv) which has among its directors or shareholders any person who would be disqualified in terms of paragraph (a)(iii) and (iv).

(2) A Primary Mining Licence for any minerals shall not be granted to an individual, partnership or body corporate unless —
- (a) in the case of an individual, the individual is a citizen of Tanzania;
- (b) in the case of a partnership, it is composed exclusively of citizens of Tanzania;
- (c) in the case of a body corporate, it is a company and —
    - (i) its membership is composed exclusively of citizens of Tanzania;
    - (ii) its directors are all citizens of Tanzania;
    - (iii) control over the company, both direct and indirect, is exercised, from within Tanzania by persons all of whom are citizens of Tanzania.

(3) Notwithstanding subsection (2), the Commission may, on recommendation of the Resident Mines Officer and upon satisfying itself that a Primary Mining Licence holder needs a technical support which cannot be sourced within Tanzania, allow the Primary Mining licence holder to contract a foreigner for the technical support.

[Cap.4 s.8]

(4) The provisions of subsection (1)(a)(iii) and (iv) shall apply in relation to engagement of foreign technical support.

(5) A mining licence for mining gemstones shall only be granted to applicants who are Tanzanians.

(6) Notwithstanding subsection (5), where the Minister after consultation with the Commission determines that the development of gemstone resources in an area of land subject to a mineral right, is most likely to require specialized skills, technology or high level of investment, he may grant a mining licence for gemstones to the applicant, where he is satisfied that the licence will be held by that person together with a non-citizen whose undivided participating shares amount to not more than fifty percent either alone, in the case of one person or in the aggregate in the case of more than one person.

(7) A mineral rights shall not be granted to an individual who, or to any partnership or body corporate or to any one of the partners, shareholders or directors of the partnership or body corporate which is in default in another mineral rights or in an expired or cancelled mineral rights: Provided that —
- (a) an individual who or partnership or body corporate which is in default; or
- (b) a partner, shareholder or director of a partnership or body corporate which is in

default, may be granted a mineral right upon rectifying the default.

(8) A prospecting licence shall not be granted to an individual, partnership, body corporate, or any one of the partner, shareholders or directors of the partnership or body corporate who owns more than twenty other valid prospecting licences, unless the cumulative prospecting areas of such other prospecting licences do not exceed 2,000 square kilometres.

[Act No.7 of 2017 s.7]

Part IV
MINERAL RIGHTS

Division B: Special mining licence and mining licence

(i) Applications for special mining licence and mining licence

39. Applicants

(1) Subject to section 42 or 51, as the case maybe, the holder of A Prospecting licence hereinafter in this Division of this Part referred to as an "entitled applicant" is entitled —

(a) on application to the Commission, pursuant to section 41, to the grant of a special mining licence;

(b) on application to the Commission pursuant to section 50 to the grant of a mining licence, for the mining within the prospecting area of minerals to which the prospecting licence applies.

(2) Where a person who is not an entitled applicant has made an application to the licensing authority for a special mining licence or mining licence in the prescribed form and tendered the prescribed fee, the application shall be registered immediately in the register maintained for such applications in accordance with this Act.

(3) The application registered under subsection (2) shall be assigned a number, date and time at which it was received shall be indicated on an official receipt and handed to the applicant or his authorized agent or sent to the applicant by registered mail.

(4) Every applicant applying for a special mining licence or a mining licence under the provisions of this Act shall submit copies of his application to such persons as the Minister may prescribe in the Regulations.

[Act No.23 of 2015 s.40; Cap.4 s.8]

(ii) Special mining licence

41. Application for special mining licence

(1) An application for a special mining licence shall be in the prescribed form and shall be accompanied by the prescribed fee.

(2) In addition to the requirements in subsection (3), an application for a special mining licence shall identify the relevant prospecting licence and provide a full description of the land within the prospecting area for which the special mining licence is sought and a plan of the

proposed mining area drawn in the manner and showing particulars as the Commission may reasonably require.

[Acts Nos.23 of 2015 s.42; 7 of 2017 s.17; Cap.4 s.8]

(3) Every application for a special mining licence shall include or be accompanied by: —

(a) a statement of the period for which the licence is sought;

(b) a comprehensive statement by the applicant, so far as he knows, of the mineral deposits in the proposed area, and details of all known minerals proved, estimated or inferred, ore reserves and mining conditions;

(c) the proposed programme for mining operations, including a forecast of capital investment, the estimated recovery rate of ore and mineral products, and the proposed treatment and disposal of ore and minerals recovered;

(d) proposed plan for relocation, resettlement and compensation of people within the mining areas in accordance with the Land Act;

[Cap.113]

(e) the applicant's environmental certificate issued in terms of the Environment Management Act;

[Cap.191]

(f) details of expected infrastructure requirements;

(g) the procurement plan of goods and services available in the United Republic;

(h) proposed plan with respect to the employment and training of citizens of Tanzania and succession plan for expatriate employees, if any as maybe required by the Employment and Labour Relations Act;

[Cap.366]

(i) a statement of integrity pledge in a prescribed form;

(j) local content plan; and

(k) such other information as the Minister may reasonably require for the disposal of the application.

(4) An application under this section shall be submitted to the Commission.

(iii) **Mining licence**

51. Rights of holder of mining licences

A mining licence confers on the holder the exclusive right, subject to this Act and the Regulations, to carry on mining operations in the mining area for the stated minerals, and for that purpose the holder, his servants and agents may, in particular —

(a) enter on the mining area and take all reasonable measures on or under the surface for the purpose of facilitating and undertaking his mining operations;

(b) erect the necessary equipment, plant and buildings for the purposes of mining, transporting, dressing or treating the mineral recovered by him in the course of mining operations;

(c) subject to payment of royalties in accordance with this Act and the Regulations, dispose of any mineral product recovered;

(d) stack or dump any mineral or waste product in a manner provided for in the applicable Regulations; and

(e) employ and train citizens of Tanzania and implement succession plan on expatriate employees in accordance with the Employment and Labour Relations Act, and may prospect within the mining area for any minerals other than gemstones.

[Cap.366]

Division C: Primary mining licences
54. Application for primary mining licence

(1) Any person not disqualified under section 8, may apply to the Commission for the grant of a primary mining licence.

(2) Every such application shall —
   (a) be in the prescribed form and accompanied by the prescribed fee;
   (b) describe the area not exceeding the prescribed maximum area over which a primary mining licence is sought, and shall be accompanied by a sketch plan with sufficient details to enable the Commission to identify the area;
   (c) include a statement of integrity pledge in a prescribed form; and
   (d) include a local content plan.

(3) An application for a primary mining licence shall contain:
   (a) in the case of an individual, his full name and nationality, physical and postal addresses and attach an identification card such as his national identity card, passport, driving licence or voter's registration card;
   (b) in the case of a body corporate, its corporate name, place of incorporation, names and the nationality of its directors including copies of their identity cards;
   (c) in the case of more than one person, the particulars referred in paragraphs (a) and (b);
   (d) environmental investigations and social study and an environmental protection plan as described in the relevant regulations.

(4) A primary mining licence shall confer on the holder the right to prospect for and mine minerals as provided for in this Division of this Part.

[Acts Nos.23 of 2015 s.45; 7 of 2017 s.21]

Division D: Mineral processing, smelting and refining
59. Mineral right holder to set aside minerals for processing, smelting or refining

The mineral right holder shall be required to set aside certain amount of minerals at such percentage as the Minister may, after consultation with the mineral right holder and the Commission, determine for processing, smelting or refining within the United Republic.

60. Application and grant of licence for processing minerals

(1) A person who is not entitled to process minerals in any area within or outside the area subject to a mineral right may apply to the Commission for a licence for processing minerals.

(2) An application under subsection (1) shall be made in the prescribed form and accompanied by —

(a) prescribed fee;

(b) environment management plan as described in relevant regulations;

(c) process plant layout;

(d) procurement, haulage and processing inputs plan;

(e) compensation, relocation and resettlement plan, if required; and

(f) such other documents and information as maybe required by the licensing authority.

(3) The Commission shall, if satisfied with the content of the application under subsection (2), register the applicant and issue the licence upon such terms and conditions as maybe prescribed in the licence.

(4) The Processing Licence issued under this section shall be valid for a period not exceeding ten years and shall be subjects to renewal.

(5) Procedures for application and granting of licence for processing minerals under this section shall be prescribed in the regulations.

TITLE THIRTEEN
ENVIRONMENTAL MANAGEMENT ACT [2004] (Excerpts)

THE ENVIRONMENTAL MANAGEMENT ACT
No.20 OF 2004

An Act to provide for legal and institutional framework for sustainable management of environment; to outline principles for management, impact and risk assessments, prevention and control of pollution, waste management, environmental quality standards, public participation, compliance and enforcement; to provide basis for implementation of international instruments on environment; to provide for implementation of the National Environment Policy; to repeal the National Environment Management Act, 1983 and provide for continued existence of the National Environment Management Council; to provide for establishment of the National Environmental Trust Fund and to provide for other related matters.

ENACTED by Parliament of the United Republic of Tanzania.

PART X
ENVIRONMENTAL QUALITY STANDARDS

141. Compliance with standards, etc

Every person undertaking any activity shall be required to comply with environmental quality standards and criteria.

143. Water quality standards

The National Environmental Standards Committee shall —

(a) prescribe criteria and procedure for measuring standards for water quality;

(b) establish the minimum quality standards for all waters of Tanzania;

(c) establish minimum quality standards for different uses of water including:

(i) drinking water;

(ii) water for agricultural purposes;

(iii) water for recreational purposes;

(iv) water for fisheries and wildlife;

(v) water for industry;

(vi) water for environment; and

(vii) water for any other purposes.

145. Air quality standards

The National Environmental Standards Committee shall —

(a) prescribe criteria and procedure for measurement for air quality;

(b) establish ambient air quality standards;

(c) establish occupational air quality standards;

(d) establish emission standards for various sources;

(e) prescribe criteria and guidelines for air pollution control for both mobile and stationary sources; and

(f) any other air emission quality standards.

150. Soil quality standards

The National Environmental Standards Committee shall —

(a) establish criteria and procedures for the measurement and determination of the quality of soil;

(b) set minimum standards for the management of the quality of soil;

(c) prescribe guidelines for the disposal of any waste in the soil, the optimal utilization of any soil, identification of the various soils and practices that are necessary in order to conserve soil and prohibition of activities that may degrade the soil; and

(d) do any other thing necessary for the monitoring and control of soil degradation.

GROUP FIVE
TAX LAWS AND REGULATIONS

TITLE FOURTEEN
VALUE ADDED TAX ACT (CHAPTER 148)
[2015] [Revised Edition 2019]

Value Added Tax Act
(Chapter 148)

Commenced on 1 July 2015

[This is the version of this document at 30 November 2019.]

[Note: This Act has been thoroughly revised and consolidated under the supervision of the Attorney General's Office, in compliance with the Laws Revision Act No.7 of 1994, the Revised Laws and Annual Revision Act (Chapter 356 (R.L.)), and the Interpretation of Laws and General Clauses Act No.30 of 1972. This version is up-to-date as at 31st July 2002.]

[GN.No.224 of 2015; Acts Nos.5 of 2014; 2 of 2016; 4 of 2017; 7 of 2017; 9 of 2017; 4 of 2018; 6 of 2019; 8 of 2019; 13 of 2019]

An Act to make a legal framework for the imposition and collection of, administration and management of the value added tax and to provide for other related matters.

Part I
PRELIMINARY PROVISIONS

1. Short title

(1) This Act maybe cited as the Value Added Tax Act.

(2) [omitted]

2. Interpretation

(1) In this Act, unless the context otherwise requires —

"**adjustment event**" —

    (a) in relation to a supply, other than a supply mentioned in paragraph (b) means —

        (i) a cancellation of the supply;

        (ii) an alteration in the consideration for the supply;

        (iii) the return of the thing supplied or part thereof to the supplier; or

        (iv) a variation of, or alteration to, all or part of the supply and which has the effect that the supply becomes or ceases to be a taxable supply; and

    (b) in relation to a taxable supply of a voucher, means the giving of the voucher in full or part payment for a supply that is exempt; or zero rated;

[Act No.2 of 2016 s.90]

"**agent**" means a person who acts on behalf of another person in business;

"**ancillary transport services**" means stevedoring services, lashing and securing services, cargo inspection services, preparation of customs documentation, container handling services and the storage of transported goods or goods to be transported;

"**association of persons**" means a partnership, trust or body of persons formed, organised, established or recognised as such in Mainland Tanzania, and does not include a company;

"**Commissioner General**" means the Commissioner General of the Tanzania Revenue Authority appointed as such under the Tanzania Revenue Authority Act;

[Cap.399]

"**commercial accommodation**" means accommodation in a building including part of a building or a group of buildings operated as a hotel, motel inn, boardinghouse, guest house, hostel, lodge, cottage, serviced apartment or similar establishment, or on sites developed for use as camping sites, where lodging is regularly or normally provided for a periodic charge, or other accommodation offered for short term occupation by person other than as the individual's main residence;

"**company**" has the same meaning ascribed to it under the Companies Act;

[Cap.212]

"**connected persons**" means —

(a) two persons, if the relationship between them is such that one person can reasonably be expected to act in accordance with the intention of the other, or both persons can reasonably be expected to act in accordance with the intentions of a third person;

(b) in the case of an individual, the individual and —

　(i) the husband or wife of the individual;

　(ii) the husband or wife of a relative of the individual;

　(iii) a relative of the individual's husband or wife;

　(iv) the husband or wife of a relative of the individual's husband or wife; and

　(v) a relative of the individual;

(c) a partnership and a partner in the partnership, if the partners, either alone or together with other persons who are related to the partner, controls ten percent or more of the rights to income or capital of the partnership;

(d) a company and a shareholder in the company, if the shareholder, directly or indirectly, either alone or together with persons who are connected with the shareholder, controls ten percent or more of the voting power in the company or the rights to distributions of income or capital by the company;

(e) a company and another company, if a person, directly or indirectly, either alone or together with persons who are connected with the person who controls ten percent or more of the shareholding rights, or the rights to distributions of income or capital in both of them;

(f) a person acting in the capacity of trustee of a trust and an individual who is or maybe a beneficiary of that trust or in the case of an individual whose relative is or maybe a beneficiary of the trust; and

(g) a person who is in control of another person if the former is legally or operationally in a position to exercise restraint or direction over the latter;

"**document**" means a statement in writing, including an account, assessment, book, certificate, claim, note, notice, order, record, return or ruling kept either in paper form or electronic form;

"**economic activity**" means —
- (a) an activity carried on continuously or regularly by a person, which involves or is intended to involve the supply of goods, services, or immovable property, including—
  - (i) an activity carried on in the form of a business, profession, vocation, trade, manufacture, or undertaking of any kind, whether or not the activity is undertaken for profit; or
  - (ii) a supply of property by way of lease, hire, license, or similar arrangement;
- (b) a one-off adventure or concern in the nature of a trade; and
- (c) anything done during or in respect of the commencement or termination of an economic activity as defined under (a) or (b) of this definition provided that "economic activity" does not include —
  - (i) the activities of providing services by employee to employer; or
  - (ii) activities performed as a director of a company, except where the director accepts such office in carrying on an economic activity, in which case those services shall be regarded as being supplied in the course or furtherance of that economic activity;

"**entertainment**" means the provision of food, beverages, amusement, recreation or hospitality of any kind;

"**exempt**" in relation to a supply or import, means a supply or import that is specified as exempt under this Act or a supply of a right or option to receive a supply that will be exempt;

"**export**" in relation to a supply of goods, means the removal of goods from a place in Mainland Tanzania to a place outside the United Republic, and in the absence of proof to the contrary, the following are sufficient evidence that the goods have been so exported —
- (a) evidence of the consignment or delivery of the goods to an address outside the United Republic; or
- (b) evidence of the delivery of the goods to the owner, charterer, or operator of a ship, aircraft or other means of transport engaged in international transport for the purpose of carrying the goods outside the United Republic;

"**fair market value of supply**" means —
- (a) the consideration the supply would fetch in an open market transaction freely made between persons who are not connected; or
- (b) where it is not possible to determine an amount under paragraph (a), the fair market value which a similar supply would fetch in an open market transaction freely made between persons who are not connected, adjusted to take account of the differences between such supply and the actual supply;

"**finance lease**" means a lease that is treated as a finance lease under the Financial Leasing Act, but does not include a hire purchase agreement;

[Cap.417]

"**financial services**" means services of —
- (a) granting, negotiating, and dealing with loans, credit, credit guarantees, and security for money, including management of loans, credit, or credit guarantees by the grantor;
- (b) transactions concerning money deposit, current accounts, payments, transfers, debts, cheque or negotiable instruments, other than debt collection or debt factoring;
- (c) transactions relating to financial derivatives, forward contracts, options to acquire financial instruments and similar arrangements;
- (d) transactions relating to shares, stocks, bonds, and other securities, but does not include custody services;
- (e) transactions involving granting or transferring ownership of an interest in a scheme whereby provision is made for the payment or granting of benefits by a benefit fund, provident fund, pension fund, retirement annuity fund, preservation fund, or similar fund;
- (f) transactions involving the provision of, or transfer of ownership of a health or life insurance contract or the provision of reinsurance in respect of such contract;
- (g) making payment or collection of an amount of interest, principal, dividend, or other amount in respect of any share, debt security, equity security, participatory security, credit contract, contract of life insurance, or futures contract; and
- (h) foreign exchange transactions, including the supply of foreign drafts and international money orders,

but does not include supply of the services of arranging for or facilitating any of the services specified under paragraphs (a) to (h);

"**fixed place**" in relation to the carrying on of an economic activity, means a place at or through which the activity is carried on, being —
- (a) a place of management;
- (b) a branch, office, factory, or workshop;
- (c) a mine, an oil or gas well, a quarry, or any other place of extraction of natural resources; or
- (d) a building site or construction or installation project;

"**goods**" means all kinds of tangible moveable property, excluding shares, stocks, securities, or money;

"**government entity**" means —
- (a) the Government of the United Republic or a Ministry, Department, or Agency of that Government;
- (b) a statutory body, authority, or enterprise owned or operated by the Government of the United Republic; or
- (c) a local government authority;

"**import**" means bringing or causing goods to be brought from outside the United Republic into Mainland Tanzania;

"**imported services**" means services supplied to a taxable person if the supply of the services is not made in the United Republic as determined under this Act;

"**immovable property**" includes —
   (a) an interest in or right over land;
   (b) a personal right to call for or be granted an interest in or right over land;
   (c) a right to occupy land or any other contractual right exercisable over or in relation to land;
   (d) the provision of accommodation; or
   (e) a right or option to acquire anything mentioned in paragraphs (a) to (d);

"**income tax**" has the meaning ascribed to it under the Income Tax Act;
[Cap.332]

"**input tax**" in relation to a taxable person, means —
   (a) value added tax imposed on a taxable supply made to the person, including value added tax payable by the person on a taxable supply of imported services;
   (b) value added tax imposed on a taxable import of goods by the person; and
   (c) input tax charged under the law governing administration of value added tax applicable in Tanzania Zanzibar;

"**input tax credit**" in relation to a taxable person, means a credit allowed for input tax incurred by the person;

"**international assistance agreement**" means an agreement between the Government of the United Republic and a foreign government or a public international organisation for the provision of financial, technical, humanitarian, or administrative assistance to the United Republic;

"**international transport services**" means the services, other than ancillary transport services of transporting passengers or goods by road, rail, water, or air —
   (a) from a place outside the United Republic to another place outside the United Republic;
   (b) from a place outside the United Republic to a place in Mainland Tanzania; or
   (c) from a place in Mainland Tanzania to a place outside the United Republic;

"**Minister**" means the Minister responsible for finance;

"**money**" means —
   (a) any coin or paper currency that is legal tender in the United Republic or another country;
   (b) a negotiable instrument used or circulated, or intended for use or circulation, as currency of the United Republic or another country;
   (c) a medium of exchange, promissory note, bank draft, postal order, money order, or similar instrument; or
   (d) any payment for supply by way of credit card or debit card or crediting or debiting an account,

and shall not include a collector's piece or, a coin medal, paper money, collected as antique;

"**net amount**" in relation to a tax period, means the amount calculated under section 67;
[Cap.4 s.8]

"**non-profit organisation**" means a charitable or religious organisation established and functions solely for —
- (a) the relief of poverty or distress of the public;
- (b) the provision of general public health, education or water; and
- (c) the supply of religious services;

"**output tax**" in relation to a taxable person, means value added tax payable by the person in respect of —
- (a) a taxable supply made; and
- (b) a taxable supply of imported services acquired;

"**partnership**" means two or more persons carrying on an economic activity;

"**person**" means —
- (a) an individual;
- (b) a company;
- (c) an association of persons;
- (d) a Government entity, whether or not that entity is ordinarily treated as a separate person;
- (e) a foreign government or a political subdivision of a foreign Government;

[Cap.4 s.8]

- (f) a non government organisation; or
- (g) a public international organisation;

"**prepaid telecommunications product**" means a phone card, prepaid card, recharge card, or any other form of prepayment for telecommunication services;

"**progressive or periodic supply**" means —
- (a) a supply made progressively or periodically under an agreement, arrangement or law that provides for progressive or periodic payments;
- (b) a supply by way of lease, hire, license or other right to use property, including a supply under a finance lease; or
- (c) a supply made directly in the construction, major reconstruction, or extension of a building or engineering work;

"**registered person**" means a person registered for value added tax under this Act;

"**registration threshold**" means the amount prescribed under section 28(4);

"**relative of an individual**" means a brother, sister, ancestor or lineal descendant of the individual;

"**residential premises**" means an area occupied or designed to be occupied and capable of being occupied as a residence, and includes —
- (a) any garage, storage space, or other space associated with the premises, so long as that space is of a type commonly considered to be part of such residential premises; and
- (b) any land that is reasonably attributable to the premises,

but does not include any premises or part of premises that is used to provide commercial accommodation;

"**resident**" means an individual whose permanent home is in Mainland Tanzania;

"**resident company**" means a company incorporated in Tanzania or issued with the certificate of compliance under the Companies Act or its centre of management and control is in Mainland Tanzania;

[Cap.212]

"**resident trusts**" means the trust whose majority of members of trustees are residents of Mainland Tanzania or the place of management and control of the trust is in Mainland Tanzania;

"**resident association of persons**" means an association of persons other than a trust —

(a) formed in Mainland Tanzania; or

(b) its place of management and control is in Mainland Tanzania.

"**resident Government entity**" means a Government entity with residence in Mainland Tanzania;

"**sale**" means a transfer of the right to dispose of goods or immovable property as owner, including exchange or barter, and shall not include an offer or exposure of goods or immovable property for sale;

"**services**" means anything that is not goods, immovable property or money including but not limited to —

(a) a provision of information or advice;

(b) a grant, assignment, termination, or surrender of a right;

(c) the making available of a facility, opportunity, or advantage;

(d) an entry into an agreement to refrain from or tolerate an activity, a situation, or the doing of an act; and

(e) an issue, transfer, or surrender of a license, permit, certificate, concession, authorisation, or similar right;

"**service directly related to land**" means service —

(a) physically rendered on land;

(b) of experts and estate agents relating to specific land; or

(c) relating to construction work undertaken or to be undertaken on specific land;

"**supply**" means any kind of supply whatsoever;

"**tax decision**" has the same meaning as ascribed in the Tax Administration Act and shall include a decision referred to under section 90;

[Cap.348]

"**tax fraction**" means the amount out of tax calculated in accordance with the following formula —

$$\frac{R}{100 + R}$$

where "R" is the rate of value added tax specified in section 5;

"**tax invoice**" means a document issued in accordance with section 86 and regulations made under this Act;

"**tax period**" means a calendar month, beginning at the start of the first day of the month and ending at the last day of the month;

"**taxable import**" means an import of goods, other than an exempt import;

"**taxable person**" means a registered person or a person who is required to be registered for value added tax under this Act;

"**taxable supply**" means —

    (a) a supply, other than an exempt supply, that is made in Mainland Tanzania by a taxable person in the course or furtherance of an economic activity carried out by that person; or

    (b) a supply of imported services to a taxable person who is the purchaser and acquires the services in the course of an economic activity if had the supply been made in Mainland Tanzania by a taxable person in the course of furtherance of an economic activity —

        (i) it would have been taxable at a rate other than zero; and

        (ii) the purchaser would not have been entitled to a credit for ninety percent or more of the value added tax that would have been imposed on the supply;

"**telecommunication service**" means a service of any description provided by a company by means of any transmission, emission or reception of signs, signals, writing, images and sounds or intelligible information of any nature, by wire, optical, visual or other electromagnetic means or systems, including —

    (a) voice, voice mail, data services, audio text services, video text services, radio paging and other emerging telecommunication services;

    (b) fixed telephone services including provision of access to and use of the public switched or non – switched telephone network for the transmission and switching of voice, data and video, inbound and outbound telephone service to and from national and international destinations;

    (c) cellular mobile telephone services including provision of access to and use of switched or non-switched networks for the transmission of voice, data, video and value added services, inbound and outbound roaming services to and from national and international destinations;

    (d) carrier services including provision of wired, optical fibre or wireless facilities and any other technology to originate, terminate or transit calls, charging for interconnection, settlement or termination of domestic or international calls, charging for jointly used facilities including pole attachments, charging for the exclusive use of circuits, a leased circuit or a dedicated link including a speech circuit, data circuit or a telegraph circuit;

    (e) provision of call management services for a fee including call waiting, call forwarding, caller identification, multi calling, call display, call return, call screen, call blocking, automatic callback, call answer, voice mail, voice menus and video conferencing;

    (f) private network services including provision of wired, optical fibre, wireless or any other technologies of electronic communication link between specified points for the exclusive use of the client;

(g) data transmission services including provision of access to wired or wireless facilities and services specifically designed for efficient transmission of data; and

(h) communication through facsimile, pager, telegraph, telex and other telecommunication service;

"**telecommunication service provider**" means a person licensed by the Tanzania Communications Regulatory Authority or an equivalent foreign body to provide telecommunication services;

"**time of supply**" means —

(a) in relation to a supply of goods, the time at which the goods are delivered or made available;

(b) in relation to a supply of services the time at which the services are rendered, provided, or performed; or

(c) in relation to a supply of immovable property, the earlier time at which the property is —

(i) created, transferred, assigned, granted, or otherwise supplied to the customer; or

(ii) delivered or made available;

"**trust**" means a person acting in the capacity of trustee or trustees of a particular trust estate;

"**trust estate**" means property held by a person or persons acting as trustee for a settlement, trust or estate;

"**value added tax**" means the tax imposed on taxable supplies or taxable imports, and includes an interest, fine or penalty payable in accordance with the provisions of this Act;

"**value added tax return**" means a return that a taxable person is required to file with the Commissioner General, in which required information concerning that person, or other person's liability to pay tax under this Act, is provided;

[Cap.4 s.8]

"**voucher**" means a stamp, token, coupon, or similar article, including an article issued electronically, which can be redeemed by the holder for supplies of goods, services, or immovable property, and includes a prepaid telecommunications product, and does not include a postage stamp;

"**Zanzibar input tax**" in relation to a taxable person, means —

(a) value added tax imposed under the value added tax law applicable in Tanzania Zanzibar on a taxable supply made to that taxable person; and

(b) value added tax imposed under the value added tax law applicable in Tanzania Zanzibar on a taxable import of goods by the person; and

"**zero-rated**" in relation to a supply or import, means —

(a) a supply or import that is specified as zero-rated under this Act; or

(b) a supply of a right or option to receive a supply that shall be zero-rated pursuant to the provisions of this Act.

(2) For purposes of this Act, goods shall be classified by reference to the tariff numbers set out

in Annex 1 to the Protocol on the Establishment of the East African Community Customs Union and in interpreting that annex, the general rules of interpretation set out therein, shall apply.

Part II
IMPOSITION OF VALUE ADDED TAX

(a) Imposition and exemptions

3. Imposition of value added tax

Value added tax shall be imposed and payable on taxable supplies and taxable imports.

4. Person liable to pay value added tax

The following persons shall be liable to pay value added tax —

(a) in the case of a taxable import, the importer;

(b) in the case of a taxable supply that is made in Mainland Tanzania, the supplier; and

(c) in the case of a taxable supply of imported services, the purchaser.

5. Value added tax rate and amount payable

(1) The amount of value added tax payable shall be calculated by multiplying the value of the supply or import by the value added tax rate, which shall be eighteen percent.

(2) Where the supply or import is zero-rated, the value added tax rate shall be zero percent.

(3) Where a supply is both exempt and zero-rated, the supply shall be zero rated.

(4) Where the supply is both exempt and taxable at standard rate, the supply shall be taxable at standard rate as specified under this section.

[Act No.2 of 2016 s.91]

6. Exemptions and rates to be specified by law

(1) Except as otherwise provided for in the provisions of this Act or the Schedule —

(a) a supply, class of supplies, import, or class of import shall not be exempt or zero-rated; and

(b) a person or class of persons shall not be exempted from paying value added tax imposed under this Act.

(2) Notwithstanding the provisions of subsection (1), the Minister may, by order published in the *Gazette*, grant value added tax exemption on:

(a) importation of raw materials to be used solely in the manufacture of long-lasting mosquito nets by local manufacturer having a performance agreement with the Government of the United Republic;

(b) importation by a government entity or supply to a government entity of goods or services to be used solely for implementation of a project funded by —

(i) the Government;

(ii) concessional loan, non-concessionalloan or grant through an agreement between the Government of the United Republic of Tanzania and another government, donor or lender of natural calamity or disaster. of concessionalloan or non-concessional loan; or

[Cap.134]

(iii) a grant agreement duly approved by the Minister in accordance with the provisions of the Government Loans, Grants and Guarantees Act entered between local government authority and a donor:

Provided that, such agreement provide for value added tax exemption on such goods or service; or

[Cap.4 s.8]

(c) importation or supply of goods or services for the relief of natural calamity or disaster.

(3) The exemption granted under this section shall cease to have effect and the value added tax shall become due and payable as if the exemption have not been granted if the said goods or services are transferred, sold or otherwise disposed of in any way to another person not entitled to enjoy similar privileges as conferred under this Act.

(4) The order issued by the Minister under subsection (2) shall specify goods or services that are eligible for exemption, commencement and expiry date of the exemption.

(5) The Minister may, for the purposes of this section and upon such terms and conditions as maybe required —

(a) appoint a technical committee which shall advise the Minister on the granting and monitoring of exemptions; and

(b) prescribe procedures for purposes of monitoring utilisation of exemptions granted under this section.

(6) The Committee appointed under subsection (5) shall comprise of representatives from the following institutions —

(a) the Ministry responsible for finance and planning;

(b) the Attorney General's Office;

(c) the Ministry responsible for local government; and

(d) the Tanzania Revenue Authority.

(7) The Committee may co-opt any person with special knowledge or skills to provide expertise on a particular matter as maybe required by the Committee.

(8) In this section, "project funded by Government" means a project financed by the Government in respect of —

(a) transport, water, gas or power infrastructure;

(b) buildings for provision of health or education services to the public; or

(c) a centre for persons with disabilities.

[Act Nos.9 of 2015 s.34; 9 of 2017 s.34; 4 of 2018 s.67; 13 of 2019 s.101]

7. Treaties

Where, an agreement approved by the Minister is entered into between the Government of the United Republic and an international agency listed under the Diplomatic and Consular Immunities and Privileges Act, and such agreement entitles a person to an exemption from tax on the person's purchases or imports, the exemption shall be effected under this Act by —

(a) exempting the import of goods imported by the person; or

(b) refunding the value added tax payable on taxable supplies made to the person upon application by the person.

[Act No.9 of 2017 s.35; Cap.356]

(b) Value added tax on imports

8. Payment and collection of value added tax on imports

(1) The value added tax payable on a taxable import shall be paid —

(a) where goods are entered for home consumption in Mainland Tanzania, in accordance with the provisions of this Act and procedures applicable under the East African Customs Management Act; or

(b) in any other case, where goods are imported for use in Mainland Tanzania, on the day the goods are brought into Mainland Tanzania and in the manner prescribed by the regulations.

(2) The liability to pay value added tax on a taxable import shall arise by the operation of this Act and shall not depend on the making of an assessment by the Commissioner General of the amount of value added tax due.

(3) The Commissioner General shall collect value added tax due under this Act on a taxable import at the time of import.

(4) Unless a contrary intention appears —

(a) the provisions of the East African Customs Management Act shall, for the purposes of this Act, apply as if the value added tax payable on taxable imports were customs duty payable under the East African Customs Management Act; and

(b) the terms used in this Act in respect of an import of goods shall have the same meaning as in the East African Customs Management Act.

[Act No.1 of 2005]

9. Value of import

The value of an import of goods shall be the sum of —

(a) the value of goods for the purposes of customs duty under the East African Customs Management Act, whether or not duty is payable on the import;

(b) the amount of any customs duty payable on the import; and

(c) the amount of any tax, levy, fee, or fiscal charge other than customs duty and value added tax payable on the import of the goods.

[Acts Nos.1 of 2005; 2 of 2016 s.92; Cap.4 s.8]

10. Value of returning goods

Where —

(a) goods are imported after having been exported for the purpose of undergoing repair, maintenance, cleaning, renovation, modification, treatment, or other physical process; and

(b) the form or character of the goods has not been changed since they were exported,

the value of the import shall be such amount of the increase in their value as is attributable to the repair, maintenance, cleaning, renovation, modification, treatment, or other physical process.

11. Deferral of value added tax on imported capital goods

(1) A registered person may, in the form and manner prescribed, apply to the Commissioner General for approval to defer payment of value added tax on imported capital goods.

(2) The Commissioner General shall approve an application under this section if satisfied that —

    (a) the person is carrying on an economic activity;

    (b) the person's turnover is, or is expected to be made up of at least ninety percent of taxable supplies;

    (c) the person keeps proper records and files value added tax returns and complies with obligations under this Act and any other tax law; and

    (d) there are no reasons to refuse the application in accordance with subsection (3).

(3) The Commissioner General shall refuse an application under this section if the applicant or a person connected to the applicant —

    (a) has an outstanding liability or an outstanding return under any tax law; or

    (b) has been convicted in a court of law in the United Republic or elsewhere for an offence of evading payment of tax, custom duty or an offence relating to violation of trade laws or regulations.

(4) The deferment granted under this Act shall cease to have effect and the value added tax shall become due and payable as if the deferment had not been granted if the applicant fails to account for deferral import value added tax, the said goods are transferred, sold or otherwise disposed off in any way to another person not entitled to enjoy similar privileges as conferred under this Act.

(5) The Commissioner General shall, within fourteen days of receiving the application, notify the applicant of the decision to approve or reject the application.

(6) Where the Commissioner General approves the application, such application shall take effect on the date mentioned in the decision.

(7) Where an application is rejected, the Commissioner General shall state the reasons for such rejection, and afford the applicant the right to object and appeal against the decision.

(8) The Commissioner General may revoke the approval made under this section if —

    (a) the person no longer meets the requirements for approval; or

    (b) the person becomes liable to fines or penalties, or is prosecuted or convicted, under this Act or any other tax law.

(9) A person who is approved under this section shall treat tax payable on taxable imports by the person as if it were output tax payable by the person in the tax period in which the goods were entered for home consumption.

(10) For purposes of this section, "capital goods" means goods for use in the person's economic activity which have a useful economic life of at least one year and are not —

    (a) consumables or raw materials; and

    (b) imported for the principal purpose of resale in the ordinary course of carrying on the person's economic activity, whether or not in the form or state in which the goods were imported.

[Acts Nos.2 of 2016 s.93; 4 of 2018 s.22]

(c) Value added tax on supplies

12. Subject matters and sub-categories of supply

(1) Anything capable of being supplied by any person other than money shall be the subject matter of a supply.

(2) For purposes of this Act, every supply that is, or capable of being made shall be recognised as —

(a) a supply of goods;

(b) a supply of immovable property; or

(c) a supply of services.

(3) For purposes of this Act, a supply of goods includes —

(a) a sale, exchange or other transfer of the right to dispose of goods as owner, including under a hire purchase agreement; and

(b) a lease, hire or other right of use granted in relation to goods including a supply of goods under a finance lease.

13. Consideration of supply

(1) For purposes of this Act, "consideration" as used in relation to a supply, means the sum of the following amounts —

(a) the amount in money paid or payable by any person, whether directly or indirectly, in respect of, in response to, or for the inducement of the supply; and

[Cap.4 s.8]

(b) the fair market value of anything paid or payable in kind, whether directly or indirectly, by any person in respect of, in response to, or for the inducement of the supply.

(2) Without limiting the scope of subsection (1), the consideration for a supply includes —

(a) any duty, levy, fee, charge, or tax including value added tax imposed under this Act that —

(i) is payable by the supplier on, or by reason of, the supply; and

(ii) is included in or added to the amount charged to the customer;

(b) any amount charged to the customer that is calculated or expressed by reference to costs incurred by the supplier;

(c) any service charge that is automatically added to the price of the supply; and

(d) any amount expressed to be a deposit paid when goods are sold in a returnable container and which maybe refunded on the return of the container.

(3) The consideration for a supply shall not include a price discount or rebate allowed and accounted for at the time of the supply.

(4) An exact reimbursement of costs incurred by agent for the payer shall not form part of the consideration for the supply made by the agent to the person paying the reimbursement.

14. Single and multiple supplies

Where a supply consists of more than one element, the following criteria shall be taken into account when determining how this Act applies to the supply —

(a) every supply shall normally be regarded as distinct and independent;

(b) a supply that constitutes a single supply from an economic, commercial, or technical point of view, shall not be artificially split;

(c) the essential features of the transaction shall be ascertained in order to determine whether the customer is being supplied with several distinct principal supplies or with a single supply;

(d) there is a single supply, if one or more elements constitute the principal supply, in which case the other elements are ancillary or incidental supplies, which are treated as part of the principal supply; or

(e) a supply shall be regarded as ancillary or incidental to a principal supply if it does not constitute for customers an aim in itself but is merely a means of better enjoying the principal thing supplied.

15. When value added tax becomes payable

The value added tax imposed on a taxable supply shall become payable at the earlier of —

(a) the time when the invoice for the supply is issued by the supplier;

(b) the time when the consideration for the supply is received, in whole or in part; or

(c) the time of supply.

16. Exception for progressive, lay-by sale, and vending machine

(1) Notwithstanding the requirement of section 15 —

(a) where a progressive or periodic supply is treated as a series of separate supplies in accordance with the provision of section 19, any value added tax imposed on each supply shall become payable —

(i) if the supplier issues a separate invoice for the supply, at the time when the invoice is issued;

(ii) at the time when any part of the consideration for the supply is paid;

(iii) at the time when the payment of the consideration for the supply is due; or

(iv) if the supplier and customer are connected persons —

(aa) for a periodic supply, on the first day of the period to which the supply relates; or

(bb) for a progressive supply, at the time of supply;

(b) where a taxable supply of goods is made under a lay-by agreement, the value added tax imposed on the supply becomes payable at each time when any part of the consideration is paid for the supply; and

(i) the amount of value added tax that becomes payable at such time is the tax fraction of the amount paid; and

(ii) where a taxable supply is made through a vending machine, meter, or other automatic device not including a pay telephone that is operated by a coin, note, or token, the value added tax becomes payable when the coin, note, or token is taken from the machine, meter, or other device by or on behalf of the supplier.

(2) For purposes of subsection (1), "lay-by agreement" means an agreement for the sale and purchase by which —

 (a) the price is payable by at least one additional payment after the payment of a deposit;

 (b) delivery of the goods takes place at a time after payment of the deposit; and

 (c) ownership of the goods is transferred by delivery.

(3) The Minister may make regulations prescribing for the value added tax to become payable under this section for —

 (a) a taxable supply that is subject to a statutory cooling off period under any other laws;

 (b) a taxable supply that occurs before the total consideration for the supply is certain;

 (c) a taxable supply made under an agreement that provides for retention of some or all of the consideration until certain conditions are met; or

 (d) a taxable supply for which the correct value added tax treatment is not known until a later time.

17. Value of taxable supply

(1) The value of a taxable supply which is made in Mainland Tanzania shall be the consideration for the supply reduced by an amount equal to the tax fraction of that consideration.

(2) The value of a taxable supply of imported services shall be the consideration for the supply.

(3) The value of a supply that is not a taxable supply shall be the consideration for the supply.

(4) The value of a supply made without payment of consideration shall be a fair market value.

18. Exception for supplies to connected person

Where a taxable person makes a taxable supply to a connected person, and the supply is made for no consideration, or for a consideration that is lower than the fair market value of the supply, the value of the supply shall be the fair market value of the supply reduced by the tax fraction of that fair market value.

19. Progressive or periodic supply

(1) Each part of a progressive or periodic supply shall be treated as a separate supply.

(2) Where the progressive or periodic parts of a progressive or periodic supply are not readily identifiable, the supply shall be treated as a series of separate supplies each corresponding to the proportion of the supply to which each separate part of the consideration relates.

[Cap.4 s.8]

(3) For purposes of determining the time of supply for each part of a lease or other supply of a right to use property, the supply shall be treated as being made continuously over the period of the lease or right of use.

20. Sale of economic activity

(1) An economic activity shall be sold as a going concern where —

 (a) everything necessary for the continued operation of the economic activity is supplied to the person to whom the economic activity is sold; and

(b) the purchaser makes the acquisition in the course of or for the purposes of, an economic activity it carries on after the sale.

(2) Without prejudice to the provision of subsection (1), part of an economic activity shall be an economic activity if it is capable of being operated separately.

(3) Where a taxable person makes supplies in Mainland Tanzania as a part of a transaction for the sale of an economic activity as a going concern by that taxable person to another taxable person —

(a) the supplies shall be treated as a single supply that is made in Mainland Tanzania; and

(b) the single supply shall be treated as if it were not a supply.

(4) For purposes of working out the supplier's entitlement to input tax credits in relation to a transaction to which subsection (3) applies —

(a) any input tax incurred in acquiring goods or services for the purposes of the transaction shall —

(i) where the supplier otherwise only makes taxable supplies be treated as relating to those supplies; and

(ii) in any other case, be calculated in accordance with partial input tax credit formula; and

(b) the value of the single supply of the going concern shall not be included in any calculations made under section 70.

21. Tax treatment on rights, vouchers and options

(1) Where —

(a) a supply of a right, option, or voucher is a taxable supply; and

(b) a subsequent supply is made on the exercise of the right, option, or in return for a voucher given in full or part payment for the subsequent supply, the consideration for the subsequent supply is limited to any additional consideration given for the subsequent supply or in connection with the exercise of the right or option.

(2) Where —

(a) a supply of a right, option, or voucher was not a taxable supply;

(b) a subsequent supply is made on the exercise of the right or option, or in return for a voucher given in full or part payment for the subsequent supply; and

(c) the subsequent supply is a taxable supply, the consideration for the subsequent supply shall include any consideration given for the supply of the right, option, or voucher.

(3) For purposes of this Act, supply of voucher shall be treated as a supply of services.

22. Reimbursements of rights, voucher and option

Where —

(a) a taxable supply is made on the exercise of a right or option, or in return for a voucher that is given in full or part payment for the subsequent supply; and

(b) the taxable person making that supply receives or will receive a payment from another person in respect of the exercise of the right or option or the acceptance of the voucher, or because of the making of the supply,

the taxable person shall be treated as having made a taxable supply to the payer and the amount received shall be treated as consideration for that supply.

23. Input tax credits of right, voucher and options

(1) The Minister may prescribe any kind of documentary evidence which, in lieu of a tax invoice, the taxable person shall hold in support of the input tax credit to which the person maybe entitled in relation to the acquisition of a voucher or of a subsequent supply in return of the voucher.

(2) In the absence of such regulations any document from which the underlying tax burden can reasonably be calculated maybe used in support of the input tax credit.

24. Pre-payments for telecommunication services

(1) This section shall —
  (a) apply to a supply, by a telecommunications service provider, of a prepaid telecommunications product;
  (b) apply to a supply by a person who acts as a distributor, agent, or telecommunications intermediary in relation to the supply of a prepaid telecommunications product; and
  (c) not apply to a supply by one telecommunications service provider to another.

(2) Where a telecommunications service provider supplies a prepaid telecommunications product to a telecommunications intermediary at a discount from the intended retail price, the consideration for the supply shall be calculated as if the intermediary had paid the intended retail price.

(3) Where a telecommunications intermediary purchases and on-sells a prepaid telecommunications product —
  (a) the acquisition by the intermediary shall be treated as if it were not an acquisition; and
  (b) the supply by the intermediary shall be treated as if it were not a supply.

(4) Where a telecommunications service provider supplies a prepaid telecommunications product through a telecommunications intermediary acting as agent for the telecommunications provider, the consideration for the supply is not reduced by the commission paid to the intermediary.

25. In kind employee benefits

Where a taxable person is an employer and makes a taxable supply to an employee as part of the employee's salary or because of the employment relationship, the supply shall be treated as having been made for consideration equal to the fair market value of the supply.

26. Cancelled transactions

(1) Where a supply, or an agreement for a supply, is cancelled and part of the consideration previously paid is retained by the supplier, any adjustments allowed or required under section 71 because of the cancellation, shall be reduced to take account of the amount retained.

(2) Where a supply or an agreement for a supply is cancelled and the supplier recovers an amount from the customer as a consequence of the cancellation, the amount recovered shall be treated as consideration received for a supply made in the tax period when the amount is recovered.

(3) The provisions of subsections (1) and (2) shall apply whether or not the cancellation has

the effect that no supply is made, and any references to supplier and customer in those subsections shall be treated as referring to the persons who would have been the supplier and customer had the transaction not been cancelled.

27. Sale of property of debtor

(1) Where a creditor supplies the property of a debtor to a third person in full or partial satisfaction of a debt owed by the debtor to the creditor —

 (a) the supply to the third person shall be treated as having been made by the debtor and its value added tax status shall be determined accordingly; and

 (b) the creditorshall be liable to pay the value added tax, on the supply and that value added tax shall be payable in priority to —

  (i) the satisfaction of the debt; and

  (ii) the return to the debtor or any other person of any part of the proceeds that is surplus to the debt.

(2) A creditor who is not a registered person but is required to pay value added tax by operation of subsection (1), shall pay value added tax at such time and manner as maybe prescribed in the regulations.

(3) This section shall apply to a representative acting for a creditor under section 92.

Part III
REGISTRATION

28. Registration requirement

(1) A person shall, in respect of any month, be registered for value added tax from the first day of that month, if there is reasonable ground to expect that the person's turnover in the twelve months period commencing at the beginning of the previous month will be equal to or greater than the registration threshold.

(2) A person is required, in respect of any month, to be registered for value added tax from the first day of that month if —

 (a) the person's turnover is equal to or greater than the registration threshold in the period of twelve months ending at the end of the previous month; or

 (b) the person's turnover is equal to or greater than one half of the registration threshold in the period of six months ending at the end of the previous month.

(3) The provisions of subsection (2) shall not apply to a person where the Commissioner General is satisfied, on the basis of objective evidence submitted to the Commissioner General, that the requirements of subsection (1) are not met.

(4) The amount of registration thresholdshall be as prescribed in the regulations.

(5) For purposes of this Part, a person's turnover shall be the sum of —

 (a) total value of supplies made, or to be made, by the person in the course of an economic activity carried out during that period; and

 (b) total value of supplies of imported services made, or to be made, to the person during the period that would be taxable supplies if the person was a taxable person during that period.

(6) The following amounts shall be excluded when calculating the person's turnover for the purpose of this Part —

(a) the value of a supply that would not be a taxable supply if the person were a taxable person;

(b) the value of a sale of a capital asset of the person;

(c) the value of a supply made solely as a consequence of selling an economic activity or part of that economic activity as a going concern; and

(d) the value of supplies made solely as a consequence of permanently ceasing to carry on an economic activity.

29. Other persons required to be registered

(1) Notwithstanding the provisions of section 28, a person shall be required to be registered for value added tax if —

(a) the person carries on an economic activity involving the supply of professional services in Mainland Tanzania, whether those professional services are provided by the person, a member or employee of that person; and

(b) supplies of such services in Mainland Tanzania are ordinarily made by a person who —

(i) is permitted, approved, licensed, or registered to provide such professional services under any other written laws; or

(ii) belongs to a professional association that has uniform national registration requirements relating to the supply of professional services of that kind.

(2) A Government entity or institution which carries on economic activity shall be required to be registered for value added tax.

(3) Notwithstanding the provisions of section 28, the Commissioner General may register a taxable person as intending trader upon fulfilling the following conditions —

(a) provide sufficient evidence to satisfy the Commissioner of his intention to commence an economic activity, including contracts, tenders, building plans, business plans, bank financing;

(b) the person makes or will make supplies that will be taxable supplies if the person is registered; and

(c) specify the period within which the intended economic activity commences production of taxable supplies.

30. Time of application for registration

(1) A person who is required to be registered for value added tax shall within thirty days from the date of such requirement, make application for registration to the Commissioner General.

(2) An application for registration of an intending trader maybe made at any time.

(3) An application for registration under this section maybe made by a representative.

31. Mode of application

The Minister may prescribe in the regulations the manner of making applications for registration.

32. Processing of application

(1) Where the Commissioner General is satisfied that an applicant qualifies for registration for value added tax, the Commissioner General shall register such person.

(2) The Commissioner General shall, by notice in writing, notify the applicant for registration of the decision within fourteen days of the application.

(3) The notice referred to under subsection (2) shall state if the Commissioner General —

(a) registers the person, the day on which the registration takes effect; or

(b) rejects the application, the reasons for the decision and the details of the person's rights to object and appeal against the decision, including the time, place, and manner of filing a notice of objection.

(4) The Commissioner General shall issue a registration certificate to the registered person.

33. Compulsory registration

Where the Commissioner General is satisfied that —

(a) a person is required to be registered for value added tax and that person has not applied for registration, subject to section 30, the Commissioner General shall register the person and, not later than fourteen days after the day on which the registration is done, notify the person on the registration; or

(b) there is good reason including protection of Government revenue, may register the person for value added tax regardless of the person's turnover.

34. Effect of failure to process application

Where the Commissioner General fails to process the application by a person who has applied for registration within the time required, the provisions of this Act shall not apply to such person until the person is duly registered.

35. Taxpayer Identification Number and Value Added Tax Registration Number

A registered person shall use a Taxpayer Identification Number and a Value Added Tax Registration Number on all documents required to be issued under this Act.

36. Registration to cover branches or divisions

The registration by a person under this Act shall be a single registration, which shall cover all economic activities undertaken by that person's branches or divisions.

37. Notification of changes

A registered person shall notify the Commissioner General in writing within fourteen days of the occurrence of the following changes —

(a) the name of the registered person, business name, or trading name of the person;

(b) the address or other contact details of that person;

(c) one or more places through which the person carries on an economic activity in Mainland Tanzania;

(d) the nature of one or more of the economic activities carried on by the person;

(e) the person's status as a registered person; and

(f) any other changes as prescribed in the regulations.

38. Transparency in pricing

(1) A price advertised or quoted by a registered person in respect of a taxable supply shall be value added tax inclusive, and the advertisement or quote shall state that the price includes both value added tax and the amount of value added tax payable on the supply, except that the prices of goods or services offered for retail supply need not separately state the value added tax included in the price if —

(a) a notice stating that prices include value added tax is prominently displayed —

(i) at or near the entrance to the premises, or on the website, where the goods or services are offered for supply; and

(ii) at the place or webpage where payments are effected; and

(b) the receipt or invoice given to the customer separately states the total amount of value added tax charged for supplies to which it refers and, if applicable, identify which items are subject to value added tax.

(2) The Minister may make regulations prescribing any other method of displaying prices for taxable supplies in relation to a registered person or a class of registered persons, except that the method involving value added tax exclusive pricing maybe prescribed only for supplies to registered persons.

(3) The price charged by a taxable person for a taxable supply shall be considered to include any value added tax that is payable on the supply, whether or not the person is registered or he separately states that value added tax is charged or took liability to pay value added tax into account when setting the price.

39. Application for cancellation of registration

(1) A registered person who permanently ceases to make taxable supplies shall apply for the cancellation of its registration in the manner prescribed in the regulations.

(2) The application referred to under subsection (1) shall be made within fourteen days after the date on which the person permanently ceased to make taxable supplies.

(3) A registered person who fails to maintain the registration threshold may apply for the cancellation of his registration in the manner prescribed in the regulations.

40. Decision on application for cancelation of registration

Where the Commissioner General is satisfied that a person applying for cancelation of registration is not required to be registered for value added tax and such person has been registered for —

(a) at least twelve months, the Commissioner General shall, by notice in writing, cancel the person's registration; or

(b) less than twelve months, the Commissioner General may, by notice in writing, cancel the person's registration, if satisfied that, it is appropriate to do so.

41. Power to cancel registration

(1) The Commissioner General may, by notice, cancel the registration of a person who is no longer required to be registered for value added tax, if the Commissioner General is satisfied

that —
- (a) the person obtained registration by providing false or misleading information;
- (b) the person is not carrying on an economic activity;
- (c) the person has ceased to produce taxable supplies; or
- (d) the person's taxable turnover falls below registration threshold.

(2) The cancellation of a person's registration shall take effect from the date set out in the notice of cancellation.

42. Persons whose registration is cancelled

A person whose registration is cancelled shall —
- (a) immediately cease to be a registered person;
- (b) immediately cease to use or issue any documents including tax invoices and adjustment notes that identify him as a registered person and surrender value added tax registration certificate; and
- (c) within thirty days after the date of cancellation of his registration, file a final value added tax return and pay all taxes due under this Act.

43. List of registered persons

(1) The Commissioner General shall maintain and publish an up to date register of registered persons, which shall include —
- (a) the name and address of the registered person;
- (b) the business or trading name or names, under which the registered person carries on its economic activities;
- (c) the Taxpayer Identification Number and Value Added Tax Registration Number of the registered person; and
- (d) the date on which the registration took effect.

(2) The Commissioner General shall maintain a complete historical record of the register identifying the person registered for value added tax and shall, on the request, make the record available to members of the public or by including the historical information on the published register.

Part IV
PLACE OF TAXATION

(a) Supplies of goods and services made in Mainland Tanzania

44. Supplies of goods

(1) A supply of goods shall be treated as a supply made in Mainland Tanzania, if the goods are delivered or made available in Mainland Tanzania.

(2) For purposes of subsection (1), goods supplied after they are imported into Mainland Tanzania but before they are entered for home consumption in Mainland Tanzania shall be treated as having been delivered or made available outside Mainland Tanzania.

45. Inbound and outbound goods

(1) Goods installed or assembled in Mainland Tanzania by, or under a contract with the

supplier shall be treated as a supply made in Mainland Tanzania.

(2) A supply of goods shall be treated as a supply made in Mainland Tanzania if the goods are dispatched or transported from Mainland Tanzania to a place outside the United Republic.

46. Supplies relating to immovable property

(1) A supply of immovable property situated in Mainland Tanzania or a supply of services directly related to land situated in Mainland Tanzania shall be treated as a supply made in Mainland Tanzania.

(2) A supply of service directly related to immovable property shall be treated as a supply made in Mainland Tanzania if —

(a) the land to which the property relates is not situated in Mainland Tanzania; and

(b) the supplier is —

(i) a resident of Mainland Tanzania; or

(ii) a non-resident who carries on an economic activity at or through a fixed place in Mainland Tanzania.

47. Supply of services directly related to land

A supply of services directly related to land situated outside Mainland Tanzania shall be treated as a supply made in Mainland Tanzania if the supplier is a non-resident who is operating through a fixed place in Mainland Tanzania.

48. Supply of essential services

Where water, gas, oil, electricity, or thermal energy is supplied through a pipeline, cable, or other continuous distribution network and delivered to a place in Mainland Tanzania or from a place in Mainland Tanzania to a place outside the United Republic such supply shall be treated as a supply made in Mainland Tanzania.

49. Services supplied to registered person

(1) A supply of services by a non-resident who is a registered person to a customer who is a registered person shall be treated as a supply made in Mainland Tanzania.

(2) Subsection (1) shall not apply if the customer is a non-resident who carries on an economic activity at or through a fixed place outside Mainland Tanzania and the supply is made —

(a) for the purpose of that economic activity; or

(b) to that fixed place.

50. Telecommunication services

(1) A supply of telecommunication services shall be treated as a supply made in Mainland Tanzania, if a person in Mainland Tanzania, other than a telecommunications service provider, initiates the supply from a telecommunications service provider, whether or not the person initiates the supply on his own behalf.

(2) For purposes of subsection (1), a person who initiates a supply of telecommunication services is the person who —

(a) controls the commencement of the supply;

(b) pays for the supply; or

(c) contracts for the supply.

(3) Where it is impractical for the supplier to determine the location of a person referred to in subsection (2) due to the type of service or the class of customer, the person who initiates the supply of telecommunication service shall be the person to whom the invoice for the supply is sent.

(4) This section shall not apply if the person who initiates the call in Mainland Tanzania is a non-resident who is global roaming while in Mainland Tanzania and who pays for the supply under a contract made with a non-resident telecommunications service provider, through a place outside the United Republic at which the non-resident is established.

[Cap.4 s.8]

51. Services supplied to unregistered person in Mainland Tanzania

(1) A supply of any of the following services shall be treated as a supply made in Mainland Tanzania when supplied to a customer who is not a registered person —
- (a) services performed in Mainland Tanzania, if the services are received by a person in Mainland Tanzania who effectively uses or enjoys the services in Mainland Tanzania;
- (b) services received for radio or television broadcasting at an address in Mainland Tanzania; and
- (c) electronic services delivered to a person who is in Mainland Tanzania at the time when the service is delivered.

(2) For purposes of this section "electronic services" means any of the following services provided or delivered through a telecommunications network —
- (a) websites, web-hosting, or remote maintenance of programmes and equipment;
- (b) software and the updating thereof;
- (c) images, text, and information;
- (d) access to databases;
- (e) self-education packages;
- (f) music, films, and games, including gaming activities; and
- (g) political, cultural, artistic, sporting, scientific, and other broadcasts and events including broadcast television.

52. Other services supplied to unregistered person within Mainland Tanzania

(1) Any other supply of services shall be treated as a supply made in Mainland Tanzania, if —
- (a) the customer is a resident of Mainland Tanzania and is not a registered person; and
- (b) the supplier is —
    - (i) a resident of Mainland Tanzania; or
    - (ii) a non-resident who carries on an economic activity at or through a fixed place in Mainland Tanzania; and
- (c) the supply is made in the course of that economic activity or through that fixed place.

(2) A supply of services shall be treated as a supply made in Mainland Tanzania, if it is not treated as a supply made in —
- (a) Mainland Tanzania in accordance with section 51; and
- (b) the supplier is —
    - (i) a resident of Mainland Tanzania; or

(ii) a non-resident and carries on an economic activity at or through a fixed place in Mainland Tanzania.

53. Progressive or periodic supplies

Where a progressive or periodic supply is a series of separate supplies, the place where each supply takes place shall be determined separately.

(b) Supplies for use outside the United Republic

54. Zero-rating of immovable property

A supply of immovable property shall be zero-rated if the land to which the property relates is outside the United Republic.

55. Zero-rating of supply of goods

(1) A supply of goods shall be zero-rated if the goods are exported within the meaning of the term "export" as provided for under section 2.

(2) A supply of goods shall be zero-rated if the goods are supplied to a tourist or visitor by a licensed duty-free vendor who holds documentary evidence, collected at the time of the supply, and establishing that the goods shall be removed from the United Republic without being effectively used or enjoyed in the United Republic.

(3) Subsection (1) shall not apply where the goods are re-imported in Mainland Tanzania.

55A. Zero-rating of supply of goods to Tanzania Zanzibar

A supply of locally manufactured goods by a local manufacturer shall be zero-rated if the goods are supplied to a taxable person registered under the value added tax law administered in Zanzibar and such goods are removed from Mainland Tanzania without being effectively used or enjoyed in Mainland Tanzania.

[Act No.2 of 2016 s.94]

56. Leased goods used outside United Republic

(1) Where goods are supplied in Mainland Tanzania by way of lease, hire, licence, or similar supply, the supply shall be zero-rated if and to the extent that the goods are used outside the United Republic.

(2) The following conditions shall apply for the purposes of subsection (1) —

(a) the use of leased goods in international territory shall be treated as a use wholly within the United Republic if immediately before that use the goods are used in the United Republic; and

(b) the supply shall not be zero-rated if the goods are a means of transport and the total period of the lease, hire, licence, or similar supply is equal to or less than thirty days.

57. Goods used to repair temporary imports

A supply of goods made in the course of repairing, maintaining, cleaning, renovating, modifying, treating, or otherwise physically affecting temporary import goods shall be zero-rated where —

(a) the goods being supplied are attached to or become part of those temporary import goods, or become unusable or worthless as a direct result of being used to repair, maintain, clean, renovate, modify, treat, or otherwise physically affect the temporary import goods; and

(b) the temporary import goods —

   (i) are imported under a special regime for temporary imports under the East African Customs Management Act, or brought temporarily into Mainland Tanzania for the purpose of the performance of the services;

   [Act No.1 of 2005 E.A.C.M]

   (ii) are removed from the United Republic after the services have been performed; and

   (iii) are not used in Mainland Tanzania for any purpose other than to enable the services to be performed or to enable the temporary import goods to be brought into Mainland Tanzania, or outside the United Republic.

58. Supply of goods and services to non-resident warrantor

A supply of goods or services shall be zero rated, if it relates to the repair or replacement of goods under warranty, and —

(a) the supply is provided under an agreement with, and for consideration given by, the warrantor, who is a non-resident and is not a registered person; and

(b) it is reasonable to presume that the goods under warranty were under this Act previously subject to value added tax when imported, unless no value added tax was payable.

59. Goods for use in international transport services

(1) A supply of goods for use in repairing, maintaining, cleaning, renovating, modifying, treating, or otherwise physically affecting an aircraft or ship engaged in international transport services shall be zero-rated.

(2) A supply of aircraft's stores or ship's stores, for an aircraft or ship shall be zero-rated, if the stores are used for consumption or sale on the aircraft or ship during a flight or voyage that constitutes international transport services.

(3) The following supplies of services shall be zero-rated —

(a) a supply of international transport services;

(b) a supply of insuring the international transport services of goods;

(c) a supply of the services of repairing, maintaining, cleaning, renovating, modifying, treating, or otherwise physically affecting an aircraft or ship engaged in international transport services;

(d) a supply, to a non-resident who is not a registered person, of services that —

   (i) consist of the handling, pilotage, salvage, or towage of a ship or aircraft engaged in international transport services; or

   (ii) are provided directly in connection with the operation or management of a ship or aircraft engaged in international transport services; and

(e) a supply of ancillary transport services of goods in transit through Mainland Tanzania in circumstances that is —

(i) an integral part of the supply of an international transport services; and

(ii) in respect of goods stored at the port, airport, or a declared customs area for not more than thirty days while awaiting onward transport.

(4) For purposes of this section —

"aircraft's stores" means stores for the use of the passengers or crew of an aircraft, or for the service of an aircraft;

"ship's stores" means stores for the use of the passengers, crew of a ship, or for the service of a ship; and

"stores" in relation to aircraft's stores and ship's stores, includes goods for use in the aircraft or ship, fuel, and spare parts, and other articles or equipment, whether or not for immediate fitting.

[Act No.4 of 2017 s.67; Cap.4 s.8]

60. Services supplied for use outside United Republic

(1) A supply of services directly related to land outside the United Republic shall be zero-rated.

(2) A supply of services physically performed on goods situated outside the United Republic at the time the services are performed shall be zero-rated.

(3) A supply of services, of which the services are physically received at no time and place other than the time and place at which the services are physically performed, shall be zero-rated if the services are performed outside the United Republic of Tanzania.

61. Services connected with temporary imports

A supply of services shall be zero-rated, if the services consists of repairing, maintaining, cleaning, renovating, modifying, treating, or otherwise physically affecting goods that —

(a) are imported under a special regime for temporary imports under the East African Customs Management Act, or are brought temporarily into Mainland Tanzania for the purpose of the performance of the services; and

(b) are removed from the United Republic after the services have been performed and are not used in Mainland Tanzania for any purpose other than to enable the services to be performed or to enable the goods to be brought into Mainland Tanzania or outside the United Republic.

[Acts Nos.1 of 2005; 2 of 2016 s.95]

61A. Zero-rating of supply of services

(1) A Supply of services shall be zero-rated if —

(a) the customer is outside the United Republic at the time of supply and effectively uses or enjoys the services outside the United Republic; and

(b) the services are neither directly related to land situated in the United Republic nor physically performed on goods situated in the United Republic at the time of supply.

(2) A supply of services is not zero-rated in accordance with the provision of subsection (1), if —

(a) the supply is of a right or option to receive a subsequent supply of something else in the United Republic; or

(b) the services are supplied under an agreement with a non-resident but are rendered to a person in the United Republic who is not a registered person.

[Act No.2 of 2016 s.96]

61B. Zero rating supply of electricity services

A supply of electricity services by a supplier of electricity service in Mainland Tanzania to another supplier of electricity service in Tanzania Zanzibar shall be zero rated.

[Act No.8 of 2019 s.48]

62. Intellectual property rights for use outside United Republic

A supply of services consisting of filing, prosecuting, granting, maintaining, transferring, assigning, licensing, or enforcing intellectual property rights for use outside the United Republic shall be zero-rated.

63. Inter-carrier telecommunication services

A supply of telecommunication services by a telecommunications service provider to a non-resident telecommunications service provider shall be zero-rated, including but not limited to a supply involving the termination of calls in Mainland Tanzania or the transmission of signals in or through Mainland Tanzania.

(c) Special rules

64. Value added tax representatives of non-residents

(1) A non-resident who carries on economic activity in Mainland Tanzania without having a fixed place in Mainland Tanzania, and makes a taxable supply for which the non-resident is liable to pay value added tax shall —

   (a) appoint a value added tax representative in Mainland Tanzania in accordance with the requirements set out in the regulations; and

   (b) if required by the Commissioner General, lodge a security.

(2) The value added tax representative shall be a resident and responsible for doing all things required to be done under this Act, which shall include —

   (a) applying for registration or cancellation of registration and fulfilling other obligations in relation to registration; and

   (b) paying any value added tax or any fine, penalty, or interest imposed on the non-resident under this Act.

(3) The registration of a value added tax representative shall be in the name of the principal.

(4) A person who is the value added tax representative of more than one non-resident shall register separately for value added tax in respect of each non-resident.

65. Services from foreign branch

(1) Where a taxable person carries on economic activities at a fixed place in Mainland Tanzania and at one or more fixed places outside Mainland Tanzania —

   (a) the person shall be treated as two separate persons corresponding respectively to the economic activities carried on inside and outside Mainland Tanzania;

   (b) the person outside Mainland Tanzania shall be deemed to have made a supply of imported services to the person inside Mainland Tanzania consisting of any benefit in the nature of services that is received by the person in Mainland Tanzania through or as a result of the activities carried on by the person outside Mainland Tanzania; and

(c) the time of supply shall be determined on the assumption that a supply has been made.

(2) Where, within twelve months from the time of making a supply referred to in subsection (1), the person outside Mainland Tanzania makes an allocation of costs to the person inside Mainland Tanzania in respect of the supply, the allocation of costs shall be treated as consideration for the supply.

(3) Where a supply referred to in subsection (1) is a taxable supply, the value of the supply —

(a) where the provision of subsection (2) applies, shall be equal to the amount of the costs allocated, reduced by that part, if any, of the amount allocated that represents —

(i) salary or wages paid to an employee of the person outside Mainland Tanzania; and

(ii) interest incurred by the person outside Mainland Tanzania; and

(b) in any other case, shall be assumed to have been made by a non-resident outside Mainland Tanzania to a connected person in Mainland Tanzania.

[Act No.2 of 2016 s.97]

Part V
RETURNS, PAYMENTS AND REFUNDS

(a) Returns and payment

66. Value added tax returns

(1) A taxable person shall lodge a value added tax return in the form and manner prescribed by the Minister on the 20th day of a month after the end of the tax period to which it relates, whether or not that person has a net amount of value added tax payable for that period.

(2) A non-taxable person who is required to pay an amount of value added tax under this Act shall file a return in respect of that value added tax at the time prescribed by the Commissioner General.

(3) A taxable person who has filed a value added tax return may, on application in the prescribed manner and not later than three years after the end of the tax period to which the returns relates, request the Commissioner General to amend the returns to correct any genuine omission or incorrect declaration made in the returns.

(4) Where a person makes an application under subsection (3), the Commissioner General may —

(a) make a decision on the application on the basis of the information provided in the application without undertaking an audit or investigation of the applicant's tax affairs; or

(b) amend the original return or accept filing of an amended return.

(5) The decision by the Commissioner General under subsection (4) shall be made not later than ninety days of receiving the application, and the decision shall be in writing stating —

(a) the details, if any, of the amendment made;

(b) the reasons for the decision and the details of the applicant's rights to object and appeal against the decision; and

(c) the time, place, and manner of filing a notice of objection.

(6) A taxable person who makes an application to amend a value added tax return before the receipt of a notice of audit or investigation, if any, shall pay the unpaid tax and the applicable interest for late payment.

(7) For purposes of subsection (1), where the 20th day falls on a Saturday, Sunday or a public holiday, the value added tax return shall be lodged on the first working day following a Saturday, Sunday or public holiday.

[Acts Nos.2 of 2016 s.98; 4 of 2017 s.68]

(b) Net amount of value added tax payable

67. Calculation and payment of net amount

(1) The net amount of value added tax payable by a taxable person in relation to a tax period shall be calculated by —

(a) adding all output tax that becomes payable by the person in that tax period;

(b) subtracting all input tax credits allowed in that tax period; and

(c) adjusting the resulting amount by —

(i) adding all increasing adjustments required to be made in that tax period; and

(ii) subtracting all decreasing adjustments allowed in that tax period.

(2) Where the amount of output tax payable in a tax period is nil, it shall not prevent the subtraction of input tax credits or the addition and subtraction of adjustments.

(3) Where the net amount for a tax period is a positive amount —

(a) it shall be accounted for and paid by the taxable person at the time when the value added tax return is due to be filed; and

(b) the liability to pay the net amount shall arise by operation of this section and shall not depend on the making of an assessment of the amount due by the Commissioner General.

(4) Where the net amount for a tax period is a negative amount, it shall be carried forward into one or more subsequent tax periods in accordance with section 81, unless an immediate refund is allowable under section 82.

(c) Input tax credits

68. Credit for input tax

(1) A taxable person shall be allowed a credit for an amount of input tax incurred by the person if —

(a) the goods, services, or immovable property on which the input tax was incurred were acquired or imported into Mainland Tanzania by the person in the course of the person's economic activity and for the purpose of making taxable supplies;

(b) in the case of a supply, the person paid, or is liable to pay, the consideration for the supply; and

(c) in the case of an import, the person paid, or is liable to pay, the value added tax imposed on the import under this Act or input tax paid under the value added tax law applicable in Tanzania Zanzibar, where the respective goods are transferred to Mainland Tanzania.

(2) The value added tax payable by the purchaser of a taxable supply of imported services shall be output tax and input tax of that person, and the purchaser shall not be allowed an input tax credit for that supply unless he has accounted for the output tax in the same value added tax return in which the input tax credit is claimed.

(3) A taxable person shall not be allowed an input tax credit for —
   (a) an acquisition of goods, services, or immovable property, to the extent that it is used to provide entertainment, unless the person's economic activity involves providing entertainment in the ordinary course of the person's economic activity;
   (b) an acquisition of a membership or right of entry for any person in a club, association, or society of a sporting, social, or recreational nature;
   (c) an acquisition or import of a passenger vehicle, or of spare parts or repair and maintenance services for a passenger vehicle, unless the person's economic activity involves dealing in, hiring out, or providing transport services in passenger vehicles and the vehicle was acquired for that purpose; and
   (d) an exportation of raw minerals, raw forestry products, raw aquatic products and raw fauna products:
   Provided that in the case of raw minerals, input tax credit shall not be allowed with effect from the 20th day of July, 2017.

[Cap.4 s.8]

(4) The restrictions in subsection (3)(a) and (b) shall not apply to acquisitions or imports used to provide in-kind benefits to employees and the supply of which is taxable under section 25.

(5) In applying this section for an adjustment event referred to in paragraph (b) of the definition of the term "adjustment event" —
   (a) references to "the supply" shall be read as if they refer to —
      (i) in the case of the value added tax previously accounted for by the supplier, the value added tax paid when the voucher was issued or sold; and
      (ii) in the case of the value added tax payable on the supply, the value added tax that would have been payable on the supply for which the voucher is given, if the supply of the voucher had not been a taxable supply; and
   (b) the limitation in section 72(1)(b)(ii) shall not apply.

(6) If an adjustment event occurs in relation to a supply of imported services, the purchaser of the services shall be treated as if he is also the supplier of the services.

[Acts Nos.7 of 2017 s.47; 8 of 2019 s.49]

69. Timing of input tax credits

(1) Where a taxable person is allowed an input tax credit, the tax period in which the credit

maybe included in the calculations pursuant to section 70 shall be the latter of:
   (a) the tax period in which the value added tax became payable under this Act on the supply or import to which the input tax relates; or
   (b) if the person did not claim the input tax credit in that period, any one of the six succeeding tax periods.

(2) The input tax shall not be deducted or credited after a period of six months from the date of tax invoice, fiscal receipt or other evidence referred under subsection (3).

(3) A taxable person shall not include an input tax credit in the calculations made in section 70, unless at the time of filing the value added tax return for the relevant tax period such person holds —
   (a) in the case of an import into the United Republic by the person, a proof for payment of tax, a Single Administrative Document or similar document bearing the name, Taxpayer Identification Number and value added tax registration number of the importer which are duly cleared by customs for home consumption in Mainland Tanzania; and
   (b) in the case of a supply made to a person in Mainland Tanzania, a valid tax invoice or fiscal receipt issued by the supplier under this Act.

70. Partial input tax credit

(1) This section shall apply to input tax incurred on goods, services, or immovable property acquired or imported into Mainland Tanzania by a taxable person in the course of the person's economic activity but only partly for the purpose of making taxable supplies.

(2) The amount of the credit allowed for input tax to which this section relates shall be calculated according to the following formula —

$$\frac{I \times}{A}$$

[Please note: formula reproduced as in original.]

Where —

I: is the total amount of input tax to which this subsection relates and for which a credit is sought in the tax period;

T: is the value of all the taxable supplies made by the taxable person during the tax period; and

A: is the value of all the supplies made by the taxable person during the tax period.

(3) The amount of the input tax credit allowed under this section shall be provisional, and an annual adjustment of the input tax credit shall be calculated at the end of each accounting year as follows —
   (a) add up all the input tax credits allowed under subsection (2) for each of the twelve tax periods occurring during that accounting year;
   (b) apply the formula in subsection (2) as if references to "the tax period" in the definitions of "I", "A", and "T" were references to the relevant accounting year;
   (c) work out the amount of the adjustment by subtracting the amount worked out under paragraph (b) from the amount worked out under paragraph (a);

(d) if the adjustment so calculated is a positive amount, the taxable person shall make an increasing adjustment equal to that amount in the person's value added tax return for the sixth tax period in the following accounting year, or such earlier tax period as the regulations prescribe; and

(e) if the adjustment so calculated is a negative amount, the taxable person shall be allowed a decreasing adjustment for that amount in the value added tax return for the sixth tax period in the following accounting year, or such earlier tax period as the regulations prescribe.

(4) For purposes of this section —

(a) supplies made through an economic activity carried on at a fixed place outside Mainland Tanzania shall not be included in A or T in the formula, unless those supplies are made in Mainland Tanzania;

(b) if T/A is greater than 0.90, the taxable person shall be allowed a credit for all of the input tax to which this section relates; and

(c) if T/A is less than 0.10, the taxable person shall not be allowed a credit for any of the input tax to which this section relates.

(d) Other adjustments
71. Post supply adjustments for adjustment events

(1) Where an adjustment event has the effect that the value added tax previously accounted for by the supplier is less than the value added tax properly payable on the supply —

(a) the suppliershall —

(i) make an increasing adjustment equal to the amount of the difference; and

(ii) issue a valid adjustment note to the customer within seven days of becoming aware of the adjustment event; and

(b) where the customer is a taxable person, he shall be allowed a decreasing adjustment calculated in accordance with subsection (1)(a).

(2) Where an adjustment event has the effect that the value added tax previously accounted for by the supplier exceeds the value added tax properly payable on the supply —

(a) the suppliershall —

(i) subject to the limitations set out in section 72, be allowed a decreasing adjustment equal to the amount of the difference; and

[Cap.4 s.8]

(ii) issue a valid adjustment note to the customer within seven days of becoming aware of the event; and

(b) where the customer is a taxable person, he shall make an increasing adjustment calculated in accordance with subsection (3).

(3) The amount of a decreasing adjustment allowed under subsection (1), or an increasing adjustment the customer shall make under subsection (2), is equal to —

(a) if the customer is entitled to a full input tax credit for the original acquisition, the amount of the difference;

(b) if the customer is entitled to a credit for only part of the input tax on the original acquisition, an appropriate proportion of the amount of the difference; or

(c) if the customer is not entitled to an input tax credit for the original acquisition, nil.

[Cap.4 s.8]

72. Limitations on adjustments

(1) A decreasing adjustment shall not be allowed under section 71 —

(a) for a customer, unless he holds a valid adjustment note issued by the supplier at the time when the customer submits value added tax returns for the tax period in which the adjustment is claimed; and

(b) for a supplier, unless —

(i) he has issued an adjustment note to the customer and retained a copy for his own records; and

(ii) if the customer is not a registered person, he has repaid the excess value added tax to the customer, whether in cash or as a credit against any amount owing to the supplier by the customer.

(2) For purposes of subsection (1)(b)(ii) —

(a) if a supplier refunds part or all of the price paid due to an adjustment event covered by paragraph (a)(i), (a)(ii) or (a)(iii) of the definition of the term "adjustment event", the amount refunded shall, unless there is evidence to the contrary, be presumed to include an amount of value added tax equal to the tax fraction of the amount refunded; and

(b) if a supplier refunds an amount because of an adjustment event covered by paragraph (a)(iv) of the definition of the term "adjustment event", the amount refunded would be presumed to be the amount of value added tax that is no longer payable, unless there is evidence to the contrary.

73. Period of making adjustments

(1) An increasing adjustment which a taxable person is required to make under section 71 shall be made in the tax period in which the taxable person becomes aware of the adjustment event.

(2) A decreasing adjustment which a taxable person is allowed under section 71 shall be —

(a) in the case of a supplier, in the tax period in which the supplier issues the adjustment note; or

(b) in the case of a customer, in the tax period in which the customer first becomes aware of the adjustment event or in any one only of the subsequent six tax periods.

[Cap.4 s.8]

74. Post supply adjustments for bad debts

(1) This section shall apply where all or part of the consideration for a taxable supply has not been paid to the supplier.

(2) Where all or part of consideration payable to the supplier for a taxable supply has been overdue for more than eighteen months and the supplier has, in his books of account, written off

the amount unpaid as a bad debt, the supplier shall be allowed a decreasing adjustment equal to the amount that remains unpaid after the tax period in which —
- (a) the amount first becomes overdue by more than eighteen months; or
- (b) the debt is written off as bad in the suppliers books of account.

(3) Where all or part of the consideration payable to a supplier for a taxable supply has been overdue for more than eighteen months and the customer claimed an input tax credit for the supply, the customer shall make an increasing adjustment equal to the amount that remains unpaid in the tax period in which the payment first becomes overdue by more than eighteen months.

(4) Where a supplier makes a decreasing adjustment for a bad debt, or a customer makes an increasing adjustment for an overdue debt, and the customer pays to the supplier part or all of the previously unpaid amount, further adjustments shall be made in order to ensure that —
- (a) in the case of the supplier, the output tax paid is equal to the tax fraction of the consideration actually received; and
- (b) in the case of the customer, the input tax credit is the appropriate proportion of the tax fraction of the consideration actually paid.

(5) Adjustment notes shall not be required in respect of bad or overdue debts in order for a supplier to be allowed a decreasing adjustment or the customer to be required to make an increasing adjustment under this section.

[Act No.4 of 2017 s.69]

75. Application for private use

(1) A person is deemed to have applied property for private use where that person uses or consumes the property for a purpose other than for the person's economic activity.

(2) A taxable person shall make an increasing adjustment if the person —
- (a) is or has been allowed an input tax credit in respect of all or part of the input tax incurred on an acquisition or import of property; and
- (b) applies the same property wholly to a private use, or having used the property wholly or partly in its taxable activity, applies it to such use from a particular time onwards.

(3) The amount of the increasing adjustment shall be equal to the lesser of the following amounts —
- (a) the amount of the input tax credit the person was allowed for the acquisition or import of the goods; or
- (b) if the property has been used in the person's taxable activity before it is applied to private use, the tax fraction of the fair market value of the property at the time it is first applied wholly to a private use, reduced to reflect the extent to which no input tax credit was allowed.

(4) A taxable person shall make an increasing adjustment in respect of property he modifies, improves, or produces, if —
- (a) the person applies that property wholly to a private use; and
- (b) a supply of that property by the person would have been a taxable supply.

(5) The amount of the increasing adjustment required to be made under subsection (4), shall

be the tax fraction of the fair market value of the property at the time it is first applied wholly to a private use.

(6) An increasing adjustment under this section shall be made in the tax period in which the property is first applied to a private use.

76. Adjustment on making insurance payment

(1) An insurer shall have a decreasing adjustment if —
  (a) he makes a payment to another person under a contract of insurance; and
  (b) he meets all the following conditions —
    (i) the supply of the contract of insurance is a taxable supply;
    (ii) the payment is not made in respect of a supply to the insurer or an import by the insurer;

[Cap.4 s.8]

    (iii) the payment is not made in respect of a supply to another person, unless that supply is a taxable supply on which value added tax is imposed at a rate other than zero; and
    (iv) the person to whom the payment is made is a resident or a non-resident who is a registered person.

(2) The amount of the adjustment shall be equal to the tax fraction of the payment made and the adjustment made shall be reflected in the value added tax return for the tax period in which the payment is made.

77. Adjustment on receiving insurance payments

(1) A taxable person shall make an increasing adjustment if —
  (a) the person receives a payment under a contract of insurance, whether or not that person is a party to the contract;
  (b) the payment relates to a loss incurred —
    (i) in the course of the person's economic activity; or
    (ii) in relation to an asset used wholly or partly in the person's economic activity; and
  (c) the supply of the contract of insurance was a taxable supply.

(2) The adjustment referred to under subsection (1), shall be made in the tax period in which the payment is received and the amount of the adjustment shall be equal to the tax fraction of the amount received, or reduced to the extent that —
  (a) the economic activity in which the loss was incurred involves the making of exempt supplies; or
  (b) the asset to which the loss relates was used in making exempt supplies or for a private use; and
  (c) if both paragraph (a) and paragraph (b) apply, whichever is most appropriate in the context of the payment received.

(3) An insurer shall make an increasing adjustment if —
  (a) he recovers an amount, other than the aggravated or exemplary damages, as a result of the exercise of rights acquired by subrogation under a contract of insurance; and

(b) a decreasing adjustment is allowed to the insurer under this section for the payment to which the recovered amount relates.

(4) The amount of the adjustment made under subsection (3) shall be equal to the tax fraction of the amount recovered and the adjustment made shall be reflected in the value added tax return for the tax period in which the amount is received.

78. Adjustment to correct minor errors

The Minister may make regulations prescribing conditions under which a person shall be allowed to correct minor errors in a value added tax return for a particular tax period by making an increasing adjustment or decreasing adjustment in the value added tax return for a subsequent tax period.

79. Adjustment on becoming registered

(1) A registered person is, at the end of the last day before the registration takes effect, allowed a decreasing adjustment in relation to goods in that person's possession if —

(a) in the six months before the person became a registered person, the goods —

(i) were imported by the person and the person paid value added tax on the import; or

(ii) were supplied to the person and the person holds a tax invoice for the supply;

(b) that person acquired the goods in the course of his economic activity, and for the purpose of re-sale; and

(c) that person would have been entitled to an input tax credit for the import or acquisition had the person been registered at the time of the acquisition or import.

(2) The maximum amount of the decreasing adjustment allowed shall be equal to the lesser of —

(a) the amount of value added tax paid by the person on the import, or payable by the supplier who made the supply to the person; and

(b) the tax fraction of the fair market value of the goods at the time the person becomes a registered person.

(3) A person who is allowed a decreasing adjustment under this section shall make the adjustment in any one only of the first three tax periods after the person becomes a registered person.

(4) A person who makes an adjustment under this section shall, in writing, give notice of the adjustment to the Commissioner General and provide such supporting evidence as maybe prescribed in the regulations.

80. Adjustment on cancellation of registration

(1) A person whose registration is cancelled shall make an increasing adjustment in his final value added tax return in respect of property on hand at the time the registration is cancelled, if the person was allowed an input tax credit in respect of the acquisition or import of that property, or for something that has been subsumed into that property.

(2) The amount of the adjustment shall be equal to the lesser of —

(a) the tax fraction of the fair market value of the property on the day immediately preceding the cancellation; or

(b) that amount, reduced to reflect the extent to which the person was not allowed an input tax credit in respect of the acquisition or import of that property or, if applicable, on the inputs to the property.

(e) Refunds

81. Carry forward of negative net amount

(1) A taxable person shall be allowed a decreasing adjustment for negative net amounts carried forward from earlier tax periods, which shall be calculated as follows —

(a) in any tax period, section 67 shall first be applied without taking into account any decreasing adjustments allowed under this section;

(b) if the result is a positive amount —

(i) the person shall be allowed a decreasing adjustment for such part of one or more negative net amounts carried forward from an earlier tax period as would reduce the net amount for the current period to a positive amount or to nil; and

(ii) negative net amounts from earlier tax periods shall be taken into account in chronological order, with the oldest being taken into account first and the most recent being taken into account last; and

(c) any part of a negative net amount for which a decreasing adjustment cannot be made shall be carried forward and applied in accordance with paragraph (b) until —

(i) it has been reduced to nil; or

(ii) it has been carried forward for six consecutive tax periods without being reduced to less than minimum amount prescribed in the regulations.

(2) A taxable person who has carried forward all or part of a negative net amount for six or more tax periods —

(a) may apply for a refund of the unadjusted amount if —

(i) the amount is equal to or greater than minimum amount same as in subsection (1)(c)(ii)); or

(ii) the sum of all the unadjusted amounts the person has carried forward for more than six tax periods exceeds that amount; and

(b) in any other case, the person shall continue to carry forward the unadjusted amount under subsection (1) until the amount has been reduced to nil or an entitlement to a refund arises because of paragraph (a)(ii) of this subsection, whichever occurs first.

(3) Notwithstanding subsection (2), a taxable person may choose to continue carrying an unadjusted amount forward and applying it in accordance with subsection (1) until such time as the person applies for a refund of the amount in accordance with subsection (2).

(4) For purposes of this section, the term "minimum amount" means the amount which would not be taken into consideration for the purpose of claiming the input tax.

82. Refund without carry forward

(1) Notwithstanding section 81, a taxable person shall be entitled to a refund of a negative net

amount if —
- (a) fifty percent or more of the person's turnover is or will be from supplies that are zero-rated;
- (b) fifty percent or more of the person's input tax is incurred on acquisitions or imports that relate to making supplies that are or will be zero-rated; or
- (c) in any other case, the Commissioner General is satisfied that the nature of the person's business regularly results in negative net amounts.

(2) A taxable person who is entitled, under this section, to a refund of a negative net amount may —
- (a) apply for a refund of the amount; or
- (b) choose to carry the amount forward under section 81 until such time as the person applies for a refund of the amount in paragraph (a) of this subsection.

83. Refund for overpayment

(1) A taxable person who has paid more than the net amount shown on the person's value added tax return for a tax period, may apply for a refund of the amount overpaid.

(2) A taxable person may apply for a refund where the person has overpaid the net amount payable for a tax period if the overpayment arose in the calculation of the net amount payable for tax period, including —
- (a) an amount of output tax, or an increasing adjustment, which exceeded the amount that should have been included in those calculations; or
- (b) an amount of input tax, or a decreasing adjustment, which is less than the amount that should have been included in those calculations.

84. Application for refunds

(1) This section applies to refunds under sections 81, 82 and 83.

(2) Where a person is entitled to apply for a refund to which this section applies, the application for the refundshall —
- (a) be made in a manner prescribed in the regulations and shall be accompanied by supporting information as the regulation may require; and
- (b) not be made in case the application is made under section 81 or 82, more than three years after the end of the tax period to which the negative net amount relates; or
- (c) not be made in case the application is made under section 83, more than three years after the overpayment was made.

(3) Where a person applies for a refund to which this section relates, the Commissioner General —
- (a) may, subject to the proof of credibility of the taxpayer, make a decision on the application on the basis of the information provided without undertaking an audit or investigation of the applicant's tax affairs; and
- (b) shall, within ninety days of its receipt, make a decision on the application and inform the applicant of the decision by notice in writing stating —
  - (i) the amount of the refund allowed; and

(ii) the period during which the refundshall be made.

(4) Where the Commissioner General is not satisfied that the refund should be allowed, or is satisfied that the amount refundable is less than the amount requested he shall give —

(a) the reasons for the decision;

(b) the applicant's rights to objection and appeal against the decision; and

(c) the time, place, and manner of filing a notice of objection.

(5) The Commissioner General shall refund if he is satisfied that —

(a) the person is entitled to a refund of the amount requested; or

(b) a lower amount represents the person's actual entitlement to a refund.

(6) The Commissioner General shall not refund the person if he is satisfied that such person is not entitled to a refund.

(7) Where the Commissioner General allows a refund to which this section relates —

(a) the refund shall not be paid unless the applicant has filed all value added tax returns which the applicant is required to file; and

(b) the Commissioner General may apply the refund first in reduction of any outstanding liability of the person for taxes payable under this Act or under another tax law, including any interest, penalties, or fines payable under this Act or under that tax law.

(8) Where the amount remaining after applying subsection (7)(b) does not exceed the minimum amount prescribed in the regulations, the Commissioner General may refund the amount or require the taxable person to take the refund as a decreasing adjustment in a tax period prescribed by the Commissioner General.

(9) Where the Commissioner General allows a refund under this section, the taxable person may, with the agreement of the Commissioner General, take the refund as a decreasing adjustment in a tax period agreed with the Commissioner General.

[Cap.4 s.8]

85. Refund to diplomats, international bodies

(1) The Commissioner General may refund part or all of the input tax incurred on an acquisition or import by —

(a) a public international organisation, a foreign government, or other person prescribed by regulations, to the extent that the person is entitled to exemption from value added tax under an international assistance agreement;

(b) a person to the extent that such person is entitled to exemption for value added tax under the Vienna Convention on Diplomatic Relations or under any other international treaty or convention having force of law in United Republic, or under recognised principles of international law; or

(c) a diplomatic or consular mission of a foreign country established in Mainland Tanzania, relating to transactions concluded for the official purposes of such mission.

(2) A claim for a refund under subsection (1) shall be made in the form and manner prescribed in the regulations, and shall be accompanied by supporting documentation as the

regulations may require.

(3) The Commissioner General shall within one tax period after the date on which an application for a refund is made under this section —

(a) make a decision in relation to the application and give the applicant notice of the decision, stating the amount refundable and any difference between that amount and the amount for which a refund is requested; and

(b) pay the amount refundable to the applicant.

[Act No.4 of 2018 s.68]

Part VI
DOCUMENTS AND RECORDS

86. Tax invoice

(1) A registered person who makes a taxable supply shall, no later than the day on which value added tax becomes payable on the supply under section 15, issue a serially numbered true and correct tax invoice generated by electronic fiscal device for the supply, which shall —

(a) be issued in the form and manner prescribed by the Minister; and

(b) include the following information —

(i) the date on which it is issued;

(ii) the name, Taxpayer Identification Number and Value Added Tax Registration Number of the supplier;

(iii) the description, quantity, and other relevant specifications of the things supplied;

(iv) the total consideration payable for the supply and the amount of value added tax included in that consideration;

(v) if the value of the supply exceeds the minimum amount prescribed in the regulations, the name, address, Taxpayer Identification Number and value added tax registration number of the customer; and

(vi) any other additional information as maybe prescribed in the regulations.

(2) A tax invoice which does not comply with the requirement under subsection (1)(b)(v) shall be valid but shall not be used to support an input tax credit claim or any refund claim.

(3) The Minister may make regulations prescribing special tax invoice requirements for all or particular kinds of supplier or supply, including regulations requiring invoices to be created using certified machines.

(4) One original tax invoice shall be issued for each taxable supply, and a person who has issued the original tax invoice may, if the customer is a registered person, provide a copy marked as such to a customer who claims to have lost it.

[Act No.8 of 2019 s.50]

87. Adjustment notes

(1) An adjustment note which is required to be issued by a supplier under section 71 shall —

(a) be issued in the form and manner prescribed in the regulations; and

(b) include the following information —
- (i) the date on which it is issued;
- (ii) the name, Taxpayer's Identification Number and Value Added Tax Registration Number of the supplier;
- (iii) the nature of the adjustment event and the supply to which it relates;
- (iv) the effect on the amount of value added tax payable on the supply;
- (v) if the effect on the value added tax payable on the supply exceeds the minimum amount prescribed in the regulations, the name, Taxpayer's Identification Number and Value Added Tax Registration Number of the customer; and
- (vi) any other additional information as prescribed in the regulations.

(2) An adjustment note shall not be invalid merely for not complying with the requirement of subsection (1)(b)(v), but cannot be used to support a claim for a decreasing adjustment.

(3) The Minister may make regulations prescribing special adjustment note requirements for all or particular kinds of supplier or supply, including but not limited to regulations requiring adjustment notes be created using certified machines.

(4) An amended tax invoice maybe an adjustment note if it complies with the requirements prescribed by the regulations.

(5) One original adjustment note shall be issued for each adjustment event in relation to a supply, and the person who issued the original may, if the customer is a registered person, provide a copy marked as such to a customer who claims to have lost it.

88. Documentation issued by or to agents

(1) Where a taxable supply is made by an agent or to an agent on behalf of a principal and both the agent and principal are registered persons, any documentation required to be issued by the principal, including tax documentation, maybe issued by the agent or to an agent in the name, address, Taxpayers Identification Number and value added tax registration number of the principal.

(2) Where a taxable supply is made to an agent acting on behalf of a principal and both the agent and the principal are registered, any documentation required to be issued to the principal, including a tax invoice generated by electronic fiscal device or adjustment note, maybe issued to the agent and shall be in the name, address, Taxpayer Identification Number and value added tax registration number of the principal.

89. Records and accounts

(1) A taxable person shall keep record of all accounts, documents, returns, and other records that are required to be issued or given under this Act, or such other tax law, including —
- (a) tax invoices and adjustment notes issued and received by the person;
- (b) customs documentation relating to imports and exports of goods by the person;
- (c) records relating to supplies of imported services to the person, whether or not those supplies were taxable supplies;
- (d) a value added tax account that records, for each tax period, all the output tax payable by the person in that period, or the input tax credit the person is allowed in that

period, and all the increasing and decreasing adjustments that the person is required or entitled to make in that period; and

(e) records showing the deposit of amounts paid to the Commissioner General under this Act.

(2) The records referred to under subsection (1) shall be maintained —

(a) for at least five years from the end of the tax period to which they relate; or

(b) until a later date on which the final decision is made in any audit, recovery proceedings, dispute, prosecution, or other proceedings under this Act relating to that tax period.

Part VII
ADMINISTRATION

90. Tax decisions

The following decisions shall be tax decisions made or deemed to have been made under this Act —

(a) a decision to register a person for value added tax;

(b) a decision to cancel a person's registration for value added tax;

(c) a decision not to pay a refund or not to allow a decreasing adjustment;

(d) the issue of an assessment, including a decision to make an assessment of an administrative penalty, and decision as to the amount of the penalty;

(e) a decision in response to a request for permission to file a value added tax return late;

(f) a decision in response to a request for an extension of time to pay an amount payable under this Act, to require payment sooner than requested, or to require the applicant to comply with other payment arrangements;

(g) a decision to declare a person to be a representative of a taxable person for the purposes of this Act;

(h) a decision not to remit all or part of an amount of interest payable in respect of another amount payable under this Act; and

(i) a decision not to remit all or part of a penalty imposed under or in respect of this Act.

91. Continuity of partnerships or unincorporated associations

Where —

(a) a partnership or other association of persons is dissolved or otherwise ceases to exist as a result of the retirement or withdrawal of one or more of its partners or members, or of the admission of a new partner or member;

(b) a new partnership or association comes into existence consisting of the remaining members, or of the existing members and one or more new members; and

(c) the new partnership or association continues to carry on the economic activity that was carried on by the dissolved partnership or association,

the dissolved partnership or association and the new partnership or association shall, for the purposes of this Act, be deemed to be one and the same, unless the Commissioner General otherwise directs.

92. Death or insolvency of taxable person, mortgagee in possession

(1) Where, after the death of a taxable person or the sequestration of a taxable person's estate —

(a) an economic activity previously carried on by the taxable person is carried on by or on behalf of the executor or trustee of the person's estate; or

(b) anything is done in connection with the termination of the economic activity,

the estate of the taxable person, as represented by the executor or trustee, shall, for the purposes of this Act, be deemed to be the taxable person in respect of the economic activity.

(2) Where a mortgagee takes possession of land or other property previously mortgaged by a mortgagor who is a taxable person and, while in possession of the land or property, the mortgagee carries on the economic activity previously carried on by the mortgagor in relation to the land or other property, the mortgagee shall, to the extent of and for the duration that it carries on that economic activity, be deemed to be the mortgagor.

93. Interaction with income tax

(1) This section has effect for the purposes of income tax.

(2) For purposes of income tax, any value added tax payable for a supply shall be treated as if it were not part of the consideration received by the supplier for the supply.

(3) Where the amount of value added tax payable on the supply is later adjusted, the amount taken into account for income tax shall be correspondingly adjusted.

(4) Input tax incurred by a person shall be included in calculating the amount of an expense or outgoing, whether of an income or capital nature, to the extent that the person was not allowed an input tax credit for that input tax.

(5) Where the amount of input tax for which a credit was allowed is later adjusted, the amount taken into account for income tax shall be correspondingly adjusted.

Part VIII
GENERAL PROVISIONS

94. Power to make regulations

(1) The Minister may make regulations prescribing for any matter necessary or convenient in order to carry out or give effect to the provisions of this Act.

(2) Without prejudice to the generality of subsection (1), the Minister may make regulations —

(a) requiring persons or classes of persons to provide information required, whether on an isolated or periodic basis;

(b) providing for application of special schemes for payment and recovery of value added tax from particular persons or classes of persons;

(c) prescribing for adjustments to be made when a taxable person applies for property for private use and for taxable activity, and the extent to which the property changes significantly;

(d) prescribing methods for suppliers of financial services to calculate the proportion of input tax that is reasonably attributable to the making of taxable supplies;

(e) prescribing methods for taxable persons to calculate the extent to which an amount of input tax maybe credited;

(f) prescribing for the manner value added tax account shall be maintained; and

(g) prescribing for the manner value added tax for goods manufactured in Tanzania Zanzibar and brought in Mainland Tanzania by a registered value added tax person shall be accounted.

(3) Without prejudice to the provisions of subsection (1), the regulations shall not have the effect of —

(a) making a supply or import exempt or zero-rated; or

(b) making a person or class of persons exempt from the payment of a tax imposed under this Act.

[Act No.2 of 2016 s.99]

95. Repeal and savings

(1) Repeals the Value Added Tax Act.

(2) Not withstanding subsection (1) —

(a) regulations, rules, orders or notices made under the repealed Value Added Tax Act and in force shall continue to be in force until they are revoked, amended or cancelled by regulations, rules, orders or notices made under this Act;

(b) where the Government of the United Republic has concluded a binding agreement relating to exploration and prospecting of minerals, gas or oil with a person before the commencement of this Act, the provisions of the repealed Act relating to value added tax relief shall continue to apply to the extent provided for in the agreement; and

(c) the value added tax relief granted to an investor licensed under the Export Processing Zone Act or the Special Economic Zone Act shall continue to apply to the extent provided for under the repealed Act.

[Act No.24 of 1997]

96. Transitional provisions

(1) Notwithstanding section 95, blank forms and other documents used in relation to the repealed Value Added Tax Act, may continue to be used under this Act, and all references in those forms and documents to provisions of and expressions appropriate to the repealed Value Added Tax Act, are taken to refer to the corresponding provisions and expressions of this Act.

(2) Every registered person who, in any one of the twelve months prior to the commencement day, filed a return under the repealed Value Added Tax Act shall be treated as a registered person for the purposes of this Act.

(3) The Commissioner General shall, within three months from the date of commencement of this Act, serve notice on every person who becomes a registered person pursuant to subsection (2) confirming the registration of that person and informing him his option to cancel his registration if he is not required to be registered for value added tax.

(4) A person who is required to be registered for value added tax and is not automatically registered under subsection (2) shall apply for registration within thirty days from the commencement date of this Act and, prior to becoming registered, shall comply with this Act as if that person was a registered person.

(5) Input tax incurred under the repealed Value Added Tax Act for —

(a) a person who was entitled to input tax for all or part of the value added tax charged on an import or acquisition by that person; and

(b) the input tax credit would have been allowed in a tax period ending after the date of commencement of this Act,

shall be allowed under this Act as decreasing adjustment against the person.

(6) The decreasing adjustment referred to under subsection (5) maybe claimed once in any of the first six tax periods ending after the date of commencement of this Act.

(7) The person shall notify the Commissioner General, in the form and manner prescribed, of the amount that is to be claimed, the tax period in which it is to be claimed, and such other information as the regulations may prescribe and the Commissioner General may disallow all or part of the amount if the Commissioner General is not satisfied that the person incurred the value added tax and is entitled to the decreasing adjustment.

(8) The value added tax imposed under this Act on a taxable supply shall become payable on the date of commencement of this Act, if —

(a) the supply is, or will be, made after the commencement of this Act;

(b) before that day an invoice for the supply was issued or a payment for the supply was made, or both; and

(c) value added tax was not paid on the supply under the repealed Act.

(9) Subsection (8) shall apply separately to each part of a progressive or periodic supply that is treated as a separate supply.

[Act No.24 of 1997]

Schedule (Section 6(1))

[Acts Nos.2 of 2016 s.100; 4 of 2017 ss.70 &71; 9 of 2017 s.36; 4 of 2018 s.69; 6 of 2019 s.30; 8 of 2019 s.51]

Part I Supplies and imports exempt from value added tax

1. Agricultural implements

No.	Implements	HSC
1.	Tractors for agricultural use	8701.90.00
2.	Agricultural, horticultural or forestry machinery for soil preparation or cultivation except lawn mower or sports ground rollers and parts	84.32

Continued

No.	Implements	HSC
3.	Harvesting or threshing machinery except machines under HS Code 8433.11.00, 8433.19.00, 8433.90.00	84.33
4.	Liquid sprayers for agriculture	8424.81.00
5.	Powder sprayers for agriculture	8424.81.00
6.	Spades	8201.10.00
7.	Shovels	8201.10.00
8.	Mattocks	8201.30.00
9.	Picks	8201.30.00
10.	Hoes	8201.30.00
11.	Forks	8201.90.00
12.	Rakes	8201.30.00
13.	Axes	8201.40.00
14.	Tractor trailers	8716.10.10
15.	New Pneumatic Tyres of a kind used in agricultural and forest vehicles	4011.61.00
16.	Rotavator	8432.29.00
17.	Poultry incubator	8436.21.00
18.	Irrigation equipment	8424.81.00
19.	Irrigation parts (sprinkler system, chemical injection system, water disinfection system, rain guns, high pressure fogging equipments, Irrigation computer, filter for irrigation system)	8424.90.00
20.	Green house system	9406.00.10
21.	Semen for bovine animal	0511.10.00
22.	Semen for non-bovine animal	0511.99.10
23.	Dam liner	3920

2. Agricultural inputs

No.	Item	HS code
1.	Fertilizers	Chapter 31
2.	Pesticides	3808.99.10 or 3808.99.90

Continued

No.	Item	HS code
3.	Insecticides	3808.91.11 to 3808.91.99
4.	Fungicides	3808.92.10 or 3808.99.90
5.	Rodenticides	3808.92.10 or 3808.99.90
6.	Herbicides	3808.93.10 to 3808.92.90
7.	Anti sprouting products	3808.93.10 or 3808.93.90
8.	Plant growth regulators	3808.93.10 or 3808.93.90

3. Livestock, basic agricultural products and food for human consumptions

No.	Food item	HSC
1.	Live cattle	0102.21.00
2.	Live swine	0103.10.00
3.	Live sheep	0104.10.10
4.	Live goats	0104.20.10
5.	Live poultry	0105.11.10
6.	Unprocessed edible animal products	Chapter 2
7.	Unprocessed edible eggs	0407.29.00
8.	Unpasteurised or pasteurised cow milk except with additives and long life milk	04.01
9.	Unpasteurised or pasteurised goat milk except with additives and long life milk	04.01
10.	Unprocessed fish	03.02
11.	Unprocessed edible vegetables	Chapter 7
12.	Unprocessed fruits	08.10
13.	Unprocessed nuts	08.02
14.	Unprocessed bulbs	0601.10.00
15.	Unprocessed tubers	0601.20.00
16.	Unprocessed cereals	Chapter 10
17.	Wheat or meslin flour	11.01
18.	Maize flour	11.02

Continued

No.	Food item	HSC
19.	Tobacco, not stemmed or stripped	2401.10.00
20.	Unprocessed cashew nuts	0801.31.00
21.	Unprocessed coffee	0901.11.00
22.	Unprocessed tea	0902.10.00 0902.20.00
23.	Sunflower seeds	12.06
24.	Oil seeds	12.07
25.	Unprocessed pyrethrum	1211.90.20
26.	Unprocessed cotton	1207.21.00
27.	Unprocessed sisal	5303.10.00
28.	Unprocessed sugar cane	1212.93.00
29.	Seeds and plants thereof	12.09
30.	Preparations of a kind used in animal feeding'	23.09
31.	Fertilised eggs for incubation	0407.11.00 0407.19.00 0407.21.00
32.	Oil-cake of soya beans	2304.00.00
33.	Oil-cake and other solid residues of cotton seeds cotton seeds	2306.10.00
34.	Oil-cake and other solid residues of sunflower seeds	2306.30.00
35.	Maize Bran	2302.10.00
36.	Wheat Bran	2302.30.00
37.	Lysine	2922.41.00
38.	Methlonine	29390.40.00
39.	Mycotoxin binders	3824.10.00
40.	Pollard	2309.90.10
41.	Rice Bran	2306.90.90
42.	Cotton cake	2304.00.00

4. Fisheries implements

No.	Implements	HSC
1.	Floats for fishing nets	7020.00.10
2.	Fishing nets	5608.11.00

Continued

No.	Implements	HSC
3.	Fishing vessels, factory ships and other vessels for processing or preserving fishery products	8902.00.00
4.	Nylon fishing twine	—
5.	Outboard engine	8407.21.00

5. Bee-keeping implements

No.	Implements	HSC
1.	Bee hive	Any Description
2.	Protective bee keeping jacket veil	6113.40.00
3.	Mask	6307.90
4.	Honey strainer	—
5.	Bee hive smoker	8424.89

6. Diary equipment

No.	Implements	HSC
1.	Hay making machine	8433.30.00
2.	Cans and ends for beverages	7310.29.20
3.	Milking machines	8434.10.00
4.	Homogenizer, Butter churn, milk pasteurizer	8434.20.00
5.	Cream separator	8421.11.00
6.	Milk plate heat exchanger	8419.50.00
7.	Milk hose	3917.31.00, 4009.12.00, 4009.32.00
8.	Milk pump	8413.60.00, 8413.70.00, 8413.81.00
9.	Heat insulated cooling tanks	8419.89.00, 7309.00.00, 7310.00.00
10.	Milk storage tanks	—

7. Medicine or pharmaceutical products

No.	
1.	Essential Human and veterinary medicine, drugs, medical equipment and packaging material which have been approved by the Minister responsible for health: Provided that, the packaging material is specifically designed for packing pharmaceutical products and printed for use by a local manufacturer whose name appears on the packaging material
2.	Food supplements or Vitamins supplied to the Government

8. Articles designed for people with special needs

No.	Articles	HSC
1.	Orthopaedic appliances, including crutches, surgical belts and trusses, splints and other fracture appliances, artificial parts of the body, hearing aids and other appliances which are worn or carried, or implanted in the body, to compensate for a defect or disability excluding other items under HSC 9021.90.00	90.21
2.	White cane for blinds or visually impaired	—
3.	Spectacle for correcting vision	9004.90.10
4.	Contact lenses	9001.30.00
5.	Spectacle lenses of glass	9001.40.00
6.	Spectacle lenses of other materials	9001.50.00
7.	Sunscreen and sun tan preparation used by albino	33.04
8.	Braille	8469.00.007
9.	Mechanically propelled tricycle for carriage of disabled persons	8713.1.00
10.	Motor vehicle specifically designed for use by persons with disability	87.03

9. Education materials

No.	Article	HSC
1.	Dictionary and encyclopedia	4901.91.00
2.	Printed books	4901
3.	Newspapers	4902.90.00
4.	Children pictures, drawing or colouring	4903.00.00
5.	Maps and hydrographic charts	4905.99.00
6.	Examination question papers	4911.99.20
7.	Instructional charts and diagrams	4911.90.10
8.	Examination answer sheet	4011.00.90

10. Health care

1.	A supply of medical, dental, nursing, convalescent, rehabilitation, midwifery, paramedical, optical, or other similar services where the services are provided: (a) by or in an institution approved for the provision of those services by the Government; and (b) by, or under the supervision and control of, a person who is registered as being qualified to perform that service under Tanzania laws, or whose qualifications to perform the services are recognised in Tanzania

Continued

| 2. | A supply of services in a nursing home or residential care facility for children, or for aged, indigent, infirm, or disabled persons who need permanent care, if the facility is approved for the provision of those services by an appropriate Government institution |

11. Immovable property

1.	A sale of vacant land.
2.	A lease, license, hire or other form of supply, to the extent that it is a supply of the right to occupy and reside in residential premises.
3.	A sale of immovable property, to the extent that the property relates to residential premises, not including: (a) the first sale of newly constructed residential premises; or (b) a subsequent sale if the premises have been occupied as a residence for less than two (2) years.

12. Educational services

| 1. | A supply of services consisting of tuition or instruction for students provided by an institution approved by the Minister responsible for education, being:
(a) a pre-primary, primary, or secondary school;
(b) a technical college, community college, or university;
(c) an educational institution established for the promotion of adult education, vocational training, improved literacy, or technical education;
(d) an institution established for the education or training of physically or mentally handicapped persons; or
(e) an institution established for the training of sportspersons. |

13. Intermediary services

1.	Supply of financial services supplied free of charge
2.	Insurance premiums for aircraft
3.	Life insurance or health insurance
4.	Insurance for workers compensation

14. Government entity or institution

| 1. | A non commercial activity carried on by a Government entity or institution, except to the extent that the activity involves making supplies of goods, services or immovable property that are also supplied or able to be supplied in Mainland Tanzania by at least the person who is a non government entity |

15. Petroleum products

No.	Petroleum product	HSC
1.	Aviation spirit	2710.12.30
2.	Spirit type jet fuel	2710.12.40
3.	Kerosene type jet fuel (Jet A-1)	2710.19. 21
4.	Petrol (MSR and MSP)	2710.12.10 and 10.12.20
5.	Diesel (GO)	2710.19.31
6.	Kerosene (IK)	2710.19.22
7.	Bitumen	2713.20.00 and 2715.00.00
8.	Liquefied petroleum and Natural gases	2711
9.	Compressed Petroleum and Natural gases	2711
10.	Compressed or liquefied gas cylinders for petroleum and Natural gases for cooking	7311.00.00

16. Supply of water, except bottled or canned water or similarly presented water.

17. The transportation of person by any means of conveyance other than taxi cabs, rental cars or boat charters.

18. Supplies of arms and ammunitions, parts and accessories thereof, to the armed forces.

19. Funeral services, for the purpose of this item funeral services includes coffin, shroud, transportation, mortuary and disposal services of human remains.

20. Gaming supply.

21. Supply of solar panels, modules, solar charger controllers, solar inverter, solar lights, vacuum tube solar collectors and solar battery.

22. Supply of air charter services.

23. Soya beans 12.01.

24. Ground nuts 12.02.

25. Supply of precious metals, gemstones and other precious stones by a small scale miner at buying stations or at Mineral and Gem Houses designated by the Mining Commission under the Mining Act.

26. A supply of precious aircraft lubricants of HS Codes 2710.19.51, 2710.19.52, 3403.19.00 and 3403.99.00 to a local operator of air transportation.

Part II Imports exempt from value added tax

Item No.	Description
1.	An import of goods given, otherwise than for the purposes of sale, as an unconditional gift to the State
2.	An import of baggage or personal effects exempt from customs duty under the Fifth Schedule of the East African Customs Management Act, 2004

Continued

Item No.	Description
3.	An import of goods including containers, if the goods have been exported and then returned to Mainland Tanzania by any person without being subjected to any process of manufacture or adaptation and without a permanent change of ownership, but not if at the time when the goods were exported, they were the subject of a supply that was zero-rated under this Act or under the repealed Value Added Tax Act
4.	An import of goods shipped or conveyed to United Republic for transshipment or conveyance to any other country
5.	An import of goods made available free of charge by a foreign government or an international institution with a view to assisting the economic development United Republic
6.	An import of food, clothing and shoes donated to non - profit organisation for free distribution to orphanage or schools for children with special needs in Mainland Tanzania
7.	Import of goods by non-profit organisation for the provision of emergency and disaster relief, and where such goods are capital goods, the goods shall be handled to the National Disaster Committee upon overtion, completion or diminishing of the disaster
8.	An import of goods by the religious organisation for the provision of health, education, water, religious services in circumstances that, if services are supplied — (a) without fee, charge or any other consideration in a form of fees; or (b) on payment of any consideration, the fees or charges does not exceed fifty percent of the fair market value
9.	An import of goods that is exempt under an agreement entered into between the Government of the United Republic and an international agency listed under the Diplomatic and Consular Immunities and Privileges Act
10.	An import of goods by a registered and licensed explorer or prospector for the exclusive use in oil, gas or mineral exploration or prospection activities to the extent that those goods are eligible for relief from customs duties under the East African Customs Management Act, 2004
11.	An import of aircraft, aircraft engine or parts by a local operator of air transportation
12.	An import of railway locomotive, wagons, tramways and their parts and accessories by a registered railways company, corporation or authority
13.	An import of fire fighting vehicles by the Government
14.	An import of laboratory equipment and reagents by education institution registered by the Ministry responsible for education to be used solely for educational purpose
15.	An import of CNG plants equipments, natural gas pipes, transportation and distribution pipes, CNG storage cascades, CNG special transportation vehicles, natural gas metering equipments, CNG refueling of filling, gas receiving units, flare gas system, condensate tanks and leading facility, system piping and pipe rack, condensate stabilizer by a natural gas distributor
16.	Firefighting equipment
17.	An import of machinery of HS Codes 8479.20.00, 8438.60.00, 8421.29.00, 8419.89.00 by a local manufacturer of vegetable oils for exclusive use in manufacturing vegetable oil in Mainland Tanzania

Continued

Item No.	Description
18.	An import of machinery of HS Code 8444.00.00, 8445.11.00, 8445.12.00, 8445.13.00, 8445.19.00, 8445.20.00, 8445.30.00, 8445.40.00, 8445.90.00, 8446.10.00, 8446.21.00, 8446.29.00, 8446.30.00, 84.47, 8448.11.00, 8448.19.00, 8449.00.00, 8451.40.00 or 8451.50.00 by a local manufacturer of textiles for exclusive use in manufacturing of textiles in Mainland Tanzania
19.	An import of machinery of Chapter 84 by a local manufacturer of pharmaceutical for exclusive use in manufacturing pharmaceutical products in Mainland Tanzania
20.	An import of machinery of HS Code 8453.10.00 by a local manufacturer of hides and skins for exclusive use in manufacturing leather in Mainland Tanzania
21.	Import of ambulance of HS Code 8703.90.10 by a registered health facility other than a pharmacy, health laboratory or diagnostic centre
22.	Revenue Stamps of HS Code 4907.00.90 [Cap.4 s.8]
23.	Electronic cash register Code 8470.50.00

TITLE FIFTEEN
CUSTOMS (MANAGEMENT AND TARIFF) ACT (CHAPTER 403) [1952] [Revised Edition 2019] (Excerpts)

Customs (Management and Tariff) Act
(Chapter 403)

[*This is the version of this document at 30 November 2019.*]

[*Note: This Act has been thoroughly revised and consolidated under the supervision of the Attorney General's Office, in compliance with the Laws Revision Act No.7 of 1994, the Revised Laws and Annual Revision Act (Chapter 356 (R.L.)), and the Interpretation of Laws and General Clauses Act No.30 of 1972. This version is up-to-date as at 31st July 2002.*]

[*Ords Nos.2 of 1952; 10 of 1955; 3 of 1958; 5 of 1960; Acts Nos.14 of 1961; 2 of 1962; 2 of 1963; 12 of 1964; 1 of 1966; 10 of 1967; 12 of 1969; 13 of 1969; 10 of 1970; 13 of 1976; 13 of 1989; 16 of 1994; 13 of 1996; 25 of 1997; 27 of 1997; 2 of 1998; 8 of 1998; 12 of 1999; 15 of 1999; 11 of 2000; 15 of 2000; 14 of 2001; 10 of 2002; 18 of 2002; 1 of 2008; 2 of 2014; EAC. Cap.27; E.A.C.L.N.49/1954; 84/1961; 1/1967; 64/1970*]

An Act to provide for the management and administration of customs, transfer tax and related matters.

Part III
IMPORTATION

Entry, examination, and delivery

28. Entry of cargo

(1) Save as otherwise provided in the Customs laws, the whole of the cargo of any aircraft or vessel which is unloaded or to be unloaded shall be entered by the owners within such period after the commencement of discharge as maybe prescribed, or such further period as maybe allowed by the proper officer, either for —

(a) home consumption;

(b) warehousing;

(c) transhipment; or

(d) transit.

(2) Where any entry is delivered to the proper officer, the owner shall furnish therewith full particulars supported by documentary evidence of the goods referred to in the entry.

(3) Entries for goods to be unloaded maybe delivered to the proper officer for checking before the arrival at the port of discharge of the aircraft or vessel in which such goods are imported; and in any such case the Commissioner-General may in his discretion permit any goods to be entered before the arrival of such aircraft or vessel.

(4) Where any goods remain unentered at the expiration of the prescribed period, or of such further period as may have been allowed by the proper officer, then such goods shall, if the proper

officer so requires, be removed by, or at the expense of, the agent of the aircraft or vessel in which such goods were imported to a customs warehouse.

29. Entry of transfer goods

(1) Save as otherwise provided in the Customs laws, any goods liable to transfer tax which are unloaded or to be unloaded from any aircraft, vessel or vehicle, shall be entered by the owners in the manner and within the period prescribed, or within such further period as maybe allowed by the proper officer.

(2) Where any goods liable to transfer tax remain unentered at the expiration of the period prescribed or such further period as may have been allowed by the proper officer, then such goods shall, if the proper offier so requires, be removed to a customs warehouse by, or at the expense of, the owner of the aircraft, vessel or vehicle in which such goods were transferred.

[Act No. 13 of 1989 s. 13]

Part IV
WAREHOUSING OF GOODS

General provisions

38. Dutiable goods maybe warehoused

(1) Subject to any regulations, goods liable to import duty may on first importation be warehoused without payment of duty in a Government warehouse or a bonded warehouse.

(2) On, or as soon as practicable after, the landing of any goods to be warehoused, the proper officer shall take a particular account of such goods and shall enter such account in a book; and such account shall, subject to sections 43 and 49, be that upon which the duties in respect of such goods shall be ascertained and paid.

[E.A.C.L.N. 1 of 1967]

39. Procedure on warehousing

(1) Where any goods entered to be warehoused are delivered into the custody of the person in charge of a warehouse, the proper officer shall, save where the Commissioner-General otherwise directs, take a particular account of such goods, whether or not any account thereof has been previously taken.

(2) The proper officer shall, in taking such account, enter in the book for that purpose the name of the aircraft or vessel or the registered number of the vehicle, as the case maybe, in which the goods were imported or, in the case of postal articles, the parcel post reference, the name of the owner of such goods, the number of packages, the mark and number of each package, the value and particulars of the goods.

(3) After such account has been taken and the goods deposited in the warehouse in accordance with the directions of the proper officer, such officer shall certify at the foot of the account that the entry and warehousing of the goods is complete; and such goods shall from that time be considered goods duly warehoused.

(4) Subject to section 41, all goods entered to be warehoused shall forthwith be removed to the warehouse for which they are entered and deposited therein in the packages in which they were

imported:

Provided that, where any goods are permitted to be repacked, skipped, bulked, sorted, looted, or packed, in accordance with section 35, then such goods shall be deposited in the packages in which they were contained when the account thereof was taken.

(5) Any person who contravenes subsection (4), shall be guilty of an offence and any goods in respect of which such offence has been committed shall be liable to forfeiture.

[E.A.C.L.N. 1 of 1967]

40. Removal to warehouse of goods entered therefor

(1) Where any goods entered to be warehoused are not duly warehoused by the owner, the proper officer may cause them to be removed to the warehouse for which they were entered.

(2) Where any goods are so removed to a bonded warehouse the warehouse keeper shall pay the cost of the removal of such goods and shall have a lien on such goods for such cost.

41. Entry of warehoused goods

(1) Goods which have been warehoused maybe entered either for —

(a) home consumption;

(b) exportation;

(c) removal to another warehouse;

(d) use as stores for aircraft or vessels; or

(e) re-warehousing.

(2) Where any goods have been entered for warehousing, they may, before they are actually warehoused, be entered for home consumption, for exportation, for removal to another warehouse, or for use as stores for aircraft or vessels; and in any such a case such goods shall be deemed to have been so warehoused and maybe delivered for home consumption, for exportation, for removal to another warehouse, or for use as stores for aircraft or vessels, as the case maybe, as if they had been actually so warehoused.

Part XVII
CUSTOMS TARIFF

194A. Payment of customs duty when importing

A person engaged in mining operations, or any person subcontracted by such person for the purpose of carrying on any such mining operations, shall be entitled in relation to any mine after the first anniversary of the commencement of commercial production from that mine to import upon payment of customs duty at a rate not exceeding five percent, explosives, fuels, lubricants, industrial items and other supplies, machinery, vehicles and other capital equipment and spare parts for such equipment, where such equipment has been verified to the satisfaction of the Commissioner — General after consultation with the Minister responsible for minerals to be reasonably necessary for, and for use solely in carrying on, mining operations in relation to that mine.

[Act No.27 of 1997 s.17]

194B. Exemption from customs duty after the first anniversary

A person engaged in mining operations which are not mining operations in respect of any mine after the first anniversary of the commencement of commercial production from that mine, or any person subcontracted by that person for the purpose of those mining operations, shall be entitled to import without payment of customs duty explosives, fuels, lubricants, industrial items and other supplies, machinery, vehicles and other capital equipment and spare parts for such equipment where such equipment has been verified to the satisfaction of the Commissioner-General after consultation with the Minister responsible for minerals to be reasonably necessary for, and for use solely in carrying on, mining operation relating to that mine.

[Act No.27 of 1997 s.17]

194C. Payment of customs duty on sale or transfer of any item

A person who sells or transfers any items which have been imported into the United Republic without payment of customs duty by any person engaged in mining operations, or any person subcontracted by that person for the purpose of such mining operations, to any person in the United Republic, shall pay customs duty on the value thereof, if any, on the date of the sale or transfer:

Provided that, no such customs duty shall be payable if that sale or transfer occurs by way of sale or assignment of any interest under the Mining Act.

[Cap.123]

[Act No.27 of 1997 s.17; Cap.123]

TITLE SIXTEEN
WITHHOLDING TAX ON PAYMENT FOR GOODS AND SERVICES PRACTICE NOTE TAX ACT [2019]

TANZANIA REVENUE AUTHORITY

Practice Note No.01/2019

Withholding Tax on payment for Goods and Services as per Income Tax Act, Cap 332

February, 2019

WITHHOLDING TAX ON PAYMENT FOR GOODS AND SERVICES

1.0 Tax Law

This Practice Note is issued under section 9 of the Tax Administration Act, Cap 438 as amended from time to time.

2.0 Purpose

The Practice Note (PN) is issued for the purpose of providing guidance for the general public and officers of the Tanzania Revenue Authority (TRA) in order to achieve consistency in the administration of Withholding Tax (WHT) on goods and services as provided for under Section 83 of the Income Tax Act Cap 332. It explains the legal and administrative aspects including procedures for treatment and computations of withholding tax on goods and services.

3.0 Interpretation

In this Practice Note unless the context requires otherwise —

"**Act**" means the Income Tax Act Cap 332 and the Tax Administration Act Cap 438.

Definitions and expressions used in this PN have the same meaning as in the Act, unless the context requires otherwise.

4.0 The Application of this Practice Note

This PN considers:

Services

i. Type of services attributable to payment of services fee that are subject to withholding tax under Section 83(1)(c)(ii) of the Income Tax Act.

ii. Payments to be included in calculating service fees

iii. Source rule for payment

iv. Application to particular type of persons v. Calculation of withholding payment amounts.

vi. Procedures applicable to withholding

Goods

Withholding tax on payments for goods supplied to corporations and its institutions by any person.

5.0 Applicable Concepts

5.1 Withholding tax

Withholding tax is a tax that is required to be withheld by the person making "payment" of certain amounts to another person in respect of goods supplied or services rendered. It is a tax deducted at source because the person making payment has an obligation to withhold.

5.2 Payment

"Payment" for this purpose is defined in the Act as —

"*Payment includes the transfer of assets or money, the transfer or decrease of a liability, the provision of services, the use or availability for use of money or asset and the creation of an asset in another person".*

5.3 Withholdee

Withholdee is a person receiving or entitled to receive a payment from which income tax is required to be withheld.

5.4 Withholding Agent

Withholding agent is a person required to withhold income tax from a payment made to a withholdee.

5.5 "Professional Service"

"Professional Service" means services rendered by a person licensed as a practitioner by any recognized professional body and shall include other services or activities of an independent business character including consultancy, legal, architectural, engineering, supervisory, accounting and auditing, medical, artistic, survey, theatrical performance, sports, exhibition, private security services, private investigation and consultancies in various disciplines or any entertainment held or given other than those for remuneration under contract of employment.

5.6 "Corporation"

"Corporation" means any company or body corporate established, incorporated or registered under any law in force in the United Republic or elsewhere, an unincorporated association or other body of persons, a government, a political subdivision of a government, a public authority, public institution, a public international organization and a unit trust but does not include partnership;

6.0 Types of withholding tax

Final Withholding Taxes are taxes in which the withholdee cannot claim any tax credit when calculating the income tax payable for a year of income.

Non-Final Withholding Taxes are taxes which the withholdee is entitled for a tax credit being an amount equal to the tax treated as paid for the year of income in which the amount is derived.

Note: This PN covers only the WHT that relates to Non-Final Withholding Taxes.

7.0 Withholding tax obligations

The law requires a resident person who makes payment to another resident or non- resident to withhold a tax at the rates specified under paragraph 4(c) of the First schedule of the Income Tax Act.

7.1 In case of —

(a) Services

Tax is withheld on payments made in respect of:

i. Service Fee with a source in URT Paid to a non-resident

ii. Service fee for provision of professional services paid to a resident person

(b) Goods

(1) Any resident corporation which makes payment in respect of goods: supplied by a resident person in the course of conducting business shall withhold income tax at the rate of 2% as provided for under paragraph 4(c) of the First Schedule.

(2) The law shall apply to a resident corporation whose budget is wholly or substantially

financed by the Government budget subvention.

For the purpose of this Practice Note the supply of water and electricity shall be regarded as goods and therefore not subject to withholding obligation under services.

Note: Water and electricity are non- transferable which is one of the key attributes of any service.

7.2 Exempt payment under Sec 83

1. Payments made by individuals unless made in conducting a business;
2. Payment that are exempt amount.

7.3 Source of Payment

A service fee payment has a source in the United Republic where the fees is attributable to rendering service:

i. In the United Republic, regardless of the place of payment. A payment has a source in the United Republic no matter where the payment is made if the service is rendered in the United Republic. Service is rendered in the United Republic where

(a) Either the activities are carried out in the United Republic; or

(b) The results of the activities are directed to or utilized or benefitted by resident of the United Republic.

ii. Where the payer is the Government of the United Republic i.e Union Government and Zanzibar Revolution Government.

8.0 Application to particular types of persons

The withholding tax deduction applies to payments made by a resident person including a domestic permanent establishment of a non- resident person to a resident person.

The tax withholding is non-final when the payment is made to a resident person. The withholdee shall be entitled to a tax credit in an amount equal to the tax deducted as paid in the year of income.

The tax deducted on a payment made to a partnership shall be allocated to the partners, proportionately to each partner's share and treated as having paid by the partners for the year of income.

9.0 Basis for calculation of the withholding payments

Withholding Tax Base

I. Tax shall be calculated on the gross amount paid without deduction of expenses or allowances

II. Withholding Tax shall be computed on the amount exclusive of VAT

Example 1:

ABC Limited invoice in relation to Consultancy services provided to Dar es Salaam City Council has the following amount:

DESCRIPTION	AMOUNT(Tsh)
Service Fee	10 000 000/ =
VAT	1 800 000/ =
Total	11 800 000/ =

Therefore:

I. W/Tax will be charged on Tsh 10 000 000/=

II. W/Tax is 5% * 10 000 000/=

WHT = Tsh 500 000/=

10.0 Inclusion of value of benefits and facilities

Where services are provided and payments are made to the withholdee of cash plus provision of benefits and facilities, the withholding tax base shall include the amount paid for the benefits or facilities. Where the benefits were not paid for, they shall be quantified at a market value at the time of payment. Furthermore, where services are provided and payments are made to the withholdee in form of service fee and reimbursements then the withholding tax base will be the full amount that is service fee plus reimbursement amount.

Example 2:

FLG Consultants were hired by Kinondoni District Council to carry consultancy work. The contract terms involved payment of reimbursement expenses which were used for accommodation in a 5 star hotel for 4 staff of FLG for 20 days by the client. The contract price was quoted at Tsh 150 000 000/= plus reimbursements. The Client Paid a total of Tsh 16 000 000/= as reimbursement expenses for accommodation of FLG staff.

DESCRIPTION	AMOUNT (Tsh)
Consultancy Fee	150 000 000/=
Reimbursements	16 000 000/=
Total	166 000 000/=

W/Tax Base

Consultancy fee   Tsh 150 000 000/=

Reimbursements   Tsh 16 000 000/=

W/Tax Base   **Tsh 166 000 000/=**

WHT Computation = 166 000 000 * 5%

WHT = Tsh 8 300 000/=

11.0 Withholding Tax Base for Mixed Supplies (Goods & Services)

If the invoice raised involves both supply of Goods and Services, separation of the amount payable must be made for value for Goods and Services. However, if the separation is not done then the full amount will be considered as supply for services.

Example 3:

XYZ was hired to conduct a Survey for Ministry of Education. The contract involved also supply of Books and Stationeries where there was a need. After completing the work, XYZ raised an invoice with the following details:

DESCRIPTION	AMOUNT (Tsh)
Survey Fee	70 000 000/=
Books and Stationeries	30 000 000/=
VAT	18 000 000/=
Total	118 000 000/=

I. W/Tax will be charged as follows:
(a) W/Tax on Goods (2% * 30 000 000/=)
$\qquad$ = Tsh 600 000/=
(b) W/Tax on Service (5% * 70 000 000/=)
$\qquad$ = Tsh 3 500 000/=

Note: Failure to separate the figures in respect of the value for goods and services attracts WHT at the rate of 5% on the entire amount (5% * 100 000 000) = Tsh 5 000 000/=

12.0 Withholding Tax Base for Construction Works

I. Section 83(3) of the ITA read together with Finance Act 2016 provides for apportionment of construction works when determining the base for WHT.

II. If payment involves Construction Works, the payment subject to WHT shall be based on the ratio of 3:2 for Materials and Services respectively.

Example 4:

Mgeni Contractors were awarded a contract to construct a new office for Ministry of Finance in Dodoma. One of the invoice raised based on percentage of completion had the following amount:

DESCRIPTION	AMOUNT(Tsh)
Value of work	600 000 000/=
VAT	108 000 000/=
Total	708 000 000/=

WHT Computation based on Construction Work Ratios

Material	Service
3	2
3/5 * 600 000 000/=	2/5 * 600 000 000/=
360 000 000/=	240 000 000/=

W/Tax on Goods — (2% * 360 000 000/=)

WHT = Tsh 7 200 000/=

W/Tax on Services — (5% * 240 000 000/=)

WHT = Tsh 12 000 000/=

13.0 Procedure Applicable to Withholding

Statements and payments of tax withheld or treated as withheld — Sec. 84

I. Time for Payment

    (a) Tax withheld is payable to the Commissioner General within seven days after the end of each calendar month of deduction.

    (b) Payment of WHT is done electronically through Revenue Gateway System

II. Filing of Withholding tax statements

Every withholding agent shall file with the Commissioner General within 30 days after the end of each 6-month calendar period a statement of any income tax withheld during the month by filling the prescribed form *ITX 230.01.E.* — *Withholding Tax Statement* —

    (a) payments made by the withholding agent during the period that are subject to withholding;

    (b) the name and address of the withholdee;

    (c) income tax withheld from each payment; and

    (d) Any other information that the Commissioner General may prescribe.

Note: A withholding agent who fails to withhold income tax as required by the law must nevertheless pay the tax that should have been withheld in the same manner and at the same time as tax that is withheld. All tax return forms can be downloaded through www.tra.go.tz

14.0 Issuance of Withholding Certificate — Section 85 of the ITA

A withholding agent is required to prepare and serve a withholding certificate to all withholdee's separately for each month within 30 days after the end of the month of deduction. However, due to the introduction of online payment module, the certificates can be viewed and printed both by the withholder and withholdee though Revenue Gateway System.

15.0 Tax Credit to Withholdee

Tax withheld is a tax credit against the withholdee's total tax liability for the year of income.

The withholdee is entitled to tax credit of an amount that is equal to the tax withheld or treated as withheld when paid on his behalf by the withholding agent. The tax credit is against the withholdee's tax liability for the year of income when the tax is withheld.

16.0 Consequences for failure to withhold — Sec. 84 of the ITA

A withholding agent who fails to withhold Income tax in accordance with the law must nevertheless pay the tax that should have been withheld in the same manner and at the same time as tax that is withheld together with interest.

A withholding agent who fails to withhold income tax but pays the tax that should have been withheld to TRA shall be entitled to recover an equal amount from the withholdee.

17.0 Consequences for failure to file returns — Sec. 78 of TAA, Cap 438

Failure to comply with the requirement will attract sanctions including interest and penalties as per Tax Administration Act, Cap 438 as hereunder: —

A withholding agent who fails to file a tax return (statement of taxes withheld and paid) on due dateshall be liable for a penalty for each month or part of the month during which the failure continues calculated as the higher of

I. 2.5% of the amount assessable per tax return less the amount of tax paid at the start of the period towards that amount or

II. Tshs 225 000 in case of a body corporate or Tshs 75 000 for an individual.

18.0 Submission of Contract Documents to TRA

In compliance with Regulation 109 of The Public ProcurementAct No. 7 of 2011 published through GN. No.446 of 2013

Which states that

"The Accounting Officer shall ensure that copies of all contracts are sent to the Authority, Attorney General, Controller and Auditor General, Internal Auditor General or Government Asset Management Division as the case may be, and the Tanzania Revenue Authority within thirty days from the date of signing the contract"

GROUP SIX
ANTI-CORRUPTION AND ECONOMIC CRIMES LAWS AND REGULATIONS

TITLE SEVEVTEEN
PREVENTION AND COMBATING OF CORRUPTION ACT (CHAPTER 329) [2007] [Revised Edition 2019] (Excerpts)

Prevention and Combating of Corruption Act
(Chapter 329)

Commenced on 1 July 2007

[*This is the version of this document at 30 November 2019.*]

[*Note: This Act has been thoroughly revised and consolidated under the supervision of the Attorney General's Office, in compliance with the Laws Revision Act No.7 of 1994, the Revised Laws and Annual Revision Act (Chapter 356 (R. L.)), and the Interpretation of Laws and General Clauses Act No.30 of 1972. This version is up-to-date as at 31st July 2002.*]

[*GN No.153 of 2007*; *Acts.Nos.11 of 2007*; *7 of 2018*; *11 of 2019*]

WHEREAS corruption is an obstacle to principles of democracy, good governance and human rights and poses a threat to peace, tranquility and security in the society;

AND WHEREAS the Government has resolved to undertake protracted measures that would ensure that Tanzania remains a corruption free State adhering to the principles of freedom, equality, justice, brotherhood, peace and wherein all people are equal and every person has a right to ownership and protection of property acquired by lawful means;

AND WHEREAS technological changes ushered in by globalization and development of science in communication and information technology has made it necessary to reinstitute the Bureau, to devise modern tactics and strategies of preventing and combating corruption, and to review the current legal framework for the purposes of enabling the Bureau to effectively control corruption and corrupt practices;

AND WHEREAS it is necessary to make comprehensive provisions for the prevention, investigation and combating of corruption and related offences and to ensure that the Bureau conducts its operations independently and performs its functions effectively;

NOW THEREFORE, be it ENACTED by Parliament of the United Republic of Tanzania as follows:

Part III
Corruption and related offences

15. Corrupt transactions

(1) Any person who corruptly by himself or in conjunction with any other person —

(a) solicits, accepts or obtains, or attempts to obtain, from any person for himself or any other person, any advantage as an inducement to, or reward for, or otherwise on account of, any agent, whether or not such agent is the same person as such first mentioned person and whether the agent has or has no authority to do, or forbearing to do, or having done or forborne to do, anything in relation to his principal's affairs or business, or

(b) gives, promises or offers any advantage to any person, whether for the benefit of that person or of another person, as an inducement to, or reward for, or otherwise on account of, any agent whether or not such agent is the person to whom such advantage is given, promised or offered and whether the agent has or has no authority to do, doing, or forbearing to do, or having done or forborne to do, anything in relation to his principal's affairs or business,

commits an offence of corruption.

(2) A person who is convicted of an offence under this section, shall be liable to a fine of not less than five hundred thousand shillings but not more than one million shillings or to imprisonment for a term of not less than three years but not more than five years or to both.

(3) In addition to a penalty provided for under subsection (2), the court shall where such person —

(a) is an agent, order him to pay to his principal, in such manner as the court may direct —

(i) the amount or value of any advantage received by him or any of its part;

(ii) part of the amount or value of any advantage received by him, and that the whole or part of the residue be confiscated to the Government; or

(b) is an agent or not, order that the amount or value of any advantage received by him, or any of its part, be confiscated to the Government.

16. Corrupt transactions in contracts

(1) Any person who offers an advantage to a public official as an inducement to or reward for or otherwise on account of such public official's giving assistance or using influence in or having given assistance or used influence to assist in the promotion, execution or procuring of —

(a) any contract with a public body for the performance of any work, the supply of any service, the doing of anything, the supplying of anything or the supplying of any article, material or substance;

(b) any subcontract to perform any work, supply of service, the doing of anything or supply any article, material or substance required to be performed, supplied, done under any contract with a public body,

commits an offence of corruption.

(2) Any public official who solicits or accepts any advantage as an inducement to or reward for or otherwise on account of his giving assistance or using influence in or having given assistance or used influence to assist in the promotion, execution or procuring of the payment of the price, consideration or other moneys stipulated or otherwise provided for in, any such contract or subcontract as is referred to in paragraphs (a) and (b) of subsection (1), commits an offence.

(3) A person convicted of an offence under this section shall be liable to a fine of not less than one million shillings but not more than three million shillings or to imprisonment for a term of not less than three years but not more than five years or to both.

(4) In addition to the penalty prescribed for under this section, the court shall, if such person —

(a) is an agent, order him to pay to his principal, in such manner as the court may direct —
- (i) the amount or money value of any advantage received by him or any part of it; or
- (ii) part of amount or money value of any advantage received by him, and that the whole or part of the residue be confiscated;

(b) is an agent or not, order that amount or value of any advantage received by him, or any part of it, be confiscated to the Government.

17. Corrupt transactions in procurement

(1) Any person who —
- (a) offers any advantage to another person as an inducement for or a reward for or otherwise on account of the withdrawal of a tender, or refraining from inviting a tender, for any contract with a public or private body for the performance of any work, the supply of service, the doing of anything or the supplying of any article, material of substance; or
- (b) solicits or accepts any advantage as an inducement for or a reward for or otherwise on account of the withdrawal of a tender, or refraining from inviting a tender, for such a contract as is referred to in paragraph (a),

commits an offence.

(2) A person convicted of an offence under this section shall be liable to a fine not exceeding fifteen million shillings or to imprisonment for a term not exceeding seven years or to both.

(3) In addition to the penalty prescribed for under this section, the court shall, if such person —
- (a) is an agent, order him to pay to his principal, in such manner as the court may direct —
  - (i) the amount or money value of any advantage received by him or any part of it; or
  - (ii) part of amount or money value of any advantage received by him, and that the whole or part of the residue be confiscated;
- (b) is an agent or not, order that amount or value of any advantage received by him, or any part of it, be confiscated to the Government.

18. Corrupt transactions in auctions

(1) Any person who —
- (a) offers any advantage to another person as an inducement to or reward for or otherwise on account of that other person's refraining or having refrained from bidding at an auction conducted by or on behalf of any public or private body; or
- (b) solicits or accepts any advantage as an inducement to or reward for or otherwise on account of his refraining or having refrained from bidding at any auction conducted by or on behalf of any public or private body,

commits an offence of corruption under this Act,

(2) A person convicted of an offence under this section shall be liable to a fine not exceeding fifteen million shillings or to imprisonment for a term not exceeding seven years or to both.

(3) In addition to the penalty prescribed for under this section the court shall, if such person —
- (a) is an agent, order him to pay to his principal, in such manner as the court may direct —
  - (i) the amount or money value of any advantage received by him or any part of it; or
  - (ii) part of amount or money value of any advantage received by him, and that the whole or part of the residue be confiscated;
- (b) is an agent or not, order that amount or value of any advantage received by him, or any part of it, be confiscated to the Government.

21. Bribery of foreign public official

(1) Any person who intentionally promises, offers or gives to a foreign public official or an official of a public international organisation, directly or indirectly, an undue advantage, for that foreign public official himself or another person or entity, in order that the foreign public official acts or refrain from acting in the exercise of his official duties to obtain or retain business or other undue advantage in relation to a local or international economic undertaking or business transaction, commits an offence and shall be liable to a fine not exceeding ten million shillings or to imprisonment for a term not exceeding seven years or to both.

(2) Any foreign public official or an official of a public international organisation who intentionally solicits or accepts, directly or indirectly an undue advantage, for himself or another person or entity in order that he acts or refrains from acting in the exercise of his official duties, commits an offence and shall be liable on conviction to a fine not exceeding ten million shillings or to imprisonment for a term not exceeding seven years or to both.

22. Use of documents intended to mislead principal

A person who knowingly gives to any agent, or an agent knowingly uses with intent to deceive, or defraud his principal, any receipt, account or other document such as a voucher, a profoma invoice, an electronically generated data, minute sheet relating to his principal's affairs or business, and which contains any statement which is false or erroneous or defective in any material particular, and which to his knowledge is intended to mislead the principal, commits an offence and shall be liable on conviction to a fine not exceeding seven million shillings or to imprisonment for a term not exceeding five years or to both.

23. Persons obtaining advantage

(1) A person who solicits, accepts or obtains or agrees to accept or attempts to obtain for himself or for any other person, any advantage without lawful consideration or for a lawful consideration which he knows or has reason to believe to be inadequate —
- (a) from any person whom he knows or has reason to believe to have been, or to be, or to be likely or about to be, concerned in any matter or transaction with himself or having any connection with his official functions or of any official to whom he is subordinate; or
- (b) from any person whom he knows or has reason to believe to be interested in or related to or acting for or on behalf of the person so concerned, or having such a connection,

commits an offence and shall be liable on conviction to a fine not exceeding ten million shillings or to imprisonment for a term not exceeding seven years or to both.

(2) In addition to the penalty imposed under subsection (1), the court shall order that the amount of money value of any advantage received by the public officer, or any part of it be confiscated to the Government.

24. Advantage received on behalf of accused person

Where any advantage has been received with the knowledge of the accused person, or by any person other than accused person, and the court is satisfied, having regard to the relationship of that other person to the accused person or any other circumstances, that such person has received the advantage for or on behalf of the accused person, or by reason of his relationship to the accused person or otherwise on account of or in connection with the official functions of the accused person, the advantage shall be deemed to have been received by the accused person.

25. Sexual or any other favours

Any person being in a position of power or authority, who in the exercise of his authority, demands or imposes sexual favours or any other favour on any person as a condition for giving employment, a promotion, a right, a privilege or any preferential treatment, commits an offence and shall be liable on conviction to a fine not exceeding five million shillings or to imprisonment for a term not exceeding three years or to both.

26. Public official to give accounts of properties

(1) Any officer of the Bureau authorised in writing by the Director-General may, by notice in writing addressed to any public official require such public official to give, within such time and in such manner as maybe specified in the notice, a full and true account of all or any class of properties which such public official or his agent possess or which he or his agent had in possession at any time during which the public officialheld any public office, and such officer of the Bureau may by the same or subsequent notice, require such public official to give a true account of how he acquired such property.

(2) In any prosecution for an offence, any statement or account in writing given by the accused person pursuant to a notice given to him under subsection (I) shall be admissible in evidence.

(3) A public official who fails to comply with the requirement of a notice addressed to him pursuant to this section, or knowingly gives a false account in relation to any property, commits an offence and shall be liable on conviction to a fine not exceeding five million shillings or to imprisonment for a term not exceeding three years or to both.

(4) In a prosecution for an offence under subsection (3), evidence of the fact that a notice under subsection (1) was given by an officer of the Bureau shall be conclusive evidence that such officer of the Bureau was authorised as such.

(5) For the purpose of this section —

"agent" means the husband, wife or child of the public official, any debtor of the public official, or any other person acting for or on behalf of the public official, and includes any person in possession or ownership of property, the acquisition of which is or was met wholly or partly by the public official;

"public official" includes any person who held a public office at any time during the five years immediately preceding the date on which a notice under subsection (1) is given.

27. Possession of unexplained property

(1) A person commits an offence who, being or having been a public official —

    (a) maintains a standard of living above that which is commensurate with his present or past lawful income;

    (b) owns property disproportionate to his present or past lawful income,

unless he gives a satisfactory explanation to the court as to how he was able to maintain such a standard of living or how such property came under his ownership.

(2) Where in proceedings for an offence under paragraph (b) of subsection (I) the court is satisfied that, having regard to the closeness or relationship to the accused and other circumstances, there is reason to believe that any person is or was holding property in trust for or otherwise on behalf of the accused or has acquired such property as a gift from the accused, such property shall, in the absence of evidence to the contrary, be presumed to be in the control of the accused.

(3) Subject to this section, a person who is convicted of an offence under this section shall be liable on conviction to a fine not exceeding ten million shillings or to imprisonment for a term not exceeding seven years or to both.

[Cap.4 s.8]

(4) The court shall, in addition to the penalty imposed under subsection (3), order the confiscation of any pecuniary gain or property —

    (a) found to be in the ownership of the accused; and

    (b) of an amount or money value not exceeding the amount or value of pecuniary gain or property the acquisition of which was not explained to the satisfaction of the court.

(5) Any application for an order under subsection (4) shall be made by the Director-General within twenty eight days after the date of the conviction, except that such order shall not be made in respect of property held by a person other than the person convicted —

    (a) unless that other person has been given reasonable notice that such an order maybe made and had an opportunity to show cause why it should not be made; or

    (b) if that other person satisfies the court in any proceedings to show cause that he had —

        (i) acted in good faith as regards to the circumstances in which the property came to his possession; and

        (ii) so acted in relation to the property that an order in the circumstances would be unjust.

(6) Nothing in subsection (5) shall be construed as limiting the court's discretion to decline to make an order under subsection (4) on grounds other than those specified in subsection (5).

(7) An order under subsection (4) maybe made subject to such conditions as the court thinks fit regard being made to all circumstances of the case.

(8) A court may make orders under both paragraphs of subsection (4) in respect of the same offence but shall not make orders under both provisions in respect of the same pecuniary gain or

property.

(9) An order under subsection (4) may make provisions for taking possession of property to which the order applies and for the disposal of such property by or on behalf of the Government.

30. Aiding and abetting

Any person who aids or abets another person in commission of an offence under this Act commits an offence and shall be liable on conviction to a fine not exceeding two million shillings or to imprisonment for a term not exceeding two years or to both.

31. Abuse of position

Any person who intentionally abuses his position in the performance or failure to perform an act, in violation of law, in the discharge of his functions or use of position for the purpose of obtaining an undue advantage for himself or for another person or entity, commits an offence and shall be liable on conviction to a fine not exceeding five million shillings or to imprisonment for a term not exceeding three years or to both.

32. Conspiracy

Any person who conspires with another person to commit an offence under this Act commits a like offence and shall be liable on conviction to a fine not exceeding five million shillings or to imprisonment for a term not exceeding three years or to both.

33. Trading in influence

(1) Any person who promises, offers or gives to a public official or any other person directly or indirectly, an undue advantage in order that the public official or that other person to abuse his real or supposed influence with a view to obtaining from the administration or a public authority an undue advantage for the original instigator to the act or for any other person, commits an offence and shall be liable on conviction to a fine not exceeding three million shillings or to imprisonment for a term not exceeding two years or to both.

(2) Any public official or any other person who directly or indirectly solicits or accepts an undue advantage for himself or for other person in order that such public official or the other person abuse his real or supposed influence with a view to obtaining from an administration or a public authority an undue advantage, commits an offence and shall be liable on conviction to a fine not exceeding three million shillings or to imprisonment for a term not exceeding two years or to both.

34. Transfer of proceeds of corruption

(1) Any person who —
- (a) converts, transfers or disposes of property knowing such property to be proceeds of corruption or related offences for the purpose of concealing or disguising the origin of the property or helping any person who is involved in the commission of the offence to evade the legal consequences of his action; or
- (b) acquires, possesses or uses property with the knowledge that such property is the proceeds of corruption or related offences,

commits an offence and shall be liable on conviction to a fine not exceeding ten million shillings or to imprisonment for a term not exceeding seven years or to both.

(2) Where the Director of Public Prosecutions has reason to believe that any person having illicitly received or acquired an advantage or property, he may by notice addressed to that person or to any other person to whom the advantage, property, the proceeds or money value, or any part of the proceeds or money value, the advantage or property money is believed to have been transferred or conveyed by the person suspected of having illicitly received or acquired it or by an agent of such person, directing the person to whom the notice is addressed not to transfer, dispose of or part with the possession of the property or money value specified in the notice.

(3) The Director of Public Prosecutions may, subject to subsection (1) issue a notice to any other person to whom the money or property under this section may pass by operation of law.

(4) Every notice issued under subsection (2) shall remain in force and binding on the person to whom it is addressed for a period of six months from the date of the notice or, where proceedings for an offence under this Act or any other written law in relation to the advantage or property commenced against any of such person until the determination of those proceedings.

(5) Any person who has been served with a notice under subsections (2) and (3) who, on contravention of the notice, transfers, disposes of, or parts with, the possession of the sum of money value or a property specified in the notice, commits an offence and shall be liable on conviction to a fine not exceeding ten million shillings or to imprisonment for a term not exceeding seven years or to both.

(6) In any proceedings for an offence under this section, it shall be a defence to an accused person if he satisfies the court that —

(a) the sum of money or other property specified in the notice was delivered to an officer of the Bureau, or to some other person as directed in the notice;

(b) the sum of money or other property specified in the notice was produced to the court and has been retained by such court; or

(c) the notice was subsequently withdrawn by the Director of Public Prosecutions by notification in writing.

[Act No.7 of 2018 s.89]

35. Presumption of corruption

Where, in proceedings under this Act, it is proved that an advantage was offered, promised or given, or solicited, accepted or obtained or agreed to be accepted or obtained by a public official by or from a person, or agent of a person holding or seeking to obtain contract from a public office the advantage shall be deemed to have been offered, promised or given, solicited, accepted or obtained or agreed to be accepted or obtained as an inducement or reward as referred to in section 18 unless the contrary is proved.

36. False pretence to be an officer

Any person who falsely pretends that he is —

(a) an officer or has any of the powers of the officer under this Act or any other laws relating to prevention and combating of corruption under any authorization or warrant under either of those laws; or

(b) able to procure an office to do or refrain from doing anything in connection with the duty of such officer,

commits an offence and shall be liable on conviction to a fine not exceeding two million shillings or to imprisonment for a term not exceeding one year or to both.

37. Offence of disclosure of identity

(1) Any person who, knowing or suspecting that an investigation in respect of an offence alleged or suspected to have been committed under this Act or any other law relating to corruption is taking place, without lawful authority or reasonable excuse, discloses to the —

> (a) person who is the subject of investigation the fact that he is so subject or any detailed of such investigation; or
>
> (b) public, section of the public or any particular person the identify of the subject person or the fact that the subject person is so subject or any details of such investigation,

commits an offence and shall be liable on conviction to a fine of one hundred thousand shillings or to imprisonment for one year or to both.

(2) Subsection (1) shall not apply to the disclosure of investigation where —

> (a) a warrant has been issued for the arrest of the subject person;
>
> (b) the subject person has been arrested whether with or without warrant;
>
> (c) the subject person has been required to furnish a statement in writing by a notice served on him under this Act; and
>
> (d) the subject person has been summoned and or his statement recorded.

(3) Without prejudice to the generality of the expression "reasonable excuse" referred to in subsection (1), a person referred to shall have a reasonable excuse as regards to disclosure of any of the descriptions mentioned in that subsection (1) if, but only to the extent that, the disclosure reveals —

> (a) unlawful activity, abuse of power serious neglect of duty, or other serious misconduct by the Director-General, a Director or any officer of the Bureau; or

[Cap.4 s.8]

> (b) a serious threat to public order or to the security of the United Republic or to the health or safety of members of the public.

38. Freezing of assets

(1) Where a person is charged or is about to be charged in any court with a corruption offence or any other related offences, the court may order, on an application by the Director of Public Prosecutions subject to such conditions as to the duration of the order or otherwise as the court deems fit —

> (a) the attachment in the hands of any person named in the order all moneys and other property due or owing or belonging to or held on behalf of the accused; and
>
> (b) the prohibition of the accused or any other person named in the order from transferring, pledging or otherwise disposing of any money or other property so attached.

(2) The court may, in respect of any order under subsection (1), specify moneys or salaries, wages, pensions, or other benefits that shall be paid to or received by the accused indicating the

source, manner and circumstances of payment or receipt.

(3) In making an order under subsection (1), the court may authorise —
  (a) the payment of debts incurred in good faith and due to creditors of the accused before the request for the order was made by the Director of Public Prosecutions; or
  (b) the sale, transfer or disposal of any property by the accused where the court is satisfied that such sale, transfer or disposal is necessary in order to safeguard the property rights of any other person claiming interest in the property.

(4) An order made pursuant to this section shall take effect forthwith and the Director of Public Prosecutions shall —
  (a) cause notice of the order to be published in the next issue of the Government *Gazette* and in at least two daily newspapers widely circulated in Tanzania; and
  (b) give notice of the order to —
    (i) all notaries;
    (ii) banks, financial institutions and cash dealers; and
    (iii) any other person who may hold or be vested with property belonging to or held on behalf of the accused.

(5) An order under this section shall, subject to any condition to the contrary imposed under subsection (1), remain in force until —
  (a) the Director of Public Prosecutions decides not to proceed with a prosecution; or
  (b) the final determination of the charge.

(6) Where an order under this section ceases to have effect or is revoked, the Director of Public Prosecutions shall cause notice to be published in the Government *Gazette* and in at least two daily newspapers widely circulating in Tanzania.

(7) Any payment, transfer, pledge or other disposition of property made in contravention of an order made under this section shall be null and void.

39. Duty to give information

(1) Every person who is or becomes aware of the commission of or the intention by another person to commit an offence under this Act shall be required to give information to the Bureau.

(2) Procedures for giving and handling of information under this section shall be as maybe prescribed by the regulations.